CW00555987

The Search for Order

£15.99
W8 (4)

The Search for Order

BIBLICAL ESCHATOLOGY IN FOCUS

WILLIAM J. DUMBRELL

Wipf and Stock Publishers
EUGENE, OREGON

Wipf and Stock Publishers
199 West 8th Avenue, Suite 3
Eugene, Oregon 97401

The Search for Order
Biblical Eschatology in Focus
By Dumbrell, William J.
Copyright©1994 Dumbrell, William J.
ISBN: 1-57910-796-6
Publication date: October, 2001
Previously published by Baker Books, 1994.

Contents

Abbreviations 7
Introduction 9

Part 1 Eschatology in the Old Testament

1. Creation, Fall, and Covenant *15*
2. Exodus, Covenant, and Promised Land *39*
3. Kingship *57*
4. Zion Theology and Preexilic Eschatology *75*
5. Exilic Eschatology *97*
6. Postexilic and Apocalyptic Eschatology *127*

Part 2 Eschatology in the New Testament

7. Matthean Eschatology *155*
8. Marcan Eschatology *181*
9. Lucan Eschatology in His Gospel and Acts *207*
10. Johannine Eschatology *235*
11. Pauline Eschatology *259*
12. Other Eschatological Voices *317*
13. Apocalyptic Eschatology *331*

Bibliography *347*
Index of Subjects *361*
Index of Scripture *371*

Abbreviations

ABR	*Australian Biblical Review*
AnBib	Analecta Biblica
AOAT	Alter Orient und Altes Testament
AV	Authorized Version
Bib	*Biblica*
BJRL	*Bulletin of the John Rylands University Library of Manchester*
BR	*Biblical Research*
BSac	*Bibliotheca Sacra*
BT	*The Bible Translator*
BTB	*Biblical Theology Bulletin*
BZ	*Biblische Zeitschrift*
BZAW	Beihefte zur Zeitschrift für die alttestamentliche Wissenschaft
CBQ	*Catholic Biblical Quarterly*
CBQMS	*Catholic Biblical Quarterly* (monograph series)
ConBNT	Coniectanea biblica, New Testament
ConBOT	Coniectanea biblica, Old Testament
E Asia J Th	*East Asia Journal of Theology*
EncJud	*Encyclopaedia Judaica*
ETL	*Ephemerides théologicae lovanienses*
EvQ	*Evangelical Quarterly*
ExpT	*Expository Times*
HAR	Hebrew Annual Review
HSM	Harvard Semitic Monographs
HTR	*Harvard Theological Review*
HUCA	*Hebrew Union College Annual*
ICC	International Critical Commentary
Int	*Interpretation: A Journal of Bible and Theology*
JBL	*Journal of Biblical Literature*
JETS	*Journal of the Evangelical Theological Society*
JSNT	*Journal for the Study of the New Testament*

JSNTSup	Journal for the Study of the New Testament—Supplement Series
JTS	*Journal of Theological Studies*
KJV	King James Version
NASB	New American Standard Bible
NEB	New English Bible
NF	Neue Folge (new series)
NICNT	New International Commentary on the New Testament
NIGTC	The New International Greek Testament Commentary
NIV	New International Version
NKJV	New King James Version
NovT	*Novum Testamentum*
NovTSup	Novum Testamentum Supplements
NRSV	New Revised Standard Version
NTAbh NF	Neutestamentliche Abhandlungen
NTS	*New Testament Studies*
OBO	Orbis biblicus et orientalis
OTL	Old Testament Library
OTS	*Oudtestamentische Studiën*
OTWSA	*Die Ou-Testamentiese Werkgemeenskap in Suid-Afrika*
Res Q	*Restoration Quarterly*
RSV	Revised Standard Version
RTR	*Reformed Theological Version*
RV	Revised Version
SANT	Studien zum Alten und Neuen Testament
SBL	Society of Biblical Literature
SBLDS	SBL Dissertation Series
SBLSP	SBL Seminar Papers
SE	*Studia Evangelica*
SJT	*Scottish Journal of Theology*
SNTSMS	Society for New Testament Studies Monograph Series
SNTSU	Studien zum Neuen Testament und Seiner Umwelt
TDNT	*Theological Dictionary of the New Testament*
TEV	Today's English Version
Th Ev	*Theologia Evangelica*
TynB	Tyndale Bulletin
VOX Ev	*Vox Evangelica*
VT	*Vetus Testamentum*
VTSup	Vetus Testamentum, Supplements
WTJ	*Westminster Theological Journal*
Wunt	Wissenschaftliche Untersuchungen zum Neuen Testament
ZAW	*Zeitschrift für die alttestamentliche Wissenschaft*
ZNW	*Zeitschrift für die neutestamentliche Wissenschaft*

Introduction

Coined in the nineteenth century by a German writer and brought into English about 1845, the word *eschatology* refers to knowledge of the end. The *Oxford English Dictionary* defines eschatology as "the department of theological science concerned with 'the four last things: death, judgement, heaven, and hell.'" But the word has both broader and narrower meanings. Some use the word *eschatology* exclusively in the narrow sense of the end of history and the commencement of the new age. Others use the word in the broad sense of the goal of history toward which the Bible moves and of biblical factors and events bearing on that goal. As evidenced by this book, I understand eschatology in the broad sense. But just what are the issues that bear on the goal of history? I shall briefly survey how I have delimited them.

Interpretation of the Bible demands a framework within which the details are set. We need to know the big picture before we look at the details. The Bible is a book about the future in light of the human failures of the past and present. In this sense the entire Bible is eschatological, since it focuses upon the ushering in of the kingdom of God, the fulfilling of the divine intention for humanity and society. In very broad terms the biblical sweep is from creation to the new creation by way of redemption, which is, in effect, the renewing of creation. Yet the end is not merely a return to the beginning, for the Bible reveals a great deal more about the divine intention than what is shown at the beginning of Genesis. Regarding eschatology, we must recognize how the Bible develops its theme of God's purpose from the beginning in Genesis to the end in Revelation.

Our understanding of the divine intention initially comes from the narratives of Genesis 1–2, the accounts of creation and the garden. The fall (Gen. 3), however, furthers our understanding of God's plan, so the issues arising out of Genesis 1–3 qualify as broad issues of biblical eschatology. The creation account, while indicating the universality of

9

Yahweh, also reveals Israel's understanding of Yahweh and of her own background through Abraham; thus, we are not surprised to find direct connections between the prime narratives and the history of Israel. Vocational and functional correspondences between Adam and Israel prepare us for the continuance of God's governmental purposes for our world through Israel. First indicated in Genesis 1–2, these purposes find their fulfilment in Jesus, who was both Israel's Messiah and the Second Adam. In the present work, I trace the connections that link Adam, Israel, and Jesus, viewing these major biblical figures as embodiments of the biblical intention. Israel resumed the role, initially given to Adam, of God's regent in a world that needs order. In becoming both Israel and the Second Adam, Jesus brings the divine purpose to its intended conclusion.

In the prophetic period, another strand is added to the web of human understanding regarding God's purposes—that of the New Jerusalem as the New Eden occupied by the redeemed people of God. By the time of the eighth-century prophets, two major developments within eschatology had occurred. The first relates to salvation, which in Isaiah is restricted to a believing remnant, a restored Israel; thus, belief becomes the criterion for a personal standing within the covenant, though the remnant seems to regard itself as a national Israel in reconstruction. The second applies to the formulation of the outlines of biblical eschatology in terms of a believing people whose center of theological interest is Jerusalem and the temple, in terms of the Gentiles' final assault on the people of God, which will be divinely thwarted, and in terms of the establishment of Jerusalem as the center of world government to which the world beyond Israel will come in pilgrimage for direction by Israel's God. Indeed, in the Book of Isaiah divine kingship and divine rule from Zion appear as the two determining factors in Israelite eschatology. And it is these factors that survive the demise of physical kingship in Israel and Judah.

The fall of Jerusalem in 587/586 B.C. marks another significant development in biblical eschatology since the event raised the question of the future of Israel and her hope. In response arose apocalyptic eschatology with its more cosmic emphasis and stress upon the reality of evil in the world as working through dominant political structures. Apocalyptic differs from prophetic eschatology (its matrix) only in its emphasis on the coming of the new age, not by historical progression as prophecy may have suggested, but by divine intervention. Thus, by the end of the Old Testament era hope is severed from the historical progress of national Israel and affixed to divine intervention, which will bring an end to the present age.

Israel's role of world mission, forfeited by disobedience, is transferred in the Gospels to Jesus, whose ministry put Israel's task and the issues that affect her before the nation again. Jesus went to the cross as Israel's Messiah and suffering Servant, achieving by his death the work of the Servant, namely, the redemption of Israel and the world. After the empowering of Pentecost, as recorded in Acts, a restored Israel resumes her role in the world. Through the mission to Israel as a distinct entity, a new people of God arises in the New Testament. The theology resulting from the emergence of this new people is traced through the Pauline Epistles.

In Paul's time, the old and new ages overlapped and tensions arose. In my presentation of this period, I treat the issues of the new age as they are found in the canonically ordered epistles. I adopted this order since the chronology of Paul's ministry is disputed and since Paul's theology seems fixed from the beginning of his ministry. Pauline eschatology culminates in the Epistle to the Ephesians, in which eschatological fulfilment for the people of God—namely, the divine intention expressed through the Second Adam—is found redemptively. Featured in this epistle is the eschatology of the one new man, by which the restraints of the middle wall of partition between Jew and Gentile are broken down.

Last of all, I survey the contents of the Book of Revelation, though most of the book is a contextual analysis of the difficulties facing the churches existing under Roman control. Revelation 21–22 is a picture of the end that capitalizes upon all the symbolism and history of the preceding biblical account. With a return to the setting of Eden at the end of the book, we find that the divine purposes for creation have been fulfilled and the people of God are set in Adam's and Israel's role as kings and priests in the New Jerusalem, now descended to earth.

The present work is concerned with the forward look of the Bible and its future orientation. Hopefully, it is a biblical theology of the last things. I attempt to trace the manner in which the biblical orientation toward the future is worked out in the course of salvation history. *The Search for Order* seems a most fitting title, for the account of creation in Genesis 1–2 exhibits a certain contingency and provisionality as the future is given over into the hands of human beings, who lapse from almost the very start. Though the task of humankind is to Edenize the world, it is clear that the task, as well as the personal and social order which stem from it, can only be achieved by divine intervention and within a divine timetable.

A general approach to eschatology, the approach I have chosen, requires that one identify the eschatological direction of the Bible and then make a subjective judgment about the themes that contribute toward the arrival at the canonical end of the New Creation. In this first connection I have argued that Genesis 1–2 sets the general eschatological platform; these chapters indicate the divine purpose for creation. I have then progressively and canonically selected for treatment those themes that seem in the movement of salvation history to bear upon or develop the general eschatological theme.

In regard to particulars: The question of what to include or exclude is less difficult in the Old Testament than in the New. In the Old Testament, revelation is tied to particular national history. In the New Testament, Jesus' message of the kingdom of God come and coming, the related Christology, the soteriology, and the fate of national Israel require treatment. In these circumstances I have offered a broad treatment of the four Gospels.

In the case of the Pauline material, I have seen as the major issues the apostle's view that in Jesus, the Jewish Messiah, the eschaton had in some sense been pulled back into the present, resulting in a now and not yet, an indicative/imperative approach to human experience. The Epistle to the Ephesians offers the consummation of Pauline eschatology in its doctrine of Jew and Gentile forming one new people of God, one new man. I have thus pursued what I have taken to be the soteriological and ecclesiological themes that relate to both of these major issues. The substitution of the Abrahamic for the Mosaic covenant and thus the status of the Mosaic torah, reconciliation, salvation, and resurrection are all basic soteriological matters. Eccesiology (which can hardly be separated from soteriology since salvation is experienced in community), considers the body of Christ, the *ekklēsia*, the union of Jew and Gentile in the one man.

As indicated earlier, I have chosen to proceed canonically, though a more generally thematic approach might have done just as well on the Pauline material. But Paul's letters are occasional and the issues discussed must be related to the purpose of the epistles. No doubt there will be differences of opinion on both my method and my treatment of content, but I set forth *The Search for Order* as the way I see the subject of biblical eschatology unfolding.

The opportunity to explore the basic ideas of this book has been provided largely by the loving concern of my wife, Norma, whose ministry to me over the years has made her such an invaluable helpmeet.

Part 1

Eschatology in the Old Testament

1

Creation, Fall, and Covenant

An understanding of eschatology cannot be gained by looking at any one biblical verse, chapter, or book, since God's plan for humankind and the world is unveiled throughout both the Old and New Testaments. Not surprisingly, however, the first indication of God's plan is found at the beginning of the Bible in the creation account of Genesis. Though Genesis 1–3 does not reveal the divine intent in its entirety, it is a starting point for the story of redeemed humankind in a renewed world.

Creation (Gen. 1–2:4a)

Three features of the creation account are key to an understanding of biblical eschatology. These are (1) the implied cosmology (Gen. 1:1–2); (2) the act of creation, including the role of humankind in the created world and God's assessment of his creation (Gen. 1:3–31); and (3) the relationship of the seventh day to the preceding six days of creation (Gen. 2:1–4a).

In the Beginning (Gen. 1:1–2)

Genesis 1:1–2 serves as an introduction to the account of creation, and perhaps to the Book of Genesis and the entire Old Testament as well. Since there is no one agreed-upon translation of the two verses, interpreting them is fraught with difficulties. Verse 1 may be translated absolutely ("In the beginning God created the heavens and the earth") or dependently ("When God began to create the heavens and the earth, . . . "). Though both translations are syntactically and contextually possible, Genesis 1:1 is best regarded as an absolute beginning, an indication of God's control over all creation as complete. That control is expressed through the verb *bārā'* (create), which always has God as its subject and which never specifies a substance from which the created objects are formed. The phrase "the heavens and the earth" points to the totality of creation, just as it does in every other occurrence in the Old Testament. Genesis 1:1 thus emphasizes the transcendence and sovereignty of God as Creator and as the assumption from which all biblical thinking commences. In the very beginning it is God who provides the explanation of ourselves and our world.

Verse 2 begins an account of the process of creation with focus upon the earth, which is made prominent by its initial position in the sentence. The syntax (in this case the initial position of a noun rather than a verb) makes clear that verse 2 is not the logical or natural sequel to verse 1. Moreover, the word order renders indefensible the so-called gap theory, which views verse 2 as documentation of the recovery of the world from the chaos into which it had lapsed between verse 1 and verse 2.

Two nouns in verse 2 indicate the condition of the earth. The first (formlessness) is the operative word, which the second (emptiness) reinforces. By themselves the two words merely point to the condition of the earth as yet unfit for human habitation. However, the clause "darkness was over the surface of the deep" may interpret "now the earth was formless and empty," in which case "darkness" of the second clause parallels "the earth" of the first. Perhaps what is depicted is the covering of the earth by the primeval waters. Furthermore, the use of *tĕhôm* (deep) may allude to ancient Near Eastern cosmologies, specifically Babylonian and Canaanite, in which a general threat to order comes from the unruly and chaotic sea. In the cosmologies, the sea is finally tamed by a warrior god—Baal in the Canaanite story and Marduk in the Enuma Elish, the Babylonian myth of creation in which the chaos monster is Tiamat (a name related etymologically to *tĕhôm*). That Genesis 1:2 reflects the chaos/order struggle so characteristic of the ancient cosmologies is probable given the many correspondences that exist between the creation account in Genesis and the Enuma Elish (Heidel 1961, 129), even if the biblical account is a polemic against such worldviews. Echoes of such a creation conflict are also found in later Hebrew poetry (cf. Job 7:12; 26:12, Ps. 74:13; 93:3–4; Isa. 51:9–10). (Another indication of the chaos struggle might be the invariably pejorative use of the word *sea* in the Bible. Consider, for example, the reference in the Book of Revelation to the advent of the new heavens and the earth, when all the forces of disorder have been swept away. Rev. 21:1 remarks that "there was no longer any sea.")

If the first two clauses of Genesis 1:2 indicate the provisional character of a creation under threat, the third clause attests to the power of God to overcome the difficulties: *"but* the Spirit of God was moving over the face of the waters" (Gibson 1981, 15). Note the phrase "Spirit of God." In the Old Testament "Spirit," the translation of a word that can also mean "wind," is connected with power and beneficent life (Judg. 6:34; 14:6; Job 33:4; Ps. 139:7; Isa. 61:1). In the account of creation, *ʾĕlōhîm* unambiguously refers in each instance to the divine name. Thus, the subject of the third clause is best translated as "Spirit of God," not as "a mighty wind" (NEB). Moreover, if the adversarial role of the Spirit is accepted (indicated by the translation of the conjunction at the beginning of the clause as "but" rather than "and"), then the verse paints a picture of order imposed upon an unruly element in creation in a way that is completely congruent with the notion of creation emerging as a result of conflict, which is found in later biblical poetry. Whatever the threat, the unruly element, we are forced to deal with the possibility that evil was present at the very beginning of creation.

The First Six Days (Gen. 1:3–31)

Genesis 1:2 may point to some primeval divine encounter in which God prevailed, but the acts of creation that begin in verse 3 are to be understood in light of the absolute and sovereign control exerted by God over all creation in verse 1. Genesis 1:3–31 presents eight acts of creation occurring in the first six days. The eight are divided into two groups of four acts, each group occurring within three days. (The account of the seventh day, found in Gen. 2:1–3, functions as the climax of the preceding six days.)

Verses 3–13 detail the four initiatives by God that took place the first three days; verses 14–31 detail the four initiatives of the last three days. In both groups, the movement is from the heavens to the waters to the earth. Progressive separations characterize the divine acts of the first three days: light from darkness (day 1), the waters above from the waters below (day 2), and the waters below from the dry land (day 3). God then "fills" his creation with essential life on the last three days. On day 4, he creates the luminaries to give light; on day 5, the sea creatures and birds; and on day 6, animals and humankind to occupy the earth. It would take us beyond the purview of this work to determine whether the chronology of creation is to be understood in literal terms or in figurative terms (the result of literary arrangement), although the latter case now seems to have a consensus. In any event, the last act of the sixth day warrants special consideration, for it was then that God created humankind.

IN THE IMAGE OF GOD (GEN. 1:26–28)

In Genesis 1:26 the uniqueness of humankind as a species is suggested by a mere few words: "Let us make man in our image." The plural address, "let us," has been variously interpreted as a vestige from a fossilized myth, as a royal plural, and as an address to the heavenly council, the latter of which is the most plausible. Though Christian expositors have tended to view the "let us" as an address to the Spirit or to Wisdom (cf. Prov. 8:30), thus indicating distinction within the divine being, such an address does not fit the evidence. In the Old Testament, Spirit is not a divine hypostasis but is God acting powerfully, and Wisdom is God acting wisely. (Moreover, the unity of the divine being is sealed by the singular verb in Gen. 1:27.) In any case, God resolves to make humankind "in our image, in our likeness." The inclusion of the phrase "in our likeness" seems designed to exclude any notion of an exact copy, while conveying the idea of some resemblance in either nature or function. Juxtaposing the words *image* and *likeness* avoids the potentially idolatrous idea of humankind's being made without qualification in the image of God.

What does it mean to be made in God's image and likeness? (The phrase "in the image of God" occurs in the Old Testament only in Gen. 1:26–27 and Gen. 9:6, though a similar phrase in Gen. 5:3 indicates that being in the image of God is a representative function transmitted by procreation.) The word *ṣelem* (image) always connotes visibility in the Old Testament, and the word's Akkadian cognate refers to a statue in the round and to a representation rather than to a model or a copy. However, even though "image" clearly conveys the notion of the external, we need to remember that humanity in the Old Testament is always a psychic unity. Thus, *ṣelem* refers to the whole of humankind viewed in terms of a representative function in the world; as a species, humanity is on view. (Note that humankind, without gender distinctions, was made in the image of God. The inclusion of biological terms for male and female in Gen. 1:27c anticipates the blessing in the next verse [Bird 1981, 146–50]. Thus, gender distinctions form no part of the divine image.) A clear understanding of the word *image* warrants another caution. "Image" should not be narrowly construed as rationality, intuitiveness, or personal awareness, although the word includes these ontological properties when it refers to the whole human being. Let us look at Genesis 1:26 further, this time noting implications of the preposition: "Let us make man in our image." If "let us make man" is a heavenly self-address by God, then "our image," which in some sense humankind is to reflect and in which humankind is made, is in heaven and possessed by the Godhead alone (Wenham 1987, 32). Having been made *in* the image, humankind is an image of the heavenly being, a representative of what is divine. (See Col. 1:15–20 in which Paul speaks of Christ as the preexistent image of God.)

In both ancient Egypt and Mesopotamia, the notion of humankind as the image of the deity is well attested. In Egypt the pharaoh was regarded as the image and the incarnation of the creation god, Re (Mettinger 1974, 413). In Mesopotamia the word *image* was commonly used to refer to the statue of a god or a king, but when used in priestly or royal designations, the human representative on view was presented as the possessor of the power and authority of the god (Bird 1981, 129–59). For instance, the king as an image of the deity was regarded as a servant of the gods, one whose royal function was a mandate from the gods to rule and who possessed divine power.

A link between image and royal authority exists in the Bible as well as in extrabiblical sources. The first instance is in Genesis 1:26c, which is translated as a purpose clause: "in order that they [humankind] may have dominion"—a kingly function. Furthermore, an exposition of Genesis 1:26–28 found in Psalm 8 declares that humankind, made a little lower than the heavenly beings (v. 5), is crowned with the divine attributes of glory and honor. The description of humankind in Genesis 1 is in royal terms. The species is God's vice-regent, placed over all creation to have dominion over it and to rule it. Under God humankind is king over all creation.

Humankind's mandate is to "have dominion" (Gen. 1:26, 28) and "subdue" (Gen. 1:28). What is signified by the verb *rādâh* (have dominion) is a superior's exercise of authority over a positionally inferior being. The word, however, does not necessarily connote the exercise of a despotic or arbitrary rule, for when this thought is required, the context supplies the appropriate qualification (Bird 1981, 151–55): "with rigor" (Lev. 25:43, 46, 53 NKJV), "with force and cruelty" (Ezek. 34:4 NKJV), and "in anger" (Isa. 14:6). The verb *kābaš* (subdue) relates specifically to humankind's relationship with the earth, and thus to the blessing of verse 28 (Westermann 1984, 151–59). Each use of the word in the Old Testament involves the exertion of some sort of force. It is used in reference to the conquest of Canaan and the subduing of the Canaanites (Num. 32:22, 29; 1 Chron. 22:18) and to forced labor (2 Chron. 28:10; Neh. 5:5; Jer. 34:11, 16). The meaning of *kābaš* as "tread down" appears in Micah 7:19, where God undertakes to tread our iniquities under his feet. Force applied against some resistant object requiring effort to bring it under control is how the word is used in the Old Testament (Bird 1981, 154).

Humankind's role in Genesis 1 may be summarized this way: having been made in the image of God, the human species is installed as God's vice-regent over all creation with power to control it and regulate it, to harness its clear potential. All this was a concentration of power in the hands of puny man! We need now look more precisely at the world over which human beings were set in control.

A PERFECT CREATION?

Six times in Genesis 1 God judges various specifics of creation as "good": light, the sea and dry land, plant life, celestial bodies, sea creatures and birds, and living creatures and beasts. Each time the phrase is used, God is the speaker, and the phrase refers to divine approval of some specific creative act. Then as the final divine evaluation of creation, God pronounces it as "very good" in Genesis 1:31.

Traditionally many views have been offered as to the meaning of "it was good" and "it was very good." Those who interpret God's pronouncement in terms of a "perfected creation" understand the words to refer to the complete harmony achieved by creation and its integration with all details. For them, both the parts and the whole of creation emerged perfect from God's hand. However, we do not see such perfection in our world today, for pain, suffering, natural calamities, and the inevitability of decay mark the world we know. Others understand "good" in an ethical sense, that is, the narrative describes the creation of humankind as the culmination of the work of the first six days. The human species then lives in perfect harmony with the animal world and the remainder of creation. Still others suggest that "it was good" records an aesthetic judgment. Creation was not only beautiful, but more importantly it conformed to the divine purpose. Thus, creation is viewed as having been adapted to the divine will, corresponding to the purpose which God had proposed. But as Claus Westermann notes (1984, 166), aesthetics and function must be kept together since they were not separated in Hebrew. In others words, every pronouncement that something is "good" includes a functional sense, that is, what it is good for. The world created by God and acknowledged as "good" is the one in which history begins and the one that will reach its goal by fulfilling the divine purpose for which it was created.

The word *ṭôb* (good) has a very broad range of meanings, and the translation of it must depend entirely on the immediate context. The adjective, which can certainly mean aesthetical or ethical good, need not be understood in terms of perfection in the context of Genesis 1. However, *ṭôb* would be the word to use if one wanted to convey the concept of ultimate perfection (whatever that would mean, since it presupposes a standard of comparison). If *ṭôb* in Genesis 1 conveys the concept of a perfect universe, the concept is without parallel in the Old Testament. In the context of Genesis 1:31 the meaning of *ṭôb* is best taken as "efficient" (Köhler and Baumgartner 1958, 349). Thus, the emphasis in the narrative of creation in Genesis 1 is upon the complete correspondence between divine intention and the universe, which was suitable to fulfil the purpose for which it was brought into being.

The view that creation corresponded perfectly to God's purpose need not mean that God created an absolutely perfect world. Indeed, a less-than-perfect creation leaves room for the absolute perfection of the new creation and for the eschatological finality we find in Revelation 21–22. There is no scientific evidence to support the notion of a perfect creation from which, as a result of the fall, there was a subsequent decline or deviation. Nor is there any scientific evidence to support a view of creation that does not posit pain, death, and the struggle for food and habitat as original and intrinsic to the created order of the animal world. In short, there is no concept of creation known to science that does not contain the natural processes and difficulties as we know them, that does not leave room for control to be exercised over nature by humankind. If we were to suggest that an absolute order emerged from Genesis 1, a perfect creation free from the illness, suffering, and death of animals and free from natural calamities, then we would appear to be at odds with the scientific data. We clearly inhabit a world subject to change.

Entropy, an operative principle in our world, indicates that there is an inbuilt tendency towards decay. The general course of this exhaustion of energies is an irreversible process in which disorder increases at the cost of order (Patterson 1983, 100–102). Going beyond the earth, the tendency extends to the whole universe. In the natural world, there are occurrences that are clearly destructive. Lightning ignites forests; volcanoes wreak havoc on arable land and pollute the atmosphere; earthquakes tornadoes, and hurricanes ravage the earth. Yet each one of these phenomena occurs under the permissive divine ordering of nature. Life in our biological world is parasitical and is sustained at the expense of other organisms. All the evidence seems to assure us that death and violence have been part of the animal world from the beginning. We do not find any biblical assertion that pain and suffering in the nonhuman biological species resulted from humankind's sin; death and decay in the nonhuman orderd seem to have been a natural part of the created order. Of course, we can attribute further unnecessary death and suffering in the natural order to the whole range of problems that have resulted from the fall—to humankind's sinful condition and forfeiture of responsibility in this world. But from a philosophical perspective, to regard animal and creature pain and suffering as a moral evil is to make an inappropriate transfer from the moral domain to the natural. While animal pain, natural disasters, and catastrophes present problem, they do not present *moral* problems. Though there is no doubt that the fall has intensified such natural suffering, it is part of our world. C. S. Lewis has aptly expressed the situation: "Try to exclude the possibility of suffering which the order of nature and free wills involve and you will find that you have excluded life itself" (1962, 34).

Our "very good" world of Genesis 1:31 was not a perfect world. Why have we considered this issue in such detail? For one thing, it impinges on questions of humankind's dominion over nature, a contingent creation that needed to be controlled and, perhaps, subdued. Genesis 2, with the garden symbolizing divine intention for humankind, makes it clear that the garden is distinct f rom the outside world to which by nature humankind belonged. But primarily, since biblical eschatology moves towards a final perfected state in which there will be no sickness, sorrow, or distress and in which the wolf will lie down with the lamb, we must note the great distinction between such an end and the limitations of the beginning as presented in Genesis 1–2. Genesis 1 draws a picture of humankind and the world that corresponded entirely to the divine intention, but we cannot ascribe to that creation our abstract notion of perfection.

The Sabbath (Gen. 2:1–4a)

Genesis 2:1 concludes the account of creation: "Thus the heavens and the earth were completed in all their vast array." God's rest, as described in the next two verses, is thus the rest of completion, not exhaustion. These verses serve to complete the story of creation presented as a seven-day scheme. Though part of the scheme, the seventh day is distinctly special and unending. No morning or evening is specified, which it was for the preceding six. Clearly the creation Sabbath is meant to provide the ongoing context from which humankind in Genesis 2 onwards is meant to operate.

While the concept of the Sabbath is clearly important, no light can be shed on the origin of the day from extrabiblical sources. An Akkadian word similar to *Sabbath* perhaps refers to a festival day, but this is uncertain. Although there is some link between the Sabbath and the day of the full moon, a regular seventh day cannot be obtained from the lunar month. Some suggest that regular weekly market days were observed in the ancient world, but there is no support for this from the Old Testament. These and other proposals (e.g., one that uses Exod. 35:3 as proof that Israel derived the Sabbath from the Kenites, a southern people who may have been smiths) are too tenuous to be helpful.

Genesis 2:2–3 declares that after God's work of creating he "rested," the translation of the verb *šābat* which basically means "stop" or "cease." Though the verb is sometimes translated as "keep Sabbath," this is a later derived meaning. Generally used with persons as the subject (Robinson 1980, 32–42), the verb occurs over seventy times in the Old Testament, but in none of these basic usages is the idea of rest or desisting from work prominent. Thus, it seems best to view the seventh day of creation as the day that caused the creation week to come to an end and thus the day that brought creation to completion. Implicit in the meaning of *šābat* is the nuance of completion or perfection in the sense of bringing a project to its designed goal. In terms of the prominence given to the seventh day as completing the creation sequence, the nuance is explicit.

Many creation texts of the ancient world convey the idea of a creation rest for the creating deity. Peculiar to the Old Testament, however, is the notion that the rest gives meaning to the account of creation and explains the end goal to which creation is directed. The rest on the seventh day into which God enters is given implicitly to humankind (since the end of the day is not noted). Such rest cannot be achieved by toil or by trial; indeed, humankind's rest in Genesis 2 simply cannot be a rest from work already done. The Sabbath day merely provides the context in which the ideal life of the garden takes place and is to be perpetuated. God's rest is the divine endorsement of creation and his willingness to enter into fellowship with humanity. Creation is fixed and settled.

The Garden and the Fall (Gen. 2:4b–3:24)

The sorry tale of Paradise gained and lost is recounted in Genesis 2:4b–3:24. Genesis 2:4b–25 indicates the nature of the fellowship that God and human beings were to share. But it is the paradox of revelation that human beings, created to enter into and enjoy divine rest, would forfeit the immediacy of the divine presence in the fall (Gen. 3).

Genesis 2:4b–7 summarizes the creative work of the first six days. Man, according to this account, is formed outside the garden, abstracted from the world at large. Then God places man within the garden (v. 8). Verses 9–17 explicate the implications of the placement, with verses 9–14 describing the nature of the garden and verses 15–17 specifying man's role in the garden as "to work it and take care of it." Concluding the account and bringing it to a climax are verses 18–25, which introduce the woman and the animals. At the beginning of the next chapter is the temptation narrative (3:1–5). Details of the fall are recounted in verses 6–7; the consequences and the respective breaches in relationships are detailed in verses 8–13. Then in three divine speeches

God condemns the serpent, the woman, and the man (vv. 14–19). The climax of the narrative (vv. 22–24) finds the first human pair just where the man was at the beginning of the account—outside the garden.

Separated from the World

What do we know about the garden that God planted? In the center of it, according to Genesis 2:9, stood the tree of knowledge and the tree of life (cf. Prov. 3:18; 11:30; 13:12; 15:4). While there are no direct parallels to these trees in the literature of the ancient Near East, there is mention of a plant that bestows life in the Gilgamesh epic. In the myth of Adapa there is the food of life, which bestows immortality. Sumerian myths allude to trees with magical properties growing between the two mouths of the river in Paradise (Wallace 1985, 32).

Another feature of the garden can be inferred from the noun used to identify it: *gan*, which comes from a verb meaning "cover" or "surround." This type of garden was a fenced-off enclosure protected by a wall or hedge. According to the Old Testament record, walls surrounded both royal gardens (2 Kings 25:4, Neh. 3:15; Jer. 39:4; 52:7) and vineyards (Prov. 24:30–31; Isa. 5:5), the latter's being protected from the ravages of animals. Thus, the garden was a special place spatially separated from its surroundings, a valued, fertile, well-watered place that was constantly cared for. Further supporting our notion of the garden is the Septuagint, the Greek Old Testament; the word for *gan* found there is a loan word from Persian that means "what is walled, what is hedged about," thus a "pleasure garden surrounded by a stone or earthen wall" (Keil and Delitzsch 1975, 80–81). To Jerome, the translator responsible for the Vulgate, the garden was "a delightful paradise."

Ancient Near Eastern literature offers abundant evidence of the existence of parks and gardens as special places. In Egyptian literature and art, gardens are places of love and happiness (Pritchard 1969, 37–41). Kings in Mesopotamia planted and boasted of extravagant gardens. Some monarchs were depicted as the deity's own gardeners (Hutter 1986, 258–62). In view of the royal allusion in Genesis 1:26, the man's role as gardener in Genesis 2:15 further casts him as a royal figure. The implications of a different outside world, the analogies to be drawn from the Hebrew noun and particularly the stance of the cherubim (3:24) who guards the way (the entrance of the garden?) to the tree of life mark the separation of the garden from the outside world.

The Garden Sanctuary

Creation accounts in the ancient world commonly connect creation and temple building (Weinfeld 1981, 502). Not surprisingly, Genesis

2:9–17 depicts the man as priest/king in the sanctuary garden, the world
center that was Eden. The description of the garden (vv. 8a, 9–14) contains motifs used in describing divine habitations in ancient Near Eastern tests. One such motif is the presence of God. Another is the depiction of the garden as the source of world fertility, of the four great rivers
(v. 10). Yet another motif that conveys the image of the garden as the
divine habitation is found in Genesis 3:22 in an address to the heavenly
council (cf. Gen. 1:26). Finally, the garden is described as the place
from which decrees are issued that affect the whole course of human
relationships (Gen. 3:16–19, 22).

Especially significant in the study of biblical eschatology is this concept of the garden as a separate place, a sanctuary. The Garden of Eden
is best seen as a special sanctuary, quite unlike the rest of the world. In
the Old Testament Canaan, which is specifically identified as a divine
Sanctuary in Exodus 15:17 and Psalm 78:54, and Eden are paralleled
(Isa. 51:3; Ezek. 36:35), quite apart from the significance of the presence of God in the restricted space of Genesis 2–3. Moreover, Eden (itself necessarily evaluated as the source of the world river system) was
clearly conceived of as a mountain sanctuary (Ezek. 28:13–14), which
is important since such mountains in the ancient world were deemed
basic points of contact between heaven and earth. Eden was the garden
of God, the earth center where God was to be found (Isa. 51:3). (In Ezek.
36:33–36 the Garden of Eden is the symbol of fertility, a fitting analogy
for the land of Palestine about to be restored. Also in Ezekiel, the divine
garden is used in reference to Zion and the temple [47:1–12; Wallace
1985, 85–86].) In the garden of Genesis 2, the sanctuary of the divine,
the man is cast in a priestly role. Consider the correspondence between
the precious stones set in the breastplate of the high priest in Exodus
28:17–20 and the adornments of the king of Tyre, who is likened to the
original inhabitant of the garden, in Ezekiel 28:13. By implication, the
original inhabitant of the garden, Adam, is a decidedly priestly/kingly
character. If Genesis 1 emphasizes humankind's kingship, Genesis 2
presents Adam as God's priest.

Dominion and Order

Before the fall, man, the priest-king, exercised dominion over nature
by worship and service in the divine presence. Man's service, indicated
by the verb ʿābad which basically means to "work" or "serve," connotes
tilling and cultivating in the context of Genesis 2:15. However, the
verb's later and frequent use in the technical sense of worship imparts
a religious connotation to man's task in the garden sanctuary, where
God is experienced directly. After man's expulsion from the garden

(Gen. 3:23), the same verb is used to describe his task regarding the earth. Seemingly, this verb is used to convey the very fundamental character of man's dominion over the earth. Divine service, that is, submission to the Creator and then to the world, is thus man's role, one that is offered to Israel in Exodus 19 and that is ascribed to the Son of man in Mark 10:45.

The nature of man's role in the garden is further revealed in Genesis 2:15 by the words "to keep it." To guard, watch, obey, retain, and observe are other nuances conveyed by the verb. In the context of the garden, this watchful role may be understood in a twofold sense. First, the verb indicates the nature of the attention devoted to the garden in the presence of the Creator from whom the mandate was derived. Second, perhaps there is a latent notion of the watchfulness man needs to exercise over against the serpent, who will appear in Genesis 3.

As a paradigm existing under ideal circumstances, the account of the garden in Genesis 2 displays the harmony that humankind's (and later Israel's) dominion was to secure for the world at large. At the same time, the account indicates what dominion is and how it is to be exercised. Dominion is the service that takes its motivation from the ultimate relationship with God, on behalf of whom dominion is exercised. But the possibility existed, even within the garden, for humankind to exercise its God-given authority independently (vv. 16–17). We know that this will happen in Genesis 3 and that it will have disastrous results for humankind's mandate and role. The fall will deny to humankind the further possibility that Eden held out: that humankind might develop and deepen the relationship by which life in God's presence would be retained, a relational immortality. Humanity, as created, was endowed with a conditional immortality, but the biblical expectation had in mind an inheritance "that can never perish, spoil or fade" (1 Pet. 1:4). It is clear that the immortality to which the Bible finally progresses is a significant advancement upon that endowed to the first pair in the garden at the dawn of creation.

Fractured Order and Harmony

The harmonious created order of Genesis 2 is fractured by the fall, resulting in a reversed order in Genesis 3 (Walsh 1977, 173–77). As established in Genesis 2:18–25, the original order of relationships was God, the man, the woman, and the animals. With a reversal of that order, chapter 3 begins. The animal world, in the shape of the serpent, takes the lead by persuasively inducing the woman to eat of the fruit of the tree of knowledge of good and evil and thus to become "like God" (v. 5). That the serpent's suggestion is no idle boast is confirmed by God himself in verse 22: "The man has now become like one of us, knowing good and evil." In verses 6–7 the woman and then the man eat the fruit. In verses 14–19 God pronounced judgment on the trio in a reverse of the established order: on the serpent, on the woman, and then on the man. The reversed order strongly suggests that sin is not merely a moral lapse; it is a deliberate human assault upon the established order of creation.

KNOWLEDGE OF GOOD AND EVIL

Uncovering the implications of the phrase "knowing good and evil" (Gen. 3:22) is pertinent to our study of biblical eschatology since such knowledge is characteristic of human beings cast out into the world and, therefore, of human beings in need of redemption. The phrase is not, as commonly understood, a synonym for total knowledge, since this certainly does not correspond to our postfall reality. Nor can it mean sexual experience or moral knowledge, for the acquisition of these would not make the human pair "like God." It seems better to understand the phrase "knowing good and evil" as a claim for moral autonomy, the ability to be self-legislating, humankind's assertion of its right to decide questions of moral choice (Clark 1969, 274–78), humanity's absolute refusal to bow to the will of God in all areas of life. Human beings are morally autonomous, that is, we can make choices, but we cannot tell whether the choices are good ones. To God alone belongs the right to determine what is good and what is evil. For guidance and direction in living, humankind remains totally dependent upon God.

CONSEQUENCES OF THE FALL

The consequences which ensue from the disobedience in the garden are recorded in Genesis 3:14–19 in successive curses that are laid upon the serpent, the woman, and the man. These three are cursed in a manner striking at the essence of their basic relationship to the other and to the world: The serpent is to be humiliated (vv. 14–15). There will be broken intimacy between the man and the woman, and the woman will feels the pangs of childbirth (v. 16). And the man is cursed in relationship to the ground. (vv. 17–19).

The curse on the serpent, in particular verse 15, has often been given a messianic, hence eschatological, interpretation. Such, in fact, is found in the Septuagint, a very early witness to a traditional interpretation, where the neuter noun *seed* of verse 15 is treated syntactically as masculine to refer to the messiah. In the Palestinian Targums, Aramaic translations of the Old Testament, a play upon a literal and a figurative meaning of the Hebrew noun *ʿāqēb* (heel, end) leads to a messianic understanding. The verse is taken to mean that the serpent and his descendants will bite the woman's descendants on the "heel" but also that there will be a remedy at the "end," in the day of the messiah (Vorster 1973, 111). (There is no evidence in rabbinic sources of a messianic interpretation.) According to Irenaeus and the earth church fathers, the woman's seed refers to humankind generally and then to Christ specifically. The nub of the matter is to what the word *seed* refers. Since the offspring of the woman is juxtaposed to the offspring of the serpent, there can be no doubt that the former refers collectively to humankind. The messianic interpretation of early Christians, therefore, reads back into the context the later theological use of the word *seed* (cf. Gal. 3:16). Moreover, all the various messianic readings ignore the immediate context of Genesis 3:15: the curse is upon the serpent.

In passing judgment on the man, God declared, "Cursed is the ground because of you" (Gen. 3:17). Exactly what is the nature of this curse? In the Old Testament most curse sayings are found in declarations of punishment, threat utterances, or accompanying legal proclamations (as in the extended presentation of covenant curses in Deut. 27:15–26). In each case the curse comes as a response to the violation of one's relationship with God. The verb *curse* (ʾārar) is thus an antonym of *bless*. To bless means to endow with potential for life, to give the power to succeed, prosper, or reproduce. Even when a human mediator intervenes, a blessing is always the gift of God. To curse means to alienate, to remove from the benign sphere, to subject to deprivation. When the ground is blessed, it may yield abundance (Gen. 27:27–28; Deut. 28:11). When the ground is cursed, it ceases to yield its natural fruit (Duet. 11:17; Jer. 23:10).

The curse of Genesis 3:17 breaks the former natural relationship between the man and the earth. What will henceforth characterize the relationship is hardship, pain, toil, and distress (the noun ʿiṣṣābôn signifies both physical and emotional suffering, i.e., pain and sorrow). Prior to his sin the man's task was to "work"; after he must "toil" with agonizing effort (cf. Gen. 3:16; 5:29). Verses 18–19 contain images that help us grasp the effects: the thorns and thistles and the sweat on the man's brow.

Before the fall, the man's work in the garden was free of grief or pain. After the fall, the man's toil is painful and disappointing. But did the change occur in the man or in the environment or both? It is often suggested that the fall caused the ground to become unyielding; thus, a change occurred in both the man and in the environment. From the fall onward, pain, suffering, and struggle penetrated the natural order as well as the human: the lion began to prey on the lamb, and pestilence entered the human sphere. Scientific opinion indicates, however, that suffering and struggle were part of the natural process from the very beginning. In keeping with our argument for the contingency of creation, we suggest that what was impaired as a result of the fall was the man's control of the ground. Let's look again at Genesis 3:17: "Cursed is the ground because of you." The phrase translated as "because of you" could also be rendered "for your sake," "on account of you," or "for the benefit of you," but the sense most suited to the context of Genesis 1–3 is "because of," that is, the ground yields a curse because of what will be the man's inappropriate control of the ground in the future.

The problem after the fall is the man's inability to rightly use the ground. The fall has left him "like God" in this way: He has power to make decisions by which the course of his own life and his world are to be controlled. However, he does not have the ability to be sure his decisions are right in themselves nor the assurance that such decisions will promote the right consequences. As a result of the fall, the man is unable to exercise proper dominion over nature, as we saw him doing in Genesis 2. His conditional but lapsible immortality, requiring the context of the garden and the presnece of God for its continuance, has now been lost. The immortality of the end however will be incorruptible and non lapsible (1 Pet. 1:4), a great movement forward. In environmental terms, it has been humankind's failure to serve the world and to exercise dominion that has resulted in the present spate of global problems confronting us. Humanity lives in disharmony with nature and itself in a world in which difficulties abound. Unable to administer its charge, humankind's mismanagement and neglect and exploitation only serve to accentuate, increase, and sharpen the innate problems of the natural world, on which humanity was charged to expend its energy as a steward of creation.

ESCHATOLOGICAL SIGNIFICANCE OF THE CREATION AND FALL

Significant for biblical eschatology are the several analogies that can be drawn between the man Adam and the nation Israel: Israel was created, as was Adam, outside the divine space to be occupied—Israel outside of Canaan and Adam outside of the garden. Both Israel and Adam were placed in divine space: Israel in Canaan and Adam in Eden. Israel was given, as was Adam, law by which the divine space could be retained. Israel transgressed the law, as did Adam. Israel was expelled, as was Adam, from the divine space (Lohfink 1969, 59–60). Clearly the creation account indicates to Israel the nature and purpose of her special status and role, which once belonged to the man. After Adam, the priest-king, failed to exercise his dominion over the world, the mantle passed to national Israel, a corporate royal priest (Exod. 19:5–6).

Also fundamental to biblical eschatology is the disruption of nature, however one defines it, caused by the fall. Paul makes clear that the disruption is something the advent of the new creation would remove (Rom. 8:18–23; see chap. 11). From the fall onward, this hoped-for restoration is an ingredient in the biblical expectation for the end. The hope for the removal of the curse upon the ground is to some degree symbolically met by Israel's gift of the Promised Land, but the hope continues and is addressed precisely in the postexilic doctrine of the new creation.

The Covenant with Creation (Gen. 6:17–18; 9:8–17)

As a doctrine of the new creation is built in biblical eschatology upon the creation and fall, in like manner a doctrine of the new covenant, to which Israel's fortunes are bound, is built upon Old Testament covenants. *Bĕrît*, the word *covenant*, occurs some 280 times in the Old Testament; its initial use is in Genesis 6:18. With Noah, a member of the godly line of Adam's son Seth, is the issue of a divine covenant first raised. The context of Genesis 6:17–18 is a promise God delivers in the very shadow of the flood: "But I will establish my covenant with you" (v. 18). From this verse, several questions arise: What is the meaning of "establish," and why is it in the future tense? What is the meaning of "covenant"; why is it used seemingly without introduction; and why is it "my" covenant? And is the covenant established with Noah personally or representatively?

Covenants, as we usually think of them, convey the notion of mutuality. And in the Old Testament some covenants between people are mutual. In covenants between God and human beings, however, there is no mutuality. Divine covenants are imposed upon the recipients, as we would expect and as the phrase "my covenant" suggests. Though the etymology of the word *covenant* probably signifies a bond or fetter, we must look at how the word is used in comparable contexts in the Old Testament in order to pinpoint its meaning. Three such contexts appear in Genesis in narratives describing the relations of Abraham, Isaac, and Jacob with others (Gen. 21:22–23; 26:26–33; 31:43–54). In each of these three narratives, the covenant does not initiate the relationship, which in each case already existed (McCarthy 1972, 65–85). Rather, the covenant gives the relationship a quasi-legal backing and guarantees its continuance. The point is instructive regarding Genesis 6:17–18 since it suggests we must look at some prior circumstance for the origin of the relationship.

The suggestion that God's relationship with Noah preceded the event of Genesis 6:18 is reinforced and taken one step further by the wording of the verse. The usual terminology for covenant initiation is "to cut" a covenant. Indeed, in every case of covenant initiation in the Old Testament, the covenant is technically begun by having been "cut" (Dumbrell

1984, 24–25). (Undoubtedly the idiom "to cut a covenant" originates in some type of prebiblical curse ritual enacted by covenant making.) In Genesis 6:17–18 and in 9:8–17, however, the covenant is not cut, but "established" (literally, "caused to stand"). In every case where "establish a covenant" occurs, the phrase refers, not to the initiation of the covenant, but to the perpetuation of a covenant previously concluded (cf. Gen. 17:7, 19, 21; Exod. 6:4; Lev. 26:9; Deut. 8:18; 2 Kings 23:3; Jer. 34:18). We may surmise then that the phrase "establish my covenant" in Genesis 6:18 (and in Gen. 9:9, 11, 17) refers to the maintenance of a preexisting *covenant* relationship.

Let's look for clues regarding the preexisting relationship. Though it has been customary to view Genesis 6:17–18 as an anticipation of 9:8–17, our study of covenant terminology indicates that 9:8–17 is not the covenant to which 6:17–18 refers. To be sure, chapter 9 treats in detail the promise to Noah found in chapter 6. In Genesis 9 the promise is elaborated to include Noah's descendants (v. 9), making it clear that Noah is representative of humanity, the animal species threatened by the flood (v. 10), and the earth itself (v. 13). Before the flood, Noah is provided with an assurance in the form of a preexisting covenant. After the flood, the covenant is confirmed and its implications are explained. The rainbow is a sign God gives to guarantee the order of creation against a future inundation.

The pledge by God after the flood to maintain the created order (Gen. 8:21), which is the substance of the covenant affirmation to Noah, seems to refer to a divine commitment to preserve the structure of creation that was given implicitly to humankind by the act of creation itself. Note that the mandate given to humanity in Genesis 1:28 ("Be fruitful and increase in number; fill the earth and subdue it") is virtually repeated to Noah after the flood in verses 1 and 7 of chapter 9. From the expanded details of the covenant outlined in 9:8–17, we find that what is being maintained is some basic arrangement with the created world whereby humankind, the animal world, and the earth itself are assured of continuance. Moreover, Genesis 1:26–28, to which the divine promise and command given to Noah in chapter 9 refer, embodies a divine purpose to be accomplished by humankind and the world. This would suggest that the covenant with Noah incorporates not only the fallen state of humankind of Genesis 3 but also the divine plan for humankind and the world of Genesis 1–2. (We must be careful not to view the world or creation as fallen, for the order of creation, the material world, was always essentially neutral. The fall refers to humankind alone, who was to exercise dominion over neutral creation.)

God's covenant with Noah can be called eschatological in the sense that it reestablishes the divine plan for creation. The later eschatological doctrines of the new covenant and the new creation, which are associated, draw together the concepts of creation, redemption, and thus the restitution of all things (Col. 1:20). Just as creation and covenant are associated at the beginning of human history, so will they be at the end.

The Tower of Babel (Gen. 11:1–9)

Through the Babel narrative, the full predicament begun by the fall is explained and carried yet another step. In a plain in Shinar, humanity gathers to perpetuate itself through the building of an impressive and symbolically significant landmark—a city with a tower reaching up to "the heavens" (Gen. 11:4). It has been suggested that the building of the tower, often viewed as a fortress tower, constituted an assault upon heaven. Though attractive, this view must be deemed unconvincing because the Hebrew idiom used to describe the tower merely indicates that the structure was sky-high. On another level, however, the use of the word *heaven* reveals the insolence of the builders (Fokkelman 1975, 18–19). In verse 5 of this carefully crafted work, the narrative turns: God comes down to inspect the operation. Every human action that is recorded in verses 1–4 is thereafter met in verses 6–9 with a divine reaction. In the first four verses the focus is upon settlement and construction, but in the second four it is upon dispersal and ruin.

The Babel narrative draws its significance from its position at the close of Genesis 1–11, the primeval history. Ostensibly the story explains the origins of the language families and migrations, but the account is far more concerned with causes than with results. Though once a unity, humanity abused that unity by seeking to build a name for itself in God's world without ever considering God. (The real contrast with the city that the people try to build is the New Jerusalem that comes down from heaven [Rev. 21:2]. In an inverse sense, Babel points to that end.) Thus, the people were scattered and their language unity was fractured. Genesis 11:1–9 culminates the spread-of-sin narratives, which began in Genesis 3: If the account in chapter 3 deals with the fall of humankind, then the one in chapter 11 reveals the fall of society. After the flood, the human race began all over again, but apparently no lessons had been learned. The Babel narratives documents the divisions that thereafter characterize the social structure of our world.

As we come to the close of the first major section of the Bible, we are not left without hope for the future. The genealogy of Shem, found following the Babel narrative in Genesis 11:10–32, provides a deliberate contrast to the activities of the boastful builders since it climaxes in Abram, around whom God will begin to erect a new center. All human hope for the future is to focus upon this one man! And an eschatological part of that hope is for the harmony of the races, the one new society, which apparently existed prior to the building in a plain in Shinar.

Not surprisingly, a presentation of biblical eschatology must include the first eleven chapters in Genesis, which have a unique role in the canon: to describe, on the one hand, the potential of the created world for order and to describe, on the other hand, the human and natural disorder into which the world progressively lapsed as a result of the human fall. Genesis 1–2 shows us a world over which humankind, at the center and in the divine presence, was to rule. As long as humankind remained God-centered, the divine purposes for the world were achievable. Genesis 3–11 shows us the consequences of the human fall and the spread of sin. By the time we reach chapter 11, we see a human society that has lost its God-centeredness. The remainder of the Bible reveals the way in which the expectation for the future is progressively and gradually expanded by the creation of a worshiping people of God and the institutions that will bind the people together to redress the disorder characteristic of Genesis 3–11. Both people and institutions will find their final expression in a God-given new creation. Since the development of the people of God and the accompanying institutions takes place within salvation history, our account of the developing character of biblical eschatology must deal with the theological and historical contexts in which the constituent elements of eschatology arise. In the Old Testament, eschatology is inseparable from Israel's development as the people of God.

The Call of Abram (Gen. 12:1–3)

As recounted in Genesis 11, the social world of humankind had been fractured, thereafter leaving humanity unable to cooperate. In stark contrast stands God's call of a man through whom the world can find a blessing and integration. Out of the disorder of Babel begins the march toward the divine reestablishment of order.

In Genesis 12:1 God summons Abram to break with his native land, his past, and his family. The divine speech and command, which are structurally similar to the speech and implicit command at the beginning of creation (Gen. 1:3), initiates a new era of history. With the potential of overcoming the sorry record of human failure, the call launches a biblical witness that ultimately leads to the new creation.

God appoints for Abram a promised land (v. 1) and assures Abram that his descendants will be a great and significant nation (v. 2). The name for which the futile builders at Babel had striven (11:4) is to be given to Abram; moreover, his name will be "great" (v. 2). Abram will provide the redemptive center for those who will be reached through him and his descendants. With hindsight, it is now clear that salvation for the world will come through Israel.

A Great Nation

One of God's plans for Abram is to make "a great nation" of his descendants (v. 2). The use of "nation" warrants scrutiny, for it is generally only applied to Israel in the derogatory sense of failed Israel (Deut. 32:28; Judg. 2:20; Isa. 1:4; 10:6; Jer. 5:9). In the Old Testament, the word *nation* is usually reserved for political, ethnic, and geographical descriptions of peoples beyond the boundaries of Israel. The word typically applied to Israel is the family term *people*. However, since it usually has separative, elective connotations, the word may not have been apt in reference to the world role of the descendants of Abram. Perhaps "nation" is used to represent a political alternative to the world assembled at Babel in chapter 11, the message being that political unity will be divinely given rather than constructed from within the world itself! In the call, God perhaps has in mind final governmental structures—those of his kingdom on earth.

The people's attempt to establish a world governmental center at Babel has been undone. God has substituted a new nucleus—Abram. Around this center will gather the great nation that will be the company of the redeemed, the new people of God. Israel in some sense foreshadows this new people and will continue as the holder of the creation charge given to Adam until it is finally and fully expressed by the redeemed. Within the context of Abram's call, the only alternative to the great nation that the Abramic descendants will become is the nondescript clans (v. 3; "peoples") of the rest of the world. If these peoples are to enjoy blessing from God, they too must find it through Abram and Israel—an idea reiterated in the New Testament. Since Israel is in Abram, salvation will flow out to the world first from the Jew (Rom. 1:16)!

God's Blessing

Blessing is a joyous theme in Genesis 12:1–3. The words *bless* and *blessing* occur five times in just three verses, in sharp contrast to the word *curse* that occurs five times in the spread-of-sin narratives (Gen. 3:14, 17; 4:11; 5:29; 9:25; Wolff 1966, 145). Though the curse alienates, the blessing integrates. In the call of Abram, we are dealing with the divine reply to the human disaster of Genesis 3–11.

An eschatological issue, the question of Israel's mission, is raised by the final use of "bless" in Abram's call: "And all peoples on earth will be blessed through you" (v. 3). How are the peoples of earth to be brought into touch with Abram? In his, and Israel's, mission to go to them? The whole discussion turns on the translation of the verb *bless*. Is it passive (as in the NIV) or reflexive ("And by you all the families of the earth shall bless themselves" RSV)? (In later contexts in Genesis where the Abramic promises are repeated, the verb is translated at times as passive [18:18; 28:14] and at times as reflexive [22:18 RSV; 26:4 RSV].) The climatic last clause of verse 3 demands an understanding of Abram as the mediator of the blessing, such as the passive supplies. The reflexive, making Abram the model for rather than the source of blessing, is anticlimactic. Possibly, neither the passive nor the reflexive does justice to the thought intended, but what is needed is a combination of the two, as in "win for themselves a blessing." This climactic rendering would mean that the peoples of the world would find blessing by coming to the Abramic descendants, rather than by later Israel's outreach. And this interpretation is consistent with the way mission is presented in the Old Testament— nations come in pilgrimage to Israel's God.

The Abrahamic Covenant and the Patriarchs

The promise of land and of descendants forms the content of what later becomes known as the Abrahamic covenant, which is concluded with Abram in Genesis 15:18. Since the promises had previously been delivered by God to Abram (Gen. 12:1–3; 15:1–17), the covenant serves to assure him the promises will be fulfilled. Unlike the covenant with Noah, which was "established," the one with Abram is "cut." But like the covenant with Noah, the Abrahamic covenant is unilateral, that is, it is imposed by God.

Terms of the Abrahamic covenant are restated in Genesis 17. Though God promises that the line of Ishmael will be blessed (v. 20), a covenant will be established with Isaac and his line (vv. 19, 21). Verses 4–6 refer to the innumerability of Abraham's descendants: he will be the father of nations and kings. Since the promise is repeated in regard to Sarah in verse 16, it cannot refer to general Abrahamic descent through Ishmael (and so to Edom, Midian, and others). More likely, the promise refers to the company of believers of whom Abraham is father (cf. Rom. 4:16–17). To symbolically reinforce the promise of progeny, God changes the name of Abram ("the father is exalted") to Abraham ("father of a multitude"; Sarna 1971, 112). The relationship between God and Abraham is now an "everlasting covenant," a term which expresses the historical continuity of the covenant in Israel's experience and which paves the way for its application to circumstances beyond the history of Israel itself.

The patriarchal narratives, which follow the Abrahamic covenant, indicate the manner in which the individual figures of Abraham, Isaac (who is less sharply delineated than the other two), and Jacob become conveyors of blessing to their age and to the somewhat circumscribed world. Each patriarch is the bearer of the Abrahamic promises (26:2–5; 28:13–15), which are also reaffirmed at the end of the patriarchs' lives (22:15–18; 26:24; 35:9–12). Abraham's intercession for Sodom and Gomorrah in Genesis 18 reveals how the promise structure is to be mediated to the outside world. The covenant promises are continued through Isaac, but the Jacob cycle (Gen. 25:19–35:29) is more important for the development of the theme of Israel. Jacob's story is told through a progressive series of alienations (from Esau, from Isaac, and then from the land). The birth of Joseph to Rachel (Gen. 30:23–24) transforms the alienation, for after his birth the return to the Promised Land begins and reconciliations take place. Both on leaving and returning to the Promised Land (Gen. 28:10–17; chap. 32), Jacob receives reassurances that his movements are within the divine purposes for the developing people of God. After Jacob's struggle with the angelic figure, which mirrors Jacob's difficulties through his life (Fokkelman 1975, 208–22), Jacob is given the name *Israel*, which probably means "God strives." He reenters the Promised Land with his new name, prefiguring his new role as the patriarch of the twelve tribes.

Judah's Eschatological Blessing (Gen. 49:10)

Judah's blessing is found within the Joseph Narratives (Gen. 37–50), the function of which is to indicate how God preserved the tribes of Israel in times of great difficulty. Driven into slavery in Egypt by his brothers, Joseph rises from prisoner to prime minister in a remarkable personal reversal. Then at a time of great famine for Egypt and the surrounding nations, life and death are in Joseph's hands. Because Joseph is the dispenser of that life (Gen. 41:57), Israel is preserved. The midpoint of the Joseph narratives comes in Genesis 45:1–11, where Joseph reveals himself to his brothers and provides for the fateful descent of the eleven tribes and Jacob into Egypt. Thus, Joseph is the providential means of the preservation of all twelve tribes. When the Book of Genesis concludes, the people of Israel are multitudinous, but outside of the Promised Land.

On his deathbed, Jacob pronounces a tribal blessing on each of his twelve sons. Verse 10 of the important oracle concerning Judah is eschatological in tenor:

> The scepter will not depart from Judah,
> nor the ruler's staff from between his feet,

> until he comes to whom it belongs
> and the obedience of the nations is his.

The translation and interpretation of the oracle rests on the key word *šîlōh* in the third line, which is complicated by some textual uncertainty. Many manuscripts indicate the word is from a root meaning "be quiet, at ease, prosper." Hence, the word is interpreted as "Peacemaker," a proper name for the messiah (Monsengwo-Pasinya 1980, 358). But there is no consensus, and the word's textual reading translation, and interpretation are much disputed. In addition to the rendering "until he comes to whom it belongs," the New International Version list two alternative readings: "until Shiloh comes" and "until he comes to whom tribute belongs." Note that none of these interpretations changes the supremacy of Judah over the other tribes. One interpretation that does, however, translates the third line as "his throne will come indeed to Shiloh." Since Shiloh was in Ephraim, not Judah, and is never associated with the Davidic monarchy, this translation cannot be supported. The more likely renderings are "until he comes to whom tribute belongs" or "until he whose it [the scepter] is comes."

Despite the variations in translation and interpretation, Genesis 49:10 is considered the first messianic declaration in the Old Testament. Indeed, later interpreters understood the verse this way. For instance, Ezekiel, provoked by the conduct of members of the royal line, forecasts the end of the line. In an oblique reference to Genesis 49:10, Ezekiel announces that the promise to Judah is about to be reversed by Nebuchadnezzar's capture of Jerusalem: "It will not be restored until he comes to whom it rightfully belongs" (21:27). Indeed, the Septuagint views verse 27 and its reference to Genesis 49:10 as avowedly messianic.

Through the Joseph narratives, the Book of Genesis concludes with one promise to Abraham fulfilled (progeny) and the other (land) assured. These promises, which are intricately bound to the role of Israel in the Old Testament, are designed to take us back to the position that Adam occupied in Genesis 1–2. Biblical eschatology progressively makes it clear how and in what sense these promises will ultimately be fulfilled in Israel and how the blessings attached to the promises potentially become the portion of all humankind.

2

Exodus, Covenant, and Promised Land

God's promise to Abraham of descendants was clearly fulfilled by the end of the Book of Genesis. Before the exodus, we are told, the more the Egyptians oppressed the twelve tribes, the greater their numbers grew (Exod. 1:12). Beginning with Israel as enslaved and ending with Israel potentially at worship, the Book of Exodus relates the manner in which God begins to fulfil the promise of land to the assembled great multitude of Israel. The covenant at Sinai, the highlight of Exodus, establishes Israel's vocation as a source of Abrahamic blessing. Since Israel fails to realize this vocation in the Old Testament and thus does not offer the Gentile world the access to her God that the covenant required, the fulfilment of Israel's obligation becomes a matter of eschatological expectation to which the New Testament will respond. Furthering the discussion of covenant and Promised Land is the Book of Deuteronomy, which deals with Israel's retention of the land by exhibiting a national life reflecting the covenant requirements.

The Exodus

The exodus is preceded by the call and authentication of Moses (Exod. 1–4). At the mountain of God, the Deity reveals himself to Moses as "Yahweh" and in so doing indicates how he will make himself known in the developing history of Israel. As testimony to Yahweh's power, the plagues and Passover of Exodus 7:8–13:16 lead to the physical deliverance of Israel from Egypt (Exod. 14).

The Song of the Sea (Exod. 15:1–18)

How Israel interpreted her deliverance is told in the Song of the Sea, which is also known as the Song of Moses. This victory song celebrates Yahweh's defeat of Egypt by use of the *sea* (the key word in chap. 14 and in 15:1–12). In verse 3 Yahweh is depicted as a warrior for the first time in the Bible. In verses 1–12 Yahweh is the Lord of nature and history, who shatters the power of Pharaoh. (In later biblical references, such as Ezek. 32:2, Pharaoh is personified as the chaos dragon itself.) Two motifs in the hymn, the sea and the victorious deity, are also found in the creation myths of Ugarit and Mesopotamia. In the Ugaritic Baal epic, Baal (also called Hadad, "the thunderer") defeats Yamm (the sea) and then claims kingship for himself. In the Mesopotamian Enuma Elish, Marduk defeats Tiamat (the saltwater chaos figure) and is then celebrated as king by his fellow members of the pantheon. Compare the use of the sea in these myths with its use in Exodus 15. In verse 5 the deep waters (*tĕhôm*, which is related etymologically to Tiamat) smother the Egyptian army, and in verse 8 the *tĕhôm* is "congealed in the heart of the sea." Though all three narratives share the motif of the sea, the three do not use it the same way. In the biblical narrative, the sea is not a foe to be overcome; it is but a passive instrument in Yahweh's hands. There is yet another shared element. The victory at the sea leads to Israel's assertion of faith in Yahweh's kingship (v. 18; Day 1985, 97–101) and Israel's erection of a sanctuary for Yahweh (v. 17; cf. 25:8). Similarly, Baal's and Marduk's victories were each associated with the receipt of kingship and the building of a palace.

The celebration of Yahweh's victory over Egypt in verses 1–12 is transformed in verses 13–18 into a celebration of the march to the Promised Land. Israel passes through astonished walls of petrified people as she had formerly passed through walls of water (Lohfink 1969, 67–68). The effortless character of the progress to the Promised Land is clearly dependent upon God's leadership. Yahweh leads the twelve tribes as their *shepherd* (a common appellation for human and divine kingship in that day) and brings them safely to the haven of promise. It is the display of divine power (vv. 1–12) and divine concern (vv. 13–17) that elicits the praise of verse 11: "Who among the gods is like you, O LORD? Who is like you—majestic in holiness . . . ?" Note that the matter of God's incomparability is raised again in Psalm 89:6–8. Verse 6b asks, "Who is like the LORD among the heavenly beings?" Interestingly, what elicited such praise was God's victory over the sea and over the chaos dragon (vv. 9–10) and the favor shown to the Davidic dynasty (vv. 19–37; McCurley 1983, 37).

Goal of the Exodus

Whatever we can learn about God's purpose in delivering Israel is important to our study of biblical eschatology, for the goal of the exodus prefigures the Christian expectation for redemption. We find the goal of Yahweh's act of deliverance expressed by three images in Exodus 15:17: God delivered Israel from Egypt to bring them in and plant them on (1) "the mountain of your inheritance" at (2) "the place, O Lord, you made for your dwelling" in (3) "the sanctuary, O Lord, your hands established." These three images of "mountain," "place," and "sanctuary" indicate the nature of the divine purpose for the people of God as expressed through the exodus. Moreover, the threefold expectation illuminates the nature of Yahweh, Israel's sovereign King, who had so conquered and led and who will reign forever.

How are we to understand the mountain, place, and sanctuary? In the cosmologies of the ancient world, at the very center of the earth and so controlling it stood the sacred mountain. At this point, the upper and lower waters of the cosmos met, and heaven, earth, and the netherworld were connected. Since the deity of the national fortunes presided at the site, sanctuaries and temples were constructed there so that communication between the human and divine worlds might take place. In Canaan, the home of the presiding deity, El, was the mountain where the upper and lower waters met. In Mesopotamia, where mountains did not play such a key role, a temple could represent the cosmic mountain. The ancient peoples would build a temple tower, called a *ziggurat*, in the temple precinct, and they believed the deity resided at the top (McCurley 1983, 131). In the Enuma Elish, after Marduk's victory over Tiamat and after his recognition by the lesser deities of the pantheon, the fashioning of just such a temple is narrated. It is clear from Psalm 78:54 that the holy mountain to which verse 17 refers is Palestine itself; the entire Promised Land is the point of contact between the divine and human worlds, the place where the God of Israel could be met. And what about "place" and "sanctuary"? We can understand the meaning of *mākôn* (place) by looking at a word similar to and synonymous with it—*māqôm*. In various biblical writings (among others, see Exod. 23:20; 1 Sam. 12:8; Jer. 7:7; 16:2–3), *māqôm* is a technical term for the "Promised Land." "Sanctuary," as verse 17 makes plain, is a place hallowed by the presence of Israel's deity. (Remember that the garden of Gen. 2 was so hallowed.)

All three images relate to aspects of the Promised Land. "Mountain" refers to the Promised Land as a point of revelation; "place" is the land viewed in terms of its geographical isolation. But the last image is the major and climactic one. "Sanctuary" connotes that the land is specially separated for divine use. And what does all this tell us about Yahweh? Look at verse 18, the remarkably early reference which controls the thought of the whole song: "The LORD will reign for ever and ever." All of Exodus 15—the cosmic victory, the subsequent leading of Israel, and the goal of the deliverance—is a reflex of divine kingship. It is an exhibition of Yahweh at work, presiding over the Israelite theocracy. From now on if the world encounters Yahweh, it must do so through Israel, legatee of the Abrahamic promises.

As we have already noted, Exodus 15:1–18 exhibits many characteristics of the Ugaritic and Mesopotamian creation myths. The narrative tells of a threat to divinely established order by a chaos power; the victory of the Divine Warrior, who does battle for the heavenly council (perhaps alluded to in v. 11); the celebration of his kingship; and the building of his sanctuary or temple. Elsewhere in the Old Testament, the motif of a battle with chaos, the principle of disorder, is associated with aspects of creation (see Ps. 74:12–17; 89:5–12; chap. 93; 104:1–9; Isa. 51:9–11). These allusions were written, no doubt, in an environment where there was general knowledge of the conflict between Baal and Yamm. Some interpret this Canaanite myth as the battle to perpetuate divine order in the world, the battle to assert divine control over the unruly elements in the universe. However, there are good grounds to view the myth as an account of creation (Day 1985, 179–89; Groenbaek 1985, 36). No matter how the Canaanites interpreted the myth, the elements are clearly associated in the Old Testament with creation.

In the poetry of Exodus 15:1–18 the exodus is presented as a new creative act. Thus, creation and redemption are brought together in a way that is continued throughout the remainder of the Bible. By the use of creation motifs, the Song of the Sea casts the great act of the divine redemption of the people of God as a renewal of the creation mandate. Redeemed Israel is hereafter the human means by which Yahweh will fulfil his purpose of bringing Eden order to the world at large. Moreover, the achievement of the biblically anticipated order must be by way of divine intervention through redemption. Yahweh's intervention for the people of God in the exodus thus foreshadows the incarnation of the Son of God by whose ministry evil will finally be overcome and creation potentially renewed (Rom. 8:18–23; Col. 1:15-20).

The Sinai Covenant

The covenant of Sinai is the next point of interest for the full emergence of Israel as the people of God and the bearer of the divine purpose for creation, which therefore entails Israel's position as the assignee of Adam's forfeited role and the promulgator of the Abrahamic blessings. It has long been a commonplace of biblical studies to view the covenant in Exodus 19–24 as different in character and kind from the Abrahamic and Davidic covenants. These two covenants, it is normally argued, are *promissory*, patterned after a royal grant, that is, a pledge freely made by a royal sovereign to a subject (Weinfeld 1972, 74–81). The Sinai covenant, on the other hand, is generally considered to be patterned after an agreement between a suzerain and a vassal, meaning the covenant demanded from Israel conditions in order that it might become operable. Pointing to the place of law within the Sinai covenant as clear indication of its demand nature, many biblical scholars have judged the covenant as conditional, fundamentally different from the unconditional covenants with Abraham and David. However, my detailed exegesis of the Sinai material, which I will note where applicable, questions whether the covenant is in fact dissimilar to the other covenants of the Old Testament (see Dumbrell 1984, 84–90).

Eschatologically, Israel based its view of its future as a nation on the Sinai covenant. The new covenant of Jeremiah 31:31–34 translates the language of Sinai into an understanding of the perfect fulfilment of that covenant. That is to say, what had been potential in the Sinai covenant was prophesied by Jeremiah to be completely fulfilled. In both Ezekiel and Isaiah 40–55, the extravagant language of restoration echoes the covenant in Exodus, for their reconstruction programs cast Jerusalem as the recipient of all Sinai traditions, the cosmic center of the world to which all nations would come in pilgrimage and by which the Gentiles would acknowledge Israel's God. Most clearly, the prophets' theology is based upon an understanding of the divine intention for Israel as expressed at Sinai.

Israel's Vocation (Exod. 19:3b–6)

The beginning of the covenant material (19:1–3a) records the completion of Israel's movement to Sinai, the immediate goal of the exodus (cf. Exod 3:12). What follows in Exodus 19:3b–6b is a self-contained unit that describes Yahweh's actions toward Israel and his future plans for the nation. Verse 4, in a three-part statement that also outlines the movement within the Book of Exodus, summarizes Yahweh's past actions: (1) redemption from Egyptian bondage ("You yourselves have seen what I did to Egypt"), (2) guidance and care on the march ("and how I carried you on eagles' wings"), and (3) the covenant assemblage at Sinai ("and brought you to myself"). Verses 5 and 6 then reveal what Yahweh has in mind for Israel. Now that Sinai has been reached, Israel is to be transformed into a worshiping people of God enjoying the liberating power of her God. Thus, the aim of the exodus release is to be realized in Israel's experience.

In order to understand the vocation God planned for Israel, we must look closely at the profound theological statements in verses 5–6. All the potential embodied in the redemption of Israel is dependent on the two conditions that introduce verse 5: "Now if you obey me fully and keep my covenant." Most expositors argue that the phrase "keep my covenant" points forward to the Sinai compact about to be concluded. But wherever this phrase occurs in the Old Testament as a required human response to a divine covenant, what is demanded is commitment to an established, not future, covenant (for virtually the same wording, see Gen. 17:9–10; 1 Kings 11:11; Ps. 78:10; 103:18; 132:12; Ezek. 17:14). In Exodus, moreover, few references to "covenant" precede 19:5a, but each (2:24; 6:4–5) refers to the patriarchal covenant, with which continuity had been established through the revelation to Moses in chapter 3. Thus it is probable that the covenant referred to in verse 5a is the patriarchal covenant concluded with Abraham.

The key term regarding Israel's vocation in verse 5 is the noun rendered "treasured possession," which has been fully treated in the past (Fiorenza 1972, 140). What the noun conveys is something like "property abstracted for special use." Though most uses of it in the Old Testament are dependent upon the Sinai context (Deut. 7:6; 14:2; 26:18; Ps. 135:4; Mal. 3:17), two uses are not. In Ecclesiastes 2:8 the term refers to private property held by royalty. And in 1 Chronicles 29:3 the meaning is similar. David, in amassing building materials and resources for the temple, proposes to devote to the project not only the revenues and resources of the empire, which he might fairly command, but also his own personal "treasure," over which he alone had control. By calling Israel his "treasured possession" in Exodus 19:5, Yahweh makes clear his sovereignty over Israel in particular.

Verse 5 ends with the clause "for all the world is mine." How does this clause relate to what precedes and what follows it? The New International Version treats the end of verse 5 as a concessional clause introducing verse 6 ("Although the whole earth is mine, you will be for me kingdom of priests and a holy nation"). By obliterating the conjunction with which verse 6 actually begins, this translation positions verse 6 as the major statement and casts the clause as a reason for or defense of God's choice of Israel. But no reasons are ever given for divine choices. Yahweh chooses because he is Yahweh, not because he is accountable. Let's look again at verses 5–6. Verse 6 begins with "and you," which signals a break with the preceding verse (as a break had been signaled by "and now" at the beginning of v. 5). We suggest that verse 5 carries the main weight of the proclamation and verse 6 elaborates upon it. In other words, verse 6 details the vocation of Israel, the role that is to be hers as a result of the divine election registered in verse 5. Therefore, the last clause of verse 5 testifies to the purpose for which the exodus redemption was instituted by God: Israel is called because the whole world ("earth") is the object of Yahweh's care. (In view of the universality of the context, there can be no thought of limiting "earth" to the land of Canaan.) If verse 4 describes the redemption and verse 5 the divine motivation, then verse 6 points to the results in Israel's ongoing historical experience.

As Yahweh's treasured possession, Israel is to be "a kingdom of priests and a holy nation" (v. 6). But what does this mean? The word *kingdom*, it is generally agreed, refers to the institution of kingship, the royal domain. Unresolved, however, is how "kingdom" relates to the word that follows it (translated as "of priests"). Is Israel to be (1) a kingdom composed entirely of priests, (2) a kingdom of which one component is the priesthood, or (3) a kingdom that is priestly in character, that is, a priestly kingdom? After a very careful examination, Elisabeth Fiorenza (1972, 114–16) concludes that "of priests" is an attribute of kingdom, the third option. Since "holy nation" is best understood as parallel to "kingdom of priests," her conclusion is sound. In the phrase "holy nation," the word *nation* is notable, for only here and in the call of Abram (Gen. 12:2; also included are references to the call) is it used of Israel in a positive sense. Without a doubt, "nation" conveys the notion of political structures. And the use of "nation" in verse 6 contrasts with "peoples" in the verse preceding ("my treasured possession out of all the peoples" NRSV). Perhaps the message is that outside of Israel there can be no other defined political structures, that there can be no acceptable political models other than the kingdom of God.

Israel's role as a priestly kingdom and holy nation means that she must serve the world by her separateness, just as a priest served his society by being removed from it. By her difference, Israel is to lead the world. The holy nation of Israel is to exhibit that character of national purity befitting one who is Yahweh's "treasured possession"; the priestly kingdom of Israel is to be a worshiping community. The priestly/kingly role that Adam exercised in Genesis 1–2 devolved upon Israel at Sinai! Particularly in the intertestamental period, Israel is viewed as God's true humanity, a parallel to Adam. In 1 Enoch we find Israel regarded as Adam's true heir (Wright 1983, 363–64); 4 Ezra 3:3–36, 6:53–59, as well as 2 Baruch 14:17–19 make similar attestations.

The call of Israel in Exodus 19:5 has the world in view. Israel is to be the community whose manner of life displays the political harmony Yahweh intended for all of society. And her call is not to be an end in itself. Israel's theocratic constitution is to be eventually, eschatologically, the world's constitution; the model of divine rule over Israel is to be the model of Yahweh's universal lordship. Exodus 19:5 thus points us to the eschatological goal to which the history of salvation is directed: the acknowledgment of all the world outside of Israel of the reality of divine kingship (see Isa. 2:2–4). As we now know, however, the vocational call to Israel in Exodus 19 is something to which she was never able to rise, and the coming of the kingdom was deferred until the advent of Israel's messiah, who embodied all that the true Israel was ever meant to be. Despite the outcome for Israel, however, it is with the exodus of Israel that we first find theology of the kingdom of God, that is, the rule of God in action displayed through Israel. Though the synoptic Gospels greatly expand on the theology, these books did not introduce it.

Giving of the Law (Exod. 20–23)

Biblical scholars generally acknowledge the distinctive character of the Ten Commandments, for which there is no parallel *collection* in ancient texts. In contrast to the case law of Exodus 21–23, the Ten Commandments of Exodus 20 are simply addressed to "you" (second person singular), that is, to no particular group, and are limited to no specific social setting. Obligatory in nature and containing virtually no defined penalties, the Decalogue transcends all social frameworks. Though it was specified to Israel first by covenant, the Decalogue is God's universal demand on all human society. Not surprisingly, therefore, either direct or implicit expression of all Ten Commandments can be found in the biblical material preceding Exodus 20 (Kaiser 1983, 82). In three chapters following the Decalogue, we find the so-called Covenant Code, case law mirroring the customary case law of ancient Near Eastern societies. Whereas Exodus 20 is identified as ten "words" (v. 1), chapters 21–23 are "precedents" (21:1). The case law defines those situations in which it was to be applied and specifies penalties for offenses. Thus the case law of Exodus 21–23 represents the application of the more general Decalogue to the society of ancient Israel (Durham 1987, 316).

The Ten Commandments flow naturally from the redemption, for they are the laws, the guidelines, within which the relationship between Yahweh and the redeemed would operate. (Note that *tôrâ*, the general word for "law" in the Old Testament, is best understood as guidance or direction for living.) Thus, the covenant relationship set the parameters, which are the Ten Commandments. In this biblical sense, law results from covenant but is not a precondition of it. Covenant implies and demands law by which the contours of the relationship can be drawn. But what are we to make of the two types of law found in Exodus—the apodictic Ten Commandments and the casuistic Covenant Code? The difference between the laws are highlighted by the posture of Moses to each. That the Ten Commandments come unmediated and the case law is delivered through Moses indicates the primary character of the Decalogue and the secondary character of the Covenant Code. While the Decalogue points us to those values emanating from an ideal demonstration of the covenant relationship, the Covenant Code, with its mundane expected infringements and defined penalties, reflects the historical reality of a murmuring Israel on the march. Thus, the idealism of Exodus 20 is tempered by the realism of Exodus 21–23. By the arrangement of these codes, we are compelled to recognize that the challenges of chapters 19–20 and the potential failures of chapters 21–23 create a tension in which the whole history of Israel within the Old Testament is set.

The Tabernacle (Exod. 25–31)

The blueprint for the tabernacle and plans for its associated institutions are the subjects of the *seemingly* digressive detail of Exodus 25–31, chapters which are largely ignored by expositors, but these chapters immediately follow the ratification of the covenant (chap. 24) and may be said to interpret it. The blueprint given to Moses is a heavenly pattern (25:9); thus, the true tabernacle, of which the earthly is but a copy, already exists in heaven. And Yahweh himself is the true builder. Who, then, can be surprised at the extraordinary role exercised within the history of Israel by the tabernacle and at the importance of its later replacement—the Jerusalem temple? What chapters 25–31 make clear is that the tabernacle/temple symbolizes God's heavenly dwelling place, that the earthly structure signifies in a political sense the rule of God. Through the covenant ratification, Yahweh's kingship is accepted by the nation. The tabernacle, set up in the midst of Israel's battle camp, concretely attests to this divine rule. Remember, too, one of Yahweh's goals in the exodus—the establishment of the Promised Land as a divine sanctuary (Exod. 15:17). The portability of the tabernacle and its movement around the Promised Land would document the whole of the Promised Land as a world sanctuary until the establishment of the temple under David and Solomon would centralize worship and alter the theological understanding.

The building of the tabernacle is significant in yet another way: it relates directly to another of Yahweh's goals in the exodus, that Israel would be a *priestly* kingdom (19:6). Israel's claim to be a community directed by Yahweh necessitated Israel's worship of Yahweh as her sovereign. Gradations of approach by different people and at different levels of holiness (in the outer court, the holy place, and the Holy of Holies) characterize the worship structure of the tabernacle. Differences such as those between the furnishings inside the tabernacle and in the outer court and between the vestments of those in the priesthood underscore that all of this is protocol designed to facilitate an approach into the inner sanctuary, the throne room of the Divine King in the Holy of Holies. In the Book of Exodus, the importance of the institution of worship is upheld even after the interruption of the sin of the golden calf (chap. 32) and the renewal of the covenant (chap. 34). Indeed, the erection of the tabernacle in chapters 35–40 is the flourish with which the book concludes.

Tabernacle and Sabbath

An injunction to keep the Sabbath both concludes the section on plans for the tabernacle (Exod. 31:12–17) and begins the account of actual construction (35:1–3). As Brevard Childs (1974, 541) points out, the tabernacle and the Sabbath are associated concepts, in fact two sides of one reality. As indicated in connection with creation, the Sabbath conveys the idea of that day which completes the sequence of the preceding six days and gives them a point and a goal. In the mythology of the ancient world, particularly that of Mesopotamia, the completion of the work of creation was followed by the building of a temple (Weinfeld 1981, 501). For instance, the gods built the temple of Esagila in Babylon for Marduk as a place for his rest. Note, therefore, that the command to erect the tabernacle was given to Moses appropriately on the Sabbath day (Exod. 24:15–16).

Eschatological Character of the Sabbath

The three concepts of Sabbath, tabernacle, and rest are brought together in the exodus and conquest narratives. For the direction of Old Testament eschatology, the concepts are of the utmost importance since they anticipate the ideal future role of the people of God. As we have noted, the Sabbath and the tabernacle are closely related. In Exodus 20:8–11 the fourth commandment brings together the Sabbath and rest. But how are we to understand "rest," which is also translated as "settle down" or "remain," as it is expressed in the Old Testament? The basic idea is simple: the state of being at *rest* is the opposite of being in motion. Thus, the verb basically conveys the notion of settling down or assuming a fixed position. No nuance of rest from labor is implied by the verb (Robinson 1980, 33–37).

Yahweh's goal for Israel is to bring the people into a settled condition in the Promised Land, where they may enjoy the benefits of this new garden of God free from internal or external disturbance. The basic direction of Old Testament eschatology is clear, having been set on course by the narrative in Genesis 2 of Adam's role in Eden. As the replacement for Adam, Israel is to worship God free from threat or hindrance in the Promised Land, which is to be the center of its world. Yet, we must note a basic difference between worship by Adam and by Israel. Worship of God in Eden was immediate and experienced directly; not so was worship in the tabernacle, a copy of God's heavenly palace. And what of Yahweh's goal for Israel? Israel would continue to repeat Adam's transgression, not fulfil his potential. The Promised Land as a historical reality proved difficult to conquer and difficult to hold; likewise, rest in the Promised Land was elusive. Israel's leaders failed to give her rest. Joshua did not, nor did David. Indeed, the basic failure of the Old Testament is the failure of Israel as occupants of the Promised Land to experience rest.

Despite the shortcomings, Israel is our model. Israel, her temple, and her Promised Land are the continuing realities that the eschatology of the New Testament takes up and transforms in Christ. Israel and her institutions are the carriers of the biblical promise. Moreover, according to the writer of the Epistle to the Hebrews, the rest that eluded Israel is to be ours: "There remains, then, a Sabbath-rest for the people of God" (4:9). The great blessing in both Testaments is the enjoyment of this quality of life in the presence of God, the renewal of the Eden experience, which is summed up in the evocative word *rest*. Rest is the great goal toward which the whole of divine revelation is moving and which finally comes to fruition in chapters 21–22 of the Revelation to John. And we must not overlook the tie to our weekly Sabbath, the day on which we are to recall the purpose of God for creation (Gen. 2:1–4a). In the sense that the divine purpose for humankind and the world is still to be recovered and in the sense that the tensions of human experience reflect the created world, the weekly Sabbath is an eschatological concept bound up with the final entrance of believers into the rest provided by God.

Moses as Mediator and the Remnant of Israel (Exod. 33–34)

The story in Exodus 32 of the great national apostasy of the golden calf interrupts the flow of the exodus narrative; then, somewhat surprisingly but with characteristic divine grace, Yahweh renews the Abrahamic promises (33:1–2). In verse 3b the narrative takes an ominous turn: Yahweh announces that he will not go forward with Israel to Canaan. With Israel at once reduced to a mere "people," the utter necessity of Mosaic mediation is evident for the first time. In chapters 33–34 the future of Israel and the fate of the Sinai covenant will be determined by the efficacy of the mediatorial office, which Moses now positively assumes.

In Exodus 33:7–11 we learn for the first time of a "tent of meeting." This tent cannot be a reference to the tabernacle, for it had not yet been constructed. It would appear that the structure was an oracular tent in which Moses would continue to experience God's presence as at Sinai, for there would be no further face-to-face contact between Yahweh and Israel as there had been in Exodus 19. Thus, a distinction is drawn between Moses and Israel—Moses is henceforth the recipient of the presence withdrawn from Israel! Through the repeated words "outside the camp" in verse 7, the separation between Moses and the people is underscored (Moberly 1983, 32–34). What follows the tent narrative is Moses' forthright intercession for Israel (vv. 12–17). Only Moses, however, is promised the significant blessing of rest (in v. 14 where the pronominal suffix is the singular *you*). Seemingly prepared to operate within this restriction, Moses appears to accept the considerable distance that now exists between Israel and Yahweh. In view of the new and onerous responsibilities that had descended upon him, Moses then pleads in verses 18–23 for his own Sinai theophany, as Israel had experienced in receipt of similar promises (Exod. 19). Moses' request to see the divine glory, however, is not granted, for the hidden dimension of God's essence remains undisclosed (McConville 1979, 153–54). Instead, as an expression of divine faithfulness to the covenant, Yahweh proclaims his name to Moses, as it had earlier been announced to Israel (v. 19; cf. Exod. 3:13–15). Yahweh does grant Moses' request that the divine presence go with Israel (v. 17), indicating that Israel is still to be set apart for divine use, but the totality of the national experience evident in Exodus 19–20 appears now to have been withdrawn.

The theophany and Moses' response to it in Exodus 34:1–7 mark a turning point in the narrative. In verses 8–9 the comments of Moses make clear that the covenant is to be renewed because of Yahweh's grace alone. Yahweh will still accompany Israel on the march, but since Israel has been undeserving, the renewal is a wonderful demonstration of Yahweh's *hesed* (loyal love), a word used in verse 6 to express a loyalty that goes far beyond what can be expected or deserved within a relationship (Sakenfeld 1975, 317–30). According to verse 10, marvels which Yahweh will hereafter do before Israel will be, it seems, the covenant renewed *through Moses* (Moberly 1983, 94). Indeed, it is significant that in verse 10 of the Septuagint Moses is the primary recipient of the covenant (indicated by "with thee"), an idea also expressed in the New International Version: "I am making a covenant with you."

Before actually renewing the covenant, Yahweh spells out a number of conditions, some of which warn against idolatry (Exod. 34:11–26). By continuing to address Moses alone (in the second person singular), Yahweh emphasizes Israel's dependence upon the mediator. (The plural is used only when specific conditions for all Israel regarding idolatry are detailed, as in vv. 13 and 15.) In verse 27 the act of covenant renewal occurs. Here we find that through Moses Israel has been included in the renewed covenant. Yahweh then rewrites the Decalogue (v. 28b; cf. 34:1), which is to form the basis for the covenant, and Moses comes down from the mountain with the two new tablets of stone.

Exodus 34:29–35, the narrative of the veiled Moses, concludes the covenant cycle found in chapters 19–34 and summarizes the status of Israel within the Sinai covenant. In these verses implications of the renewed covenant and its limitations for Israel are set forth; at the same time the prospects for Israel as the nation moves under Mosaic leadership into the Promised Land are implicitly under review. Moreover, at this end of the extended covenant narratives, the mediatorial role of Moses is designedly underscored. The glory which suffuses Moses' face as he comes down from the mountain with the tablets of stone terrifies Aaron and Israel (v. 30). Moses then allays their fears and summons them to him (v. 31), indicating by this summons that the radiance upon his face is not something before which they must quail, aweful as it is. Rather, the radiance bespeaks the intimate relationship that Moses as the successor to the Sinai revelation now enjoys with Yahweh. The leaders first approach Moses; then the congregation is summoned (v. 32); and what Yahweh has told Moses is conveyed to Israel. It is when he finishes speaking with Israel that Moses veils his face (v. 33).

How are we to interpret this veiling of Moses? Since Moses is unveiled when delivering revelation to Israel, as he is unveiled when receiving revelation for Israel in the presence of Yahweh, it doesn't appear that calming the people's fear is the underlying motive. Moses is veiled *only* when he is not acting as a receptor or mediator of revelation. Also, we cannot accept that the veil was put on to hide a fading glory, a notion drawing support from neither this context nor from traditional Jewish exegesis. As dangerous as the glow on Moses' face may have been, the phenomenon was more of a sign than a threat—a sign authenticating the covenant renewal activity and Moses' delivery of the divine word. As for the veil, Paul explains in 2 Corinthians 3:7–18 that covering represents denial of access to the deity, a veil which is withdrawn as the gospel is received.

The covenant narratives of Exodus 19–34 make clear that the prospects for fulfilling the Sinai covenant will not lie with national Israel. In Egypt, on the march, and at Sinai with the golden calf, the nation proves herself unworthy. During the trek through the wilderness, Israel will murmur again. No, one can have no confidence in the historical fortunes of national Israel. But the role of Moses shows us that the expectations of Sinai can be preserved by an Israel *within* an Israel. From the debacle that was national Israel's on Sinai, God raised up Moses, in whom the covenant hopes for Israel would be continued and fostered. Yet, Moses was simply a representative of faithful Israel, for God would continue to move the hearts of pious men and women in Israel through whom the concept of a worshiping community, drawn together at Sinai, would be realized. In short, the prospects for the fulfilment of the Sinai covenant in the experience of Israel would continue as an eschatological hope. As later developed by Israelite prophecy, the prospects would be carried, not by the nation with whom the covenant was first made, but by a remnant within the nation with whom, in Moses, the covenant had been renewed.

Still another point can be drawn from the covenant narratives. The Sinai material, particularly Exodus 19:3b–6, is Abrahamic in tenor—Israel's separation from her environment; Israel's invitation to obey an existing covenant; and Israel's call to be, in effect "a light to lighten the Gentiles" (Luke 2:32 KJV), the model for the world. The biblical record makes the continuity with Abraham explicit (see Exod. 3:13–15; 6:1–8). The Sinai covenant was in fact a particularization in Israel's experience of Genesis 12:1–3. Israel was called outside of the land that would be hers, as was Abraham. Israel was promised to be a great nation occupying the land of promise, as was Abraham. And the world would look for its source of blessing in this Israel, as it had in Abraham. Though disappointing for the *nation* Israel, the events of Exodus 19–34 laid the groundwork for an eschatology in which the conditions of Sinai would be fulfilled in the life of a new people of God, a worshiping company of kings and priests (Rev. 1:6; 5:10; 20:6). Within the Old Testament, the fulfilment of the goals of Sinai is a future prospect, which is realized only at the end of the canon. In other words, the Sinai covenant points to an ideal that by necessity must find an eschatological fulfilment— one God will bring to pass once all human endeavors have failed. Though there is no national fulfilment of the Sinai expectations within the Old Testament, there is a progressive emergence from within Israel of a confessing people of God, who in the New Testament as a result of the work of Jesus will provide the matrix into which the Gentiles may come.

The Promised Land (Deut. 26)

The Book of Exodus ends in chapters 35–40 with the building of the tabernacle and with the journey to the Promised Land still awaiting Israel. The next two books in the canon, Leviticus and Numbers, deal mainly with concerns peculiar to national Israel. It is not until chapter 26 in the Book of Deuteronomy that the foundations are further set for an eschatology regarding the Promised Land.

The concept of the land as Israel's *inheritance* directly connects the gift of the land to the patriarchal promises. Indeed, there are in the Book of Deuteronomy some eighteen explicit references to the land as the promise given to the patriarchs (Miller 1969, 454). The note of election in these passages signifies selection of the land, a portion of property cut off from a wider whole belonging to Yahweh. Though the land is perceived as a divine gift, the necessity for conquest is not overlooked; rather, the concept of divine gift underscores the nature of divine participation in what will be the wars of conquest. Israel will possess the land as an inheritance because Yahweh and Yahweh alone will wrest it from the original inhabitants.

Land of Promise

In Deuteronomy 26 guidelines are set for the grateful Israelites' celebration of the Feast of First Fruits at the central sanctuary. By bringing a gift of nature in return for the gift of history, the worshiper acknowledges the sovereignty of Yahweh over the whole land and confessionally recognizes that Israel had been formed outside of the land with no natural claims to it (vv. 1–3). Additional reminders regarding the Levitical tithe and the fair sharing of the bounty of the land are found in verses 12–15. Then in verses 16–19 the subject shifts to a demand that Israel keep the law, for life in the land is protected by national conduct in keeping with the covenant. Resting on no prior claims, Israel's occupation of the land is totally dependent upon the goodness of Yahweh.

The Promised Land, as described in Deuteronomy, exceeds every wish Israel could have hoped for: it lacks nothing in its natural bounty for abundant life. To be sure, occupants of the land eat heavenly fare— milk and honey. Watered by heaven itself (Deut. 11:11), the Promised Land abounds in fertility from brooks, fountains, and springs which flow into rich valleys (8:7). There are cisterns Israel did not dig, olive trees she did not plant, and houses she did not build. In this land Israel will be blessed above all peoples (7:14); all sickness (7:15) and every threat to Israel's security will be removed. God's care rests upon the Promised Land. His eyes are always open upon it, and his concern for it is undying (11:11–12).

Deuteronomy presents the Promised Land as Eden recaptured. As the exodus narrative anticipated, the land will be an Eden sanctuary for Yahweh staffed by priests/kings. The many parallels between the land and Eden and between Adam and Israel (see p. 29) position Israel as Adam's spiritual successor. Unfortunately, Adam's failure is to be Israel's, and her apostasy will cause her to lose the land.

Promise of Rest

The Book of Deuteronomy frequently associates the land and the issue of "rest" (3:20; 12:9–10; 25:19). For instance, the anticipation of "rest from thine enemies round about" (25:19 KJV) precedes Israel's ceremonial response to the gift of the land (chap. 26). This concept of rest sets before Israel the objective of a permanent condition of settled life in the land. Rest points to a time when Israel can live in the land, enjoying life to the full and experiencing the bountiful goodness of God in creation. Blessed by the divine presence in the land, Israel is to enjoy the Promised Land as Yahweh's sanctuary dwelling.

That a connection would be made between rest and God's sanctuary was inevitable. In Deuteronomy it appears this way: when the exodus goal of rest is achieved, then God will choose a site for his sanctuary presence in the land (12:5). Though Deuteronomy 12:5 is often cited as providing for a *sole* sanctuary, it is better understood as providing for a *central* sanctuary among many. (It is suggested frequently that the notion of Yahweh's causing his name to dwell at the sanctuary [cf. v. 5] reflects a doctrine of the presence of God in Israel that is newer and more sophisticated than the supposed older and more materialistic doctrine from the exodus of God's immanence manifested by occasional theophany. This is not so, however, for the formula "to cause the name to dwell" is a fairly common assertion of property ownership with which Israel would have been accustomed [Wenham 1971, 114].) Only after Israel has entered the inherited land and been given rest is she to erect Yahweh's central sanctuary. By taking her offerings to the central sanctuary, rather than worshiping as the Canaanites do (12:2–4), Israel recognizes Yahweh's ownership of the whole land (12:5–12).

As we know, the Deuteronomic expectation of the good life lived in the land where Yahweh's presence would be an ongoing national experience was never realized. Rather than the promised blessings, the curses of the covenant, the blights upon the land (chap. 28), fall upon Israel. Even though under David and Solomon the conquest is completed, political stability is achieved, and the central sanctuary is erected, rest is never more than Israel's hope in the Old Testament period. Yet Israel did not surrender the theology of the Promised Land. In the New Testament, particularly in the Epistle to the Hebrews and in the Book of Revelation, the notions of a heavenly Canaan and a heavenly Jerusalem find their place, reflecting the Christian hope for a restored Eden-like life. Since the ideal of Eden recaptured, which the Old Testament theology of the Promised Land incorporates, is integral to the divine purpose for the people of God, the hope could not be surrendered. As the Revelation of John will finally make clear, the people of God must worship God continually in the place of *God's* appointment, finally fulfilling the role projected for Israel in Canaan.

3

Kingship

Debate about Kingship

During the latter part of the period of the judges, when Israel moved toward an urbanized society, there arose a debate about the relevance of kingship. It is necessary to look at this debate and the emergence of kingship in detail, for it relates to a matter integral to the eschatology of Israel, that is, the concept of messiahship. Kingship did not finally come to Israel until the election of Saul in about 1020 B.C.., though by that time surrounding peoples had lived under kings for at least three hundred years. The puzzle is why kingship came to Israel so late. To understand the phenomenon, we turn to the Book of Judges, finding therein portrayals of various attitudes toward kingship that help us understand Israel's ambivalence.

Gideon's Orthodoxy (Judg. 8:22–28)

On Gideon's return from his successful campaign against the Midianites, Israel offers him not only kingship but dynastic kingship: "Rule over us—you, your son and your grandson—because you have saved us out of the hand of Midian" (Judg. 8:22). That Gideon was recognized as fit for such high office is apparent from Judges 8:18, in which Gideon is said to resemble the son of a king. Gideon's refusal to accept the royal role is couched in terms of an impeccable orthodoxy that attests to Israel's theocratic basis: "I will not rule over you, nor will my son rule over you. The LORD will rule over you" (8:23). The subsequent narrative depicts the frailty of this great man. His surprising lapse into idolatry, evidenced by the ephod made from Midianite spoils (8:24–27), perhaps reveals just how lucky Israel was to have escaped a reign by Gideon, a hero of the tribe of Manasseh.

Abimelech's Treachery (Judg. 9)

After the account of Gideon, the Book of Judges plunges into a narrative about Abimelech, Gideon's half-Canaanite son, who attempts to replace family leadership with autocratic kingship (Judg. 9:2). In an abortive reign, Abimelech establishes himself as king over the significant principality of Shechem. Since Abimelech is the only "king" described in Judges, the episode discredits the institution by relating it to the career of this renegade fratricide (Malamat 1976, 163–64) and reveals what granting the monarchy to Gideon's family would have meant in the long term for Israel. In the midst of the story about Abimelech, moreover, is a fable that seems to have been born in a context in which kingship is regarded as a real threat (Judg. 9:7–15). The fable, attributed to a representative of orthodoxy known as Jotham, ridicules kingship as that to which only charlatans and time-servers aspire.

Abimelech, the one person who actually exercised kingship during the period of the judges, is depicted as the very antithesis of all that a judge of Israel should be (Malamat 1976, 163–64). His rise to power by personal astuteness and his use of mercenaries to establish his position denies any element of spiritual spontaneity to his office. Through Jotham's fable and the narrative of Abimelech, Judges 9 presents kingship as a humanistic alternative to the great series of divine initiatives that maintained Israel's position through the activity of successive heroic figures. Thus, the author of the Book of Judges leaves us in no doubt as to where he stands on the issue of kingship.

An Editorial Comment (Judg. 21:25)

One other assessment of kingship is offered in the Book of Judges: the concluding verse proclaims, "In those days Israel had no king; everyone did as he saw fit" (21:25). At first glance these words, by contrasting the days when Israel faced extreme anarchy with those when Israel under the monarchy would be firmly and authoritatively regulated, seem to convey the writer's negative appraisal of the period of judges. Positioned at the end of the judges period and the beginning of the monarchical age, verse 25 seems to identify the source of Israel's problems as the absence of authoritative leadership, the kind the later monarchy would provide. Yet, does verse 25 condemn judgeship and advocate kingship? To answer this, we must look at the type of leadership the judges provided. Ever since the work of Max Weber early in the twentieth century, Israel's leadership during the period of judges has been conventionally characterized as *charismatic*, which to the term's popularizer meant the exhibition of the talents of extraordinarily brilliant and gifted individuals for whom *historical circumstances* had provided opportunity. When applied to the judges' leadership, however, the label *charismatic* refers to the Spirit-directed, nonrepeatable character of leadership that had been raised up by *Yahweh* to meet successive crises in Israel's affairs. That is, the judges continued the kind of Mosaic leadership to which Israel had become accustomed from Sinai days onward. Since we may expect that proponents of kingship would have been at odds with this entrenched office, it is difficult to imagine that the period of the judges would end with a positive appraisal of kingship.

Judges 21:25, rather than recommend monarchy, does no more than indicate the persistence of Israel in a period of absolute disorder. Surveying the period of the judges, the writer is appalled by its social and religious disintegration. Though at the beginning of the Book of Judges Israel was united in consolidating the conquest, by the end tribal unity has been fractured and Israel is virtually in shambles. Thus, the point made by Judges 21:25 seems to be a simple one: the ideal of Israel has been preserved despite Israel herself. No political system, no platform of tribal cooperation, can account for the Israel found at the end of the period. The preservation has depended not upon social or governmental forms of any type and certainly not upon the existence of a bureaucratic institution such as monarchy, but upon the continued interventions of Israel's Deity. Israel breached the covenant over and over again, but at this time there was a commitment to Israel that Yahweh would not break. Whether or not there would be a future for Israel depended upon one factor alone—the willingness of Yahweh to continue with this people whom he had brought into being.

In summary, Judges 21:25 denies neither the disordered political conditions nor the blatant individualism of the era of judges. But in spite of the tremendous social upheavals of the age, in spite of the lack of strong authoritarian administration, something of value remained at the end of the era. Even after the people's glaring apostasy, Yahweh preserved the ideal of a united Israel. By implication, the author of Judges is suggesting that the pattern of direct divine intervention and theocratic leadership had never been so solidly demonstrated as it had been in the period of judges. At a time when Israel's political framework was being acquired, Yahweh was pleased to preserve Israel and would not violate the covenant arrangement. The concept of Israel, located in an elective ideal to which Sinai had given political expression, was bound to the divine purpose and would survive as a result of divine election alone, not as a consequence of leadership or political forms.

Israel's Demand for Monarchy

Shortly after the close of the period of the judges, a dynastic monarchy emerged in Israel. The Books of Samuel further wrestle with issues raised in the premonarchical period, particularly the matter of Israel's leadership. First Samuel begins at Shiloh, where degenerate priests kept watch over the ark of the covenant, and Second Samuel concludes with David's purchase of the temple site (chap. 24). Within the scope of the two books is the provision of stability for Israel's worship structure. Since Israel's worship was the community's response to the exercise of Yahweh's kingship, the religious reforms of the Book of Samuel—the elimination of abuses, the purification of worship, and the provision for a centralized shrine—demonstrate a proper regard for Yahweh's kingship over the nation. Inseparable from this movement from debased to acceptable worship is the emergence of the offices of kingship and prophecy, both of which are testimony to the exercise of Yahweh's authority over Israel.

Messianic Leadership and Divine Will (1 Sam. 1–7)

The first three chapters of 1 Samuel demonstrate fulfilment of the divine intention expressed in the Song of Hannah (2:1–10), that is, the exalting of the humble and the humbling of the exalted. In telling the story of Samuel's rise and the house of Eli's fall, chapters 1–3 detail Samuel's family background and the peculiar circumstances of his birth, which marked him for high office. However, Hannah's song, in emphasizing how God rescues the lowly and reverses the order of human expectations in the interest of justice, also relates to God's purpose beyond the life of Samuel, specifically to the gift of the messiah (v. 10). Thus, 1 Samuel 1–3 prepares us for the power struggle ahead by assuring us God will prevail and will provide a model of messianic leadership.

The manifestation of divine power over Israel is the focus of the narratives in 1 Samuel 4–6. Yahweh disassociates himself from corrupt institutions, and the ark, an emblem of the tainted cult at Shiloh, is surrendered. The terms used to describe the loss of the ark indicate that its capture by the Philistines amounts to Yahweh's abandonment of the Promised Land and Israel's return to captivity. Not surprisingly, the language of the exodus is reversed in these chapters (e.g., 4:8; 5:6; 6:6) to underscore the seriousness of the entire nation's defection into idolatry. And it should be no surprise that all of Israel is at fault. If the central shrine at Shiloh is so polluted that Yahweh rejected it and its worship, what could be expected of the nation, which takes its lead from the worship center? In chapters 4–6, from which Samuel is notably absent, the crisis facing Israel takes shape and grows. In the next chapter, Samuel returns as the man whom Yahweh has raised up to meet the crisis, the last great figure of the era of the judges. Operating as a prolog to the institution of the monarchy, chapter 7 depicts Samuel as saving Israel from external threats posed by the Philistines (vv. 5–14) and preventing internal disruptions by wise administration (vv. 15–17).

Transition to Kingship (1 Sam. 8–12)

Chapters 8–12 stand between the formal closing of the period of Samuel and the beginning of the reign of Saul. Understandably given their location, these chapters move from kingship raised as a problem to be overcome to kingship engrafted onto the Sinai covenant.

COVENANT BREACH (1 SAM. 8)

Rejecting the leadership of Samuel's family because of its similarity to Eli's, Israel demands that Samuel appoint a king (v. 5). Though such a move had been previously sanctioned in the Book of Deuteronomy (17:14–20), the demand is put by the elders in such a way as to deny Israel's covenantal exclusivity: "Appoint a king to lead [Heb. "judge"] us, such as all the other nations have" (v. 5; cf. vv. 19–20). If Israel's monarchy is to be patterned after that of other nations, then the elders are tacitly demanding dynastic kingship, which would deny Yahweh's prerogative to determine Israel's leadership and its succession. Moreover, the elders' request exhibits an internal tension. On the one hand, asking for a "king" calls for a departure from the past. On the other hand, asking for someone to "judge" seeks a continuance of the past—when in a time of crisis leadership was appointed directly by Yahweh. Above all, the request is tantamount to a unilateral breach of the covenant. At Sinai, Israel had been called to be a kingdom under Yahweh separated from her world; her distinctiveness lay in the difference between Israel and the surrounding nations. Based upon her separateness from the world, Israel would serve the world by her spiritual attractiveness. The elders' demand signifies that distinctions absolutely basic to the preservation of the Sinai covenant are to be abandoned and thus the covenant is to be rejected! To be sure, the demand in verse 5 simply repeats the request anticipated in Deuteronomy 17:14; however, the expectation in Deuteronomy is moderated by the remainder of that chapter. Since kingship will come to Israel, kingship itself is not the issue, but at issue is the *type* of kingship for which Israel will settle.

DIVINE MODIFICATION OF ISRAEL'S DEMAND (1 SAM. 9)

Though 1 Samuel 8 presents kingship as a potential threat to the covenant and Yahweh's leadership, the next chapter shows kingship as a force to be reckoned with. And the reckoning takes the form of an office set up to contain whatever threat kingship may pose to the covenant. From 1 Samuel 9 on, the Mosaic office of *prophecy*, whose function it was to recall for Israel the fact and implications of the Sinai compact, gains institutional prominence. Henceforth the prophet acts as Yahweh's prime minister sent with power from Yahweh to regulate by Yahweh's word the political structures of Israel. By constant superintendence over Israel's official leadership and in particular over Israel's king, the prophet presides over Israel's political affairs. Thus, the prophet is depicted as the preeminent divine messenger, functioning with full divine authority, coming from the court of the Divine King.

SAUL—ANOINTING AND OPPOSITION (1 SAM. 10–11)

As an initial step in the appointment of Saul as Israel's first king, Samuel anoints him to the office of "leader" (1 Sam. 10:1). This office seems to have been integral to the evolution of the monarchy as Israel emerged from her tribal background. Indeed, in the historical books all persons anointed as leader eventually became king (1 Sam. 13:14; 25:30; 2 Sam. 5:2; 6:21; 7:8; 1 Kings 1:35; 14:7; 16:2; 2 Kings 20:5, 2 Chron. 11:22). Thus, Saul becomes king designate.

Anointing is attested in the ancient world. Egyptian officials were anointed, as were Egyptian vassals in Syria. Although kings were not anointed in Egypt and in Mesopotamia, they were in the empire of the Hittites in Asia Minor, where nobles had greater power than in Egypt or Mesopotamia. The basic purpose of anointing was authorizing one to act on behalf of another power or agent. For this reason, the Israelite king, at least in the early stages of Israelite kingship, is known as Yahweh's "anointed," that is, *messiah*. Since in the Old Testament the term *messiah* always appears in a phrase that means "Yahweh's messiah" (where appropriate the possessive pronouns *my*, *your*, or *his* might be used), it is clear that the relationship established is between Yahweh and the king, not between the king and the people. Moreover, the non-public character of the anointing of Saul and David makes it clear that the ceremony does not relate the king to the populace but does relate the king to God. (Note the parallel to the baptism of Jesus.) After Saul, David, and Solomon, the practice of anointing is only occasionally attested and ceases entirely with the exile. Though Jehoahaz, whose succession may have been disputed, is the one southern king to be anointed (2 Kings 23:30), no northern king after Saul is ever called messiah.

Despite Saul's anointing and his flush of success against the Ammonites, opposition to his kingship was still very real (1 Sam. 11:11–12). It cannot, however, be said that the overall tenor of 1 Samuel 8–12 is antimonarchical since kingship will be established in Israel, we are told, because Yahweh himself has willed it (8:22). Indeed, in these chapters only Samuel expresses definite opposition to kingship (Eslinger 1983, 66), and his is only an initial reaction to the suggestion. Once Yahweh explained the choice and the concept of kingship, then even Samuel falls into line. The prophet continues to be critical only in regard to Israel's wish to be like the surrounding nations, the point at which Yahweh himself is critical. Neither Yahweh nor Samuel is antimonarchical; rather, they are procovenantal (Vannoy 1978, 239). In asking for a king who will act as a military commander against the Philistine threat, the people search for security and endeavor to guarantee their future. Samuel's acute perception into the people's improper motives elicit his displeasure.

Theological Basis for Kingship

In view of the ambiguity that surrounded kingship and the elders' mixed motives in seeking appointment of a monarch, the nature of Israel's new office needed to be clarified and engrafted to the covenant. This gradual integration of kingship and covenant is the function of 1 Samuel 9–12, where we find the development of a theology of kingship, which would undergird the institution and make it work.

Here it is necessary to reflect upon parallels between the selection of Saul and David, for with them an ideal framework of kingship is established. Both Saul and David are the subject of deliberate divine choice (cf. 1 Sam. 9:16; 16:1). Saul's search for his father's lost asses leads Saul to Samuel, and Samuel passes over Jesse's seven sons before settling on David. In both cases Samuel had been advised beforehand of the circumstances that would unite him with Yahweh's choice. Both Saul and David are anointed by Samuel, which brings them into a special relationship with Yahweh as the Lord's messiah (cf. 10:1; 16:13). Thus, Saul and David are authorized to act as Yahweh's representative. Both are empowered for office by the reception of the Spirit (cf. 10:10; 16:13). (In fact, Saul begins to act like a prophet upon receipt of the Spirit.) Note that David's reception of the Spirit is followed immediately in 1 Samuel 16:14 by the Spirit's withdrawal from Saul, indicating the transfer of leadership. Finally, both Saul and David are publicly attested through mighty acts (cf. chaps. 11 and 17). In chapter 11 Saul mobilizes all Israel to punish Nahash and the Ammonites. In chapter 17 David fights the battles of the LORD as his messiah. This sequence of events in the elevation of Saul and David (election, anointing, gift of the Spirit, and public demonstration) provides theological undergirding for the office of kingship from the very beginning of its institution in Israel (Knierim 1968, 31–35). Furthermore, we see that messiahship was not something Israel constructed as a result of historical disappointment with kingship, not a projection of ideal kingship into the future to combat failure. Rather, messiahship was written into the very structure of Israel's kingship from the inception of the office and gave to kingship a distinctively Israelite character.

The selection of no other Israelite king exhibits the four features of election, anointing, Spirit endowment, and public demonstration, which characterize the selection of Saul and David. These two monarchs are used to depict an ideal kingship—one impossible to duplicate in the experience of later northern and southern kings. Elsewhere in the Old Testament (see Isa. 7:14–16; 9:1–7; chap. 11), Davidic messiahship is used eschatologically to describe the ideal ruler who will operate under the Spirit to bring about the desired conditions of the eschaton. Also, the presentation in Isaiah 40–55 of Israel's ideal suffering figure, the Servant, is couched in language very similar to that in the election of David and Saul. It is no surprise, then, that the selection of only one biblical figure fully exhibits the features of David's and Saul's call. When Jesus of Nazareth is called to be Israel's Messiah, we know that in him all the expectations of Jewish messiahship are fully met.

Kingship and Covenant

After Saul's victory over the Ammonites, Saul's kingship is integrated into the covenant before the assembly of all Israel at Gilgal (1 Sam. 11:14–15). Verse 14 states the purpose of the assembly in these words— "And there reaffirm the kingship." As it is used in this verse, the verb *reaffirm* means to repair something which has lapsed into a state of deterioration (Vannoy 1978, 64; cf. 2 Chron. 15:8; 24:4; Isa. 61:4). Since Saul had just been publicly recognized at Mizpah (10:12) and had not yet been made king formally by Samuel, why would Saul's kingship need assistance? It would not, but the covenant relationship between Yahweh and Israel had fallen into a state of neglect and needed to be repaired (Vannoy 1978, 66–67). "Reaffirm the kingship" refers, therefore, to the kingship Yahweh exercises over Israel. In view of the threat posed to the covenant by Israel's request for a king, the relationship between Yahweh and Israel is indeed at risk.

As Israel moves closer and closer to kingship, she wrestles with how the civil rule of a king can be integrated with the kingdom-of-God society established at Sinai. First Samuel 11:14 identifies the solution—kingship must become a vehicle for Yahweh's continued rule over Israel. Precisely because the kingship of Saul is about to be formally conferred by all Israel (1 Sam. 11:15), Israel needs to reaffirm that her fidelity to the kingdom of Yahweh will not be subordinated to the new political rule. And by the sacrifice of peace offerings in verse 15, it seems clear that Saul's kingship is to be placed within the broader framework of a renewed covenant fellowship. Only after the reaffirmation of Yahweh's kingship is Saul attested as king for the first time.

The narrative of Saul's installation as king and of his reign, which begins in 1 Samuel 13, is interrupted by an address by Samuel in chapter 12. The placement of this address forces us to recognize that alongside the new king stands another—the prophet. Samuel begins by defending his public and private conduct (vv. 1–5) and then turns to consider events leading up to Israel's request for a king. After summarizing Yahweh's hand in the exodus and in the period of the judges (vv. 6–11), Samuel affirms that Israel may now have a king (vv. 12–13). Verses 14–15 restate the covenant terms on which kingship is acceptable to Yahweh, and verses 16–22 challenge Israel to covenant fidelity in the new order. Though it has often been suggested that verses 23–25 mark Samuel's withdrawal from public leadership, by no means is this the case. Rather, in these verses Samuel looks forward to a relationship with the new regime.

Fulfilment of Israel's Demand

In 1 Samuel 13:1 the narrative of Saul's kingship officially begins with the formula by which a reign is normally announced: "Saul was [thirty] years old when he became king, and he reigned over Israel [forty]-two years." The numbers indicating Saul's age and length of reign are missing in the Hebrew, but more important is the content of the narrative that follows. It seems that the end of Saul's reign is in sight almost as soon as it begins.

Rejection of Saul (1 Sam. 13–15)

Could beleaguered Saul do anything right? As king, he inherits the continuing threat of the Philistines. Samuel had already stipulated that Saul must wait seven days before committing Israel to battle (1 Sam. 10:8). When Samuel doesn't appear after Saul's agonizing wait, Saul himself offers the necessary sacrifices. At once, Samuel appears. It seems his command to Saul in 10:8 had been, "You must wait seven days *until I come to you*" (emphasis added). The point made by the incident is profound: kingship must be subject to prophetic direction, as arbitrary as that direction may at times appear. In short, messiahship must always be subordinated to the divine will. The fortune of Saul is no better in chapter 14. His attempt to be cultically circumspect and to fulfil every divine requirement puts him at odds with Israel over his indiscreet ban on food during battle. As a result, Saul loses public support. The final blow to Saul's kingship comes in chapter 15. Though he is directed to destroy the Amalekites totally, his destruction is not complete, and thus he fails to observe the holy-war code of the consecration to Yahweh of the spoils of battle. In chapter 13, after Saul's failure to obey Samuel's command, the prospect of a dynasty for Saul had been rejected (vv. 13–14); now after the breach of the code of war, Saul himself is dismissed as king (15:23, 26). From the experience of Saul, we know that imposed upon the Israelite ruler are extreme demands, ones that cannot be met without further divine gifting. Israel's messiah must be perfect (Knierim 1968, 38).

Choice of David (1 Sam. 16–2 Sam. 5)

Yahweh's rejection of Saul is followed in 1 Samuel 16 with the election, choice, and anointing of David for high office. David publicly demonstrates his new authority in chapter 17. Israel's new messiah is now portrayed as the achiever of Yahweh's victories (vv. 45–47). The chapters that follow in 1 Samuel are generally concerned with David's rise to power, his careful conduct during this time, and the increasingly evident rejection of Saul. At the end of 1 Samuel, Saul and Jonathan are slain in battle with the Philistines at Gilboa (chap. 31). David, who had distanced himself from any suggestion of complicity in Saul's death, is then made king over Judah at Hebron (2 Sam. 2:1–4). David's demand for the return of his wife Michal, Saul's daughter, further strengthens David's claim to Saul's throne. Finally, David is made king over Israel as a whole (2 Sam. 5:1–5). His subsequent victory over the Philistines (2 Sam. 5:17–25) means that David succeeded where Saul had failed.

Choice of Jerusalem (2 Sam. 6)

After David captures Jebusite-held Jerusalem, he makes it his political capital (2 Sam. 5:7–9). The groundwork for the move to this centrally situated city, however, had been laid long before, for David had carefully determined what course he should follow. For instance, on David's rise to power before having been made king, he had established a network of coalitions through political marriages to strengthen his position in the south and elsewhere. Thus, the move to Jerusalem must be seen in light of the various sociological, geographical, religious, and political factors to which it points.

Once Jerusalem is established as the political capital, David seeks to rationalize his choice of location by moving the ark there too (2 Sam. 6:1–15), thereby making Jerusalem the religious capital as well. For twenty years, the ark had been exiled in Kiriath-jearim. By bringing the ark back, David would consolidate old tribal ties and centralize all of Israel's sacral traditions. Moreover, the return of the ark would lay the groundwork for David's desire to build a temple (2 Sam. 7). Before we examine the actual return of the ark, we need to explore more fully why it was so utterly necessary.

The sociological and political milieu most closely parallel to that of David's Jerusalem and Israel is that of the Mesopotamian city-state. Since the city-state was recognized as the property of a deity, it was under the deity's control (Frankfort 1948, 258–61). As steward of the divine ruler and administrator of the deity's territory, the king was considered to be the protector of the country and people, particularly when it came to constructing cities and temples. The temple was viewed as the embodiment of the deity's cosmic presence, a replica of the holy mountain on which the deity was thought to reside. So, a proposal to build a temple meant, in effect, that the deity had declared his intention to take up residence in the city-state. The actual choice of a temple site was no incidental thing but was thought to be evidence of divine disclosure. It follows naturally, then, that the erection of a temple was viewed as an assertion of divine control over the political and religious life of the city-state. In the context of this Mesopotamian milieu, the relationship between the return of the ark and David's desire to build a temple should be clear. In 2 Samuel 6 Yahweh indicates that he will take up residence in the new Davidic capital of Jerusalem *through* the return of the ark. Once the residency is established, then David can act on his desire to build a temple.

Found in 2 Samuel 6:1–15, the narrative of the return of the ark is quite instructive regarding the relationship between David and Yahweh and the choice of Jerusalem. There is no doubt that David had carefully calculated the ark's return from its virtually self-enforced exile on the perimeter of Israelite-controlled territory. But there is a hitch—David had left Yahweh out of his calculations. His first attempt fails (v. 10). The ark then resides three months in the house of Obed-edom. Only after assurance of Yahweh's favor through the blessing of Obed-edom and his house will David try again. The appellation *King* in verse 12 indicates that success will attend this second venture (Carlson 1964, 85–

91). On the way to Jerusalem, sacrifices are offered every six paces (v. 13), suggesting a progressive sanctification of the territory through which the ark passes. That the ark is successfully brought to Jerusalem signifies Yahweh's choice of the city, despite David's premature arrangements. As only Yahweh had been responsible for the ark's capture (1 Sam. 4), so only Yahweh can bring it back.

The absence of the ark had corresponded with a theological interlude in the nation's history, but that era was over. The ark's presence is immediately taken to mean that the Divine King of Israel is in Jerusalem. Yahweh is now prepared to place himself at the center of Israelite life. The ark, the footstool of the divine throne over which God is in some way enthroned, is brought to the newly endorsed divine residence (2 Sam. 6:17). In the ancient world, it was customary to deposit written oaths or political agreements that founded a society at the feet of the deity or to bury them under the image of the god in the temple. In keeping with the custom, Israel kept the Sinai foundational documents in the covenant ark.

The joyful reception that the ark, the cult symbol of all Israel, receives (2 Sam. 6:15) is in recognition of God's hand in its return. (An analogy for the sacrifices and the festival banquet that David holds for all Israel is found in annals of Assyria describing the arrival of national gods at a new national capital [McCarter 1984, 178–82].) The return heralds a new beginning in the fortunes of David and his house and prepares the way for the covenant arrangements found in 2 Samuel 7. And the return brings to an end the tenuous kingship of the house of Saul, with which the ark had not been associated. With the dismissal of Michal, Saul's daughter, in 2 Samuel 6:20–23, David precludes the house of Saul from participating in Davidic succession.

Choice of the House of David (2 Sam. 7)

Second Samuel 7 considers the nature of David's kingship and through promises of an eternal throne for David and his house operates as a charter for a Davidic dynasty. However, the chapter opens by considering not David's house but Yahweh's. Capitalizing upon the return of the ark, David raises the question of a suitable dwelling place for it, that is, whether at this stage of his monarchy a temple should be built in Israel (vv. 1–2). The impulse for David's desire to build is stated as Yahweh's having given David "rest from all his enemies around him" (v. 1). This peace, a state of affairs foreshadowed in Deuteronomy 12:10, is recognized as double-edged: while peace can render Israel complacent and ungrateful for what Yahweh has done (Deut. 8:12–14), peace can also bring rest—the great blessing associated with prosperous life in the land. The implications of 2 Samuel 7:1 seem clear. In the wilderness wanderings that preceded the conquest, the ark, which resided within the Israelite camp, was perceived as the agent of victory; by its presence within Israel, it had promoted hope of rest in the form of the settled occupation of the Promised Land (Num. 10:35–36). By David's defeat of the Philistines, the immediate goal of the conquest, the general occupation of Palestine, had been achieved. With the ark's arrival in Jerusalem, a place had been established from which the rest could emanate. David's response to peace is meritorious, for he proposes to take advantage of the rest achieved by building a central sanctuary. Thus, what David proposes is in accord with what Deuteronomy 12:11 requires of Israel when such conditions prevail (Carlson 1964, 100–102).

Nathan's unqualified endorsement in 2 Samuel 7:3 of David's initial proposal to build may be seen as a premature prophetic rejoinder, for that very night Yahweh speaks to Nathan regarding David's plan (v. 4). Verses 5–16 reveal the content of Yahweh's message, which can be characterized as both "good and bad news." On the positive side, Yahweh exalts David's position and calls him "my servant" (v. 8), a title which in Israel's past had been reserved for the likes of Abraham, Moses, and Joshua. Furthermore, the title implies a leadership role for David, one that is alluded to in verses 10–11: David has accomplished what the judges could not. Indeed, Yahweh's exaltation of David affirms the characterization of him in 2 Samuel 5:2 as Israel's ideal shepherd. On the negative side, Yahweh refuses David's request to build a temple.

Why was David kept from building a temple? Some have seen the refusal as a victory for older Israelite prophetic traditions, which Nathan supposedly represented. According to this view, Israelite tribal religion could not without proper preparation entertain the notion of a fixed residence for the Deity, for previously Yahweh had wandered about with his people (2 Sam. 7:9) and had not required a temple. To be sure, the mobility of the ark throughout Israel endorsed the whole of occupied Palestine as a divine sanctuary. When a semipermanent shrine had been built at Shiloh, the result was a corrupt priesthood and a debased institutionalism (1 Sam. 1–3). To build a house, a temple, for Yahweh was unthinkable. But was it? Since permission to build a temple is given to David's son in Samuel 7:13, such characterization of the refusal founders.

Without a doubt, the building of a temple would bring about major theological changes. But 2 Samuel 7 is testimony to Israel's recognition of this fact and desire to reconcile dynastic kingship and the covenant, to find a solution to the difficulties under which Israelite kingship labored as a human institution during the reign of Saul. Let's look more closely at Yahweh's refusal. In 2 Samuel 7:5 through Nathan, Yahweh asks David, "Are you the one to build me a house to dwell in?" On one level, the question serves as a rebuke. As David should have learned when he tried on his own to take the ark to Jerusalem (2 Sam. 6:1–15), the initiative must be God's. On another level, the question can be variously interpreted, depending on the word emphasized. For example, if emphasis is placed on the word *dwell*, the question infers the utter impossibility of building a sanctuary in which Yahweh would be enthroned. If emphasis is placed on the word *me*, Yahweh's reply to his own question comes in verse 11: "The LORD himself will establish a house for you." And if emphasis is placed on the word *you*, Yahweh's reply comes in verse 13: "He [Solomon] is the one who will build a house for my Name." Though words are repeated and played upon in verses 5, 11, and 13, the counterpoint is between verses 5 and 13. ("You" in v. 5 contrasts with "he" in v. 13.) Though David may not build, Solomon, through whom the Davidic house is continued, may build.

Yahweh's choice of Solomon over David as temple builder is not a display of divine arbitrariness. Good reasons for deferring the project existed, and these are later given. First Kings 5:3 indicates that David put off building because of lack of opportunity, that is, he was fully engaged in the business of building an empire by the subjugation of enemies. First Chronicles 22:8 attributes the postponement to David's preoccupation with bloody conquest (see also 1 Chron. 28:3). And in 2 Samuel 7 is set the theology that accounts for the delay in temple building. On the one hand, rest had been given to David (v. 1); yet on the other hand, rest is still to come (v. 11). This second allusion to rest is part of a projection of what is still in store for David (vv. 9b–11; Carlson 1964, 111–14). Three important elements spell out what is ahead: Yahweh will (1) make David's "name great" (v. 9b), (2) "provide a place" for Israel (v. 10), and (3) give David "a rest" from his enemies (v. 11a), which presumably will eclipse the provisional respite already given (cf. v. 1). Only after these things are accomplished will a dynasty follow (v. 11b). What God has in store for David is reminiscent of what was promised to Abraham. The establishment of the Davidic empire will set the ideal borders of the Promised Land, which the promise to Abraham had foreshadowed (cf. v. 10 and Gen. 15:18; note that these borders are defined in Deut. 11:24 as Israel's "place"). At the same time, the foundation of the empire will bring David the Abrahamic great name (cf. v. 9 and Gen. 12:2).

According to 2 Samuel 7:9b–11, only when the Promised Land has been fully occupied and when rest has been bestowed will a Davidic dynasty be assured. Then once the line of David is sure, a temple will be constructed by Solomon (2 Sam. 7:12–13). Verse 13 specifies that the house will be built "for my [Yahweh's] Name," a formula which some view as a conscious theological adjustment to the concept in verse 5 of Yahweh's presence in the temple. That is, Yahweh himself will not sit enthroned in the temple, but only a reflex of himself, his name, will take his place there. Those who view the formula as a weakening of the concept of the Deity's dwelling in the temple ascribe its addition to the Deuteronomist, who had a transcendent view of God's presence. But we have noted that the phrase "to cause the name to dwell" (cf. Deut. 12:11) is a well-attested ownership formula in the prebiblical world (Wenham 1971, 114). Therefore, the use of "for my Name" in verse 13 is an assertion of Yahweh's kingship and ownership over Israel, and it is only within the context of that assertion that David's line can be permanently established. Verse 13, then, reaffirms the very close link between divine and human kingships.

The eternal kingship of the Davidic line is stated in 2 Samuel 7:13b in absolute terms: "And I will establish the throne of his kingdom forever." Though verse 14 provides for chastening, the new covenant promises will not be withdrawn. The Davidic house will stand forever, but this divine pronouncement appears to contrast markedly with historical realities that eventually bring about the dissolution of the Davidic empire. From this apparent conflict springs the question of whether the promises to David are conditional or unconditional. In the Old Testament, there is evidence supporting both responses. Second Samuel 23:5 attributes the following words to David: "For he has made with me an everlasting covenant" (NRSV). Also, Psalm 89:33–37 goes to extraordinary lengths to emphasize the unchanging character of the David covenant. Yet, the covenant is cast as conditional in 1 Kings 2:4, 8:25, 9:4–5, Psalm 89:29–32, and 132:12. How can the covenant be both conditional and unconditional? The Scriptures distinguish between the unconditional generality of the promise and the conditional particularity of an individual in the line of David. That is, though the line will not fail, covenantal promises may be withdrawn from individuals in David's house. In physical terms the Davidic line failed when Jerusalem fell to Nebuchadnezzar in 587/586 B.C., but in spiritual terms Jesus of Nazareth eschatologically consummates the promises given to the house of David.

Though the word *covenant* is not found in 2 Samuel 7, it is used to label the promises given to David in the first half of the chapter. How do the Davidic promises relate to the existing covenant between Israel and God? It is clear from verses 6–16, in which the fortunes of David are interwoven with the unfolding of the history of Israel, that the promises are given to David as Israel's representative. Moreover, David is the agent through whom the exodus deliverance, that is, the rest in the Promised Land, is finally to be achieved. So the sonship terms previously applied to Israel (Exod. 4:22) are now applied to David (v. 14). David as king is the representative carrier of the promises to Israel! Through the noted allusions in 2 Samuel 7 to Genesis 12:1–3, the Davidic promises take on the tenor of the Abrahamic covenant. Furthermore, the blessing of rest, secured by the sanctuary presence of God, holds out hope that the covenant blessing of creation might be restored. Even beyond the promises of 2 Samuel 7, Davidic kingship is linked to Israel's covenant. For example, Psalm 110 asserts the priestly nature of the Jerusalem, and thus the Davidic, kingship (v. 4). The person of the king embodies the covenant expectations of Exodus 19:6 that Israel itself would become a priestly royalty (see p. 45). All of these correspondences make clear that the covenant with David fits within the covenant structure of Israel.

The tenor of David's prayer in 2 Samuel 7:18–29 indicates that David understood the covenantal significance of the divine promises and their effect upon humanity as a whole. And a curious phrase in verse 19 might indicate David's precise understanding of the relationship between the promises to him and the covenant. A survey of various biblical versions shows no consensus on the translation of the phrase. In the Revised Standard Version, it appears in the margin as "this is the law for man." In the New Revised Standard Version, it is the exhortation "May this be instruction for the people." But in view of extrabiblical parallels for the phrase, it is best translated as "and this [i.e., the new addition to the promise doctrine] is the Charter for all mankind" (Kaiser 1974, 315). That is to say, in the oracle delivered to him David rightly sees the future and the destiny of the human race. Built upon the broad history of God's covenants from creation onward, the promises to David convey the divine intent for human development. And David is fully aware of the covenantal connections.

Eschatological Significance of Davidic Kingship

An understanding of the development and role of David kingship in Israel is crucial to an understanding of biblical eschatology. Through the occupant of the throne of Israel, Davidic kingship is to reflect the values that the Sinai covenant requires of the nation. The Davidic king is the representative of his people, he embodies them and incorporates their functions and their hopes. The Davidic king operates as Yahweh's vice-regent, who bears Yahweh's rule over the nations of the world. The Davidic covenant goes back to the divine intention not merely for Israel through Sinai but for humanity through Abraham, and thus to the manner in which the debacle of Genesis 3–11 is to be reversed and Eden is to be restored. Through Davidic kingship, divine government through Yahweh's appointed intermediary, to whom the world must be subject, is established. Thus, Yahweh's full intentions for the human race will be realized through wise administration by Israel's messiah. The notions of the charter for humanity, of the dominion which that is to confer, and of kingship over Israel exercised by the Davidic representative were all finally brought together and fused in the person of Jesus of Nazareth, who as son of David was son of Abraham, yet also Son of God.

4

Zion Theology and
Preexilic Eschatology

Solomon's reign marks the fulfilment of various Abrahamic and Davidic promises. With the very small exceptions of Tyre and Sidon, the Promised Land is secure in Israelite hands. Israel is a great nation—with people too numerous to be counted (1 Kings 4:20). And Solomon, having achieved political rest, begins to build the temple (1 Kings 5:4–5). The sanctuary, which in earlier days had been equated with the Promised Land as a whole, is now the completed Jerusalem temple, thus fulfilling the expectations of Deuteronomy 12:5–11. When the ark is deposited in the temple sanctuary, the exodus cloud fills the temple (1 Kings 8:10). From this point on, the Sinai and Davidic covenants are formally linked, and the temple is the centralized bearer of the salvation-history traditions and hopes.

Early Beginnings of Zion Theology

The Solomonic narratives (1 Kings 1–11) reveal the extent to which the promises to Abraham and David were fulfilled and the influence of the Israelite kingdom in the world. During the time of Solomon, Jerusalem becomes an international center. Moreover, the beginning of eschatological expectations associated with the city, known as Zion theology, appear. Originally a name referring to the southeast hill of the temple site, Zion is the theological name for Jerusalem in the Old Testament. Basic to the theology is the belief that Jerusalem, inhabited by the saved remnant of Israel, will become in the new age the governmental center of the kingdom of God to which the world will come in constant pilgrimage.

Jerusalem as a World Center (1 Kings 10)

As people learned of Solomon, they began to travel to Jerusalem from all nations, from all the kings of the earth, to hear his wise counsel (1 Kings 4:34). Though the pilgrimages to Jerusalem were many (1 Kings 10:24), the visit of one particular individual indicates the extent of the influence exercised by the Israelite court in Solomon's day. First Kings 10 records the visit of the queen of Sheba, the ruler of the greatest trading empire of its time, the vast Sabean kingdom of the Arabian peninsula.

Solomon, as portrayed in chapter 10, is a king equipped with wisdom that confounds the world and surrounded by a court that far surpasses other courts in splendor. At the height of her political power, Israel exercises her attractiveness over all the world. And the queen of Sheba is overcome by the magnificence of what she sees, only the half of which had been told to her previously. Confessing the special election of Israel, her eminent place in the world, and the permanent place the nation will occupy in the divine plan (v. 9), the Sabean queen offers to Solomon the homage of the world by her gifts (v. 10). This narrative of the queen's visit to Jerusalem is probably the paradigm from which was drawn later prophecy of the eschatological pilgrimage of the nations to Zion (Isa. 2:2–4; chaps. 60–62). As the queen of Sheba came to Jerusalem for wisdom, so shall the Gentile nations come to Zion to receive wisdom and the Torah.

Notion of a Godly Remnant (1 Kings 17–19)

Out of 1 Kings there emerges another precursor to a fundamental tenet of the theology of Zion—the notion of a remnant. Chapters 17–19 comprise narratives from the northern kingdom about the prophet Elijah. The prophet bursts onto the scene coming from the Transjordan region, which may have remained relatively unaffected by the syncretism growing in Israel. Declaring a three-year drought, Elijah challenges the gods of Canaan and asserts Yahweh's, not Baal's, control of life and fertility (1 Kings 17:1–7). Then by demonstrating that Yahweh is able to restore life (vv. 8–24), Elijah further challenges the supremacy of Mot, the Canaanite god of death and the underworld. These events lead to an inevitable confrontation between Elijah and a syncretistic royal establishment led by Ahab and his wife, Jezebel, the Tyrian princess and daughter of the leading proponent of Canaanite practice in the Mediterranean area.

First Kings 18:19 records Elijah's challenge to the 450 prophets of Baal and the 400 prophets of Asherah, the consort of the high god in the Canaanite pantheon. Together with these prophets all Israel gathers at the ancient coastal sanctuary on Mount Carmel, where Elijah asks Israel to decide between Baal and Yahweh: "How long will you waver between two opinions? If the LORD is God, follow him; but if Baal is God, follow him" (v. 21). By putting the words of the first commandment before Israel, Elijah in effect asks Israel to return to the covenant. Since the challenge is met by silence, Elijah invokes a trial by fire. The prophets of Baal endeavor at length to conjure up their deity, but have no success (v. 29). Then Elijah rebuilds the twelve-stone altar of Yahweh on Carmel, thereby indicating the indissolubility of the covenant people of Israel (vv. 30–32), and Yahweh dramatically answers Elijah by fire (v. 38). The prophets of Baal are then slain (v. 40), and the rain which had been withheld for the three years past is now given (v. 45).

In view of Elijah's prophetic triumphs in chapter 18, it is surprising that the next chapter begins by describing Jezebel's rage and Elijah's fright and flight for his life into the deserts of the south (19:2–3). Mosaic typology is evident throughout the narrative, in which Elijah is transformed into a Moses-like figure and links are established between Horeb and Sinai. Strengthened by an angelic presence, Elijah proceeds on a journey of forty days and nights to Horeb (vv. 4–8; cf. Exod. 24:18), where he lodges in a spot that the text identifies as "the cave" (v. 9). In light of the many Mosaic associations in the chapter, it appears that "the cave" is the cave of the Mosaic theophany in Exodus 33:22. It seems further that Elijah, alone among faithless Israel, attempts to replicate the Mosaic experience of the exodus period. Moses had been faced with a similar pattern of rebellion and apostasy and had turned the sword on fellow Israelites (Exod. 32:25–29), as Elijah had ordered against the Carmel apostates. But instead of a Mosaic-type theophany, there comes to Elijah at Horeb a question that inescapably seems to be a rebuke: "What are you doing *here*, Elijah?" (v. 9, emphasis added). Why here, Elijah, when the business of the kingdom calls there, up in Israel? In reply, Elijah retells what has happened: Israel's prophetic representatives have been slain by apostates, the covenant has been forsaken, and only Elijah himself is left as a prophetic voice (v. 10), as Moses had been in the episode of Exodus 32.

A theophany of the dimension of Sinai as given to Elijah. All the traditional elements—earthquake, wind, and fire—are present to announce, not constitute, the divine presence. Then afterwards there comes to Elijah the "gentle whisper," or specifically "the voice of drawn-out silence" (v. 12). Puzzled by the absence of communication, for nothing appears to have been heard by Elijah, the prophet moves to the entrance of the cave, and the divine question is put to him again (v. 13). Clearly, Elijah has learned nothing from the theophany; thus, it seems that God had nothing to add to what had been communicated on Sinai to Moses. After Elijah responds to the question as he had before (v. 14; cf. v. 10), Yahweh attaches a very definite political commission to Elijah's prophetic office (vv. 15–17). In short, Elijah is commissioned to go back to where the difficulties had been experienced and to act steadfastly on the basis of the Yahwistic faith. Yahweh then reveals that Israel is not bereft of witnesses; in fact, there are some seven thousand who have not bowed the knee to Baal (v. 18). This is the first biblical attestation of a group of believers within the nation, different from the nation itself. Though previously remnant terminology had been used to indicate survivors of historical and political catastrophes, this is the first time the terminology is used theologically. So at Horeb no addition to Israel's faith comes to Elijah, for there is no need. A community of faith—seven thousand steadfast believers—exists in the kingdom of Israel.

Prophetic Eschatology

The Books of Kings survey the Davidic empire from its rise to its fall—including promises to David, promise fulfilment under Solomon, divided kingdom, disintegration in the north and south, attempts at reform, end of the northern kingdom with the fall of Samaria in 722 B.C., and virtual end of the southern kingdom with the fall of Jerusalem and the beginning of the Babylonian exile in 587/586 B.C. And it is the prophets who wrestle with the questions posed by these political events. If God chose the Davidic dynasty and Jerusalem, what did their end mean? Would Israel as a people of God continue? If so, how?

The eighth-century prophets Amos, Micah, and Isaiah, faced with the impending exile of the north and the continuing apostasy of the south, reassess the theological role of Jerusalem and consider further the matter of divine choice and the divine purpose for Israel, the people of God. As a result, the roles of both Jerusalem and Israel are redefined: (1) the city of Jerusalem would meet with physical punishment, and (2) the carriers of the covenant hopes would be a remnant of believers within the faithless nation, rather than national Israel. In the seventh century, Zephaniah continues the notion of a remnant—one that will be saved from God's holy war against Judah.

Amos

The Book of Amos addresses the question of Jerusalem's religious significance for the whole of Israel, the north and the south. Indeed, references to Jerusalem, which stands parallel to Zion (1:2), frame the book. At the beginning, the LORD through Amos roars from the Jerusalem sanctuary in condemnation of the northern apostate shrines (1:2). The prophet's frequent condemnation of such shrines rests upon a theological base: the centrality of the Jerusalem temple. At the end, Amos envisages an eschatological restoration of the united kingdom of Israel under David (9:11–15). The enigmatic reference in verse 11 to raising "the booth of David that is fallen" (NRSV) may be to Jerusalem since hopes for the city are linked to the future of Davidic rule (cf. Isa. 1:8). If the fallen booth is indeed the city, this is the first instance of the eschatological expectation of a New Jerusalem. And Israel's eschatological possession of "the remnant of Edom and all the nations who are called by my name" (v. 12) indicates a final triumph of the people of God over the typical enemy. (This passage prophesying the final supremacy of God's people is later used in Acts 15:16–18 to justify inclusion of the Gentiles into the body of believers.)

Remnant terminology is used in the Book of Amos in theological contexts. It is used, for example, to identify those to whom divine mercy is to be shown: "Perhaps the LORD God Almighty will have mercy on the remnant of Joseph" (5:15). (Though the verse may be referring to a faithful remnant, the suggestion that the reference is ironic or derisive should not be dismissed [Hunter 1982, 94].) It is argued by Gerhard Hasel that the remnant notion is also found in chapter 9 (1974, 207–15). Here the sinners who will die (vv. 8–10) stand in contrast to the returning exiles (vv. 11–15). Note also Yahweh's promise in verse 8 that the house of Jacob will not totally be destroyed.

Micah

Micah, with much the same emphasis as his contemporary Isaiah, pronounces judgment upon the people of God, that is, historical Israel and Judah. In the book are alternating messages of judgment and salvation. In chapters 4–5, a prophecy of salvation, Micah speaks of divine rule exercised from Zion as the hope for the future. The seven oracles in this section each report some threat to Zion and its removal, thus indicating an eschatological vindication of Jerusalem. For example, the threat at the beginning of chapter 5 is the Assyrians—a threat removed by verse 6. In the midst of this oracle is a depiction of ideal Davidic rule (v. 2; cf. Matt. 2:6), suggesting, perhaps, that only ideal rule of this character will be the solution to the nation's political difficulties. The prophet foresees an eschatological Jerusalem that is identical to the one Isaiah describes: the city as the worship center of the world to which all the nations will flow in pilgrimage (4:1–5; cf. Isa. 2:2–5).

Micah makes a distinction between a holy remnant and the nation, as does Isaiah, for he prophesies that God's redemptive action will be directed toward the faithful. In Micah 4:7 the prophet describes how Yahweh will restore the ravaged flock—the lame and the rejected. By this supernatural and invincible action, says Micah, preeminence will come once again to Zion (v. 8). The notion of the remnant is carried further in Micah 5:7–9, where the prophet examines the faithful's role. As life-refreshing dew from the divine source (v. 7), the remnant will be a channel of blessing in the world. But as a lion among sheep, the remnant will be an agent of international judgment (v. 8), exacting retribution from the former punishers of Israel.

The Book of Micah ends with a long hymnic expression of hope (7:7–20). Jerusalem speaks in verses 8–10, expressing strong confidence in Yahweh. In verses 11–13 the prophet tells Jerusalem of the good that is to come, but verses 14–17 show Israel in trouble again. At this point Micah calls for an exodus-type intervention to end the humiliation imposed by the nations. And the prophet is sure that God will respond to this appeal—because of God's immeasurable capacity to forgive and his steadfast adherence to the Abrahamic covenant (vv. 18–20).

Isaiah 1–39

The Book of Isaiah, particularly the first half (chaps. 1–39), explores such theological issues as the role of Jerusalem, the holy remnant, and Davidic kingship. In Isaiah 1, which serves as an introduction to the whole book as well as to the first subsection (chaps. 1–2), the prophet denounces Jerusalem for its apostasy. According to his indictment of the period before 701 B.C., the worship structure of Jerusalem and Judah, the very center of the nation's corporate life, had been infected by blatant apostasy. Thus, God will no longer receive the products of the sacrificial system, for they have become an abomination to him (vv. 11–13a). Moreover, God will no longer tolerate the people's prayers (v. 15). Such shows of perfunctory repentance will no longer avert the punishment that must soon be administered (vv. 18–20). Jerusalem must be cleansed, and judgment must be visited upon her. But the assurance is given in the eschatological oracle of Isaiah 2:2–4 that once this has been done, Jerusalem will emerge again as the divine world center—Zion, the city of righteousness. Before we examine Isaiah's eschatological assurance, however, we must consider the nature of the thoroughgoing rejection of Jerusalem in Isaiah 1 in light of the entire prophecy.

It is clear from the tenor of the Book of Isaiah that the judgment to be visited upon Jerusalem is for purposes of cleansing only. Though Isaiah begins with Jerusalem under judgment, it concludes with the choice of the New Jerusalem and the divine purpose for her (chaps. 65–66). The role of Jerusalem and her function within God's plan are the themes that bind the Book of Isaiah together as a theological unit. To illustrate, let's look at movement within the book more closely. In chapter 39, which concludes the first half of the book, the prophet forecasts the punishment of Jerusalem and the despoliation of the temple for King Hezekiah's foolishness in showing the treasures of the temple and palace to the ambassadors from Babylon. Isaiah makes clear that Jerusalem will be destroyed and the people of Judah will be exiled. In the very next chapter (40:1–11), the prolog to the second half of the prophecy (which we consider in the later discussion of the exilic and postexilic situations, which the material of 40–66 seems to project), the prophet sees the prospect of the early termination of the exile and the exaltation of Jerusalem as the city of God once again. Thus, chapters 1–39 move from the prospect of judgment upon Jerusalem to certainty of it; chapters 40–66 move from the prospect of the exiles' return to the city to the emergence of the New Jerusalem, which is to arise as the centerpiece of the new creation (chaps. 65–66). Jerusalem is the key to the movement in the book. And it is the notion of the centrality of Jerusalem and its role as the city of God, the center of the world, that binds the total prophecy of Isaiah together and that takes us to the limit of Old Testament eschatological projections.

Eschatological Role of Jerusalem/Zion

Isaiah's prophecy of hope in chapter 2 follows upon the projected desolation of Jerusalem in chapter 1. Though Isaiah 2:2–4 describes a Jerusalem fitted as Zion for her role as the world governmental center, this will happen only after the judgment foreshadowed in Isaiah 1 has been administered. Indeed, the oracle in Isaiah 2:2–4 is one of Zion's elevation in the *latter days*. Tracing the development of the concept of Jerusalem indicates that Isaiah's prophecy likely grew out of existent eschatological hopes regarding Jerusalem/Zion and that such expectations are presupposed in oracles such as his. In other words, the residents of Jerusalem and Judah in Isaiah's time and before had certain expectations for Jerusalem as the divine city of God and the Davidic royal city and for the temple.

Zion never completely eclipses Sinai, but the city does receive, especially in Isaiah, prominence as the temple mountain and progressively develops into the major symbol carrying Israel's hopes for the future. In the monarchical period, Zion is prophetically identified as the cosmic site from which Yahweh, who was enthroned in Jerusalem, would rule the world. This concept of the cosmic mountain serving as the divine abode was pervasive throughout the ancient Near East, extending even to featureless Egypt. As a place set apart because of divine activity or presence, the cosmic mountain was viewed as an ordering or stabilizing principle for the world (Clifford 1972, 7). Since the ancient peoples thought the base of the cosmic mountain rested in the netherworld and the summit projected into the very heavens themselves, the mountain is seen as the place of communication between the two spheres and the point at which the divine and earthly spheres intersect. Divine presence and governmental rule coalesce in the notion. (The mountain of El, the titular head of the Canaanite pantheon, in Ugarit was the place where the divine council of the gods decided issues that affected the universe [Clifford 1972, 190–91].) In Psalm 48:2, where Zion is compared with Baal's mountain dwelling in Canaan, Zion is perceived as the cosmic mountain. It seems clear from Ezekiel 28:11–15 that the cosmic mountain is further identified with Eden, the garden paradise of God. In later rabbinic theology, Zion is the capstone which keeps in check the forces of chaos, the containment of which made creation and all civilization possible (Levenson 1985, 133). Moreover, the foundation stone of the temple bars the way to sheol. Were it not for the temple of Zion the contained chaos waters would surge forth undoing creation, as they had done in the time of the flood.

What was the theology regarding Zion as reflected in the Book of Isaiah? It is generally agreed the theology contains these points:

1. Zion is the cosmic mountain, the center of the world (Isa. 2:2; cf. Ps. 48:1–2), and has been chosen by Yahweh as the world governmental center (Isa. 2:3–4; cf. Ps. 78:68; 132:13).
2. Zion is thus the meeting place of the divine council, which in mythic thought is the ruling body of lesser deities presided over by the head of the pantheon (Isa. 6:8; cf. Ps. 82; 89:5–7).
3. Zion is the center from which emanates the divine decrees (Isa. 2:3; 14:26–27; cf. Ps. 2:4–7; 50; 93:5).
4. Zion is the source of the river of Paradise, of the special streams proceeding from it (Isa. 33:21; cf. Ps. 46:4; Ezek. 47:1–12).
5. At Zion, Yahweh has triumphed over the forces of chaos (Isa. 27:1; cf. Ps. 46:3) as well as over the historical embodiment of the chaos forces, namely, the kings and their nations (Ps. 46:6; 48:4–7; 76:5-8), destroying the weapons of war as a result (Ps. 76:3).
6. Identified as the Garden of Eden or the embodiment of it, Zion is the location of plenty and perfection, which the people of God will share (Isa. 11:6–9; cf. Ps. 36:8–9; 50:2).

7. To Zion, the nations will make a pilgrimage at the end time (Isa. 2:2–4; chaps. 60–62; cf. Ps. 72:8–11; 102:12–22), for Zion will be the center of the new creation in which all human life and values will be transformed (Isa. 35:1–10; 65:17–18).

Implicit in these theological points is the doctrine that Zion will not fall to any foe, protected as she was by Yahweh's presence (Ps. 46:5, 7, 11; 76:2). This doctrine of Zion's inviolability, which is accepted as an old tradition, seems to have emerged as a result of the Davidic capture of Jerusalem, Yahweh's choice of the city as his site for the temple, and the transfer of the ark.

Central to the Zion tradition is the tenet that at Zion Yahweh dwells among his people by means of his presence in the temple. In a confessedly old psalm, Yahweh is described as the King of Glory, who inhabits Zion as King and enters into his sanctuary (Ps. 24:7–10), which in Isaiah is described as the mountain of Yahweh (11:9). The enthronement psalms (47, 93, 96–97, 99) depict Yahweh as King on Zion. It seems clear that, once Jerusalem was captured and the temple was built, all the older creation and salvation motifs were transferred there. Zion is regarded as the creation of Yahweh (Isa. 14:32). Indeed, Yahweh had founded Zion as a sure stone, that is, the cornerstone of his house (Isa. 28:16). But Zion is also closely connected with Davidic kingship (Ps. 132), for from there Yahweh protects Israel's king, Yahweh's anointed.

Zion's Future (Isa. 2:2–4)

Isaiah's assurance regarding Zion found in chapter 2 begins with the words "in the back of days" (v. 2; "in the last days" NIV), a phrase that in part reveals how the ancient Israelites understood the eschaton. The phrase occurs for the first time in Jacob's blessing on the Israelite confederacy as the blessing of Abraham was passed on to Israel at large (Gen. 49:1). In this blessing of Jacob, the future for Israel had already been fixed by past promises uttered by God. Thus, the way for the future is, at least in some sense, a fulfilment of the prospects sketched out in the past. The phrase "in the last days" refers to the uncertain future, whether near or remote, and its general meaning cannot be pressed further but must be determined from individual contexts. In Isaiah 2:2 the context suggests that Jerusalem's remote, or ultimate, future is on view.

The Jerusalem temple, the earthly palace of Israel's God, is pictured in Isaiah 2:2 as a world mountain, the point of contact between heaven and earth. Thus, the verse subordinates geographical reality to biblical eschatology, for the hillock of Mount Zion is elevated in theological thought to the highest of the world's mountains, the central point of the world, the place where heaven and sheol meet. It is with the universal recognition of the divine mountain that the passage is concerned, and this is underscored by the absence of hostilities and the nation's new attitude toward the city. In the last days, Zion will exhibit an overwhelming, even inexplicable, drawing power, a pull that defies gravity: "And all nations shall *flow* to it" (v. 2 NKJV, emphasis added). In verse 3 the phrase "house of the God of Jacob" has a sonorous patriarchal ring, reminding us of Yahweh's choice of Zion and fulfilment of the patriarchal promises. For it is God's presence within Israel that blesses her, provides living space for her, and has brought political fulfilment of the Abrahamic promises.

From Zion will go Israel's law, her covenant possession (v. 3). Since in the Bible a covenant context is prerequisite to operative law, the Torah's going forth implies that the Abrahamic covenant will be universally operative. Such universality will accomplish Israel's mission to be a light to the Gentiles (Isa. 42:6; 49:6), since God's wise provisions will be shared on a worldwide, rather than national, basis. And in the cosmic sphere, Yahweh as Lord of the universe, and acknowledged as such, will guarantee the peace (v. 4), exercising his rule over redeemed humanity in the way intended at creation.

Isaiah 2:2–4, responding to the message of somber judgment for Jerusalem found in chapter 1, encapsulates a firmly entrenched eschatology that is expanded upon at the end of the book. In these three verses are typical prophetic hopes for Jerusalem and Israel and the essentials of prophetic eschatology. Since Micah 4:1–4 virtually repeats Isaiah 2:1–4, it is likely that both prophets drew upon a tradition that preceded them. It is difficult to overestimate the impact of the ancient oracle. Chapter 1 rejects Judah's own religious paraphernalia, including pilgrimages to the holy city, but the oracle sets before us the ultimate of eschatological pilgrimages. Outsiders will flock to Mount Zion from every quarter of the inhabited earth. Though Judah had refused Yahweh's wisdom and counsel, the world will struggle in pilgrimage to Zion to receive it. The passage presumes, however, that the world's perception of Yahweh's presence and being will be altered radically: it will take a frightful day of reckoning in order for God to be esteemed above all other possible alternatives and possessions. In Israel's case, it will take exile, forgiveness, return, and a new national heart before she is ready to receive the world. For the world, it will take an understanding of what God's mission really involves. As the detail of the Book of Isaiah makes clear, it will take the mission of the Servant, despised, rejected, but finally acknowledged by Israel and the Gentiles as an offering for sin.

Exodus 15:17 reveals that God would choose the entire Promised Land as a holy mountain; however, in time Zion would develop into the divine choice from which the Promised Land and eventually *the world* would be regulated. That Israel's eschatology is universal in scope is not surprising, for Israel's vocation of Sinai has the wider world in view. Her mission is to draw the world into the relationship that she enjoys with Yahweh. The way of life directed and guided by Yahweh's Torah is to be the path the world itself will travel. In the ancient world mountains and hills symbolized pride, and in Israel's experience they were generally places of illicit worship (Isa. 1:29–30; 2:12–16). But Isaiah is stating in 2:2–4 that Zion will be the only legitimate place of worship and Yahweh, the sole object of worship. In the future, no other hill packed with capricious deities could challenge Yahweh's holy hill. Peoples and nations would flow into Zion to receive what emanated from her: the law of Yahweh and the word of the LORD, which alone could guarantee that life would issue from Zion.

With good reason, some commentators view the Zion oracle in Isaiah 2:2–4 as the reversal of the Babel event in Genesis 11. There the peoples of the earth were to be scattered because they themselves constructed the supposed point of contact between heaven and earth, the pseudocosmic mountain whose top would reach to the heavens. Yahweh at that time expressed the desire to scatter the boastful builders by beginning with these words, "Come, let us go *down* . . . " (v. 7, emphasis added). According to Isaiah, who was considering the cosmic mountain called Zion, the scattered peoples at the end of history will say, "Come, let us go *up*" (2:3, emphasis added). Mount Zion will not bring division to the world's society, but will offer healing and peace. Since Yahweh will be the final authority and absolute judge with no human intermediaries, life will be regulated wisely. The plows and pruning hooks into which the weapons of war will be turned are life-yielding tools (v. 4), and those who come to Zion will wield them to propagate the new life they will receive there.

Isaiah's eschatological oracle mentions nothing about Davidic messiahship exercised from Jerusalem. Nevertheless, it seems clear that the prophet presumed Davidic kingship would be exercised from the world center, for the omission must be balanced by the messianic oracles found in Isaiah 7–11. To be sure, elsewhere in the book Davidic kingship is treated as the essential ingredient for divine rule over Israel (9:1–7; chap. 11). What follows the prophet's assurance about Zion indicates that his contemporaries will not respond to his message in a positive way; their pride will get in the way (vv. 5–22). Thus, Isaiah's realization leads him to call in chapter 3 for the cleansing of Zion and its leadership and to proclaim salvation for the remnant of Israel (4:2–6; Sweeney 1988, 36).

A HOLY REMNANT

The theological concept of a holy remnant first appears, as shown in this chapter, in the narrative of Elijah and is also found in the prophecy of Amos. But in the Book of Isaiah, the notion of an Israel within Israel leaps to great prominence. Isaiah 4:2–6 refers to Yahweh's eschatological gathering of the people of God; it begins, "In that day the Branch of the LORD will be beautiful and glorious" (v. 2a). This oracle of hope follows a description in chapter 3 of upheaval caused by the reversal of societal roles and of thoroughgoing judgment upon Israel. Though "the Branch of the LORD" is a technical term for the messiah in Jeremiah (23:5; 33:15) and Zechariah (3:8; 6:12), it is used differently here. Its parallel in verse 2b is not, as we might expect, the Davidic monarchy but "the fruit of the land." The remainder of verse 2, "the pride and glory of the survivors in Israel," makes it plain that Isaiah uses the word *branch* figuratively to refer to the remnant of Israel. Isaiah's use within the oracle of the names *Israel, Zion,* and *Jerusalem* indicates further that the election tradition associated with these names will be transferred to the remnant, thus identifying the survivors as the new people of God. In redeemed Jerusalem, as described in verses 5–6, the protecting presence of God will be available continually, a presence represented here by the old exodus symbols of cloud and fire. For the remnant, God's judgment will not be destructive but purifying, and those saved will owe their continued existence to Yahweh and his faithfulness (Hasel 1974, 269–70). Since Yahweh will have judged and purged these people, the remnant is deemed "holy".

Isaiah 6 reveals that the purpose of the prophet's ministry is to announce a terrible conflagration that will leave the land decimated. The people of Judah will be exiled; with the land depopulated, the cities will lie waste (v. 11). The once-proud national tree will be felled (v. 13). It is a picture of terrible desolation. However, Isaiah also proclaims that a holy seed will emerge from the stock of the national tree (v. 13). Though only a stump will be left, there is potential in it and all will not be lost. In a different setting in chapter 7, the prophet holds out hope of a remnant again. During the reign of Jotham in Judah, Syria and Israel formed an alliance to prevent the western incursions of Assyria and wanted Judah to join them. When Judah refused, the confederates attempted to coerce her by military action. As Jotham's successor, Ahaz, set out to view the defenses of Jerusalem, Yahweh sent Isaiah and his son to intercept the king (v. 3). The notion of the remnant appears in the name of the prophet's son—Shearjashub, which means "*only a remnant* shall return." (Emphasis is placed on the noun in the translation because of its emphatic position in the Hebrew.) At first glance it might appear that the name symbolically prophesies a national defeat from which only few will survive. But since the verb *return* is often used metaphorically to mean "repent" or "turn back in faith to Yahweh," more is probably intended (Hasel 1974, 281–82). The prophecy symbolized by the name, then, is that only a remnant will take the prophetic advice offered by Isaiah to the house of David and, in so doing, will turn back in faith to Yahweh.

The message of a community of faith emerging from the destruction of the body politic is a pervasive notion in Isaiah 1–39 (e.g., 1:24–26; 4:2–3; 7:1–9; 10:20–23; 28:5–6; 30:15–17): imperial Israel will give way to the community of faith. From Isaiah's time on, this is the new note that the classical prophets will sound. Isaiah's message of an emerging remnant community is repeated in preexilic prophecy (Mic. 4:6–7; 5:7–9; Zeph. 2:9; 3:12–13) and is further developed in material reflecting the exilic and postexilic periods, such as Isaiah 40–66, Jeremiah, and Ezekiel.

DAVIDIC, DIVINE, AND MESSIANIC KINGSHIP (ISA. 6–11)

Integral to a discussion of Zion theology is the matter of leadership, that is, the question of who rules, or will rule, the city. To put it simply, who is king? In chapter 6 the prophet Isaiah confronts this issue of kingship, which is quite complex indeed, for there are three types of kingship to consider—Davidic, divine, and messianic.

Isaiah 6 begins with Judah at the peak of prosperity but concludes with the saving of only the faithful remnant of the nation (v. 13). Exile has taken hold of the people of Judah, and only a stump—as potential and as a remnant of the once-proud national tree—remains. Isaiah receives a vision in the year that King Uzziah died (v. 1). Having reigned for fifty-two years, Uzziah had been in political terms an exemplary ruler. He had restored the southern kingdom, extending Judah into the territory of the Philistines in the west and incorporating Edom to the south. He undertook measures to revive southern agriculture and fortified Jerusalem. With the king's death, it may have seemed to Isaiah that Judean politics had taken a turn for the worse. And perhaps Isaiah was left wondering who would guide the ship of state and how the political future of Judah would be secured. Then as Isaiah mediated upon Judah's future after the death of this most able and successful king, Isaiah sees the Lord, the one from whom all history takes its departure. Moreover, since Isaiah sees the retinue surrounding Yahweh in the heavenlies, the prophet understands the nature of Yahweh's heavenly majesty. Seated on a throne, Yahweh is ministered to by a seraphim band who unceasingly chant a doxology of praise (v. 3). The foundations of the temple shake, and the building becomes filled with smoke (v. 4).

The prophetic reaction to all this is described in verse 5. Overcome with a feeling of personal sinfulness, Isaiah cries, "Woe is me, for I am undone! Because I am a man of unclean lips, and I dwell in the midst of a people of unclean lips; for my eyes have seen the King" (NKJV). But the prophet's confession is not merely prophetic reticence or a feeling of personal inadequacy for the task. Isaiah cries out because of the universal sinfulness of Judah, "a people of unclean lips." Yet, what does this characterization of the people mean? Verse 3 provides a clue, a point of comparison. The seraphim's lips proclaim the glory of God as King of heaven and earth; their worship acknowledges Yahweh's divine kingship and betrays a right attitude to it. As for Isaiah and Judah, their sin is their inability or unwillingness to properly acknowledge the kingship of Yahweh and to culticly worship Yahweh as the seraphim do. The cause of the rejection of Judah's cult and of the punishment foreshadowed in Isaiah 1:10–20 now seems clear. Remember that Judah's worship was based on the acknowledgment of Yahweh's covenant lordship. The people constituted the kingdom of priests, and Yahweh was their king. Right worship always meant the recognition of Yahweh's right to rule. Since the people's worship through prayers and sacrifices had become perfunctory and indifferent, this clearly constituted a rejection of Yahweh's kingship over Judah. Perhaps the nation had been beguiled, as Isaiah had, by the success of Uzziah's reign.

Isaiah's confession in 6:5, especially the reference to Yahweh, reveals the subject of chapter 6: Davidic versus divine kingship. In verse 1 the prophet identifies the dead Uzziah as the king of Judah, but in verse 5 he proclaims Yahweh's divine rule over all creation. Set before the prophet is the clash of two imperia, the earthly and the heavenly. However, the use of the article in verse 5 to name Yahweh as *"the* king" makes clear which kingship will prevail. What Isaiah comes to see and what he must announce to Judah is that the control of history rests, not with the Uzziahs of the day, but with Yahweh.

Isaiah is then sent to Judah with a message of unavoidable judgment (6:8–13), judgment on the people but also on Judah's earthly kingship. Indeed, much of chapters 6–9 deals with the rejection of the kingship of the house of David. Events of the later eighth century see the prophet's predictions dramatically carried out. The Assyrian response to the revolt led by Syria and Israel would spell the end of the northern kingdom in 722 B.C. Then Assyrian ravages gradually devastate Judah until in 701 B.C. her hold on the Promised Land is reduced to a besieged Jerusalem. Only divine intervention can avert complete destruction at this time (Isa. 36–38). Though the judgment announced by Isaiah is severe, the prophet's message is not without hope: hope in the form of the surviving remnant and in the form of a new type of king.

Isaiah 7–11 contains considerable prophecies regarding Israel's messiah. The first is occasioned by Isaiah's and Shearjashub's interception of Ahaz as the king set out to inspect Jerusalem's fortification against an attack by Syria and the northern kingdom (7:1–3). Isaiah advises Ahaz not to rely upon fortifications nor, perhaps, upon an appeal to Assyria to save Judah. The language of verse 4, "Be careful, keep calm and don't be afraid," calls upon Judah to trust totally upon Yahweh, taking no action to involve herself with alliances to ward off the present threat. The prophet further reveals that Syria and Israel will not prevail (v. 7) and that Israel will cease to be a kingdom in the very short future (v. 8). In verse 9 Isaiah announces the consequence of disbelief, "If you will not believe, surely you shall not be *established*" (NKJV, emphasis added). That the oracle is directed not merely to Ahaz but to the Davidic house and concerns its future is suggested by the verb *establish*, which appears also in 2 Samuel 7:16 in a promise of an eternal line for the Davidic house. (Note that in v. 13 Ahaz is addressed as a representative of the royal house of David.) Just in case Ahaz has any doubt about his course of action, the prophet tells him to ask for a sign. (v. 11). The king, who apparently has made up his mind, somewhat hypocritically refuses (v. 12). In this exchange between the prophet and the king, the future for Ahaz becomes apparent through a change in possessive pronouns. Yahweh is Ahaz's ("your") God in verse 11, but the prophet's ("my") in verse 13. In other words, though Ahaz had been included in the household of faith, his refusal to ask for a sign has, in effect, excluded him from it.

Despite the king's refusal to request a sign, Yahweh gives Ahaz one anyway. This messianic prophecy, which appears in 7:14–17, begins with these words: "The virgin will be with child and will give birth to a son, and will call him Immanuel" (v. 14). What are we to make of this prophecy? Who are this woman and this child? The passage is extremely difficult to interpret, and the various interpretations are heavily contested. If the word ʿalmâ is taken literally as a young woman of marriageable age, then her virginity would be presumed. Some identify the virgin as Isaiah's wife, but this is unlikely since she and the prophet have a son. It is also unlikely that the prophecy refers to the wife of Ahaz and the crown prince, Hezekiah, since Hezekiah's birth seems to have antedated this event. The one interpretation that is true to the prophecy's corporate character directs the prophecy to the royal house of David and views it as foretelling the future of the Davidic house. That is, at some future time a messianic deliverer will arise; thus, Isaiah's prophecy looks forward ultimately to the birth of Jesus. Such an interpretation requires that what happens in verse 16 is to take place before what happens in verse 15. This in turn requires an understanding of verse 15 as referring to the purpose for which the honey and curds are chosen, that is, Immanuel will eat his desert fare "that he may know" (RV margin, emphasis added) how to reject the evil and choose the good. Before the birth of the ideal ruler, according to verse 16, the imminent invasion of Judah by Syria and Israel will be terminated, but the Assyrians will come (vv. 17–25). These verses deal with the Assyrian invasion of 701 B.C., which failed to capture Jerusalem but which nevertheless desolated the land of Judah. (The message of desolation continues in chap. 8.) Isaiah proclaims the child's name in 7:14 as Immanuel, "with us is God." To be sure, God will be with Judah in *judgment*. Yet, as the ambiguity of the child's name allows, God will be with the remnant in salvation. In the long term, the future of the Davidic line is guaranteed.

In 9:1–7 Isaiah issues another prophecy regarding the messianic restoration, which is even more fully developed in chapter 11. Verse 1 establishes the historical context: the invasion of Zebulun and Naphtali, tribes of northern Israel, by Assyria and that empire's annexation of part of the northern kingdom in about 732 B.C. (cf. 2 Kings 15:29). The prophet's announcement affirms the national faith in the ideal of messianic kingship as Israel's ultimate mode of government under Yahweh. Though some have suggested that verses 1–7 celebrate the enthronement of Hezekiah in 715 B.C., the language seems far too exalted. Extremely militaristic, the vocabulary betokens a change from gloom to joy as a result of some divine initiative. Verse 2 describes the relief for Judah that the Assyrian treatment of the north has brought, and in verse 3 God is praised for the people's newly found hope. Verses 4–6, which list the reasons for rejoicing, seem to refer to the cessation of the north's domination of the south, the end of the north's military power, or the withdrawal of the Syro-Ephraimite menace. The reference in verse 4 to "the day of Midian" signifies a military reversal of the magnitude of that achieved in the unsettled period of the judges (see Judg. 7:15–25).

Accompanying the divine intervention will be the gift of a king (v. 6). Though the word *king* is not used per se, it is clear from verse 7 that the Davidic representative is intended. Verse 6 may refer to either the king's birth or coronation since the language of adoption as God's son was customarily used of the king in the Old Testament (2 Sam. 7:14; Ps. 2:7; 89:26–27). At the end of verse 6, the prophet announces a series of throne names or titles that the messianic son will bear: "Wonderful Counselor, Mighty God, Everlasting Father, Prince of Peace." The Hebrew points to four double names, and most English versions translate accordingly. On the basis of Egyptian throne names that the pharaoh received in the enthronement ceremony, some argue that five names are to be found here, but this argument is forced. It is just possible, however, that the series of four names is meant to counter the familiar title accorded to Babylonian and Assyrian kings: "king of the four quarters of the earth."

If indeed there are four titles, some interesting observations can be made about them. In each title, one element relates to the earthly realm (Counselor, Mighty, Father, Prince), and one to the heavenly (Wonderful, God, Everlasting, Peace). Offering another point of view, William Holladay observes that two governmental titles (Wonderful Counselor and Prince of Peace) surround two divine titles (Mighty God and Everlasting Father; 1978, 108). The first title, Wonderful Counselor, signifies that the king will not be dependent upon outside advice, for his own plans will achieve their ends. The second title, Mighty God, conveys the fulness of his power. Only here, and possibly in Psalm 45:6, is the king called divine. The third title, Everlasting Father, indicates his enduring fatherly rule, while the fourth, Prince of Peace, represents the messiah as the one who will bring human destiny to its sense of purpose and wholeness. (Note that in 2 Sam. 23:1 David is accorded what essentially are four titles: "David the son of Jesse, / . . . the man whom Elyon has set up / the man anointed of the God of Jacob / the favourite of the warriors of Israel" [Kaiser 1972, 130].)

With the coming of the messianic king, the human race will enter upon an age of profound peace, putting an end to strife, unrest, and devastation. Operating as the representative of the kingdom of God, the promised one will bring to the earth an all embracing salvation. (By referring to the day of Midian in v. 4, Isaiah is perhaps serving notice that the messianic figure will conduct a direct theocratic rule of the type exercised in the judges period.) Isaiah is looking beyond the limits of historical kingship since the exalted language used in 9:1–7 rules out any earthly king; the prophet looks forward to the ultimate king of the Davidic line (v. 7), the royal messiah. But much will happen before the restoration of the Davidic king and the onset of the messianic age. Isaiah 9:8–10:4 describes a period of great distress. Then the process leading to the restoration will begin as Assyria, the punishing agent, will herself be punished for her arrogance (10:5–34; Sweeney 1988, 42).

In chapter 11, perhaps with reference to 6:13 and the desolation by Assyria in 701 B.C., Isaiah prophesies further about the messianic king, who is described as a new shoot emerging from the family tree of David (v. 1). Verse 1 supposes a return to the beginnings of the Davidic line back to Jesse himself, not the mere continuance of the line but a total new reestablishment of it (von Rad 1965, 170). Then the prophet characterizes this new David rather fully. He will permanently possess the Spirit, for it will "rest" upon him (v. 2). And what is this Spirit? As spelled out in verse 2, it is the Spirit of wisdom and understanding. Isaiah then adds the words *counsel* and *knowledge* to emphasize the great wisdom of the messiah. Such a depiction presupposes that the messiah will possess the skill necessary for practical planning and the discernment critical for implementation. Possessing "the Spirit of counsel and power," the messianic king will make appropriate judgments and will have the might needed to carry them out. His being gifted with "the Spirit of knowledge and of the fear of the LORD" means the messiah will not only possess intellectual knowledge but will demonstrate the character of God, for "the fear of the LORD" is the cast of mind and heart requisite for the manifestation of the divine character, the development of a right attitude to God.

Not surprisingly, a monarch in possession of the Spirit will have anything but an ordinary reign. He will not judge by appearances (v. 3b) nor in the interest of sectional groups. His powers of judgment, not limited by knowledge of the empirical world, will transcend what he can observe (Gowan 1987, 35). Dispensing equity and fairness and thereby protecting the underprivileged, the messiah will fulfil the principal requirement of kingship. The authority that backs this divine office will be able to bring instant death by the very utterance of a word (v. 4d). His only clothing will be righteousness and faithfulness, that is, a proper attitude to covenant relationships and steadfastness to the covenant with Yahweh. Verses 6–9 prophesy the outcome of the messianic reign: universal peace and the restoration of Eden-like relationships in the animal kingdom. Thus, peace will prevail in the holy mountain of God (the Promised Land or Jerusalem), and a knowledge of God will pervade the world. Isaiah 11:10 envisages Davidic adjudication of international disputes. Nations will then flock to the banner of the messianic king, to his seat of power in the New Jerusalem. And the political fortunes of the people of God will change as well. They will be reunited from the four quarters of the earth (vv. 11–12), and they shall be one family with the former divisions between north and south, Ephraim and Judah, eliminated (v. 13). Moreover, the restored kingdom will eliminate every threat to its safety (v. 14). And all of this will be set in motion by a new exodus from Egypt and from Assyria for the remnant that is left (vv. 15–16).

CITY OF CHAOS AND CITY OF GOD (ISA. 24–27)

Judgment is a common thread running through the Book of Isaiah. Chapters 5–12 deal with judgment against Judah and Israel and chapters 13–23, with judgment against the foreign nations. And the next four chapters (24–27) foretell another judgment—the last judgment of the world with the resurrection of the righteous dead and the imposition of Yahweh's final world order. In these chapters, the prophet goes beyond the rise and fall of nations to a new world, even beyond death itself when on the last day to come the people of God will be summoned by a great trumpet blast and will worship the Lord on the holy mountain at Jerusalem. Eschatological themes taken up in later biblical works appear in these chapters, and their depiction here may be taken as typical and as typological. Chapters 24–27, held together by a heavy Jerusalem/Zion emphasis, pit the chaos city, perhaps a representative of the world at large, against Zion, the city of God. We know that during the world judgment the chaos city will be destroyed and the city of God will be protected, but it is difficult to identify the cities more precisely than this.

Isaiah pronounces judgment against the earth in 24:1–6. Present structures will be demolished, and creation will be reduced once again to a distorted chaos, with a twisted surface and scattered inhabitants (v. 1). And the judgment is universal: all social structures will be leveled (v. 2) and all will be condemned for transgressing the eternal covenant (v. 5), perhaps the creation covenant by which rules regulating the natural order had been established. But the righteous remnant, like in number to the few olives left on the tree after the harvest, will wait for the reckoning and lift their voices in praise (vv. 14–16; Sawyer 1984, 208–9). Then judgment, described as a cosmic catastrophe, will seize the remainder of humankind (vv. 17–20). Verses 21–23 extend the judgment to the heavenly realm. When the last earthly and heavenly foes are vanquished, God will at last be enthroned in Zion. Isaiah 25 opens with a song of praise (vv. 1–5), which is occasioned by the destruction of the wicked city, the representative of human power. The eschatological oracle of verses 6–10a describes a universal feast of fat things on the holy mountain, to which all people's will come in recognition of Zion's position as the world center. The sorrow and sadness that lie so heavily over the world will now be taken away, and death, as the last enemy, will be swallowed up (v. 8). Thus, the inauguration of the new age occurs. Isaiah 26:1–6, a song of victory, contrasts the fate of Zion (vv. 1–2) with the destroyed world power (vv. 5–6). Verses 7–19 deal with the present suffering of the people of God who wait for this eschatological turn of events, the intervention of God's judgment in the earth. Culminating the judgment will be the triumphant resurrection of Yahweh's righteous (v. 19), an act in clear opposition to the final deaths of the wicked (v. 14). The promise of the physical resurrection of Yahweh's faithful is associated in verse 19 with fertility-producing dew that comes down from the divine world of light to the earth to revive the dead, or the "shades" (RSV). The idea of continuous existence after death was found in Israel from a very early period on; in this regard, the word *shades* denotes the dead in a weakened condition. Chapter 27 returns to the defeat of the chaos powers when God will swiftly punish the tyrants, who are identified with the Canaanite chaos dragon, Leviathan, (v. 1). Reversing the condemnation passage in 5:1–7 known as the Song of the Vineyard, 27:2–6 speaks of Israel's deliverance. Israel, who will be adequately punished by the trampling of invaders and by exile (vv. 7–8), will be led to repentance (v. 9). The chapter concludes with Israel's restoration, whereby the scattered will be summoned from exile to the Promised Land to worship at Zion, the mountain of God (vv. 12–13).

Jerusalem Under Judgment and Beyond It (Isa. 28–35)

Isaiah 28–32 pronounces the judgment to befall Jerusalem arising from the Assyrian campaigns at the end of the eighth century. In these chapters is drawn a picture of the people of God before the restoration of Yahweh's kingship and the introduction of everlasting peace. Chapters 33–35 detail Yahweh's assumption of kingship and the worldwide justice and overcoming of all opposition resulting from it.

A comprehensive picture of the new age is found in Isaiah 33:17–24, where for the first time kingship and Zion are associated. Though verse 22 refers clearly to Yahweh's kingship, verse 17 perhaps indicates a role for messianic kingship (Gowan 1987, 13). No more threats will be raised against Zion (vv. 18–19, 21), the prophet proclaims, assuring us of Jerusalem's security in the age of the kingdom of God. Nothing will threaten this Zion of the future—not war, sickness, judgment, or even sin (v. 24).

In chapters 1–39 Isaiah deals with the punishment to be exacted from the city of Jerusalem and with the emergence of a faithful remnant and a cleansed Zion. God's attitude toward Jerusalem appears ambivalent. The vulnerability of historical Jerusalem is always made plain (cf. 1:21; 10:27d–32; 24:10; 29:1–4; 32:13–14), while at the same time the survival of the Zion ideal is emphasized (7:1–9; 10:33–34; 14:28–32; 29:5–8; 30:27–33; 31:1–9). In Isaiah, there is always a clear separation of the Zion ideal from the fortunes of the earthly Jerusalem, the power base of national Israel.

Zephaniah

In the preexilic period, the eschatology of Zephaniah is more explicitly universal than that of the other prophets. Among the eschatological features of his prophecy we find the day of Yahweh, universal judgment, the gathering of the nations, and the emergence of remnant Israel. Zephaniah, who probably prophesied shortly before the Josianic reforms of 621 B.C., declares holy war on Judah. Judgment is now to begin with the household of God (1:1–2:3). Likening Yahweh's judgment on Judah to a sacrifice, the prophet portrays Judah as the guilty party and the attacking armies on the day of Yahweh as the attendants and participants at the cultic meal. Chapter 2 turns to judgment on the foreign nations (vv. 4–15), and chapter 3 begins by recapitulating the judgment against Judah brought on by corrupt leadership (vv. 1–4) and the conflagration involving all nations (vv. 6–8).

The remainder of Zephaniah's prophecy is cast as a significant message of hope. The punishment and divisions of Babel will be reversed (3:9), and the world will find its center in Yahweh as Lord. As nations come in pilgrimage to Jerusalem, the divine center (v. 10), they will bring with them the scattered people of God (vv. 11–13). The prophet invites Zion to rejoice in her new-found salvation (vv. 14–16), for Yahweh is the King in her midst (v. 17). Zephaniah ends his prophecy with an Abrahamic flourish of salvation presented in terms of making a name for the gathered in Jerusalem. The universality of salvation, which concludes the prophecy, balances the universal judgment with which it had begun.

In the prophecy of the eighth and seventh centuries, particularly in the Book of Isaiah, Zion theology took shape. To Jerusalem, the divine center, the world would come in submissive pilgrimage, and in this way the Gentiles would receive the blessings of the Abrahamic covenant. Moreover, the prophets drew a clear distinction between the nations of Israel and Judah and the remnant of faith that was to come from both. The eschatology of the preexilic period was thus set. While exilic and postexilic prophets would nuance basic features of the eschatology, they would not substantially alter it.

5

Exilic Eschatology

The period at the end of the seventh century B.C. and the beginning of the sixth proves calamitous for Judah. In 597 Jerusalem surrenders to the Babylonians; the temple is looted; and the king, other royals, and high officials are deported to Babylon. It is easy to view these events as Yahweh's attempt to discipline his people, but much more is to come. In 587/586 Jerusalem falls to the Babylonians led by Nebuchadnezzar. The walls are leveled to the ground, and the city is set aflame. Thus, the exile officially begins.

The prophets of the late preexilic and exilic periods must face not only the decline of national Israel but also the fall of Jerusalem, when all the externals of Jewish faith—temple, ark, priesthood, and sacrificial system—will be gone. As we know, Davidic kingship and even the land itself will go. All these events raise questions: How intrinsic to the true nature of Israel is the apparatus of national institutionalism? What, or where, is the true Israel? Will there be a future for Israel, and what will be the nature of it? Will a new individualism replace the old nationalism, and will personal faith replace state commitment? And the exilic prophets, Jeremiah, Ezekiel, Joel, Obadiah, and Isaiah 40–66, wrestle with and attempt to address these concerns.

Jeremiah

Commissioned as a prophet to the nations (Jer. 1:5, 10), Jeremiah summons Judah to come to terms with Babylon's emergence to world leadership and to face the fall of the Judean state and the demise of the nation's external fabric. But his is not a prophecy of doom alone. Jeremiah looks to the future and even lays the foundation for it by prophesying the reconstitution of the new people of God under a refurbished Sinai arrangement, the new covenant. Jeremiah sees clearly that the future of the people of God lies with the exiles taken to Babylon by Nebuchadnezzar in 597 B.C. (24:4–7). Indeed, they are soon to be joined by their compatriots! And the prophet understands that the exile will not effect the needed reforms and changes of attitude in the exiles but rather that God will use the time of exile to give his people there a heart to know him (24:7).

State Failure and Fallen State

In his programmatic temple sermon (chaps. 7, 26) Jeremiah blames the imminent removal of all externals of worship on the failure of the state, exemplified by the temple cult, to protect the faith. He vigorously denounces those who promote reliance on the doctrine of Zion's inviolability and on misconstrued Sinaitic ideals resulting from the jingoistic legacies of Josianic reform. This prophet from Anathoth challenges the prophetic institution of his day, charging it with false prophecy, as in his clash with Hananiah, who is pictured in chapter 28 as a blind advocate of the Zion traditions. The nation has failed to recognize, according to Jeremiah, the temple as the point of reference for the exercise of Yahweh's authority over Israel and her world. Instead, the people view the temple as a guarantee of the divine presence and as a talisman warding off destruction. Jeremiah's message comes across clearly through a play on the word *place*, which in 7:3 connotes the temple and in 7:7, the Promised Land: Judah's failure to relate properly to the temple means her failure to secure the Promised Land. Right action at the center would have secured the whole. But it is not to be. Condemning temple sacrifices and all the cultic trappings, Jeremiah anticipates their end.

The New Covenant

Jeremiah makes a distinctive contribution to prophetic eschatology through his prophecy of the new covenant (31:31–34). This particular prophecy is found within the so-called book of consolation, a sequence of chapters (30–33) generally concerned with the restoration of the fortunes of Judah and Israel after the exile. In view of the impending changes in the political fortunes of the country, destruction of the temple, and demise of Davidic kingship, Jeremiah quite understandably looks past the Davidic covenant to the one on which it was built—the

Sinaitic covenant. With the imminent removal of the institution of kingship, the questions of Israel's political status and her understanding of her relationship to Yahweh are raised afresh. Jeremiah addresses these questions in a prophecy based on the covenant at Sinai. By analogy, then, the new covenant must be preceded by a new exodus and a new entry into the Promised Land. Chapters 30–31 deal almost entirely with the return of the scattered peoples of Israel and Judah. In his presentation, Jeremiah sees the futures of these two warring factions as intertwined in the prophetic hope of one Israel.

Jeremiah's new covenant passage begins with words that announce an age in transition: "The time is coming" (31:31). This phrase points to the indefinite but not necessarily remote future. What follows is a series of first-person assertions that spell out the divine initiatives to be taken and make clear that the new covenant will not result from negotiation between Israel and Yahweh, but will be imposed unilaterally. Thus, Yahweh will "cut" (i.e., initiate) a covenant. (Note that the word *cut* preserves the traditional language of the beginning of a covenantal arrangement.) And the prophet describes the covenant as "new," an adjective that carries both qualitative and temporal nuances. Though the word used in the Septuagint connotes qualitative newness, perhaps we should retain both nuances of the Hebrew. That is, the new covenant, while having continuity with the past, will be both a qualitative advance upon the Sinaitic and Davidic covenants and a temporal advance in the course of salvation history.

Through the new covenant, the difficulties presently experienced by Judah and those experienced in the past by Israel will be overcome; in fact, the two historical kingdoms will become one. Note how Jeremiah forges such a union in words. Verse 31, reflecting the present historical reality, mentions the two kingdoms separately as "the house of Israel" and "the house of Judah," but verse 33 refers to "the house of Israel" alone. To suggest, as it often is, that "the house of Judah" in verse 31 is a scribal addition is to misunderstand the intent of the prophecy, which is the reconciliation of the split between the two kingdoms and the unification of the people of God in a New Israel. As expressed so well in Ezekiel 37:15–28, the recall of Judah and Israel from exile will graft the warring brothers into one. With the healing of the long-standing breach, the united kingdom of David will once again herald God's people and give expression to the prophetic understanding of Israel's nature as the unified people of God.

Verse 32 clearly identifies a qualitative difference between the new covenant and the covenant at Sinai: while the Sinaitic covenant could be broken by Israel, and was repeatedly, the new covenant will be unbreakable. In Jeremiah's time, there could be no clearer testimony to the fallibility of the Sinai arrangement than the abject national failure to implement the reforms of Josiah. And verse 32 makes it plain that the failure was Israel's, not Yahweh's. Despite Israel's provocation, Yahweh continued to exhibit tireless faithfulness to the exodus commitment and never defected from his part of the Sinai pact. Through the familiar symbolism of marriage, Jeremiah demonstrates divine faithfulness to a bond that could not be dissolved by divorce even though Israel was unfaithful. How different the new covenant will be, for it will not be possible for the human partner to breach this arrangement!

To prevent a breach in the covenant, Yahweh intends to put his law in the heart of the New Israel (v. 33). Since the problems with the old covenant had arisen entirely on the human level, putting the law within the people may seem to be a decided advance. But is this inward change radically different from the conditions under the Sinai agreement? No matter the level of inwardness under the new covenant, it would be wrong to suggest that there had never been an appropriate level under the old. Let's examine this matter of inwardness a bit further. Under the Sinaitic covenant, it was always presumed that ideally law would be kept by the aligning of the national will, or heart, to the will of Yahweh (Deut. 6:4–6; 11:18). And this implies, rather than precludes, the aligning of the personal will. Though the concept of the law in the heart is usually found in Deuteronomy in the context of a command (6:4–5), such an imperative presupposes an ideal state that presumably can be achieved. Moreover, the issue of inwardness is found in Moses' final address to Israel. There he predicts that a return from exile will only begin after Yahweh circumcises the national heart (Deut. 30:6). In the Old Testament, the law's lodging in the heart is an assumed prerequisite for individual godly experience (Ps. 37:31; Prov. 40:8). Thus, the Old Testament frequently demands personal renewal, cleansing of the heart, and creation of a new heart. Furthermore, acts of contrition always stem from the heart (Ps. 51:10, 17; 73:1; Prov. 22:11; Isa. 57:15). The prophet Isaiah, in anticipation of a return to Jerusalem and a new covenant, addresses the exiles as "you who know righteousness, you people in whose heart is My law" (51:7 NKJV). Jeremiah himself makes it clear that the nation must undergo a change of heart before a return to Yahweh is possible, and he uses the language of circumcision in this connection (4:4; 9:25–26). Thus, all this accumulated evidence indicates that the newness of the new covenant does not comprise God's placement of the law in the heart alone.

The content of verse 33 fits comfortably within the parameters of the Sinaitic covenant. Indeed, the verse ends with a formula derivable from the Sinai experience: "I will be their God, and they shall be my people" (cf. Exod. 6:7; Lev. 26:12; Ezek. 37:27). Undoubtedly, verse 33 points to an ideal arrangement by which the insertion of the law in the heart will operate in an unfettered way to secure complete obedience to the new covenant. Though this would be an advance upon the realities achieved under the Sinai covenant, it would not be outside the ideal state contemplated by Sinai. Holding up for us an idealization of the Sinaitic covenant, Jeremiah draws a qualitatively new picture of an old truth and expects a radically different level of obedience from that which was exhibited under the old covenant. The Bible makes much of the tension between the placement of the law in the heart and the obedience that ought to arise from it. Obviously, the problem with the Sinaitic covenant had been the weakness of the human partner, but under the new covenant that weakness of character, epitomized by the contest between spirit and flesh, will disappear with the advent of the kingdom.

Two words in Jeremiah 31:34 signal the radical change that is to take place under the new covenant—"No longer." Since the covenant of Sinai was mediated to Israel within institutional relationships, such as priesthood and prophecy, it required constant reinforcement through teaching and correction. Under the new covenant, however, "no longer" will institutional reinforcement be required, for all will know the Lord. Thus, the fervent wish of Moses that all the Lord's people would be prophets (Num. 11:29), that is, channels through which the divine will could be reflected, will be fulfilled. And since no more mediatorial services will be required, we can assume that all will be priests, thus fully implementing the mandate for Israel in Exodus 19:5–6. Both prophecy and priesthood were concessions to sinfulness, but in the totally new economy prophesied by Jeremiah there will be no need for specialization. In fact, there will be no sacrificial system and no need for teaching the Torah.

What will allow the dissolution of mediatorial services in the new age is the new element of the new covenant, and it is expressed at the end of verse 34: "I will forgive their wickedness and will remember their sins no more." It was the sacrificial system through which forgiveness was usually extended, but in the new age no longer will sins need to be confessed and will atonement be required. And Jeremiah's words point beyond forgiveness, for the sins will no longer be "remembered." The word *remember*, especially when used of Yahweh, means more than the power of mere psychological recall. When Yahweh "remembers," it means that he will reactivate an issue or carry through a promise. So God "remembered" Noah and took action by causing the flood waters to subside (Gen. 8:1). God also "remembered" Hannah, and his promise that she would bear a son became a reality (1 Sam. 1:19–20). Thus, a determination by God not to remember does not simply mean that God will forget formally. It means that sin will have been dealt with so comprehensively in Israel that no further action regarding sin will be necessary. At once we see that this verse points beyond the present experience of the Christian believer to a time when the total efficacy of the cross of Christ will be implemented. Jeremiah's eschatological age will witness a changed society, a New Israel in which the Word and the Spirit will have free reign. In the new age, sin will be foreign to human experience.

Jeremiah 31:31–34 does not contrast life under the law with life in the Spirit, nor does it point to a new measure of forgiveness that goes beyond that provided in the Old and New Testaments. But it points to the full implementation of forgiveness in the experience of humankind, to a level of obedience to the divine Word that can never be faulted. The age that Jeremiah prophesies is the age of the new creation, when the New Jerusalem will descend and when God will dwell in the midst of his people (Rev. 3:12; 21:2–4). Though this glorious future contemplated by the prophets does not come in postexilic experience, we must not view the concept of a new exodus from Babylon to Palestine as a prophetic deception. The fulfilment of their hope for a postexilic Promised Land, a recaptured Eden, is simply postponed for Israel, for the new exodus will be accomplished and the new covenant will be made through the death of Jesus, Israel's Messiah. Moreover, the full expression of the new forgiveness and the new era resulting from it will await the final manifestation of the kingdom of God.

We must be careful not to over individualize the new covenant arrangement, for clearly Jeremiah envisages a reconstituted Israel. The focus on Israel emerges from the Sinai analogy in verses 31–34 and also from the passage that follows (vv. 35–37). The choice of Israel was as firmly fixed within the divine plan as the decrees of creation; furthermore, that Yahweh could give up on Israel is incomprehensible. Verses 38–40 continue with plans for the redevelopment of Jerusalem. Nothing in these prophecies forecasts the incoming of the Gentiles, but this is understandable from Jeremiah's point of view. Firstly, Jeremiah ministers to a nation in crisis; therefore, his major concern is to place before her the nature of her election and role. Secondly, the incoming of the Gentiles is dependent upon the reconstitution of Israel, with which Jeremiah is concerned. Once this is effected, as is clear from other Old Testament sources (e.g., Isa. 2:2–4), then the Gentiles will be incorporated into the new theocracy.

Ezekiel

A further aspect of prophetic expectation for Israel is contained in the Book of Ezekiel, which refers to events in Israel's exile between the prophet's call in 593 B.C. and the latest dated prophecy in 571 B.C. (29:17). Three visions, as described in chapters 1–3, 8–11, and 40–48, control the prophecy, whose major motif is the construction of the new temple, which would usher in the age of the rule of God. In general, Ezekiel's expectation is one of struggle and suffering that must be undergone and of order which is finally achieved. The structure of the book is testimony to the prophet's expectation. Chapters 1–24 focus on judgment against all the institutions of Israel during the exilic period. Chapters 25–32 deal with oracles against those foreign nations that have persecuted Israel. The suffering and struggle of chapters 1–32 is then followed by Israel's blueprint for the future. In most idealistic terms, chapters 33–48 offer prophecies of restoration. A magnificent depiction of the goal to which the call of Israel is directed, chapters 40–48 end the prophecy with the worship of God in the new age, as is unfolded in the temple vision.

Restoration of Israel (Ezek. 33–39)

In the Book of Ezekiel, judgment precedes restoration. The vision of chapters 1–3 depicts Yahweh, enthroned on the mobile ark of the covenant and escorted by cherubim, as descending from the heavenly palace in judgment against the temple in Jerusalem. Through the vision, Ezekiel is called, and his vocation is made clear: his mission is to be one of undeviating judgment against present Israel and her oppressors until Jerusalem falls (cf. Ezek. 24; 33:21). However, even before the fall, the prophet promises continuance and a new exodus, when God will reestablish his people and bring them back to the land of promise (20:34).

Following Ezekiel's denouncement of both Jerusalem and the foreign nations, chapter 33 begins the oracles of restoration. Verses 1–20, which repeat the watchman address of 3:16–21, renew the prophet's commission. But now Ezekiel is to bring messages of hope for Israel. As soon as Ezekiel learns of Jerusalem's fall, six prophecies come to him, thereby connecting the fall of Jerusalem with the message of hope that is to follow. Each prophecy is identified as "the word of the LORD." The six appear in 33:23–33, chap. 34, 35:1–36:15, 36:16–37:14, 37:15–28, and chaps. 38–39.

Ezekiel clarifies the nature of the Abrahamic promises in the first prophecy (33:23–33) by explaining that the occupancy of the Promised Land is contingent upon Israel's obedience. Chapter 34, the second prophecy, thus reviews the faulty leadership because of which the Promised Land has been forfeited and the people have been exiled. In a future age God will reign over and shepherd Israel (vv. 7–24). Though a Davidic shepherd is part of God's plan, he is named as a "prince," not a "king," indicating his minor position (v. 24). As a result of the restoration of divine leadership, conditions of paradise-like peace will follow (vv. 25–31). The third prophecy (35:1–36:15), which foretells the desolation of Edom, Israel's inimical enemy, discloses the removal of all enmity from the Promised Land.

A review of the factors that led to the loss of the land begins the fourth prophecy (36:16–37:14). Ezekiel makes it clear that the promised restoration will only come about because God intends to vindicate his holy name, that is, to bring about his declared purposes, through Israel (36:21–23). Verses 24–38 outline the expected restoration. People and land will be brought together in a new exodus (v. 24). Then God will make provisions so that the people will occupy the land in a manner consistent with the new covenant. Israel will be cleansed (v. 25) and given a new corporate heart (v. 26). In possession of a new spirit, the people will be capable of obedience (v. 27). These various elements of Ezekiel's prophecy add some detail to the program of restoration sketched by Jeremiah. Verse 28 makes clear the dual nature of the restoration, that is, of the land and of the covenant. Indeed, Sinai is evoked with the formula, "You will be my people, and I will be your God" (cf. Exod. 6:7). What Ezekiel foresees—the occupancy of the land and obedience to the Torah—is in continuity with the Sinai covenant. By the action of renewal, the Promised Land will become like the garden in Eden, where all Israel will exercise Adam's role and will become kings and priests (cf. Exod. 19:6). With an interweaving of the many material blessings to flow from the spiritual restoration (vv. 29–38), the chapter ends. Ezekiel 37:1–14, still part of the fourth prophecy, looks at the program of restoration from another point of view. In the valley of his call (37:1; cf. 3:22), the prophet witnesses the results of his prophetic ministry of judgment upon Israel. What remains of the house of Israel is a valley of dry bones. Then, in a manner reminiscent of the creation of the man in Genesis 2:7, God breathes his Spirit into the bodies of the dead and effects a national resurrection (vv. 5, 10). Thereby Israel and Adam are linked (Niditch 1986, 223). And what of Israel's restoration? In the valley of bones, Ezekiel learns that the restoration requires a resurrection of the entire nation from the death of exile.

In the fifth prophecy (37:15–28), we learn the significance of the national resurrection. The two previously warring factions, geographic Israel and Judah, come together in the Promised Land under Davidic leadership as a united people of God, a New Israel. This time an everlasting covenant of peace (cf. Isa. 54:10) is made, and the creation and Abrahamic promises of being multiplied and blessed are reinvoked (v. 26). By promising to place his tabernacle in the people's midst, God indwells the New Israel in a new relationship (v. 27).

In chapters 38–39, the sixth prophecy, Ezekiel describes a full assault on Zion at the end of time (Levenson 1976, 15). The prophet pictures the nations' assault upon the city of God, which is peaceably held by God's redeemed and restored people. Gog, the embodiment of Israel's foes, is a personification of the mysterious foe from the north, which was conjured up to add depth to the Babylonian menace (see Jer. 1:15). (At this time, the north is the area from which all threats are thought to come as well as the mysterious place of Baal's dwelling and mountain.) As described in these chapters, the combat between Gog and God moves out of history and into the domain of apocalyptic (Aharoni 1977, 15), a case for which can be made on the basis of apocalyptic characteristics exhibited by the account. The listing of enemies in 38:5–6 is an idealization, for these groups of people who were not contiguous and never were actual enemies of Israel could not conceivably aggregate from the north. Furthermore, the size of the threat against peaceful and pastoral Israel is greatly exaggerated: Israel takes seven months to bury the slain (39:12–15), and captured weapons serve as Israel's fuel for seven years (39:9). But how does this apocalyptic assault relate to the restoration? This threat to the restored people of God is the final challenge to be overcome before the temple is built and eternal peace is given to the land. Whether chapters 38–39 are arranged chronologically in the book is uncertain, but they indicate without doubt that the new age will not be ushered in until evil has been utterly destroyed.

Temple Vision (Ezek. 40–48)

The eschatological building of the temple in Ezekiel 40–48 at the brink of direct divine rule will follow the extinguishing of all opposition to the kingdom of God (Ezek. 38–39). Yet, the prophet had anticipated the reconstitution of the nation of Israel and its worship on God's holy soil (20:40; 37:24–28). The cosmic character of the temple vision is revealed by its delivery on a very high mountain upon which the new temple will itself be situated (40:2). Though unnamed, the mountain is clearly depicted as Mount Zion (Levenson 1976, 7). Chapters 40–48 draw their theological inspiration from Israel's remote past, especially from the age of the exodus and conquest, and the influence is easily discerned. The climax of the Sinai and exodus events was the erection of the tabernacle on the mountain of revelation, which followed the reception of a blueprint from heaven (Exod. 25:9) and the renewal of the covenant (Exod. 34). As at Sinai, the blueprint for the new temple is handed down from heaven (43:10–12), and the covenant is renewed (37:26–27). Completing Yahweh's plan for Israel through the exodus, the construction of the tabernacle constituted Israel as a worshiping people and began the age of the conquest. So the building of the new temple will usher in the new age.

Ezekiel offers a detailed description of the temple area (Ezek. 40:1–43:12), as he is led on a tour by the divine guide (until God appears in 43:6). Moving from the outer wall (40:5–16) to the outer court (vv. 17–27) to the inner court (40:28–41:26) and back to the outer court (42:1–14), the tour concludes outside the wall (vv. 15–20). At the center of the description is the structure of the new temple itself (40:48–41:26). With the tour completed, the prophet is brought to the east gate of the complex through which God will enter (43:1–5; cf. 10:19). What Ezekiel describes is similar to a vision by Isaiah (Isa. 6:1–4)—God sweeps in through the east gate and fills the temple. But Ezekiel's description also echoes the Sinai encounter as it is recounted in Deuteronomy 33:2, Judges 5:4–5, Psalm 68:8, and Habakkuk 3:3–4. In both Ezekiel's encounter and the one at Sinai, the Lord comes from the east, and the manifestation of the divine presence is thunderously audible. When the prophet refers in verse 3 to the visions of judgment he earlier received (chaps. 1–2; 8–10; Parunak 1980, 72), he sends a clear message: In the vision, the nation has been judged, and the restoration under divine kingship has begun.

With God as a guide, the temple tour resumes. In the first of two messages (43:6–44:3; 44:4–46:24), God claims the temple as his eternal dwelling place (43:7). Within the worship structure, the central object is the altar of burnt offering. God's second pronouncement deals with the temple's use in worship. In the new age, the Levites will do the menial work of the temple, and only the descendants of Zadok, the faithful priesthood of the Solomonic temple, will do altar service. Carefully removed from the new temple are all former political associations (42:20; 44:6–9), and the message is very clear. The new temple is a priestly domain, and Yahweh is the sole ruler in the new age (20:33). Note that the ideals of the monarchical period have been passed over for theological parallels from the exodus/conquest period.

The sanctifying influence that building the temple will have on the land, which means that the eschatological temple now becomes the world spiritual center that the Garden of Eden was (Wright 1992, 264), is then forecast in Ezekiel 47:1–12. The prophet sees waters trickling from under the east gate rise quickly to an unfordable stream that fructifies the land and transforms the desert into a paradise. On both sides of the stream, trees of life are planted (47:12). In contrast to an earlier time, the fruit of these trees may be eaten freely, while their leaves may be used for healing. Verses 13–23 reveal that the land, cleansed and renewed by divine possession, will be divided among the twelve tribes.

No conquest will be needed this time. Before identifying the allotments, God cites the boundaries, which correspond to the ideal borders of Numbers 34:1–12. Allotments will be first given to the seven
tribes in the north (48:1–7). Then, the apportionment is interrupted
while provisions are made for the sanctuary, as it was in Joshua's distribution (Josh. 18:1; Parunak 1980, 74). In verses 8–12 the holy site is
allotted to the Zadokites, the purified priesthood, and in verses 13–22
the Levites, the public, and the prince receive their portions. God resumes the land division among the remaining five tribes in verses 23–
29 with the handmaid tribes of Gad, Asher, Naphtali, and Dan the far-
thest from the temple.

As a protection against contamination the sacred shrine will be surrounded by the tribe of Levi. Judah will be directly north of the shrine
and Benjamin directly south, thus obliterating the old north and south
divisions. The new society is so designed as to redress the economic and
political imbalances of the past. Though the tribes will receive equal allotments, their location in relation to the sanctuary is determined by
the narratives concerning their origins. The twelve city gates (three on
each side) will bear the names of the twelve tribes, though Ephraim and
Manasseh will be combined as Joseph to insure the inclusion of Levi (v.
32; Greenberg 1984, 202). That the shrine and the city are no longer in
Judah and that Zion is referred to only obliquely appear to be explicit
rejections of the Jerusalem royal theology. In short, Ezekiel symbolically returns to the patriarchal promises through land distributed anew
to the people of God. No pattern from Israel's history can account for
the order of the tribes, though the tribal arrangement around the sanctuary recalls the battle order from the wilderness marches. That there
are no Levitical cities also implies a preconquest structure. By reaching
back into Israel's history to the exodus and conquest, Ezekiel implicitly
rejects the monarchical period and its attendant doctrines.

Ezekiel's emerging new-temple theology is not a blueprint for postexilic restoration. Yet, this much is clear: Israel's future is entirely in
the hands of Yahweh, the ultimate controller of history, who will effect
a new beginning with himself at the center. Note that the motif of Davidic kingship does not appear in Ezekiel's prophecy, which is understandable given the prophet's theocratic emphasis. Moreover, the issue
of the messiah does not arise in chapters 40–48. (We meet only the
nameless and unconnected "prince," who is the political ruler in the
new age [cf. 44:3; 45:7–8, 16–17; 46:2; 48:21–22].) The future of the people of God depends not on a Davidic king or messiah but on God entirely, and the building of the new temple will be his work. By the sym-
metry of the temple vision and the description of the holy city as
removed from direct political association and tensions, Ezekiel offers

an exalted doctrine of the presence of God, which is further accentu-
ated by the centrality of worship in the New Jerusalem of the new age.
Never ending blessings flow in divine abundance from the divine palace, the new temple.

In a grand panorama the Book of Ezekiel moves us from the Jerusalem temple under judgment to the heavenly temple from which that
judgment emerges. Finally, the holy city and temple will become the
world center around which the new society will be constructed. Though
Ezekiel's concern, like Jeremiah's, is the reconstitution of Israel, in the
elaborate picture of the temple city Ezekiel reveals how the reconstituted people of God will live in the new age.

Joel

The two halves of the book of Joel are bound together by the theme
of the day of the Lord. In the first half (Joel 1:2–2:27), in which the
prophet records the occurrence of a plague of locusts and considers its
deeper meaning, the day is one of historical judgment against Israel. In
the second half (3:1–21), the eschatological day will bring salvation.
What is the day of the Lord? The phrase appears about twenty times in
the Old Testament, all in prophetic books. Amos, the earliest user of the
phrase, reveals that the day of the Lord was popularly anticipated with
great desire. Some have linked the origin of the concept to prebiblical
mythology that divided world history into fixed ages and viewed "the
day" as the time when the old order passed away and was superseded
by the new, when one age gave way to the next. Such an origin would
likely have left an indelible eschatological cast on the phrase, to which
its use by the prophets does not bear witness. Other expositors, citing
such passages as Isaiah 13, Ezekiel 7, and Joel 2, have traced the background to holy war and the day of God's decisive intervention for Israel
against her enemies. But again not all of the references fit. Still others
have suggested that the day refers to divine intervention to exact punishment for Israel's breach of covenant (Weiss 1966, 29–60), but this
suggestion suits some references but not all.

Common to all the prophetic references to the day of the Lord is Yahweh's appearance; however, there is no unanimity as to the nature of
that presence, that is, whether it would be a blessing or a curse for Israel. It is certainly a day on which Yahweh would do battle with his enemies—if we allow Israel to be counted among them. Let's consider
briefly the earliest Old Testament use of the phrase. Amos 5:18 indicates that the day of the Lord was popularly conceived as a manifestation of Yahweh for Israel's benefit, and the context in which it appears
suggests a connection with the cult. Perhaps the phrase originated in

the cult to denote the demonstration of Yahweh's kingship and to betoken Yahweh's support for Israel during national crisis, but no matter what the origin may have been Amos used the phrase to threaten his audience with divine judgment. Thus, the concept of the day of the Lord, as considered by the prophets, is not singular in meaning; the connotation can be determined only by examining each context in which the phrase appears.

The centerpiece of the Book of Joel is the famous prophecy on the outpouring of the Spirit (2:28–32). Poised between the two halves of the book, the passages emerges out of the first half's particular judgment of locusts and yet points toward the second half's judgment against Israel's enemies. To understand the significance of the passage, it is necessary to see it in context. What precedes the passage in chapter 2 can be broken down as follows: a description of the historical day of the Lord (vv. 1–11; the plague of locusts), the call for national repentance (vv. 12–17), and the promise of covenant renewal (vv. 18–27).

Verse 28 then begins with the words "And afterward," and the eschatological tenor cannot be missed. By the outpouring of the Spirit "on all flesh" (NRSV), prophecy will be democratized, that is, in the last days, the new age, there will be no need for intermediaries. (In Acts 2 Peter uses Joel's prophecy to explain the significance of the Pentecost Spirit.) Note that this same verse brings together the great opposites of Spirit (divine nature with unlimited potential) and flesh (human nature with handicaps and limited potential) in a grand anticipation of the reality of the new creation. Like the last Adam (1 Cor. 15:45), all flesh (that is, all Israel) will become the partakers of the life-giving Spirit. When all become recipients of the divine mind through the Spirit and when all will be in direct communication with God, all social divisions and barriers will be removed (v. 29). This complete renewal of the remnant of Israel will bring to fruition Moses' wish that all God's people might be prophets (Num. 11:29), and thus Israel will become the community for which she had been vocationally marked (Exod. 19:3b–6). Verses 30–31 point unmistakably beyond the plague of locusts to a cosmic covenant, Israel's enemies will be defeated. And the last verse of the passage prophesies salvation for a remnant in Jerusalem and Mount Zion (v. 32), which is presumably the site of the divine visitation.

Completing the context of the outpouring of the Spirit are the judgment and the blessing of Joel 3. In verses 1–12 Yahweh calls satirically to the nations to join in holy war against him using instruments of peace as weapons of war, thus reversing the expectations of Isaiah 2:4. Judgment, which in the first half falls on the household of God, is now extended to the whole world. Verses 13–16 and 19–21 describe the fate of the opposing Gentiles in the language of the harvest, thus returning to the plague language of 1:13–20. Joel 3:15 then repeats 2:10 and in so doing indicates that the locust plague is indeed an anticipation of the judgment of the last day. God the Warrior intervenes in both episodes (cf. 2:11; 3:16). Joel concludes with the promise of a restored paradise for the people of God centered at Zion (vv. 17–18). As the world center, Jerusalem dispenses fertility in the New Eden (v. 18). There is no mention of a world pilgrimage to Jerusalem, for the passage is concerned only with divine judgment (vv. 19–21) and thus with divine vindication of Israel's election.

The cleansing, comfort, and restoration of the people of God is the theme of the last passage of Joel. If the book was indeed written in or around the exilic period, the unifying theme of Judah's desolation followed by restoration and covenant blessing echoes the new-covenant theology of the period. Joel's prophecy of Israel's redemption, world judgment, and a regained paradise is typical of prophetic eschatology.

Obadiah

The Book of Obadiah bears witness to mainstream prophetic eschatology. While addressing the historical realities of his day, the destruction of the temple and the exile, the prophet proclaims that the future of the people of God is secure. As Obadiah considers recent events and conflicts, he views them as foreshadowing the inbreaking of the kingdom of God.

Verses 1–14 indict Edom for hostility against Israel. With the reference to the day of the Lord in verse 15, the prophecy takes a decidedly eschatological turn. Not only Edom but all the enemies of Israel will be punished. Gathered on Mount Zion, the remnant will act as the arm of God's judgment (vv. 17–21). In addition to Judah's and Israel's return to the Promised Land (vv. 19–20), Obadiah prophesies the final theocratic rule of the kingdom of God for "saviors shall come to Mount Zion . . . , and the kingdom shall be the LORD's" (v. 21 NKJV). Obadiah's program of the restoration of Israel in the Promised Land, the judgment upon the Gentiles, and divine rule at the end of time make him a prime example of prophetic eschatology of the exilic period.

Isaiah 40–66

Isaiah 1–39, the first half of the book, ends with the prospect of exile for Judah (39:5–7). The second half of the prophecy (chaps. 40–66) begins with comfort extended to Jerusalem and the exiles then in Babylon (40:1–11). Though Isaiah 40–66 is unified by the theology of a renewed city of God, these chapters can also be divided into two units—chapters 40–55 and 56–66. Almost entirely eschatological, chapters 40–55 concern the return of the exiles to Jerusalem, the Servant's task to effect the return, and the significance of the return. Chapters 56–66, a blend of history and eschatology, expand on the material of the preceding sixteen chapters.

Ministry of the Servant (Isa. 40–55)

The motifs of comfort and hope evident in the prolog to the second half of Isaiah's prophecy (40:1–11) are maintained throughout chapters 40–55. The prophet is insistent, even emphatic, that Israel must be aroused from her exilic torpor, for her punishment is over and her return to Jerusalem is sure. Linked to the exiles' return is a new figure in prophetic eschatology—the Servant. The four Servant passages (42:1–4; 49:1–6; 50:4–9; and 52:13–53:12), which fit their contexts and contribute to the overall message of Isaiah 40–55, shed light on the Servant's ministry and function. Though the identity of the Servant has been the subject of much speculation and debate, the more important issue, and the one we will consider first, is the Servant's role. It is demonstrable that the function of the Servant—who clearly is Israel in some form (Wilson 1986, 253)—is integrally and instrumentally bound to the redemption of Jerusalem. Indeed, it is the Servant's task to effect Israel's return to the holy city.

COMFORT TO JERUSALEM (ISA. 40:1–11)

Yahweh issues a directive in Isaiah 40:1–2 to the heavenly council: "Comfort, comfort my people. . . . Speak tenderly to Jerusalem, and proclaim to her." Jerusalem is tenderly acknowledged by Yahweh as "my people," and Yahweh is "her God," language that evokes the relationships of the Sinai covenant (Exod. 6:7; cf. Lev. 26:12), which is now to be reinaugurated. In the words of the prophet, "Jerusalem" and "my people" are parallel constructions and, therefore, can be taken as synonymous, yet throughout the prophecy Jerusalem is also the idealized location of the people of God. Thus, Jerusalem connotes the Abrahamic dimensions of both people and place. Two commands appear in both verse 1 and verse 2, a similarity that serves to link the verses. (Note that whenever a double command occurs in chaps. 40–55, it is followed by further commands [51:9, 17].) This doubling ("Comfort, comfort") emphasizes the urgent need while revealing the richness and significance of the divine command. God has neither forgotten nor forsaken his people! The phrase *speak tenderly* ("speak upon the heart") foreshadows an imminent change of fortune (see Gen. 34:3; Judg. 19:3; 2 Sam. 19:7; Hos. 2:14). And what is to be spoken to Jerusalem? In the words of Isaiah, Jerusalem will be told "that her hard service has been completed, that her sin has been paid for, that she has received from the LORD's hand double for all her sins." Let's look briefly at the three causal clauses of verse 2, which offer the reasons for the main statement of verse 1. It seems clear that the comfort to be extended to Jerusalem is not consolation in the midst of sorrow but the proclamation that the sorrow has been removed (cf. 2 Sam. 12:24), for she has paid for her sins—doubly. Does this imply calculation or some strict doctrine of equivalent punishment? No, the prophet seems to be saying simply that Jerusalem's sufferings have gone beyond the limits of endurance.

Isaiah 40:3–5 is a divine herald's summons for the preparation of a divine way through the wilderness by which the process of comfort will begin. Elsewhere in Isaiah 40–55 (42:16; 43:16–19; 49:9c–11; 51:10), the return from exile is depicted as a new exodus. In view of this, the way prepared through the wilderness appears to be a call to the people of God to come out in a second exodus—this time from Babylon. Every impediment to the return, whether physical or spiritual, will be removed (vv. 4–5b). Before the final coming of Israel's God in his glory, that is, in his manifested sovereignty, the total face of nature will be changed. None of this will be done unobtrusively, as verse 5 recognizes, for all flesh, corporately not individually, will join in the public recognition of the great change. It is possible, as many commentators suggest (Stuhlmueller 1970, 74–82), that the image of the way also reflects language of the divine enthronement of the Babylonian deity Marduk. The image could conceivably have held both connotations for Isaiah—one from the religious and historical past of Israel and one from the environs of the exile. What is significant, however, is what Isaiah does with the image, that is, to recognize Yahweh's kingship because of the people's salvation through the "way."

Verses 6–8 raise another herald cry, one understood as the prophet's address to himself. Identifying completely with his people, the prophet no longer believes in the possibility of a new beginning because of human frailty and the transience of all things. Isaiah's words reflect the air of defeat and despair that controls the exilic mood. In verse 8 the voice of the herald replies to the prophet. Though all flesh is indeed grass, the seemingly hopeless situation will now be confronted by the supreme power of the divine Word. God's Word will shape history and will change its course!

Isaiah 40:9–11 concludes the prolog to the second half of the prophecy. Though the text of verse 9 is ambiguous, the general context dictates that Jerusalem be evangelized, rather than be the evangelist: "You who bring good tidings to Jerusalem, lift up your voice with a shout." And what are the good tidings? The message is disarmingly simple: God is coming as Jerusalem's king! Though the message isn't stated explicitly in verses 9–11, it is so stated in Isaiah 52:7; moreover, the shepherd imagery of verse 11, which was frequently used for royal kingship in the ancient world, implies the kingship of Yahweh, The arm of Yahweh (v. 10; cf. 52:10), the saving instrument of the first exodus, will achieve a new exodus, which will reveal Yahweh's royal power. Thereafter, Yahweh will reestablish his covenant with Israel, who is to be gathered to the divine center at Jerusalem. Recognizing the despair of the exiles, God is now willing to meet their needs (v. 11).

Both the opening and closing verses of the prolog (vv. 1–2, 9–11) offer material relating to Jerusalem. That is, the message at the heart of the prolog is enveloped by the Jerusalem theme. Chapters 40–55, the message of which is summarized in 40:1–11, are basically concerned with the return of the exiles to Jerusalem. By the divine Word, the manifestation of Yahweh's power in the world, the exile will be achieved. Three basic themes emerge from the prolog; not surprisingly, these are developed in chapters 40–55. The theme of Isaiah 40:1–2 and 9–11, consolation for Jerusalem, is developed in 49:1–52:12. The theme of verses 3–5, the return from exile as a new exodus, is developed in 40:12–48:22. That of verses 6–8, the power of the divine Word, is developed in 52:13–55:13.

PRELUDE TO THE SERVANT (ISA. 40:12–41:29)

Isaiah 40:12–41:29 represents the anterior context of the first Servant passage, which is found in 42:1–4. Forming a continuous argument, what precedes the Servant passage can be divided into two smaller units—40:12–31 and chap. 41. The first unit is the beginning of a dispute between Yahweh and the exiles over those Israelites who have been disposed to adopt paganism or have begun to doubt Yahweh's ability or willingness to help Israel. Through a series of rhetorical questions, the answers to which the people addressed would surely know, the argument moves from common to specific knowledge (Gitay 1981, 83) as the prophet attempts to answer this basic question: What kind of a god is the God of Israel?

Verse 12, in language that points to Yahweh's sovereignty over his creation and his control over the cosmic waters, the heavens, and the earth, elicits the acknowledgment that Yahweh is the Creator. In verses 13–14 the prophet refers to the infinite wisdom of Yahweh, who, unlike his contemporaries in the heavenly council, acted alone to create the world (Clifford 1984, 80). The argument proceeds to Yahweh's rulership of the world as Isaiah compares the power of the triumphant nations occupying the Promised Land with the power of God (vv. 15–17). As a speck of dust, the nations would be blown away by Yahweh, who controls the wind. Verse 18 then leads Israel to consider to whom Yahweh can be compared. Of course, Isaiah supplies the answer: Yahweh cannot be compared, certainly not to any visible likeness which is the product of human ingenuity (vv. 19–20), not to the contemptuous princes (vv. 21–24), and not to Babylon's astral deities, who themselves were created by Yahweh (vv. 25–26; Clifford 1984, 81–82). The actual content of Israel's complaint against God emerges in verse 27: God has ignored Israel's fate within history, her present plight as exiled. But Isaiah's rejoinder in verses 28–31 is that Yahweh's changelessness and inexhaustible resources guarantee his ability to protect Israel. Rather than grow faint, Yahweh gives strength to the weak (vv. 28–29). God has not forsaken his people.

Isaiah 41:21–29, which immediately precedes the first Servant passage, concerns Yahweh's dealings with the nations. The chapter opens with a trial (vv.1–4). At issue is the identity of the force behind King Cyrus of Persia, that is, who is responsible for Cyrus's present success and who gives Cyrus the power and authority he exercises. By his feats, Cyrus had burst upon the ancient Near Eastern world in 550 B.C. and thereafter menacingly, yet gradually, moved towards Babylon, finally taking the capital city in 539 B.C. and bringing the Babylonian Empire to an end. In verse 1 Yahweh ostensibly calls the peoples of the foreign nations as witnesses, though really Israel is indicted for her refusal to trust, for her lack of confidence in Yahweh, her defender. Who is responsible for these events? In verse 4 Yahweh reveals himself as the one, the Lord of history.

In reaction to Yahweh's revelation, the nations are shaken (41:5–7). Their idols can give them no support, and there is nothing upon which the nations can rely. Israel's situation, however, is quite different, for she can rely upon Yahweh (vv. 8–13). Yahweh will act in behalf of Israel because of her tie to Abraham (v. 8) and her election as Yahweh's choice and servant (v. 9). Yahweh's choice of Israel guarantees her protection against her enemies, but in turn Israel has a task as Yahweh's servant. In verses 14–20 Isaiah delivers a message of salvation to humiliated Israel, a mere worm, for whom Yahweh will overcome all obstacles in order to completely restore Israel.

In the remainder of chapter 41 (vv. 21–29), the gods of the nations are placed in the dock. Yahweh challenges them to bring forth evidence of their divinity (vv. 21–23). Since they offer no proof of fulfilled prophecy or extraordinary action, Yahweh declares they are nothing (v. 24). In verses 25–28 we find proof of Yahweh's divinity. Yahweh has called Cyrus to be the restorer of Jerusalem (v. 25) and has been the only one to predict Cyrus's advent (vv. 26–27). The chapter concludes in verse 29 with a reiteration that the gods are nothing (cf. v. 24).

PRESENTATION OF THE SERVANT (ISA. 42:1–4)

Isaiah 42:1–4 continues the address to the divine council though Israel, who has been exhorted by the preceding trial scenes (40:12–41:29) to turn from apostasy, is addressed indirectly. Verse 1, uttered by Yahweh, functions as a formula of introduction or presentation of the Servant, who is cast in both royal and prophetic terms. For example, part of verse 1 may be a coronation formula: "whom I uphold ["take by the hand"]." Then there are the striking parallels between the appointment of the Servant and the royal messiah. For example, the designation of the Servant corresponds closely to the choice of David in 1 Samuel 16:1–13, and the titles *Servant* and *chosen one* in Isaiah are applied in exactly the same way as they are to David in Psalm 89:3. The gift of the enabling Spirit, found in both verse 1 and 1 Samuel 16:13, is often used as evidence that the Servant is a prophetic as well as royal figure.

Yahweh divinely empowers his Servant with the Spirit for a mission. To be sure, in the call narrative of Isaiah 42:1–4 the structure reveals that the Servant's role is emphasized (Beuken 1972, 3). A simple summary of the content of the four verses uncovers the structure. In verse 1 Yahweh designates his Servant, equips him, and reveals his mission. In verses 2–3 Yahweh reveals the Servant's behavior and mission. In verse 4 God reveals his Servant's destiny and mission. Three times the mission is addressed. Each time the key word appears—*mišpāṭ* (justice). What does Isaiah mean by the word *justice*? In chapter 40 the prophet associates justice with Yahweh's total work of creation (vv. 12–14), a divine act which provided the principles of harmony that sustain and enable the universe to function. In Isaiah's response to Israel's complaint, aimed at Yahweh, about the manner in which the fortunes of history had swung against her, the prophet associates justice and "way" (40:27). Isaiah 41:1, part of the first trial narrative, uses *mišpāṭ* (judgment) in the establishment of Yahweh's case against the nations. Thus, for Isaiah justice is Yahweh's supremacy in the processes of history, shown particularly by the elevation of Cyrus, whose exploits will result in the liberation of Jerusalem. Justice is nothing less than Yahweh's superintendence of the created order. Yet, justice also concerns Israel and Yahweh's covenant with her since the justice to be brought by the Servant to the nations will vindicate Israel's special position. It is clear from Isaiah that Israel's understanding of Yahweh must be broadened, for Israel's history is not Yahweh's only concern. As the creator of the vast universe. Yahweh controls and shapes all history. When assessing justice, Israel (and ourselves as well) must take into account Yahweh's immeasurability, incomparability, and unassailed mastery over the entire universe, not merely Yahweh's dealings with nations or peoples.

After the introduction of the Servant in Isaiah 42:1, the next two verses indicate how he will go about fulfilling his ministry. In verses 2–3 the Servant is described in negative clauses that reveal what he will *not* do: for example, "A bruised reed he will not break, and a smoldering wick he will not snuff out" (v. 3a). These figures of the bruised reed and smoldering wick are not Palestinian but Mesopotamian (Jeremias 1972, 36–37). If the Babylonian background is pressed, they refer to the release of a condemned man who is near to death (cf. Isa. 43:17; 2 Sam. 14:7). Thus, the prophet reveals that by the ministry of the Servant grace will be extended to Israel, that is, Israel will be raised up from the near death of exile.

Verse 4 discloses the Servant's tirelessness in fulfilling his mission, which is specified as (1) to "bring justice to the nations" (v. 1c), (2) to "in faithfulness . . . bring forth justice" (v. 3c), and (3) to establish "justice in the earth" (v. 4b). "Faithfulness" in verse 3 (from ʾĕmet, "truth") basically signifies an attitude or action characterized by steadfastness, reliability, and enduring loyalty. Note W. A. M. Beuken's suggestion that the expression translated as "in faithfulness" should be taken directionally as "with truth in mind," meaning so as to establish truth or so as to display steadfastness (1972, 3). Through the covenant steadfastness to be displayed by the Servant, Israel's covenant history will be consummated. Verse 4 ends with these words: "In his law [Torah] the islands will put their hope." Though it has been suggested that the verb in verse 4 (and in 51:5) should be translated "wait in dread" (see N. H. Snaith as cited in Hollenberg 1969, 32), consider that the verb is never used in connection with Yahweh with other than confident hope in mind. In such contexts, the verb never has negative connotations. What the islands await is tôrâ (Torah), a very general concept meaning "that which shows the way." The occurrence of the word in this context suggests the very similar eschatology of Isaiah 2:2–4, in which Yahweh is depicted in the future as dispensing Torah from Jerusalem as he teaches Gentile pilgrims his "ways." (v. 3).

The certainty foretold in the first Servant passage is this: the Servant will establish Yahweh's justice, and this will lead to the proclamation of the Torah from Jerusalem (cf. 41:27–29). Viewing this prophecy in light of Isaiah 2:2–4 indicates that Yahweh's designs for divine rule from Jerusalem will be brought to fruition by the Servant's ministry. Thus, by the Servant's mission to institute the new covenant Jerusalem will become the world center from which the blessings of salvation will flow. Moreover, the city's elevation to world governmental prominence as the city of God will go far beyond the restoration contemplated in Isaiah 40:1–11.

COMMENT ON THE SERVANT (ISA. 42:5–9)

Isaiah 42:5–9 functions as a comment upon 42:1–4, which identified the Servant and revealed how he will accomplish his mission. The address by Yahweh to the Servant found in verses 5–9 provides evidence of what the Servant will do. In verse 5 the context is broadened to include Yahweh's lordship over creation, thus providing a vast backdrop against which the Servant's call is to be measured. Yahweh states his intentions for the Servant in verses 6–7 and reveals himself in verses 8–9.

Isaiah 42:6 summarized the Servant's vocation: Yahweh has called the Servant in righteousness, that is, in fidelity to his creative purposes (cf. Isa. 41:9–10) to effect a new covenant for Israel. What is distinctive about this covenant is its worldwide ramifications, for the Servant will be "a covenant for the people and a light for the Gentiles." This difficult phrase has been variously interpreted. It is probably best to view the two components as referring to the Servant's work for Israel, which will then affect the whole world. The translation "covenant people" violates Hebrew grammar, but "covenant for the people," with the Servant as the carrier for redeemed Israel of the traditions that once belonged to the nation as a whole, is plausible. What the Servant will do will initially involve Israel but thereafter will affect the world through her. When released, redeemed Israel will call other nations to her, and they will come running (55:3–5). Kings and queens will be in attendance on Israel (49:23), nations will bow down before her (49:23; cf. 45:14), and nations who oppose her will be consumed (49:26). In chapter 41 the prophet envisages the salvation of nations who confess that their own gods are nothing (v. 11). In chapter 45 Yahweh invites all the nations to turn to him and be saved (vv. 14, 22). Clearly the salvation of all the nations is contemplated *after* the submission to Israel. This attitude toward the nations evident in Isaiah 40–55 indicates that, though Israel is conceived of as only a saved remnant, this conception is still in unmistakable nationalistic terms.

THE SERVANT AND THE RESTORATION OF ZION (ISA. 49)

The second Servant passage (Isa. 49:1–6) is a typical prophetic call, though it is addressed to the nations (v. 1). The nations are a significant motif, moreover, in the entire chapter, for they are integral to the Servant's vocation. Successively throughout the chapter, the nations are called to recognize the Servant (vv. 7, 22–23), to render homage to Yahweh (v. 7), and to bring the exiles to Zion as the nations themselves come in pilgrimage (vv. 12, 18, 22–23; Wilson 1986, 275). It is implicit, therefore, that the Servant's work will effect the regathering of Israel from afar, the reestablishing of the nation, and the restoration of Zion.

Thus, the Servant's exaltation is inextricably tied to Zion's glorification (Wilson 1986, 286).

As we are told in Isaiah 44:28 and 45:13, the victories of Cyrus will result in the restoration of Jerusalem, the rebuilding of the temple as the focus of Yahweh's rule (a necessary consequence after Yahweh's victories; cf. Exod. 15:17), and the return of a renewed Israel. By all this, Yahweh will be vindicated in the sight of all nations for the international glorification of the Servant (49:7; cf. 42:12; 52:13). God's sovereignty will be established in Zion, a shrine to be honored by all the nations, and Zion will thus fulfil the expectations of the psalmist and the prophets (Ps. 47; 68:29–33; Pss. 96–98; Isa. 2:2–4; Wilson 1986, 232). The procession to Zion will be accompanied by the earmarks of a new creation, the desert in bloom with all nature transformed and rejoicing (49:9–11; cf. chap. 35; 41:17–20; 55:12–13). Upon the nations' recognition of the sovereignty of Yahweh (45:4–5), the eschatological reign of God will begin. Then the submissive nations will be blessed, and the idolatrous will be purged (Wilson 1986, 248).

EVALUATION OF THE SERVANT'S MINISTRY (ISA. 52–53)

The third Servant passage only slightly nuances the content of the two preceding passages. Found in 50:4–9, the third summons the Servant to persevere in spite of difficulties. But the material of the fourth passage (52:13–53:12) evaluates the effectiveness of the Servant's ministry. Since what precedes the fourth Servant passage outlines the achievements of the ministry on which the evaluation is based, it is necessary to look briefly at 52:1–12. Verses 1–6 challenge Zion to prepare for the return of the captives. The messenger then comes to Zion announcing God's return to Jerusalem and, thus, the comfort of his people that this return constitutes (vv. 7–10). With the return, Jerusalem is redeemed. Verses 11–12 then call for the captives to move out in a new exodus. What follows is an evaluation of the Servant's ministry (52:13–53:12) with further assessments appearing in chapters 54–55. We must recognize the emphasis Isaiah places on Jerusalem in connection with the ministry of the Servant. But does Zion, as the Servant city, play the role of the Servant? Though this proposal possesses some attractive features, tying the ministry of the Servant to the redemption of Jerusalem accounts neither for the prophetic ministry of the Servant to the wider world nor for the substitutionary suffering of the Servant described in chapter 53.

The fourth Servant passage begins by drawing our attention to the Servant's active obedience and blessedness: "See my servant will act wisely; he will be raised and lifted up and highly exalted" (52:13). The Servant's action is wise and well thought out. But if the Servant is acting obediently and living rightly in covenant relationship with Yahweh, why does he suffer? The answer lies in Isaiah 53, for it is by the way in which the Servant performs his task of suffering that the speakers of 53:1–9 are given peace and are healed (v. 5). Who are these speakers? The situation does not seem to apply to the nation Israel, who remained unperceptive throughout the exile. Indeed, understanding for her can only come after the exile (cf. Isa. 41:20). Though the speakers are not identified in chapter 53, clues to their identity might be found in 52:15—among the "startled" (NRSV) nations and the mute kings. Thus, the speakers of Isaiah 53:1–9 could be the Gentile kings of 52:15, but are they? Determining the speakers depends heavily on the identity of the Servant.

The appellation *servant* is given to Jacob/Israel in the body of Isaiah's prophecy (e.g., 41:8, 9; 44:1; 45:4). But passive Jacob/Israel is blind, deaf, and without understanding—a sharp contrast to the Servant, who exhibits the kind of obedience that stems from complete trust. Moreover, the punishment incurred by Jacob/Israel is merited, while that of the anonymous Servant is not. Though guiltless, the Servant suffers vicariously and is spurned and rejected by his own people (Watts 1990, 53).

Rikki Watts has observed that the association between Jacob/Israel and the Servant is absent from Isaiah 49–55, those chapters in which the mission of the Servant has center stage (1990, 56–59). Noting that the bulk of the salvation oracles in chapters 49–55 are future oriented, Watts suggests that there has been a postponement of the full hopes for the new exodus since Jacob/Israel's response to the divine initiatives through Cyrus made it clear that the nation is incapable of fulfilling the Servant's role spelled out in 42:1–9. So in chapters 49–55 the prophet looks forward to the future when the role of the Servant will be fulfilled, in the manner indicated by 52:13–53:12, by someone yet unknown. The pronounced notes of individualism in the Servant material, especially in 52:13–53:12, indicate that the remnant community, who was meant to be the idealized Servant community upon whom Israel's hopes reposed, has been reduced to one. At some time in the future, the solitary Servant figure will redeem remnant Israel and extend the revelation of God to the world at large. Thus, Watts plausibly suggests that chapters 40–55 serve as an explanation for the nonmaterialization of the new exodus and the glorious promises associated with the return of Israel from exile. But the divine intention is sure: the day of the Lord will come, the new exodus will occur, and remnant Israel will function as a light to lighten the Gentiles.

Isaiah 52:13–15 paints a picture for us of the Servant. The vocabulary of verse 13 suggests the elevation of a victorious king whose face has been disfigured by violence or putrefaction. He is perceived as corrupted, judged, and thus ignored. So startling is his appearance that notoriously hardened Gentiles and kings will be appalled (v. 15). In the words of the ideal confession of faith of 53:1–9, it is redeemed Israel who stands astonished at the Servant's ministry and her realization of its atoning significance. The elevation of this Servant will in turn mean the elevation of restored Israel, and the nations will discover that their future blessing depends upon Israel and her God (45:14). Moreover, without the redemption of Israel, there could be no world redemption (45:20–25) and no return to Eden. Such a world redemption would mean the universal acknowledgment of Yahweh's Torah and justice. Through the mediation of the law, which demonstrates Yahweh's will for the world, Israel would fulfil her vocation defined in Exodus 19:3b–6 and become a light to lighten the nations. In the closing chapters of Isaiah 40–55, we learn how such a world redemption will come about: as a result of the ministry of the Servant, the nations will gather around a New Israel (chap. 54) and a new David (55:3–5). Thus, the Servant is a mysterious figure of the future.

Israel's acknowledgment in Isaiah 53 of the significance of the Servant's atonement will lead finally to Israel's ministry to the world, since the Servant appears to be an incarnation of faithful Israel. Israel herself confesses that she had totally misunderstood the Servant's relationship to God as well as her own, but that she now sees these relationships in quite a different light. She had been in the wrong, and the Servant in the right. A changed perception of this character means a religious and moral conversion leading to a restored Israel. And this conversion provides the essential ground for the Servant's exaltation, for he has seen light from his travail, the success of his ministry and his teaching, and his intercession for the transgressors (Isa. 53:11–12). All this is the spoil that he was destined to receive. Though this theology is formed in Isaiah's time, its major application is in the future. The fourth Servant passage is not clear as to what triggered remnant Israel's reversal, though in part it must have been the Servant's willingness to die for the sake of his message and for his vocation. As the text tells us (53:11), this willingness to suffer was based on the Servant's knowledge, that is, his understanding of the revelation of God in history (Ward 1978, 129). A prophetic critique (53:10–11) and a divine assessment of the ministry (v. 12) follow Israel's confession of 53:1–9.

In the Aramaic translation, the Targum, of Isaiah 53, the Servant is defined as the messiah. Thus, there is an intermixing of roles between the Servant and Israel: the messiah prospers, but Israel suffers. However, the messiah does not suffer for Israel beyond being despised by the nations (v. 3); his role is intercessory only, not substitutionary. The tension displayed in the Targum about the prospect of a suffering messiah is resolved by depicting Israel as suffering and the messiah as triumphant. But this unmistakable paradox will not be finally revolved until Jesus of Nazareth is identified at once as the expected Messiah *and* the fulfiller of Israel's destiny to suffer for the world. Since the exile had clouded over the patriarchal promises, there was now a need for a new covenant, a new Moses, a new David, and, most importantly, a New Israel—a people willing to abandon idolatry in favor of faithfulness to Yahweh. And the mystery of Isaiah 40–55, which the New Testament finally uncovers, is that what is needed could only come into being by the atoning suffering of Israel for its world. The Servant representing faithful Israel will bear sin for the many (53:12), uniting in himself priestly atonement (Lev. 10:17; Num. 18:1, 23) and prophetic intercession for others (Wilson 1986, 301–6).

CONSEQUENCES OF THE SERVANT'S DEATH (ISA. 54–55)

In Isaiah 54–55 the consequences of the Servant's death are spelled out for us in terms of a new covenant based upon Zion and her world position. Not surprisingly, imagery suggestive of the old covenants abounds in chapter 54. The metaphors of the barren woman, who will possess the nations, and the children she will bear (vv. 1–3) are obviously Abrahamic, taking us back to the imagery of Genesis 18:1–19 and 22:17. In verses 4–8 the image of the woman is transformed to assume more directly the image of Zion, the concern of the whole chapter. We learn in these verses of a widowed mother, the wife of Yahweh's youth, and of the reproach of her youth, which seems to have been the period before the call of Israel in Egypt. The shame of her widowhood seems to be a direct reference to the exile. Zion, in whom the hopes for Israel have been gathered together, is depicted as a woman who was espoused in her youth, cast off because of her sins, but then recalled to the status of a wife. In this personification is a direct reference to Sinai since marriage is a frequent prophetic metaphor for the covenant (especially in Jeremiah and Hosea). Isaiah's use of the terms "Holy One of Israel" and "Redeemer" in verses 5 and 8 also invokes Sinai (cf. Exod. 15:13; 34:6). Thus, the events of Sinai are looked upon by the prophet as the time when Israel was called into political nationhood. The comparison with the time of Noah in Isaiah 54:9 adds to the covenant motifs to complete the picture of Zion. By such a comparison we are taken back to the time of the flood—when the deluge was an interruption but not a dissolution of the creation covenant. All this imagery prepares us for the covenant of peace (v. 10), which indicates that the period of the exile is a temporary check but not a negation of God's promises and which seems to be a reference to the new-covenant theology of the exilic period. According to the prophet, never again will the position of Zion be threatened. Indeed, Zion's security in the new order will be as unchallengeable as the fixed elements within nature, for nothing can be more permanent than the mountains and the hills to which Isaiah appeals in verse 10.

God's address of Zion in Isaiah 54:11a reveals the depth of the difficulty which has come upon the people of God: "O afflicted city, lashed by storms and not comforted." In contrast to what has been is what will be—the beauty and splendor of Zion (vv. 11b–13). (The figurative description anticipates the magnificent one we find of the new city of God in Rev. 21.) Since the maker and builder and Zion will be God, the city's foundations will be divinely laid (v. 11c) and will thus be unshakable (cf. v. 10). Moreover, Zion's outward glory will be reflected in the inward glory of all her sons, who will be taught by the Lord (v. 13; cf. Jer. 31:33). Verses 14–17 then set forth the consequences of the new covenant. A key term in these verses and one that serves to enclose them is "righteousness" (vv. 14, 17 NKJV; Beuken 1974, 61). However, this righteousness is not Israel's response to the new arrangement, the parading of established conduct by the redeemed people of God; rather, it is the display of *divine* righteousness, that is, divine fidelity to all covenant arrangements, which alone will guarantee access to the new age. Isaiah's use in verse 17 of the word *heritage*, which is Promised Land terminology also translated as "inheritance," foreshadows the goal of perfect occupancy of the land and the enjoyment of that rest, the presence of God in the land, which had ever been the hope of Israel.

Isaiah 55 builds upon the preceding chapter. In verses 1–2 the faithful are invited to participate in the messianic banquet on Mount Zion (Wilson 1986, 222), in the new life that will flow forth from Jerusalem as waters of life from this New Eden. It will be a life lived in proximity to Yahweh's shrine, thus affording participation in the presence of God. Remember that in 54:2 Mother Zion had been invited to enlarge the place of her tents in prospect of the large number of children about to return. This invitation to restored Israel is made on the basis of the covenant with David (vv. 3–5), for the redeemed must now assume Israel's position of kings and priests (Exod. 19:6). Because of Yahweh's cosmic victories, Israel is empowered—as David was of old—to summon the nations, who come running to serve and glorify her (Wilson 1986, 226). Hope for the future is thus grounded upon the "sure mercies of David" (v. 3 NKJV). These are not David's faithful acts but Yahweh's promises to David, God's fidelity to the Davidic covenant. Verses 6–7 is a summons to participate in the new exodus to the sanctuary, and verses 8–11, as an elaboration of the holiness of the sanctuary, call for the putting aside of all human devices and conduct that would prevent the assumption of the divine will (Clifford 1983, 31). The democratization of God's promises extends not to all—only to those who come in obedience to Mount Zion to respond to the divine call. And those who respond will embark on the new-exodus procession to Zion and the temple by the miraculously transformed way (v. 12), which will be identified by the victory of fertility over sterility (v. 13). This sign of the new exodus and conquest will thereafter stand as a memorial to the Lord (Clifford 1983, 34).

The placement of Isaiah 54–55 suggests that all this—the covenant of peace, the restoration of Zion, the new exodus, and the exiles' return—will be achieved by the suffering and death of Yahweh's Servant (chap. 53). The significance of his world-shaping ministry, anticipated by the language of Isaiah 42:1–4, now becomes clear. He will do nothing less than usher in the new era, the age of the new creation. So prominent in the prophecy of chapters 40–55, the restoration of Jerusalem provides the trigger for the advent of the new age. In the terms of Isaiah 2:2–4, whose eschatology underlies and is amplified in chapters 40–55, the weapons of war will become the instruments of peace as the world rejoices in the everlasting rule of God.

Historical and Eschatological Expansion (Isa. 56–66)

Isaiah 56–66, whose perspective is predominantly postexilic, is intimately related to chapters 40–55 and carries forward their eschatology of hope. In the last eleven chapters of Isaiah, grand promises appear alongside pedestrian domestic matters. Much of the material is concerned with difficulties of the Israelite community arising from the return from exile. Yet within these chapters, though the presentation is somewhat muted, the worldview of Isaiah 40–55 prevails: Israel will take her place at the center of the world.

Isaiah 56 begins with a sign of the new age, that is, the admittance of the foreigner and eunuch into the community of God's people come to Zion (vv. 1–8). With the old exclusions of Deuteronomy 23:1–8 cast aside, the only requirement for covenant admission is the keeping of the Torah. Foreigners and eunuchs will now be among the new people of God and will have full access to the new temple, and their sacrifices will be acceptable in God's eyes. Isaiah 56–66 intersperses such new-age oracles with material that arises directly from the postexilic period. For example, the oracle at the beginning of chapter 56 is followed by denunciations against apostates within the community (56:9–57:13).

Building upon the promises of Isaiah 40–55, chapters 60–62 describe the wonderful future in store for Jerusalem. Isaiah 60:1 announces the dawning of the new age, which will be heralded by the nations' coming in pilgrimage to Zion and bringing Zion's scattered children with them (vv. 2–9). Though the promise of world influence by Zion, legatee of the

Davidic promises, has not yet been achieved, it will be soon. The description in verse 10 of foreign dignitaries and kings rebuilding Zion's walls graphically reflects their subjugation. And in fulfilment of the Abrahamic promises, the nations will stream into Zion with their wealth (vv. 11–22).

Isaiah 61 opens with the commissioning of a Servant-like figure by Yahweh's Spirit (vv. 1–3; cf. 42:1–4). Cast in terms of the messianic expectations associated with the new age (see Isa. 11), the figure's task is to bring a message of hope to the poor, who seem to be the Jewish community in Palestine continuing to wait for fulfilment of the promises. What awaits the poor is the binding up of the brokenhearted and the release of the captives. In verses 4–11 the restoration of Zion is the issue once again. Foreigners will rebuild the city (vv. 4–5). Now restored to the world, Israel will be the world's priesthood charged with the responsibility of teaching the Torah (v. 6; cf. 42:4). The prophet's vision of Israel in the new age is notable—Israel is destined not for political importance but for service to Yahweh by maintaining world peace presumably through distribution of justice and the Torah. World homage will be offered to the bride Zion (v. 9), and the world will also be witnesses of the salvation bestowed on God's people (vv. 10–11). However, the nations will come in service and pilgrimage because of what God has done for Israel, not for any achievement on her own part (Phillips 1979, 114).

The subject of Isaiah 62 is the specific election of Zion to privilege. In verses 1–2a Zion is vindicated and restored. She is given a new name (vv. 2b–4a), and her future is cast in the covenant imagery of marriage (vv. 4b–5). Verses 6–9 reveal God's faithful intention to fulfill the promises made to Zion, while verses 10–12 call the people of God to enter Jerusalem as a sanctified people and to occupy that holy space. All this—Zion's vindication and restoration—will result from Yahweh's *prior* act of establishing the primacy of Mount Zion.

Isaiah 65–66 concludes the prophecy with a magnificent description of the restored age: the saints will come back to Zion to live in peace when the conditions of the new creation prevail and when nature once more experiences the harmony of its orders. But we should not think the return is universal. While a remnant will be saved (65:8–10), Yahweh will destroy his enemies (65:1–7, 11–12). Yahweh's servants will be blessed (65:13–16), enjoying the advent of the New Jerusalem and the unparalleled prosperity of the new creation (65:17–25). The prophecy ends fittingly on the grand note of the manifestation of the reign of Yahweh, who comes with the fire of judgment and destroys all enmity (66:15–17). The world will acknowledge Yahweh's rule (66:18), for the remnant will evangelize the Gentiles (66:19). In this new age of universal worship, all the world will come to Jerusalem (66:20, 23), and all Israel will be qualified for priestly service (66:21).

Isaiah's prophecy emphasizes the restoration of Jerusalem. In the book, Jerusalem is clearly a symbol that unites the worship center and those who inhabit it, combining sacred space and sanctified people. For Isaiah, there could be no thought of a restored Israel without the prior restoration of Zion. Yet, it is Yahweh's presence alone that makes Israel the saved people of God, the New Israel. Since Isaiah 40–66 deals primarily with the ultimate end, little space is devoted to the Davidic king and temple. Isaiah's Zion ideal was the reign of Yahweh from Jerusalem over the perfected community of the righteous—the banner to which the whole world would rally. In God's good time the enigmatic Servant would by his death usher in the new age.

6

Postexilic and Apocalyptic Eschatology

The prophets of the postexilic period were faced with the failed materialization of the extravagant promises of Isaiah, Jeremiah, and Ezekiel, but they fulfilled the traditional role of Israelite prophecy with no apparent diminution of vigor. Haggai and Zechariah (ca. 520 B.C.) and Malachi (ca. 460 B.C.) met this failure by maintaining the eschatology while also redressing present community problems. Haggai and Zechariah 1–8 viewed the rebuilding of the Jerusalem temple as a precursor to the new age. Malachi focused on the checking of priestly and social corruption. Zechariah 9–14 and the sixth-century Book of Daniel brought a different perspective as they moved from classical prophecy to apocalyptic. For these apocalyptic writers, Israel's salvation could no longer be sought in terms of changes within the historical structure, for God would yet bring history to a close by his final salvific intervention. Ezra-Nehemiah (ca. mid-fifth century) attempted to implement reforms designed to control the emerging dominance of the Jerusalem priesthood. When these reforms failed, the Chronicler (ca. 400 B.C.), the theologian of eschatological enthusiasm, proclaimed a message of expectation that God would yet act to make the promises of Isaiah 40–55 a reality in Israel's experience.

Prophetic Eschatology

Haggai

Haggai's prophecy focuses on the reluctance of the returned exiles to rebuild the temple. For the prophet, the erection of it is an indispensable precursor to the advent of the kingdom of God, which is to be centered at Jerusalem. Upon Haggai's rebuke, the people acted and led by Zerubbabel, the Davidic prince, gave themselves to rebuilding.

The basic prophetic message Haggai proclaims in 1:4–11 to the returnees who were placing community interests before a faith commitment can be summarized in just a few words: "seek first the kingdom of God" (Matt. 6:33 NKJV). The building of the temple was to have priority over all other concerns. Haggai's message had an effect, and the people's appropriate covenant response is recorded in 1:12–14. The "remnant of the people" referred to in verse 12 appears to be the returnees who in obedience to Yahweh work on the rebuilding of the temple and receive the covenant renewal promise of "I am with you" (v. 13). The prophet presents them as the carriers of the ancient covenant blessings (cf. Zech. 8:12).

In Haggai 2:1–9 the disillusionment of the community over the unpretentious character of the second temple is met with the encouragement that the God of the exodus is still with Israel (v. 5). Presumably the second-exodus blessings of the new covenant and the firm reoccupation of the Promised Land will still be experienced. Though Israel has yet to be the nation that will attract her world (v. 7), the Jerusalem temple will become the eschatological world center. The opponents of the temple building are rebuked in 2:10–14, and the returned community is exhorted in verses 15–19 to continue the charge to build. The final verses (vv. 20–23) are addressed to Zerubbabel, the temple builder, and language applied by Jeremiah to Jehoiachin, the exiled king of the Davidic line is transferred to Zerubbabel, who is hardly a messiah, but much more a figure of continuity (v. 23; cf. Jer. 22:24).

There is no evidence of any so-called decline in prophecy in Haggai. His program does not pursue the concerns of empty preexilic nationalism, and he is not given over to pedestrian and cultic matters. His is a great message that God will orchestrate his great promises to Israel with the small disillusioned community of the return. Through her the world will be blessed, and from her there will arise the eschatological people of God.

Zechariah

Zechariah's prophecy dates from the same period of time as Haggai's. It is not surprising, then, to find similar concerns in the two books, that is, rebuilding of the temple and expectation of the eschatological era. The Book of Zechariah is often divided into two sections: chapters 1–8, and interweaving of postexilic history and temple-oriented visions, and chapters 9–14, an apparent apocalyptic commentary on the expectations of chapters 1–8.

JERUSALEM AND THE TEMPLE (ZECH. 1–8)

Zechariah 1–8 focuses in large part on temple and cultic matters and at first does not seem to exhibit a marked eschatological interest. However, the rebuilding of the temple by Joshua, the high priest of the returned community, and Zerubbabel, the Davidic prince and heir to the Jerusalem throne, is undertaken to endorse Jerusalem as the world's religious and revelatory center to which the nations will come in pilgrimage (8:20–23). The last chapter of this section, chapter 8, describes the ideal future of the people of God. God's people will be restored to the Promised Land (vv. 7–8), which will yield abundantly (vv. 10–12). This remnant of Israel will dwell in a New Jerusalem, which will be called "the City of Truth" because of the indwelling presence of Yahweh (v. 3). The integrity of God's people will reflect the divine presence. As the possessors of all things (v. 12), the people will live according to the Torah (vv. 16–17). Thus, in the eschatological age the nations will voluntarily come to Jerusalem (vv. 20–23). Moreover, as the Zionistic expectations of Isaiah 2:2–4 are fulfilled, carried out as the purposes of God (vv. 2, 6, 11, 13b–14), peace and security will be the portion of all.

THEOLOGICAL COMMENTARY (ZECH. 9–14)

Without question, Zechariah 9–14 is more enigmatic and difficult to interpret than the first eight chapters. However, it is noteworthy that both sections begin and end with the same subject matter. Chapters 1 and 9 begin with the return of Yahweh to Jerusalem. Chapters 8 and 14 end with the role of Jerusalem after the defeat of the oppressing nations and the completion of the temple. Therefore, chapters 9–14 can possibly be viewed as a theological commentary on the more historically oriented first section.

Zechariah 9:1–7 describes a march to Jerusalem by Yahweh and the defeat of Israel's traditional enemies on the way (Hanson 1975, 291–324). Thereafter Yahweh will reign in Jerusalem through the eschatological King (vv. 8–10). God's rule will be marked by the release of captives (vv. 11–12), the manifestation of Yahweh as Divine Warrior (v. 14), and the transformation of the natural order (vv. 15–17). The next two chapters (Zech. 10–11) deal with problems of leadership.

Zechariah 12–14 focuses our attention upon the end-time conflict and its resolution. Though conflict will engulf Jerusalem (12:1–3), she will be divinely delivered (vv. 4–9). With a description of the reception of the Spirit and the resultant change in the attitude of God's people, the chapter ends (vv. 10–14). To be sure, all the community leader-

ship—royal, prophetic, and priestly—will have been cleansed. Eschatological cleansing is addressed again in 13:1–6, this time coupled with
the removal of idolatry. The final chapter presents a symbolic picture
of the ushering in of the day of the Lord, by which the new creation will
be introduced (Hanson 1975, 369–401). Nations will be impelled by
Yahweh to fight against Jerusalem (14:1–2). Though only a remnant
will be saved, Yahweh will deliver victory (vv. 3–5). And the mountains
will be leveled (v. 4) to make a processional way for Yahweh as he once
again enters his city (cf. Isa. 40:3–5). What will result is a new created
order on the earth, a transformation by living waters flowing from
Jerusalem (vv. 6–8; cf. Ezek. 47:1–2). Verses 9–10 proclaim the universal reign of God from Jerusalem, the geographical description of which
is notably similar to Jeremiah 31:38–40. (We may thus presume the operation of the new covenant.) When the territory surrounding Jerusalem is flattened as the city is elevated (v. 10), Jerusalem will be thrown
into complete relief as a world symbol (Isa. 2:2). With Jerusalem's security unchallenged (v. 11), covenant curses will afflict her enemies (vv.
12–15). And the nations will come in pilgrimage to Jerusalem yearly,
under the pain of withheld fertility (vv. 16–21). At last, Jerusalem and
the temple will become the world center. Described in the last two
verses as a sacred site, the temple and city effectively merge (vv. 20–21;
cf. Ezek. 48:35).

Malachi

Malachi, which concludes the prophetic corpus, strikes a pronounced note—that of covenant and renewal. Through a series of in-
dictments of various groups within the community, the prophet raises
various covenantal issues. Since Malachi presupposes the existence of
the second temple, the book is later than 516 B.C. Probably written
about the mid-fifth century, the Book of Malachi may have served as a
stimulant for the Ezra-Nehemiah reforms. The prophet describes a
community thoroughly consumed with materialism and introversion,
quick to complain, and unable to offer praise for blessings received. In
3:1 God threatens to send a covenant messenger on a mission of judgment to the community. Though in 4:4–6 this messenger is identified as
Elijah, the tenor of chapter 3 points to someone about to appear on the
scene. It may be, as many have suggested, that Malachi is alluding to
the ministry of Ezra.

The prophet identifies a remnant ("those who feared the LORD") as
the beneficiaries of Yahweh's exodus promises (Mal. 3:16–17; cf. Exod.
19:3–6). This remnant will be the "special possession," the Israel of God.
Closely following this identification is an apt statement of the point of

the book: Yahweh is always faithful to his covenant, but it requires a response from the community (4:4–6). Before the final day of the Lord comes, the real issues pertaining to God's people will be exposed by an Elijah-type figure, who will call the people of Israel to repentance. Thereafter will come the day of the Lord. If the initiatives fail, then the final covenant curses will fall on Israel. On this note of the cleansing of the community as a prelude to covenant renewal, the Septuagint concludes. Thus, Israel is potentially under a curse, for her assent to covenant in name alone will finally destroy her.

Apocalyptic Eschatology

We now turn to the place of apocalyptic in the developing eschatology of the Old Testament. The word *apocalypse* derives from the Greek word for revelation, and as a label for a genre of biblical literature and for a movement, it is taken from its occurrence as the first word in the Revelation of Saint John the Divine. The apocalyptic movement arose when problems during and after the exile called for radical answers, when the old patterns of revelation, such as nationally oriented messages, could not deal with the difficulties. During the exilic period, the great cry was for God to reveal himself in a new way, such as the prophet's cry in Isaiah 64:1 that God would rend the heavens and come down. Apocalyptic was thus raised up to meet the crises of the nation's end.

From the first third of the nineteenth century onward, biblical scholars have argued and discussed the basic definition and characteristics of apocalyptic. There is a general consensus regarding the class of writings on which the label *apocalyptic* should be bestowed. A minimum core includes Daniel 7–12, Revelation, and the extracanonical books of 1 Enoch, 4 Ezra 3–14, and 2 Baruch. Difficulty in reaching agreement as to the outer limits of the literature has really never been resolved. The problem stems from the circularity of the mode of definition and classification, that is, the literature is first identified and then features are extracted from it according to which the literature is classified. A further difficulty arises from terminology that overlaps and almost defies rigid application. As used in this book, the word *apocalypse* refers to a literary genre; *apocalyptic* refers to the particular perspectives reflected by writings in the genre; and *apocalypticism* denotes the sociological ideology that stamps the literature as distinct.

What is this literary genre known as apocalypse? To back up a step, what is a genre? By *genre* is meant a group of texts marked by distinctive recurring characteristics that constitute a recognizable and coherent class (Collins 1981, 85). Both form and content are considered in the classification of an apocalypse since the framework, or form, is the manner in which the material is conveyed and the content embraces historical and eschatological events from a temporal point of view as well as otherworldly contacts, so characteristic of this literature, from a spatial point of view. In an apocalypse, revelation may come through visions, epiphanies, auditions, otherworldly journeys, dreams, and mediators; the identification of the recipients of the revelation is often characterized by remarks noting their personal circumstances or emotional states (cf. Dan. 10:2–3). The content of an apocalypse embraces the attitude to history assumed by the particular apocalyptic movement, the eschatological purposes that are being worked out, the otherworldly beings who intervene, and the regions from which they have been sent. In apocalyptic, judgment and salvation are only for Israel's faithful (note the difference with prophecy in which judgment and salvation normally are pronounced for the whole nation). Central to apocalyptic thought are the elements of divine intervention and cosmic transformation, for the issue at the core dealt with by any apocalyptic movement is whether the ultimate meaning of human life can be found within life and its institutions or must be found beyond this world and historical experience.

Is it possible, from among the various characteristics, to identify a chief mark of apocalyptic literature? One characteristic often ascribed to the writing is the judgment of the present age as irredeemably evil, which leads to the placing of all hope in the intervention of God and an escapist attitude toward history and the problems of the age. Though many critics plainly state that the apocalyptic movement views history in extremely negative terms (Carroll 1979, 19–21), such statements are overgeneralizations of the apocalyptic position. Others argue that the approach of apocalyptic to its age is undeviatingly deterministic, a principle that separates apocalyptic from prophecy, but we must be careful to distinguish between strict determinism and the foreknowledge of God (McKane 1982, 81). Clearly, apocalyptic literature could not have made, as it did, an appeal to steadfastness unless human beings possess the freedom to make decisions. Perhaps, as has been argued, divine foreknowledge is an assurance that though God is never taken by surprise, God is always able to adjust strategies to cope with human attempts to frustrate divine purposes. Similar caution must be exercised regarding the claim that apocalyptic's chief characteristic is dualism, the division of the universe into opposing spheres of good and evil. Scholars who identify the chief mark as eschatology seem to make the most accurate assessment. During and after the exile, the prophetic hope for Israel and for God's restoration of Israel within the historical process seemed illusory. The glorious hope for the future became less and less certain. Then appears apocalyptic eschatology, which conceives the hope for a new age beyond, not within, history, contrary to preexilic prophetic expectations for a nationalistic destination for Israel as the people of God. Marked by opposition between the old and new ages, eschatology in apocalyptic literature points to nothing less than the end of history. In the Book of Daniel, for instance, imperial power becomes more and more corrupt and takes an irreversible course within history. In these circumstances, the challenge for believers is to develop such a hope that would permit them to maintain moral and spiritual initiatives and keep them faithful until the end.

Search for Origins

The search for the origins of apocalyptic is usually concentrated upon exilic and postexilic literature, although our historical and social knowledge of this period is scanty. That both prophecy and apocalyptic share a common hope for Israel after judgment indicates some kind of connection between the two, but there are real differences between them as well. Some scholars see a direct link between prophecy and apocalyptic. For example, Paul Hanson (1975, 209–79) cites material from Isaiah 56–66, Zechariah 1–8, and Haggai as providing direct evidence of conflict between a postexilic visionary group who saw themselves as continuators of the prophetic traditions and a postexilic priestly group who sought to put into place Exekiel's proposals for a priestly controlled, temple-based return community. Hanson argues that the visionary group eventually lost the struggle and as a result began to look for God's direct intervention, rather than for change within history of which they had increasingly despaired. The visionaries expressed their hopes in revived language of myth by picturing general expectations without translating myth into historical terms as exilic prophecy had (cf. Isa. 51:9–11). Myth was used by the visionaries to provide the language of escape from history into the unhistorical (cf. Isa. 59:15b–20; Hanson 1975, 133). In Isaiah 65, which Hanson dates to the last quarter of the sixth century, we see evidence of the widening schism between the visionaries and the temple adherents through the former's view that the restoration of the new community will take place only after a series of cosmic upheavals through which Yahweh will create a new order (1975, 194). Isaiah 66 continues the apocalyptic view by announcing the end of the age and the centrality of the temple in Jerusalem in the new era.

The acrimonious character of the controversy is readily seen in Isaiah 56:9–57:13 (Hanson 1975, 194–95). Increasingly seeking solutions beyond history, the visionaries became more and more displaced from the mainstream of decision making. The Zadokite priestly party rose to power and, as we see from the books of Ezra and Nehemiah, transformed Judah into a priestly state. During the exile, the Levites, who had been expelled from temple participation by the Ezekiel program, had made common cause with the visionaries to reform the cult along non-Zadokite lines. After the exile, the Zadokites sought to give expression to the reforms of Ezekiel 40–48. Backed by Persian support, the priestly party enjoyed the blessing of the prophets Haggai and Zechariah (chaps. 1–8). After the temple was completed in 516 B.C., the Zadokites became more and more unyielding. (Zech. 9–14 represents a visionary response to Zadokite narrowness and oppression.)

Hanson's brilliant reconstruction offers a plausible sociological background for the events of the postexilic period, but it relies too heavily on polarization within the community, as if this were a new thing. In one form of another, polarization between groups had always been a part of Israelite society (Carroll 1979, 19). Also, Hanson sees the division between prophecy and apocalyptic too schematically as the division between history and myth, for both used myth. Perhaps the weakest part of Hanson's thesis is his speculative treatment of the reconstruction of the problems of the return community. Hanson relates Zechariah 1–8 to Ezekiel and Zechariah 9–14 to Isaiah 56–66, but as we have pointed out, Zechariah 9–14 seems to be a detailed apocalyptic interpretation of the historical period represented in chapters 1–8. It is too doctrinaire, moreover, to separate temple and apocalyptic expectation, as Hanson does, since in the postexilic period hopes for Israel's future were bound up with the rebuilding of the temple, not narrowly with the cult. However, Hanson is correct in downplaying the effect of non-Israelite (i.e., Persian and Hellenistic) influences on apocalyptic. And he clearly demonstrates a direct connection between prophecy and apocalyptic.

The discussion of the origins of the apocalyptic movement does not end, however, with a consideration of prophecy. The thesis, which goes back to the nineteenth century, that the wisdom movement provided the matrix for the apocalyptic movement has been revived in modern discussion by Gerhard von Rad (1972, 263–83). Von Rad observes that Daniel, Enoch, and Ezra (titles of apocalyptic books) represented historical personalities who were wise men and that the concern of apocalyptic literature was with esoteric knowledge and nature, not only with a universal view of history. Apocalyptic writers showed no interest in the progress of history, for they felt, von Rad argues, that everything had been predetermined by divine decisions. The purpose of the apocalyptic movement, like that of the wisdom movement, was to provide a theodicy, that is, a justification of God's absence from history. And further like the wisdom movement, apocalyptic ignored the confessional nature of Israel's and salvation history. Even the interpretation of dreams, an accepted mode of revelation in apocalyptic, was the province of the wisdom movement (as an example von Rad cites the Joseph narratives of Genesis).

Yet von Rad's thesis is not convincing. For one thing, he is not able to account for the occurrence of eschatology in the apocalyptic movement, as in Daniel, and the complete absence of eschatology in wisdom, as in Ecclesiastes. For another, von Rad emphasizes the matter of apocalyptic's determinism, but it was also a commonplace of prophecy that God controls events. Moreover, the wisdom movement's determinism was not expressed in relation to history as it was in apocalyptic. The clearest similarity between the two movements—wisdom and apocalyptic—is not to be found by comparing apocalyptic literature with Israel's canonical wisdom literature but with the so-called mantic wisdom of the Babylonian period, which gave itself over to technical predictions based on omens and auguries in a way similar to what we see in the Book of Daniel, for Daniel's world was concerned with the interpretation of dreams and the receipt of visions. Also, insofar as the apocalyptic movement concerned itself with the wider world and an analysis of its problems, the difference between apocalyptic and Israel's wisdom, which was also world centered, is merely one of degree.

As we have suggested, perhaps mantic wisdom left its influence on apocalyptic literature. And it is possible that Persian influences were responsible for some of apocalyptic's sharply dualistic presentations. But some other claims of non-Israelite influence cannot be supported. That the periodization of history, the division of history into epochs, was a product of Persian-period influences can be rebutted with reference to earlier genealogical structures such as the Book of Genesis provides. The oft-made suggestion that apocalyptic's eschatological woes, supernatural forces of good and evil, and notion of resurrection were of Persian origin can also be countered, for earlier Old Testament writings could just as well have provided the motivating influence. In the final analysis, however, we must look primarily to Old Testament prophecy for the matrix of Old Testament apocalyptic, the more so as apocalyptic later consciously became the interpreter of Old Testament prophecy (e.g., Dan. 9).

Interpretation of Apocalyptic Literature

As a special literary genre, apocalyptic presents us with another world and calls for careful interpretation. Its dreams, visions, angelic mediation, cosmological emphasis, war in heaven, numerology, revelation of heavenly secrets, and bizarre, esoteric symbolism make literal interpretation impossible, and this was probably so intended. Symbolism is designed to convey a deeper sense of reality. Though symbols themselves are often conventional, they rarely become fixed or formalized in meaning (Osborne 1991, 229), and thus their interpretation is rarely obvious. We cannot read apocalyptic literature looking for precise questions regarding the chronology of the future, and we cannot proclaim interpretations of the future as absolute truth. More often than not, the meaning of apocalyptic literature is conveyed in general rather than particular terms. Thus upon reading the Book of Daniel, for example, we might summarize the meaning in this way: God will bring to an end the present course of history, which is so inimical to his people, and the new age in which God's purposes for creation will be fully displayed will dawn.

Often apocalyptic literature has been depreciated because of the intermediary character of its revelation, but this judgment ignores that the communications were still supernatural and that the developed eschatology represents the consummation of Old Testament theology. The function of the literature is clear—it was designed to give hope during a very difficult time in which the church and state were on a collision course. Believers were and still are to take comfort that the future lies with the people of God—no matter how unpromising or difficult the present may be.

Daniel

The Book of Daniel is found in the Writings of the Hebrew canon, not in the prophetic books. Though some use this placement in the Writings as evidence that the book was written about 166 B.C. during the Maccabean period and after the prophetic canon had been closed (Davies 1985, 14), the placement simply stamps the book as recognizably different from prophecy and justifies the labeling of it as apocalyptic (Baldwin 1978, 21). With major ingredients of Daniel drawn from the background of prophecy, the book witnesses to the reaction of pious groups in the exilic and postexilic periods to the loss of nationalism and to the cessation of institutionalism and prophetic revelation while it endeavors to maintain the faith once delivered to the saints.

Daniel begins with the approaching dissolution of historical Israel and the reasons for it, but ends with the resurrection of the faithful in Israel. Primarily, the book deals with how the faith of Israel is sustained in a most unpromising world in which all the symbols that could have been used to promote the faith have vanished and in which the Promised Land is not even occupied by the faithful. What the exile reveals so strikingly is that the faith could bridge geographical, social, and cultural boundaries, that is, it could travel. Daniel's concerns were major ones concerning God's kingdom; at the core, the question posed for him was how could he maintain contact with his society while refusing to compromise and while remaining distinct and Israelite.

THE SURVIVOR (DAN. 1)

Daniel 1 serves as an introduction to the entire book. The point of the chapter can be simply stated: Jews who rise to influence at the foreign court do so because their wisdom is given to them by God. God gives wisdom to those servants who faithfully obey his laws. It is wisdom of this character that makes Daniel a great survivor; thus, when the dust of history has settled upon the period of Babylonian power and the age of the Persian Empire has been ushered, Daniel lives on (1:21).

Verses 1–2 establish the scene by reporting Nebuchadnezzar's attack on Jerusalem in the time of Jehoiakim (ca. 605 B.C.). With this, the age of the Gentiles has arrived, and a new era has begun. Some of the cherished symbols of the faith, the temple vessels, were taken in the attack and carried off. What was utterly unthinkable happened, namely, the temple of Jerusalem, the site where Yahweh's presence was thought to reside, was violated. In the ancient Near East, the capture of divine emblems (usually statues or images of the gods) would be a clear assertion that the victor's deity enjoyed supremacy over the vanquished's deity. So, the gods of Babylon exhibited their superiority over Yahweh! Verse 2 reveals an even more disturbing matter: Yahweh himself had placed Judah and Jerusalem into the hands of the Babylonian king!

Nebuchadnezzar carried the temple vessels, we are told, to the "land of Shinar" (v. 2; "Babylonia" NIV). This phrase, found only four time in the Old Testament, and its wealth of connotations help reveal the real issues of the Book of Daniel. "Land of Shinar" occurs in Genesis 10:10 as a geographical reference, but the other occurrences are significant for our purposes. The phrase is used in Zechariah 5:5–11 to indicate that Babylon is the epitome of wickedness. Zechariah envisions wickedness in the form of a woman in a measuring basket. Taken from the Promised Land, wickedness is conveyed to the "Land of Shinar," where a "house" that is, a temple, is built for it and presumably where it is deified (v. 11). The most significant reference, however, occurs in Genesis 11:2 in the tower story. There the people of the earth, who had congregated at the land of Shinar, gave expression to their search for unity. They built for themselves a city and a tower, whose top might reach to heaven, and they did this to make a name for themselves, lest they should be scattered and lose their shared sense of belonging. In this ancient narrative, the humanistic dream of one world, one culture, one language, one ethnic stock, and one social structure is given expression; it is the search for a human center within the structure of society itself. The search is misplaced—God comes down and scatters the boastful builders, confounding and confusing their language. As a result of God's judgment in the land of Shinar, all the divisions that make it impossible for human beings to cooperate at the level of culture and society were imported and have become permanent markers of our fallen state. In Daniel 1 we see that Nebuchadnezzar's search for a shared human bond—one religion, one language, one culture, and one common education—revives the Babel mentality. Nebuchadnezzar conducts the old humanistic search for a unified world that is human centered. As the Babel builders had done, he leaves the Creator out of his calculations. Daniel is thus called to submit to a Babylonian education (v. 4), to learn the language of the Chaldeans (v. 4), and to receive a Babylonian name (v. 7).

What spurs Daniel to take a stand seems to be the assignment of this new Babylonian identity, for his receipt of a Babylonian name raises the issue of how far he would compromise his Israelite principles before calling a halt. The use of the cultic word *defile* in verse 8 indicates that Daniel's aversion to the king's food is motivated by religious piety. In his firm resolve, Daniel is to be contrasted with the exiled Jehoiachin, the last of the Davidic kings, who in 562 B.C. is released from prison, clad in new raiment, and given a food allowance at the Babylonian king's table for the remainder of his life (2 Kings 25:27–30). The Books of Kings thus end with this picture of the last representative of the Davidic throne: lampooned and compromised in exile, the puppet monarch Jehoiachin eats defiled food from a pagan king's table. In contrast, Daniel is the great survivor of the exile, for he lives until the first year of Cyrus, thus outlasting the Babylonian empire and seeing its overthrow by the Persian conquerors (Dan. 1:21).

The first chapter of Daniel sets the tone for the book as a whole. A contest will unfold between the imperium of men and the kingdom of God. But chapter 1 makes clear that there is a God who controls the course of history and to whom all must yield. In the clash of the two imperia, the otherworldly kingdom sustained by otherworldly values will prevail.

DREAMS AND REVELATION (DAN. 2)

All the main themes of the Book of Daniel are to be found in chapter 2. Though the chapter pertains to Nebuchadnezzar's dream and its interpretation, the focus is not to be placed upon the content of the dream, but on the ability of the representative of the people of God, Daniel, to interpret the dream and thus to provide a key to the future.

Among the themes and motifs presented in Daniel 2 are the testing of God's people and their subsequent elevation, pagan splendor and intellectual skills, the periodization of history, the advent of the unending kingdom of God, God's providence and sovereignty in regard to his control of history, judgment from heaven that destroys the kingdoms of humankind, and the ultimate triumph of the Divine King with a display of everlasting righteousness. All these are typical features of apocalyptic, and while it has been customary to deny chapters 1–6 the label *apocalyptic*, there seems to be no justification for doing so.

Daniel 2:1 establishes the context as early in the reign of Nebuchadnezzar, when he is at the peak of power and no political threat is in the offing. Despite all these advantages, however, Nebuchadnezzar is quite unable to control his inner life, for he experiences a troubling repetitive dream. The prognosticators of the day, the religious experts, are unable to help Nebuchadnezzar. What is happening to the king? Revelation in the form of a dream comes to the king from God. Thus, in the midst of the material splendor of the Babylonian kingdom, God communicates the future to Nebuchadnezzar through otherworldly contact. Paradoxically, it is the dream that reveals the harsh realities to come while the seeming permanency of the king's power and authority, which he exercises day by day, is a great delusion.

The key question for Nebuchadnezzar, whose spirit is troubled (2:1), is the interpretation of the dream, for the reality it discloses is anything but clear. In the dream is one major element—a great image representing the totality of humanity. In Daniel 2 three major figures complete the scene: Nebuchadnezzar, Daniel, and God. Nebuchadnezzar, representing pagan power and cruelty, is unable to master the real issues which underlie the political decisions of the day. Then there is Daniel, who is an amazing show of confidence before the divine answer to his prayer is given assures the king that he can interpret the dream (v. 16). As we learn from verse 19, Daniel is given the same dream as the king *along with* the interpretation. Even before the truth of the matter is confirmed, Daniel thanks God (vv. 20–23). In Daniel's address to the king, we clearly see the outlines of two opposing worldviews (vv. 27–30). For Daniel, "there is a God in heaven" (v. 28). In verses 31–35 Daniel divulges the content of Nebuchadnezzar's dream. The glorious image fabricated of metals valued by human society reveals the fragility and instability of society. Its composite character underlines its potential lack of durability. Daniel's interpretation, which is found in verses 36–45, makes plain that all the events between Daniel's time and the end of the world are in the hands of God, who will finally usher in the kingdom of heaven.

Though Nebuchadnezzar dreams of a single image, Daniel discloses that it represents a sequence of four empires, interpreted from one point of view as the succession of the Babylonian, Persian, Grecian, and Roman empires. What can we make of this strange mixing of unity and sequence? Consider that the succession might represent a unity of world government. Since the image is destroyed as a unit by the advent of the kingdom of God, the point might be that any historical succession betrays relatively minor changes to the basic human attitudes that world government, whatever its aims or supporting ideologies, displays. There is no substitute for, or alternative to, the government of the kingdom of God. Thus, successive world empires are merely the legatees of previous civilizations, embodying them and their ideas albeit with slight changes. This attempt at the human control of history will finally be swept away in the wake of the coming of the everlasting kingdom, which is represented in the dream as a cut stone that dashes to pieces the feet of the image (v. 34). Then the heavenly stone, so described because it is not cut by human hands, becomes a great mountain and fills the whole earth (v. 35). Thus, the ushering in of the eschaton will not result from human achievement; on the contrary, the kingdom of God will be ushered in by an act of God that will terminate history and human achievement. The mountain symbolism, probably an allusion to the world mountain as the point of contact between heaven and earth, has overtones from prophetic eschatology of Zion. Zion, whose glory and splendor will dominate the world, will be the world mountain of the new age.

Through the dream, God reveals to Nebuchadnezzar that human political power, the great counter-image (anachronistically the Antichrist), must fall before Christ, the true image, and must be destroyed before the advent of the kingdom of God. (The concept of humankind in the image of God and ruling in God's power from Gen. 1:26–28 is given total expression here.) The chapter ends in verses 46–49 with the picture of Daniel as the representative of the coming kingdom of God to whom Nebuchadnezzar and his successors, that is, all people, must pay homage.

It is commonly suggested that apocalyptic literature represents a flight from history and a disinterest in its course, but Daniel 2 demonstrates otherwise. The apocalyptists were interested in the total course of history, as opposed to the strictly national-Israel interest of the prophets. Furthermore, the amount of space devoted to the consideration of history in apocalyptic writings makes it difficult to view this use of history as a mere device by which to justify speculations about the future. In other words, there appears to have been a close interest in history for its own sake and not merely for the bolstering of predictions.

In the Book of Daniel, the rise and fall of empires is shown to be part
of the divine plan for history, a plan whose center of interest is the fate
of the people of God. There is no suggestion that God has lost control
of history or that God has abandoned history. What was implicit in the
earlier biblical reviews of history, namely, that there is a hidden meaning in history, is made explicit in apocalyptic writings. Certain elect individuals have an insight into history, which is being guided to its goal
by God as a struggle between God and the powers of evil. Such is the
view of history generally offered by Old Testament material; the apocalyptic emphases are mere shifts. In apocalyptic, the center of interest
is the last days, but since its view of history is no longer dominated by
the predetermined fate of a historical people of God, the revelation of
the secret purposes of God and history's course to the saints is now
necessary.

Judgment for the Saints (Dan. 7)

Daniel 7 sets the tone for the second half of the Book of Daniel, as
chapter 2 had for the first. (We pass over chaps. 3–6, for they represent
particular applications of the general message of Dan. 2.) Verses 1–14
describe Daniel's vision, and verses 15–28 disclose the interpretation of
it. What Daniel first sees are the four winds of heaven breaking upon
the great sea (v. 2). Since the image of the sea in the Bible usually bears
negative connotations (e.g., see Gen. 1:2; Ps. 74:13; Job 7:12; 26:12;
Mark 4:41; Rev. 21:1), the four beasts who arise out of it seem to represent paganism's opposition to the kingdom of God. The number *four*
suggests the totality of the threat, though it is not clear whether the
beasts arise concurrently (Casey 1979, 180) or consecutively (Goldingay 1989, 161). Representing Israel's enemies as wild beasts is not new
to biblical literature (Ps. 68:30; 74:19; Ezek. 29:3–5; Hooker 1967, 19),
but these animals have anomalous and frightening features (vv. 4–7).
We find parallels for the anomalies in the tradition of mantic wisdom.
In Akkadian omen texts, anomalous animal births invariably portend
future political adversity (Porter 1983, 29). In terms of symbolism, the
beasts in Daniel 7 present an assault upon the very order of creation, a
rebellion which is finally defeated by Yahweh himself. The background
for this symbolic political opposition poised against the people of God
appears to be the ancient combat myths of creation (see pp. 16–17) even
though the "one like a son of man" (v. 13) is not depicted as an active
victorious figure.

The beasts are historicized as world empires in the second half of
Daniel 7, the interpretation, as in Daniel 2. Note, however, that the
thought of Daniel 7 is much more complex and the opposition to
human imperia is greater due to the demonstration of their misuse of

power and authority in chapters 3–6. Moreover, the major details of the vision, including the four winds, the great sea, and the humanlike features of the beasts, are not reflected in the interpretation; to be sure, somewhat little space is given to it. Thus, the author seems to be relying upon the evocative power of the vision, which is not then exhausted by the interpretation. A major focus of interest in both the vision and interpretation is the fourth beast, which is so extraordinary that the author cannot adequately describe it. Having been identified anachronistically as the Antichrist, the beast represents the consummation of opposition to the people of God.

Daniel 7:9–14, the climax of the vision, takes place in the heavenly throne room: "As I watched, thrones were set in place" (v. 9 NRSV). That the word *thrones* is plural has whetted much speculation, particularly among Jewish scholars. Rabbi Akiba (A.D. 130) thought that the plural intended to specify a throne for Israel's messiah (in addition to the one for Yahweh) at the judgment scene; however, in view of the passivity throughout the scene of the "one like a son of man" (v. 13) this does not seem probable. In all his unsullied innocence, majesty, and wealth of experience, God alone is judge (Ferch 1979, 150), even though the Son of man is associated with this eschatological scene. It seems more likely that the additional thrones are for members of the celestial court. Thus, the Ancient of Days (note the Ugaritic appellation for El as "King, Father of Years"), who is clearly God, comes for judgment. Seated on a wheeled throne blazing fire, God is surrounded by his innumerable heavenly hosts (vv. 9–10). Then the books are opened, indicating the finality of the event. Similar Old Testament references to a book convey the notion of records of the deeds of people and nations (cf. "the book of life," Ps. 69:28; "a book of remembrance," Exod. 32:32; Ps. 56:8, Dan. 12:1; Mal. 3:16). This judgment scene, for which the author depended heavily on Ezekiel 1, is thus set.

The gaze of the seer, Daniel, is now directed earthwards (7:11–12). The terrifying fourth beast is slain and plunged into the fire of judgment, but history is not yet at an end. The remaining three beasts are left intact for "a season and a time" (v. 12). Thus, the foreign nations and empires temporarily triumph over the people of God. Their success is historical and short-lived, for eventually they are brought before the judgment throne of God. Yahweh's struggle with the monsters and the people's struggles with their enemies are facets of the same process, and it is divine victory that will restore the people's well-being.

There now appears "one like a son of man," and sovereignty and dominion are given to him (7:13–14). In the description, the element of likeness is not meant so much to approximate the figure to humanity as to highlight in apocalyptic's allusive manner his superiority over the beasts of the vision. That he comes on clouds attests not to his divinity but to his theological importance, since clouds are the method of divine transportation. Furthermore, there is no indication as to whether his coming is an ascent or a descent, and clearly this is not a matter of importance for the author. Though there are many possibilities, the identity of the figure cannot be established with any degree of certainty. Some have suggested that the Son of man is an angelic being, perhaps Michael or Gabriel (Collins 1977, 144–47), though where angels appear elsewhere in Daniel their identity is clear (e.g., 3:28; 6:22; 8:15–16; 9:21; 10:5–6). It also seems unlikely that the Son of man is a divine figure, for the book was written in defense of the Israelite faith in an age of monotheistic fervor. If we take the phrase "son of man" at face value in terms of its use in the Old Testament, then it refers to man in his humanness, in his weakness (cf. the extensive use of the phrase in Ezek., Caragounis 1986, 53–57). Maurice Casey's suggestion that the Son of man is a symbol representing the saints of the second half of the chapter is partly correct (1979, 39), but does not account for allusions to Genesis in the chapter, such as creation and dominion. These allusions suggest that the Son of man is glorified, transformed humanity, who is displaying at the end of days the mandate to rule that had been given to Adam and then to Israel. While in Daniel 7 the Son of man represents faithful Israel directly, insofar as the Son of man represents the destiny of humankind, he is an inclusive figure.

Verses 15–28 focus on the application of Daniel's vision. In the summary statement of verses 17–18, the beasts are identified as kingdoms. Then the emphasis shifts to "the saints of the Most High" (v. 18). The customary interpretation of the "saints" or the "holy ones" as terrestrial beings, as faithful Israel, has been rejected by many in recent years. On the grounds that "saints" is customarily reserved in the Old Testament for divine beings, these critics identify the holy ones as angels. Apart from some inconclusive contexts (Deut. 33:3; Ps. 16:3; Prov. 9:10; 30:3), the term usually does refer to angels. In fact, the only sure reference to humans is found in Psalm 34:9. But this sure reference and the most natural translation of verse 27 as "the people, the holy ones of the Most High," where the second phrase is in apposition to the first, support the customary interpretation. Thus, the Israelite elect will receive the kingdom—presumably because the Son-of-man figure already has—but not before a defined time of terrible persecution (vv. 19–21, 23–25). Finally, with the coming of the Ancient of Days, that is, the advent of the day of the Lord, judgment is given for the saints (v. 22). Thus, God's elect are vindicated. It is noteworthy that in the final judgment the saints possess the kingdom, taking the place in this final scene that the Son of man occupied in verse 13.

The meaning of Daniel 7 is clear. Judgment has been pronounced for the saints, for the high court in heaven has convened and the decisions that will affect the course of history have already been made. Hereafter, all that needs to happen is to hand down the decisions in particular cases. These facts are to provide encouragement for the saints. As they struggle in the world with the empires and tyrannies of the time, the holy ones of any age can seek consolation in the certainty that history's course has been determined, the lot has been cast, and their cause has already been championed in heaven. God has not forgotten them. The saints will be vindicated, and they will inherit the promises that God long since gave to Israel.

VICTORY OF THE GREEKS (DAN. 8)

Daniel 8 continues, as do chapters 9–12, the sequence of vision and interpretation established in the preceding chapter. Verses 1–7 deal with the victory of the Greeks, depicted as a he-goat, over the Persian Empire. The four horns that come up out of the he-goat's broken horn in verse 8 clearly represent the successors of Alexander the Great. Then in verse 9 the focus shifts to the little horn arising out of one of the four: the Seleucid emperor Antiochus IV Epiphanes, who ruled from 175 to 164 B.C. His desecration of the Jerusalem temple is depicted as an attack on the heavenly army (vv. 10–11), a defiance of the "Prince of the host," that is, of God himself. Antiochus erected in the temple a pagan altar that stood for 3 years and 10 days (Goldingay 1989, 213). This period of time is quite close to the 2,300 mornings and evenings, that is, 1,150 days, given as the duration of the temple's profanation (v. 14). The vision of verses 1–14 is followed in verses 15–27 by the interpretation. Though the vision is explicitly labeled for Daniel as one concerning "the time of the end" (v. 17), the details of the chapter point to the Antiochene persecution and the desecration of the temple. Antiochus is presented as a satanic figure, and the enigmatic "Prince of princes" in verse 25 must be God himself.

SEVENTY WEEKS OF YEARS (DAN. 9)

In Daniel 9 Gabriel reveals to Daniel a new understanding regarding the seventy years of exile forecast by Jeremiah (Jer. 25:11–14; 29:10). The seventy years of exile have become open-ended, that is, the exile will last seventy weeks of years until the ushering in of the kingdom of God. Thus, we find in this chapter two concerns typical of apocalyptic—the advent of the rule of God and the end of history. Daniel 9:1–2 establishes the context for Daniel's prayer, which is found in verses 3–19. Then comes Gabriel's reply in verses 24–27.

Verse 24 summarizes Gabriel's prophecy, with particular details set forth in the remaining verses. The six verbs of the summary can be divided into two sets. The first three ("to finish transgression, to put an end to sin, to atone for wickedness") take up the issue addressed by Daniel's prayer, namely, the people and their sin. The last three ("to bring in everlasting righteousness, to seal up vision and prophecy, and to anoint the most holy") concern the implementation of Yahweh's plan for the future. Three actions will do away with sin, and thus the age of righteousness will be ushered in.

Details of what will take place during the seventy weeks of years are set forth in verses 25–27, but no consensus exists as to the interpretation of these details. In looking at the verses, we will cite specific translation problems as well as a sampling of interpretations, while recognizing that any attempt to establish a timetable is fraught with difficulties. A problem arising from the punctuation of verse 25 concerns whether there are two periods of time, with seven weeks from the decree/word until the coming of the anointed one (Cyrus the Persian, who captured Babylon in 539 b.c.) and then sixty-two weeks during which time Jerusalem will be rebuilt and after which a second anointed figure (Jesus, v. 26) will be cut off, or whether there is one period of sixty-nine weeks (combining, as does the LXX, seven and sixty-two), which covers the rebuilding of Jerusalem and culminates in the appearance of the one anointed figure, that is, Jesus (vv. 25–26). The Hebrew text supports the former, which is reflected in the following translation: "From the going forth of the commandment to restore and to build Jerusalem unto the anointed one, the prince, shall be seven weeks: and threescore and two weeks, it shall be built again" (RV; see also AV, RSV, and NRSV). However, the Septuagint points to the latter, which is reflected in this translation: "From the issuing of the decree to restore and rebuild Jerusalem until the Anointed One, the ruler, comes, there will be seven 'sevens,' and sixty-two 'sevens'" (NIV; see also NASB). Though the Greek translation violates an introductory clausal pattern found in the Hebrew text of verses 25–27, decisions on the translation are often made on the basis of the content, that is, how one believes the weeks are to be distributed.

The difficulty with verse 25 does not end with the distribution of time. When do we begin counting the seventy weeks of years? According to the verse, clocking begins with "the issuing of the decree to restore and rebuild Jerusalem." But there are several possible decrees: (1) the decree of Cyrus the Persian in about 538 b.c. permitting the first return of the exiles and the rebuilding of the temple (Ezra 1–2), (2) the decree of Darius I in 519/518 b.c. confirming Cyrus's decree (Ezra 5:8–6:13), (3) the decree of Artaxerxes in 458/457 b.c. permitting Ezra's return (Ezra 7:12–26), and (4) the decree of Artaxerxes in 445/444 B.C. permitting Nehemiah's return (Neh. 2:1–8). (Though it is arguable that only the last decree deals with the rebuilding of the city, it is hardly likely that the temple would have previously been rebuilt and the city left desolated.) To which decree does Daniel 9:25 refer? (To complicate the picture, the word *decree* may mean simply "word" [NRSV], thereby referring to Jeremiah's prophecy of the seventy years, which may be a round figure, of Babylonian exile [Jer. 25:12; 29:10].) Do we choose the one that best fits the chronology, whatever that is determined to be, of the seventy weeks of years? Suppose we select 458 B.C. as our starting point. The 69 weeks of years (483 solar years) specified in verse 25 would end in A.D. 26, perhaps the year of Jesus' baptism (Hoehner 1975, 55; Feinberg 1981, 212, 215). But then we face problems with the chronology of Jesus' life (his crucifixion is normally set in A.D. 30 or 33) and with the detail of verse 26, which would be set in 23 B.C. (According to supporters of the 458 B.C. decree, the last week of years, detailed in v. 27, is usually divided into two parts: the first ending with the crucifixion and the last with the stoning of Stephen, by which the gospel was taken to the Gentiles.) However, the reference to an anointed prince, a messiah, in verse 25 points to Cyrus, for he is designated as anointed in Isaiah 45:1 and is the facilitator, as the messiah was expected to be, of the rebuilding of Jerusalem and the temple (Isa. 44:26, 28). But if we commence from 538 B.C., it is impossible to arrive, at least by simple calculation, at a date within the ministry of Jesus.

The customary view of Daniel 9:24–27, which commences with the decree of Cyrus in 538 B.C. and locates the terminus of the prophecy in 166 B.C. during the Maccabean period, does not fit the 490-year chronology. Yet, according to this view, the anointed prince of verse 26 is Onias III, the Jewish high priest deposed in 175 B.C. and murdered by Antiochus IV Epiphanes in 171 B.C. Then the destruction of the city and the temple referred to in verse 26 is the plundering of the Jerusalem temple in 169 B.C. (1 Macc. 1:20–28) or its desecration in 167 B.C. (1 Macc. 1:54). The last week (v. 27) refers to Antiochus IV's attempt to Hellenize Palestine, which lasted approximately seven years from 171 to 164 B.C., during which he proscribed sacrifice and oblation, and it ends with the rededication of the temple. Though this customary view, which has many defenders, is superficially plausible, the events of the Maccabean period only generally fit the detail of verses 26–27. For example, the temple and the city were not destroyed by Antiochus IV, and he did not make a covenant with the Jews.

Another view of Daniel 9:24–27, which can be described as an eschatological messianic view, has enjoyed some popularity, though it sacrifices chronological identification and understands *seven weeks, sixty-*

two weeks, and *one week* as indicators of comparative lengths of time. This understanding of the time periods is based on the recognition that in the ancient world the number *seven* was associated with fullness. So seven weeks would indicate the fullness of time, and seventy weeks would represent the fullest time. Moreover, such an understanding of the time periods is consistent with general characteristics of apocalyptic: its use of symbolic language and its disinterest in strict chronology. Thus, the eschatological messianic view assigns the first seven weeks of years to the work of rebuilding, the commencement of the sixty-two-weeks period to 516 B.C., the year of the completion of the second temple, and the end of this period to some point in the life of Christ. Verses 25–26 are then understood as a reference to the Messiah. Two events described in verse 26 are set after the period of sixty-two weeks but before the beginning of the last week: the Messiah will die a violent death, and the city of Jerusalem and the temple will be destroyed. According to this eschatological view of Daniel 9, these events are the crucifixion and the destruction of the temple in A.D. 70. The existence of some interval between the end of the sixty-ninth week and the beginning of the seventieth week is further supported, some suggest, because the goals of 9:24 have not yet been realized (Feinberg 1981, 212–13). This lapse of time and the events of the last week point to the second coming. The events of the seventieth week refer to the activities of the Antichrist, a time of domination by the end-time ruler, the "prince" of verse 26 and the "he" of verse 27. For some short period of time, this prince, the little horn of Daniel 7 (vv. 8, 23–24), will make an agreement with his followers allowing the rebuilding of the temple and the reinstitution of the sacrificial system. In the midst of this agreement, the Antichrist will go back on his word and cause the entire temple system to cease. But his end has been decreed by God, and he will be removed by divine judgment.

In chapter 9 Daniel pleads for those things Jeremiah had predicted would follow the end of the exile—the restoration of the temple and the city of Jerusalem and, above all, the forgiveness of Israel for her unfaithful past. Though by the prophecy of the seventy weeks the exile is shown to be open-ended, the chapter as a whole is hopeful. The numbers in the chapter were likely used symbolically, as is typical of apocalyptic style. Given the allusive and figurative character of apocalyptic literature, we should refrain from pressing the chronological details too far.

SELEUCID ERA AND LAST JUDGMENT (DAN. 10–12)

Daniel 10–12 constitutes a unit consisting of a vision (10:1–11:1), an interpretation (11:2–12:4), and an epilog (12:5–13). This final prophecy of the book is a further expansion of the symbolic material of chapter 7.

Chapter 10 admits us to the otherworldly conflict of good and evil angels, a conflict between the kingdom of God, represented by Jerusalem and its sanctuary, and the kingdom of Satan, represented by the nations. In verses 1–3 Daniel receives a vision of this great conflict and an understanding of it. He receives another vision and a message in 10:4–14, in which is found an allusion to the heavenly battle (v. 13). Brought by an angel, the message concerns the destiny of Israel in the last days. Daniel 10:15–11:1 records Daniel's reaction to the message and the angelic messenger's reassurance and revelation of the conflict between the satanic prince of Persia and the satanic prince of Greece.

An explanation of Daniel's vision begins in 11:2. Verses 2–4 deal with the defeat of the Persian Empire at the hands of Alexander the Great and the affairs of the Greeks until the victor's death in 323 B.C. Verses 5–20 concern the wars between the Ptolemies (Alexander's successors in Egypt) and the Seleucids (Alexander's successors in Asia Minor and Syria). For about a century after Alexander's death, the Ptolemies controlled Palestine; then in 198 B.C. at Panias the Seleucids, led by Antiochus III, defeated the Egyptian army and took control of Palestine. His successor, Antiochus IV Epiphanes, is the subject of verses 21–45. Antiochus IV's threat to Israel took the shape of great persecution from 175–164 B.C. (He is depicted in Dan. 8:9–12, 23–25 as the little horn who will suspend worship in the Jerusalem temple.) After the successful commencement of his reign (vv. 22–24), Antiochus invaded Egypt in 169 B.C. (vv. 25–26). At about the same time, a clash on the religious level occurred between Antiochus and the Jews (v. 28), and on his return from Egypt he entered and pillaged the temple. He invaded Egypt a second time (168 B.C.) but was forced by the Roman legate (Popilius Laenas) to withdraw. Verse 31 refers to the temple sacrilege committed by Antiochus IV in December 167 B.C.: daily services were abolished, and a statue of Zeus was set up in the temple, which was renamed as the temple of Zeus Olympius. The Maccabean revolt began at this time (v. 32), and the course of this resistance movement is told in verses 33–35. In three years Jerusalem was regained and the sanctuary cleansed. The details of verses 36–39 neatly fit a portrayal of Antiochus, but those of verses 40–45 do not. In these final verses, we find not a specific picture of Antiochus but a general presentation of the antichrist, who will come into direct conflict with God himself (Baldwin 1978, 199–203). Then Michael, the patron angel of Israel, will intervene (Dan. 12:1). Michael will stand up, or arise, as the defender of Israel (the verb *stand up* probably has legal overtones; cf. Esther 8:11; 9:16; Nickelsburg 1972, 11–12). In verse 1 Michael is also called the "prince." Since the word might be better translated as "army captain" (1 Sam. 17:55; 1 Kings 1:19; 2 Kings 4:13; 25:19), perhaps

Michael is being depicted as the head of the angelic host (cf. Dan. 10:13, 21; Josh. 5:14). History has now completely given way to eschatology, as the evils of the last days, a typical eschatological motif, are depicted. It will be a time of great trouble, unlike anything that has ever happened before.

Daniel 12:1 prophesies deliverance for "everyone whose name is found written in the book." The concept of a register is not unique to Daniel. For example, Isaiah 4:3 concerns the naming of the remnant. In Malachi 3:16–18 the names of those written in the book of remembrance are those who survive the judgment and live as citizens in the New Jerusalem. In Psalm 69:28 the register of the righteous who have survived the judgment of God is called the book of life. Daniel 12:2, the interpretation of which is subject to much debate, tells us something more about those to be delivered: they will be resurrected. According to verse 2, "multitudes who sleep in the dust of the earth will awake." "Sleep" is a euphemism for death; quite naturally then, "awake" is the word used to convey revivification (cf. Jer. 51:39, 57; Job 14:12). "Dust" is also associated with death elsewhere in the Old Testament (Job 7:21; 20:11; Isa. 26:19). One question regarding the interpretation of the verse concerns whether it refers to a general or partial resurrection. The two possibilities are reflected in the following translations of the subject of verse 2: "multitudes who sleep" (NIV) or "many of those who sleep" (NRSV). Since the latter translation reflects the most natural sense of the Hebrew phrase and since verse 2 displays similarities to Isaiah 26:19, which concerns the resurrection of the righteous, the latter translation is preferable. If verse 2 does indeed describe resurrection of the righteous only, then the dead wrongdoers remain dead and do not rise (cf. Isa. 26:14). Thus, the two groups identified as "some" and "others" (NIV) are not two divisions within those resurrected but two divisions within the one group of the dead (Delcor 1971, 252–53). The sense then is that the righteous dead ("some to everlasting life") are resurrected, while the unrighteous dead ("others to shame and everlasting contempt") are not.

Verse 3 then describes what will happen as a result of the resurrection—the righteous who turn many to righteousness will shine forever as bright stars in the firmament. These righteous ones are identified as *maśkîlîm*, that is, "wise." The related verb *śkl* is used in Isaiah 52:13 to identify the activity of the righteous Servant. Thus, verse 3 indicates a democratization of the Servant's task, for many are elevated and share the status of angels ("like the stars"; cf. Judg. 5:20; Collins 1974, 33). Promising vindication for the servantlike community of Daniel's day, Daniel 12:3 promises resurrection of the righteous as well. Daniel's prophecy is then sealed (v. 4).

The epilog (12:5–13) is a revelation to Daniel regarding the duration of the final crisis. In verses 5–7 he is referring to the time when the saints will be overwhelmed and when God will intervene. A final commission comes to Daniel in verses 8–13. Verses 11–12 allude not to the eschatological end but to the persecution under Antiochus IV. The references to 1,290 and 1,335 days are difficult to interpret, though both may be associated with the Maccabean crisis. A pertinent question, however, is raised regarding the interpretation of these days: Was the book written to foretell the future in specific terms of days or to uplift the community? For an indication of the answer, note how the book ends—with an admonition and implicit promise—"But you, go your way, and rest; you shall rise for your reward at the end of the days" (v. 13 NRSV).

The Book of Daniel provides the consummation of Old Testament theology. It addresses the problem of the persecuted church living in a hostile and indifferent world and views history as being under divine control. The book urges the saints of any era to come to terms with this uncertain world, but also to place hopes amid the difficulties of life in God, for the books have been opened, the issues have been judged, and the saints have been vindicated.

The Chronicler

The Hebrew canon closes with Chronicles. Since the work is probably the latest composition within the Old Testament, it is fitting that we conclude our discussion of Old Testament eschatology with a general consideration of the two books and a more specific treatment of 2 Chronicles 36:22–23, the final two verses.

Until perhaps the last twenty-five years, Chronicles has been linked as a theological precursor to the work of Ezra-Nehemiah, primarily because 2 Chronicles 36:22–23 is repeated in Ezra 1:1–3. Thus, the traditional understanding has been that the books serve to support the proposed reforms of Ezra and Nehemiah. More recently, however, scholarship leans toward separating the works, fitting the Books of Chronicles into the period at the end of the discredited Ezra-Nehemiah reforms. If this is the case, as I believe, who was this Chronicler, and what was his purpose in writing?

The Chronicler was not the southern sectarian that he is alleged to have been. No, his theology has a reconstituted Israel clearly in view. Though the Chronicler's Davidic-Solomonic emphasis is clear, this concentration upon the age and achievements of David and Solomon serves as an example of promise and fulfilment (Williamson 1977, 141). Rather than showing personal interest in David and Solomon, the

Chronicler views them as architects of a theocratic policy he endorsed. Rather than promote Davidic messianism, the Chronicler examines the operation of the kingdom of God. Consistent with the way in which the Chronicler uses the stories of David and Solomon is his ending his treatment of Solomon with the world recognition, as depicted through the Sabean queen, of the splendor, wisdom, and achievements of the Solomonic court (2 Chron. 9). As the Chronicler would have us understand, the court is symbolic of a higher reality, and the visit symbolic of a Gentile pilgrimage to the divine city. The Chronicler's preoccupation with the temple and its builders is understandable, for he regarded the building of David's temple as the necessary precondition for the establishment of the eternal dynasty. Moreover, the preoccupation finds its logical and theological conclusion in the temple-restoration edict of Cyrus, with which 2 Chronicles ends.

The closing verses of 2 Chronicles (36:22–23) informs us that the end of the exile, as prophesied by Jeremiah (Jer. 25:12), occurred in the first year of Cyrus, the Persian king. Having been stirred up by Yahweh, Cyrus issued an edict throughout his kingdom, which in effect set his realm in the context of a general world rule by God. Through the proclamation, the exiled Jews were directed to return to Jerusalem to rebuild the temple of Yahweh. The edict fulfills predictions regarding Cyrus found in Isaiah 40–55, namely, that Cyrus would restore Israel to the Promised Land and would rebuild Jerusalem and its temple (44:28). These events were to take place within a new covenant, a new exodus, and a new creation. Thus, the return to the land, the second-exodus theology associated with it, and the building of the sanctuary were compounded in the summary edict of 2 Chronicles 36:22–23.

If Chronicles was completed after the Ezra-Nehemiah period, as is generally agreed, is it appropriate that the work ends with the edict of Cyrus? We can answer with an emphatic yes! Through the edict the Chronicler indicates that the failed reforms of Ezra and Nehemiah set a course which should be maintained. The aims of Ezra and Nehemiah's temple state would come about in some future, eschatological time. Understanding that the exile was open-ended (Dan. 9) and that the projections of Isaiah 40–55 were still to come, the Chronicler proclaims that the kingdom of God will come, the second exodus will occur, and the Gentile kings will come in pilgrimage to Jerusalem. Ezra-Nehemiah's temple-centered society becomes the model to which Israel is referred.

The two verses at the end of Chronicles preserve the tenor of traditional prophetic eschatology (cf. Isa. 2:2–4; Mic. 4:1–5). Cyrus's edict is an endorsement of all that postexilic Israel could have hoped for in a divine overriding of the political climate of the day. The Chronicler's burden was to ensure that the postexilic disappointments did not cloud the hopes that the prophets had promoted. Bolstering a tired community, the Chronicler assures his people that God will never withdraw from his Abrahamic commitments, that the Promised Land will once again be Israel's, and that a theocracy will be established. Whatever the present disappointments, they can be endured if a theology of hope can be maintained. Thus, the Chronicler emerges as a theologian of eschatological enthusiasm. He belongs to the prophetic movement—one that would never give up on Israel's hope. Notwithstanding the disappointing conclusion to the Ezra-Nehemiah period, the reforms had set covenantal directions, and such directions would guide the future hope of Israel.

The witness of the Hebrew Bible concludes on a future note—one looking for Jerusalem to be the world center to which the nations would come in pilgrimage and from which the rule of the kingdom of God would extend over all the world. The Old Testament hope, which will be extended in the New Testament, is fundamentally a hope geared to this world, a universalist move for a new society to be constructed on the base of the old. It is also a national hope, devoid of the strong personalism we meet in the New Testament. Perhaps this is why there is such little emphasis in the Old Testament on the ultimate fate of the individual (Gowan 1987, 122). But the Old Testament makes it clear that the realization of the hope lies well beyond the scope of human achievement. The timing of the fulfilment, the ushering in of God's kingdom, remains in the hands of God.

Part 2

Eschatology in
the New Testament

7

Matthean Eschatology

The first Gospel bespeaks a Jewish-Christian origin and point of view. While recognizing the ministry of Jesus as originally directed to national Israel (Matt. 10:5–6; 15:24), Matthew views the ties with Judaism as having been cut. Thus, the mantle is understood as having been taken from Israel (21:43) and given to a new people of God. Rather than narrow Jewish concerns, the Abrahamic promises motivate this community to act. These people of God perceive the death of Jesus as inaugurating a new era (27:51–54), and the mission to Israel and the world begins (28:16–20). Clearly focused on the rejection of national Israel and the end of an era, the Gospel of Matthew examines the implications of this rejection for a Gentile mission and for the eschatology of the early church.

Jesus' Early Years (Matt. 1–2)

Matthew 1–2 serves as the prolog to the Gospel answering the questions *who* and *where* in regard to the birth of Jesus. Chapter 1 identifies Jesus as the Son of God who was wonderfully born through the activity of the Spirit. Nevertheless, the birth is also rooted in the traditions and expectations of Israel, for the genealogy in verses 1–17 makes it clear that Jesus came to revive the hopes of Davidic kingship, to fulfil the Abrahamic promises, and to offer Israel the possibility of a new beginning in world history. Through its focus on Gentile homage to the messianic King, chapter 2 reveals that Israel's vocation of being a source of blessing and salvation to the wider world will be achieved through

Jesus. Moreover, the family's sojourn to Egypt and return to Palestine, a remarkable second exodus, raise expectations for a new future for the nation. The remainder of the Gospel narrative will show in a remarkably redefined way how these expectations are paradoxically fulfilled.

Lineage (Matt. 1:1–17)

Exhibiting a distinct Israelite regard, Matthew's genealogy of Jesus identifies him at once as son of David, a title given prominence by its position, and then as son of Abraham (Matt. 1:1). Jesus, as Davidic king, issues from the messianic line and is Israel's heir to the worldwide promises given to Abraham. The tripartite family history, which begins in verse 2, reverses the order of verse 1. The first section (vv. 2–6a) begins with Abraham and concludes with the birth of David the king. The second (vv. 6b–11) commences with David and concludes with the exile. The third (vv. 12–16) begins with the exile and ends with the birth of Jesus.

The genealogy is conventionally structured, but the strict movement of *A* begot *B* and *B* begot *C* is interrupted by additions, thus emphasizing specific members. In the first section, the conventional formula is augmented five times. The addition of "and his brothers" in verse 2 draws attention to the primacy of the Davidic tribe of Judah at the time of Israel's beginnings as a confederation. Verses 3 and 5 name three women—Tamar, Rahab, and Ruth—thus singling them for special notice. Through the appellation *King* in verse 6a, the significance of the Davidic period and empire is stressed. David thus concludes the era which had as its aim the magnification of the Davidic house as the fulfilment of the political expectations of Israel. The second section of the genealogy covers the period of the monarchy, that is, the decline and fall of the Davidic dynasty. In this section, additions to the formula appear two times. Verse 6b identifies Solomon's mother as "Uriah's wife," a woman we know as Bathsheba. As in verse 2, verse 11 adds the words "and his brothers" to the formula, this time referring to Jeconiah (Jehoiachin), the last king before the exile, and pointing out that the fragmentation of Judah under the leadership of Jeconiah offset the earlier move to tribal ascendancy by Judah. Thus, the expectations raised by the twelve-tribe confederation at the beginning of Israel's history are negated by the exile. From this low point of Israel's fortunes, the third section moves to the high point of the advent, to the birth of Jesus. In this section, all additions to the formula appear in verse 16. Jesus is born under exceptional circumstances; his mother is Mary, the wife of Joseph. Moreover, Jesus is called "Christ," indicating that the high point in Israel's fortunes noted in verse 6 by kingship under David is recalled but also surpassed in the Messiah, Jesus of Nazareth.

Verse 17 summarizes the family history, specifying the generational count in each section as fourteen. Since the title *son of David* is a notable one in Matthew's Gospel, appearing nine times to refer to Jesus, it is likely the number *fourteen* relates to the numerical value of the Hebrew letters in the name *David*. Through this device Matthew underscores the Davidic character of the genealogy and the role of Jesus as Israel's King, one examined throughout the Gospel. While the count is correct in the first two sections, only thirteen members appear in the last one. Perhaps "Jesus," referring to the earthly ministry, is the thirteenth generation, and "Christ," referring to the postresurrection ministry, is the fourteenth (Stendahl 1960, 101). Thus, the title *Christ* anticipates the more universal postresurrection period in which the expectancy of Jesus' royal return counters the rejection experienced by him in his coming to earthly Israel.

Matthew's inclusion of the five women in the family history is significant, for it departs from customary genealogical practice. Why are they included? Perhaps the women foreshadow the universal ministry of Jesus, or perhaps they represent the remarkable way in which God sustained the history of Israel—remarkable, for instance, since four were Gentiles (Tamar and Rahab were Canaanite; Ruth, Moabite; and Bathsheba, Hittite [see 2 Sam. 11:3; 23:34]). Though these four women disrupt the genealogical flow, the severest disruption of all occurs in verse 16, where it is reported that under the strangest of circumstances, including a highly irregular and suspect conception, Jesus was born to Mary, whose husband was only the reputed father of the child! Is this an indication that God, having sustained Israel by the most unexpected means, would continue to work paradoxically with his people?

Matthew's view of Israel's history that emerges from 1:1–17 identifies three periods that have passed, the third one ending with the *birth* of Jesus. Implicitly then, verse 18 begins the story of the fourth period. Matthew's Gospel will focus on this fourth period, the new age of Israel, the life and ministry of Jesus. Jesus' coming will be more portentous for Israel than the coming of Abraham, the kingship of David, or the uprooting of Israel at the exile (Combrink 1983, 76).

Birth (Matt. 1:18–25)

The remainder of chapter 1 deals with the significance of the birth of Jesus for Christian expectations. Joseph, the father of Jesus, bears remarkable similarities to his patriarchal counterpart in Genesis 37–50. Both Josephs had fathers named Jacob; both were righteous men; and both received divinely initiated dreams. The earlier Joseph had preserved Israel by a descent into Egypt, as the father of Jesus also would.

Moreover, both Josephs operated on the eve of a great movement of redemptive activity by Israel's God.

Verse 20 acknowledges the Davidic ancestry of Joseph, and thus implicitly of Jesus. The narrative progresses through two parallel verses (vv. 21 and 23; Soares Prabhu 1976, 238–40) that foretell Jesus' birth to a virgin (see also vv. 18 and 20) and pronounce what he shall be named: Jesus in verse 21 and Immanuel in verse 23. Explanations for the two names follow. Jesus explained as "Yahweh saves" in verse 21 corresponds to Immanuel as "God with us" in verse 23, meaning that salvation will signify the presence of God with us. Thus, this most significant period of all Jewish history will witness the advent of God, who will be with us in the human sphere and who will complete and perfect for Israel and for the world through Israel the redemption for which Israel had always hoped (Ps. 103:3–4). But as the genealogy has led us to expect, all this will happen in a way that will run contrary to popular expectation.

In verse 23 Matthew cites Isaiah 7:14, taking us back to the Old Testament context of King Ahaz's meeting with Isaiah. The prophet counseled the king not to become embroiled in an alliance with Assyria against Syria and the northern kingdom. When Ahaz refused Isaiah's invitation to ask for a sign, the sign of the future birth of the messianic child, Immanuel, was given anyway. Isaiah 7:14–16 looks beyond the present circumstance of Judah to a future messianic king, to the birth of a child associated with the formation of a remnant community, who would greet and usher in the new age. Taking into account the context of Isaiah 7:14 and the parallels between Matthew 1:21 and 1:23 that "his people," the ones who will be saved, in verse 21 refers not to Israel but to the remnant community of the new age. Likewise "they" who "will call" in verse 23 alludes to the new community of faith, that is, the believing community that will arise as a result of the ministry of Jesus to national Israel. This new people who will hail the ministry of Jesus will be distinct from the nation, comprising a group within it.

Matthew 1:18–25 begins the story of Israel's fourth period of history. Unlike the earlier three periods, this one is open-ended—it has begun but has not yet closed. Presumably this historical period will extend from the advent to the parousia. Verses 18–25 also continue the motif found in verses 1–17 of Davidic and Abrahamic ancestry, serving to remind us that the promises to Israel that culminated in Davidic kingship were the result of prior promises given to Abraham. Though Jesus is the son of David, he is equally the son of Abraham. At the outset, Matthew's Gospel insists upon these wider connections, and at its conclusion, it culminates in the universal commission to the new people of God (28:16–20). Providing the basis for the commencement of Jesus' mission to Israel are the covenant promises to Israel through Abraham, and the Gospel concludes with the nucleus of a New Israel, which is to unfold blessings to the Gentiles on the basis of the Abrahamic promises. Moreover, the role of the Holy Spirit in the conception of Jesus as described in verse 18 shows that human connections are not enough and that the gospel which Jesus will proclaim can only be understood in the light of his divine origins as Son of God.

Geographical Roots (Matt. 2)

Whereas Matthew 1 deals with the family history of Jesus, chapter 2 focuses on his geographical origins (Stendahl 1960, 104), and in doing so underscores Jesus' role as Messiah of Israel. Matthew 2:1 identifies the historical setting as "during the time of King Herod," and thus we are brought face to face with the politics of the day. Herod's claim to Kingship, however, is implicitly challenged by the Easterners' inquiry. regarding the birthplace of the "king of the Jews," the Christ of Jewish expectation (v. 2). Ironically, Israel's representatives are able to identify the birthplace but leave it to the Gentiles to approach the messianic child (v. 5). A portent of fulfilment of Isaianic prophecy (see Isa. 2:2–4), which will depend on Jesus' death and resurrection, the pilgrimage of the Gentiles to Israel's King thus foreshadows their response to the later proclamation of the gospel.

Matthew's use of Old Testament material in 2:6 (cf. 2 Sam. 5:2; Mic. 5:2) sustains the Davidic motif with which the Gospel begins. After all, Bethlehem was the ancestral home of David as well as the place where David was anointed by Samuel. There arises in Matthew, then, a detectable conflict between Davidic Bethlehem and Herodian Jerusalem, one that is stacked in Bethlehem's favor. In 2:1 Bethlehem is listed before Jerusalem, and in 2:6 Bethlehem is the place from which a ruler for all of Israel will arise. The conflict between the cities mirrors the one between Herod and Jesus. Guiding the magi from Jerusalem to Bethlehem, the star heralds the birth of the King (vv. 9–10). Possibly an allusion to Numbers 24:17, the star serves as a Davidic and messianic symbol (Nolan 1979, 205–9). Once the magi worship the child (v. 11) and present (a verb Matthew uses in 5:23–24 and 8:4 for offerings presented to God; see Bauer 1988, 118), their offerings, Herod is no longer identified as "king." The future downfall of Herod's city is certain when the magi bypass it on their way home (v. 12; Nolan 1979, 39).

Matthew's further use of Old Testament Scripture in chapter 2 (vv. 15 and 18) links the preceeding Davidic motifs, representing the choice of David, with the two other pivotal episodes in Israel's history: the exodus from Egypt and the exile from the Promised Land. Jesus' return from Egypt was anticipated in the flight, for the citation of Hosea 11:1, "out of Egypt I called my son," is found in the narrative of the descent (Matt. 2:15). The similarities between circumstances of Jesus' flight to and return from Egypt and Israel's oppression in Egypt and the exodus are notable. Both Pharaoh and Herod seek to destroy the savior child at birth; both massacre infants; and both die, thus enabling a return of the oppressed. Both Moses and the family of Jesus set off for the Promised Land from Egypt under inspiration. Jesus then is the one who recapitulates historical Israel's exodus experience, and through Jesus Yahweh's promise of a new exodus (Hos. 11:1) is fulfilled. Herod's slaughter of the children (2:16) evokes Matthew's reference to Jeremiah 31:15. Recalling the trauma of the Babylonian exile, the passage depicts Rachel, the mother of Israel, weeping over the plight of Israel at Ramah, the point of departure for the exile of 586 B.C. So too did mothers weep over the loss of their sons at Herod's command.

Verses 19–23 complete the birth narratives and appeal once again to fulfilment of earlier prophecy. According to Matthew's account, revelation prompts Joseph to locate Jesus in Nazareth, in half-Gentile territory, thus ominously portending the Jews' rejection of the Messiah. Matthew's use of the plural in "through the prophets" at verse 23 seems to indicate a general appeal to a prophetic background, rather than citation of a particular passage. The move to Nazareth fulfils the prophetic statement, "He will be called a Nazarene." What does this mean? Three interpretations of this difficult statement are usually offered: it is (1) a messianic reference to Isaiah 11:1, (2) a reference to Jesus' background as a Nazarite (see Num. 6), and (3) a reference to being from the place called Nazareth. Of the three, the last seems the most plausible.

Preparation for Jesus' Ministry (Matt. 3:1–4:11)

The implementation of the aims of the prolog begins with Matthew 3:1–4:11, which lays the groundwork for the public ministry of Jesus through narratives of the ministry of John the Baptist (3:1–12), of Jesus' baptism (3:13–17), and of Jesus' experience in the wilderness (4:1–11). Using motifs and themes from Israel's story in the Old Testament, Matthew sets the account of Jesus and John in a context of prophecy, judgment, wilderness wandering, covenant renewal, and recognition of God's sovereignty.

John the Baptist (Matt. 3:1–12)

John the Baptist ushers in the new age, hoped for by Old Testament prophetic and apocalyptic speculation, by preaching a message that

Jesus will later proclaim: "Repent, for the kingdom of heaven is near" (Matt. 3:2; cf. 4:17). In the desert wilderness round about the Jordan where Moses operated as a convenantal figure, John, garbed as an Elijah figure, is sent to prepare the way of the Lord (v. 3). John's appeal for the formation of a processional way back from exile in a new exodus is uttered earlier by the prophet Isaiah (40:3). In the context of Isaiah 40–55, the ministry of the Servant leads to the reestablishment of Jerusalem. We may suppose that the ministries of John and Jesus were designed for the same end, namely, the establishment of Jerusalem as the site from which light and life would go forth to the Gentile world. In fact, we know that this will happen in the most paradoxical of ways—blessing will emanate from the cross of the Messiah, crucified outside the Jerusalem walls, to all nations.

The Baptist's affinity to Elijah strongly suggests that God is offering covenantal renewal to all Israel. Once again Israel is to stop tottering between two opinions (cf. 1 Kings 18:21) and to return to the God of the covenant. Malachi proclaimed that an Elijah-like prophet would bring the last divine word to Israel before God's coming on the great and terrible day of the Lord (4:5–6). Matthew thus depicts John's ministry as the culmination of all the prophetic ministries. In the repentance which John offers, he holds out possibility of covenant renewal for the people of God. Here, as in the Old Testament, repentance means returning to the point of origin and striking out in a new direction. John's prophetic voice urges the nation to go back to the beginning of its journey, back to the crossing of the Jordan, and once again to set out into the Promised Land, but this time in a new national direction into a new eschatological age. Israel is summoned by the Baptist to return to the region of the Jordan Valley, where the covenant had been renewed before Israel entered the Promised Land. Covenant renewal under Moses had made possible the occupancy of the Promised Land. Could a spiritual revival under John and Jesus have the same effect? Through the baptism of verse 6, John calls Israel to repeat the Red Sea/Jordan crossing, which had become fused in Israelite theology (Ps. 114). A purified Israel is to emerge from the crossing, a corporate and national Israel fit once again to occupy the Promised Land.

The imagery of judgment pervades John's message, for he comes to warn the people of the advent of Jesus (Meyer 1979, 115), the eschatological judge (Matt. 3:8–12). Matthew uses the image of the wilderness to further the judgment motif, and it seems we are to embrace the image with its full range of meaning from the Old Testament, that is, its use as a sign of as well as its representation of a disciplinary point at which God could begin again (e.g., Hos. 2). Though John's reference to Abraham in verse 9 makes clear that John addresses all Israel as legatees of the Abrahamic promises, he expects a divided response, for he speaks of impending judgment and division between wheat and the chaff (v. 12). This judgment would result in a division within the ranks of national Israel. John the Baptist defines only one way by which Israel could meet Yahweh the Judge—through a cleansing and washing resulting in a renewed and purified Israel—but there is no sure contemporaneous analogy for the unusual baptism John offers as the mode of cleansing. The regular ritual washings of Qumran were of a different character. Proselyte baptism, which was ritualistic and political, would not account for John's emphasis on the forgiveness of sins. Interestingly, there was a rabbinic view that Israel was prepared for Sinai by means of a similar washing (Jeremias 1971, 44; cf. 1 Cor. 10:1–12). The Baptist demands that the nation repent. Though the Abrahamic connection provided ancestral links, it offered no spiritual guarantees, and all claims to a unified nationalistic stance were to be surrendered (vv. 9–10).

John calls for a reconstituted Israel, but at the same time he draws attention to the limitations of the baptism that he brings (Matt. 3:11). He expects performance and demands fruits, but is merely preliminary. John baptizes them with water; however, the mightier one to come, who presumably is Jesus, will baptize them "with the Holy Spirit and with fire" (v. 11). Let's look at the phrase more closely. Since there is only one preposition, the phrase is perhaps best translated as "with the Holy Spirit and fire," indicating that Spirit and fire are coordinate ingredients of the baptism. It does not seem that John is referring to the event at Pentecost in Acts 2, for he addresses a particular group of representative Israel assembled at the Jordan about a prospective Spirit-and-fire baptism to be undergone by the nation. Further, the reference to the coming Pentecost experience in Acts 1:5 talks only of baptism with the Holy Spirit, making no mention of fire. In the Old Testament, fire was often related to purification arising from judgment, as in Isaiah 1:25: "I will turn my hand against you; I will smelt away your dross as with lye and remove all your alloy" (NRSV). Perhaps John's coordinated "Spirit and fire" refers to the possible twofold effects of such a baptism—(1) Israel's cleansing and purification and (2) removal of the nation's dross.

The Baptism of Jesus (Matt. 3:13–17)

After the introduction to John the Baptist, Matthew describes the baptism of Jesus himself at the hands of John. The scene models for Israel the covenant obedience that is required, with the baptism giving complete expression to the covenant relationship (Matt. 3:15). Israel's Messiah in the person of Jesus submits for Israel to the preached demands of John. By his endorsement of John's message, Jesus fulfils all of Israel's covenant requirements. Through apocalyptic imagery of the opening heavens (v. 16), Matthew indicates that a new phase of revelation is beginning with Jesus.

Once Jesus is baptized, the Spirit of God, which had been silent since the close of the Old Testament prophetic age, comes down from heaven and alights on Jesus (Matt. 3:16). According to Acts 10:38, this Spirit comes not to regenerate Jesus but to authorize him for office and commission him for ministry. Though the depiction of the Spirit as a dove may be an oblique reference to the end of the flood in Genesis 8:9–12 as the dawning of a new day of revelation, the heralding of God's peace for humankind, it is better seen, in accordance with contemporaneous rabbinic thought, as an image of Israel for whom Jesus was the total replacement (Strack and Billerbeck 1922, 123–25). The heavenly pronouncement in verse 17, "This is my Son, whom I love; with him I am well pleased," echoes eschatological motifs from the Old Testament. To describe God's relationship to Jesus, Matthew uses both Psalm 2:7, in which the title of God's adopted son was bestowed on Israel's messiah and Isaiah 42:1, in which the Servant, who was both a prophetic and a royal figure, would vindicate Israel within history.

Jesus in the Wilderness (Matt. 4:1–11)

Matthew continues the typology of Jesus as Israel in chapter 4. Depicted as God's Son, just as Israel had been in the past (Exod. 4:22; Isa. 1:2), Jesus is led into the wilderness (Matt. 4:1), the place where after the crossing of the Red Sea Israel had been tempted and had failed (Deut. 8:2). Israel was tested through the forty-year march so that God might know what was in her heart (Deut. 8:2) and so that she could be exalted (Deut. 8:16). And what of Jesus' testing? Most certainly it was not to corroborate his sonship, for in verses 3 and 5 even the tempter presumes Jesus' role ("if you are the Son of God," but possibly better translated as "since you are the Son of God"). Rather, the tempter schemes to have Jesus take the easy path to the realization of God's kingdom. Note the connection between the sites of Jesus' temptation and the kingdom of God. Each site—the wilderness (v. 1), the temple (v. 5), and the mountain (v. 8)—was a place where eschatological events were expected. The Qumran community had moved to the wilderness in preparation for Israel's eschaton while both the Jerusalem temple and the world mountain were associated with eschatological events (Donaldson 1985, 96).

Representing appeals for Jesus to conform his messianic ministry to popular expectations, the temptations touch the nature of Jesus' call to messiahship. Satan taunts Jesus to provide new manna to ease his hunger in the wilderness (Matt. 4:3), to demonstrate divine authorization for his ministry by jumping from the pinnacle of the temple (v. 6), and to achieve world sovereignty through political means without any sacrificial costs (v. 9). But, as the message of Israel's history in the Old Testament had made clear, only by the submission of Jesus as Son to the will of the Father would Jesus fulfil his vocation. Jesus' call was to involve a dependence upon God for the servicing of all his needs, a trust in God's presence, and the acceptance of God's sovereignty on God's terms. In the wilderness, Jesus recalls God's covenant promises, which Israel under similar circumstances had forgotten, and Jesus triumphs over temptation. The angels who come and minister to him (v. 11) foreshadow Jesus' lordship over all creation and confirm his status as Son and thus also as Israel.

The Ministry of Jesus (Matt. 4:17–25:46)

Matthew reports in quick succession Jesus' temptation (4:1–11), John's arrest (v. 12), and the beginning of Jesus' public ministry (v. 17). The narrative of Jesus' teaching ministry to Israel extends from 4:17 to 25:46. On the basis of this ministry, the call will go forth to the new people of God; during the course of the ministry, political Israel will be rejected.

Sermon on the Mount (Matt. 5:1–7:27)

In Matthew's Gospel, the Sermon on the Mount follows the commencement of Jesus' public ministry. Exhibiting possible Sinai overtones (Davies and Allison 1988, 423), the sermon perhaps aims at the reconstitution of scattered Israel. Matthew depicts Jesus as distancing himself from his disciples and the crowd, addressing both groups as would a teacher (5:1–2; 7:28–29). And what is the teaching?

A word used repeatedly in Matthew 5:3–11 helps us understand the first part of Jesus' message, known as the Beatitudes (vv. 3–12). Jesus begins each of nine pronouncements with *makarioi*, "happy are" (as in the TEV). This introductory word signals not a benediction upon would-be entrants into the kingdom of God, but a commendation of those who have already entered. The Old Testament bears witness to a word used similarly to describe the state of the believer. Referring to a condition brought about by the prior bestowal of blessing, the root ʾšr signifies an observable state of blessing (e.g., Deut. 33:29; Job 5:17; see Janzen 1965, 225). As eschatological blessings (Bauer 1988, 119), the Beatitudes are recommendations to the audience of characteristics demonstrated by those who have entered the kingdom of God, rather than conditions for entry into the kingdom. Jesus' pronouncements describe and warmly recommend the nature of the life of the kingdom adherent. Like the Old Testament Torah, the Beatitudes do not prescribe conditions that must be met before entering into the covenant, but conduct that is to flow from the grace of covenant acceptance.

Jesus uses the word *makarioi* to draw attention to a group whom he identifies as "poor in spirit" (Matt. 5:3). These are the people who have responded to the call of the gospel; presumably they are the little group of disciples seated with him. The first four Beatitudes (vv. 3–6) are concerned with the inner attitude of these believers, and the next four (vv. 7–10) deal with the outward conduct (if "pure in heart" in v. 8 is taken as "integrity"; see Hatton and Clark 1975, 132–38) that flows from such an inward disposition. Isaiah 61:1–4 is the context from which the first four have been drawn (Guelich 1976, 427–28). It is prophesied in the Isaianic passage that a royal and prophetic individual anointed by God and endowed with divine power will come to the depressed community with a message of impending salvation. Through the Beatitudes, Jesus declares that this time has now come. Present membership in the kingdom of God stems from the renewed covenant relationship while the future will bring incorporation into the manifested kingdom.

Persecution is a repeated motif in the last three verses of the Beatitudes (Matt. 5:10–12). The prophetic-type sufferings to which Jesus refers is not some future persecution to be experienced by later Christian groups after his death. Rather, Jesus' use of the perfect passive participle "those who are persecuted" in verse 10 makes clear that he expects the life-style of the kingdom-of-God adherent to result in persecution. Thus, he makes a general reference to persecution that is triggered by discipleship. The specific reason advanced for such persecution is "for righteousness' sake" (NRSV). The parallel phrase "for My sake" (NKJV) appears in verse 11. What will spark the persecution is not the disciples' conduct, but their relationship to Jesus. In the prose expansion of verses 11–12, we are told that the Old Testament prophets experienced similar persecution, an indication that the disciples' persecution will be more psychological than physical, such as rejection by the community (Hare 1967, 117).

Immediately following the Beatitudes, Jesus uses two images to depict the eschatological community of those responding to the gospel— salt in verse 13 and light in verses 14–16. Clearly, there are various ways to relate the metaphors. For instance, the image of the community as the light may repeat the salt image, or perhaps light advances upon salt. We propose that the image of salt reflects the first four Beatitudes, the ones concerning inward attitude, while the image of light reflects the next four, the ones dealing with outward conduct. Let's look closely at the images to uncover their relationship to what precedes them.

In verse 13 Jesus declares, "You are the salt of the earth." Some have argued for a connection between salt and proverbial wisdom, so that Jesus' saying becomes a proverb for the pithy and pungent effect that the new community has on its world (see Dumbrell 1981, 11). This connection may be apt for the use of salt in Mark 9:50 and Luke 14:34, but Matthew's highly personalized statement is not based upon these contexts. Underlying the use of salt as an image in the Old Testament is the notion of durability, rather than what we might expect—preservation. Though salt was an essential feature in covenant sacrifices (Exod. 30:35; Lev. 2:13; Num. 18:19), its use may have been natural because of meals associated with the sacrifices. Note that in Leviticus 2:13 salt is mentioned as "the salt of the covenant," while in Numbers 18:19 the phrase "everlasting covenant of salt" focuses on the enduring quality of the substance (Rabbinowitz 1971, 710–11). Any doubt one may have about the use of salt as a symbol of continuity and permanence should be removed by the reference in 2 Chronicles 13:5, where the enduring, indissoluble covenant with David (cf. 2 Sam. 7:16) is described as a "covenant of salt." Consider also Ezra 4:14 in which the writer presumes the existence of a binding and enduring obligation to the Persian king because the men "share the salt of the palace" (NRSV). Not purity but fidelity to an established arrangement lies behind the use of salt as a symbol in the Old Testament. Thus, we suggest that when Jesus calls his disciples "the salt of the earth" in Matthew 5:13 he is referring to the enduring inward commitment specified by the first four Beatitudes.

The metaphor of Jesus' disciples as "the light of the world" appears in Matthew 5:14. There can be little doubt as to what Jesus means. By further reference in the same verse to a city set on a hill, he provides us with a clear image. Jesus envisages an eschatological replacement whereby the small community he addresses has already assumed the function as the world center that the Old Testament Zion was meant to be. Behind the reference to light is Isaiah 2:2–4, in which the hillock of Zion becomes the towering world mountain bound up with the Sinaitic and Davidic traditions. Some have argued that identifying parallels to Jerusalem is difficult because of the indefinite character of "a city" in verse 14 (see Dumbrell 1981, 16), but such eschatological contexts do not dictate precision. Furthermore, it appears that the apocryphal Gospel of Thomas understood Jesus to be referring to Jerusalem. To Matthew's statement that "a city on a hill cannot be hidden," the apocryphal Gospel adds a note that a fortified city cannot fall (Log. 32; see Meyer 1992, 3), a somewhat obvious allusion to the prophetic doctrine of Zion's inviolability. Thus, the disciples and the new community are the replacement for Zion, to which the nations were expected to come in pilgrimage in the end time. The added comment in verse 16, "Let your light shine before men, that they may see your good deeds and praise your Father in heaven," links the Torah, light, and Israel's vocation in a way that was customary in the Old Testament and in Judaism of Jesus' day (Trilling 1964, 140). Directed to the new community and indicative of its role as the complement of Israel, verses 14–16 address the vocation of the disciples primarily as a corporate body and secondarily as individuals. The group will reflect the behavior required under the new covenant by the Beatitudes in Matthew 5:7–10.

In order to be true light of the world, the new community must first be the salt of the earth, building on the promises of the Old Testament directed in the first instance to Israel. It is possible that Jesus' phrase "salt of the earth" is more restrictive than "light of the world," for early in the Gospel Matthew uses *gē*, "earth or land," to refer to Palestine or the Promised Land. Perhaps Jesus is identifying the new people of God as the continuant between Israel and the renewed Israel. As the community that has come out of national Israel, this people is the guarantee that God's promises to Israel will not lapse even if the political unit of Israel is rejected. The new community is to embody in its function the mark of Isaiah's servant community (chap. 61), who by its very constitution provides a guarantee of the future operation of the covenant with Israel. This covenant continuity makes possible the mission to the world, to the Gentiles, since salvation is of the Jews.

The implied linkage in Matthew 5:16 of Torah and vocation is then logically followed in verses 17–20 by an explication of the relationship of Jesus and Torah. Two questions arise from these verses. Firstly, why does Jesus broach the subject of the law at this point, and secondly, what does Jesus' elaborate statement of his relationship to the law mean? Let's begin by considering the first question. Verse 17 bursts forth with these words: "Do not think that I have come to abolish the Law or the Prophets." The construction used for "do not think" signifies that Jesus is not trying to correct his listeners' previously held opinions, and there is nothing in the immediate context that has raised the question of Jesus' possible violation of the Torah. Yet, in an endeavor to prevent any misunderstanding of his ministry, Jesus categorically rejects the notion that his ministry would be involved in the demolition of Israel's Torah during the time frame he sets in verse 18. Jesus' broaching the subject of the law at this point flows from the identification of his disciples as the New Jerusalem in verse 14. According to prophetic expectation of the last days, the Torah of the Lord would go forth from the city on the hill. Since Jesus identifies the city, he reassures his listeners that prior teaching regarding the going forth of the Torah has not changed.

What does Jesus say about his relationship to the Torah? An answer to this question depends on how one interprets the phrase "the Law or the Prophets" in verse 17. If the phrase is viewed as a designation for the Old Testament canon, then Jesus is saying little more than that his message stands in complete agreement with biblical traditions. An objection to this interpretation may be raised on the grounds that in verse 18 Jesus refers to the law alone. In light of this verse, it seems best to assume that in the phrase "the Law or the Prophets," Jesus refers to (1) law as given by Moses and (2) law as interpreted in its widest prophetical sense. His ministry then, Jesus avers, will not only sustain the law in its essence but also at the point of its widest application. Jesus is saying that he comes "to fulfill" the widest expectations of the law, that is, law functioning as an instrument of divine rule, regulating the world in this scenario of the community as the bearer of the law. But what does it mean to fulfil the law? Since this verb is not used with law in the Septuagint, the verb does not likely carry the notion of putting the law into practice (Meier 1976, 75). It is further unlikely that Jesus is referring to his fulfilling and thus replacing the law, for the verb does not carry the sense of actualizing or bringing to completion in either the Septuagint or in the Greek New Testament. Jesus is concerned with the place of the law in his own teaching in the new age. In verses 17–20 Jesus demonstrates fulfilment of the law by giving a prior scriptural concept wider validity (Meier 1976, 82). Thus, the law will find its prophetic center, not its end, in the ministry of Jesus. Just as prophetic eschatology had defined the role of the law, Jesus endorses it as the teaching instrument of the last days. Once the new community's responsibility for the cosmos had been raised, the new community was viewed as having taken over Israel's eschatological function. Israel's reconstitution through the ministry of Jesus would mean blessing for the world. The nations would be drawn to this new light, and God's law would go forth from this community and would be the means by which future life would be controlled. Jesus is now the interpreter of the law, but he sets a time limit for its operation: "until heaven and earth pass away" and "until all is accomplished" (v. 18 NRSV). These phrases point to a time when the restriction regarding the abrogation of the law may be lifted. The passing away of heaven and earth at the end of an age to usher in a new age was a recurrent figure of speech in Old Testament and intertestamental thought and writings (Meier 1976, 63). Perhaps Jesus was saying that his death and resurrection would signal the end of the age of Israel and the beginning of the period of universal salvation.

In Matthew 5:21–48 Jesus goes beyond customary exposition to lay bare the real nature of the law, which was self-forgetfulness (Meyer 1979, 146), and by his teaching the Torah would be brought to its eschatological goal of completeness. Jesus views his own ministry as removing the distinctions and barriers set up by the traditions of Judaism and enforced by scribes and Pharisees. It is going too far, however, to suggest that Jesus substitutes love as the meaning of law since love as the practical outworking of law is intrinsic to the original Deuteronomic exposition of law; that is, love does not replace other demands but is the base from which all demands proceed. It is clear from the listeners' reaction in Matthew 7:28–29 that Jesus' teaching was not customary and that his authority was viewed as overarching and supplanting that of the Mosaic economy. Jesus perceives the law in terms of commitment to a new way of life, just as Moses had understood the role of the Torah in the covenant at Sinai.

Jesus' sermon turns in Matthew 6–7 to the practical implications of being disciples, the salt of the earth and light of the world. In crystal-clear terms, Jesus identifies the first business of his disciples: "But seek first his [God's] kingdom and his righteousness" (6:33). Neither one's own righteousness (6:1) nor that of the scribes and Pharisees (5:20) is adequate. The righteousness of the Pharisees and scribes arose out of a certain interpretation of the law, but God's righteousness demands living according to the law as it is interpreted through Jesus (Przybylski 1980, 99). This new righteousness, however, ultimately comes through God's gift. Jesus undercuts human observance of commandments, demonstrating that humankind cannot be classified or "judged" by a religious system such as Pharisaism (7:1–6). On the contrary, a member of God's kingdom is thrown totally upon divine resources for which he must continually and dependently ask (7:7–11). Ultimate dependency upon God, and thus self-forgetfulness (7:12), is the "law" that prevails in the kingdom. Jesus concludes his sermon with the eschatological warnings concerning the two ways (7:13–14) and false prophets (7:15–20) and with the parable of the two builders (7:24–27). Through all this, Jesus challenges Israel with the new covenant. Having been confronted with the demand for national and personal change, Israel is called to make a decision.

Ministry to Israel (Matt. 8:1–16:12)

The story of Jesus' ministry to Israel is, as we shall see, also the story of Israel's response to him. Having attracted great crowds on the mountainside (Matt. 8:1), Jesus shows himself to be Israel's Messiah through teaching and numerous healings (chaps. 8–9). Two episodes in particular attest to the messianic character of his ministry. In the first episode, two blind men perceive what Israel fails to see—that the one who teaches and heals is the Messiah (9:27–31). In the second, Jesus, appearing as the shepherd of Israel, has compassion on the leaderless throng, who are unable to accept the word Jesus brings, despite their being in desperate need (9:35–38). This need appears as the reason for the call of the Twelve (v. 38). Israel will reject them, as she will reject Jesus.

REJECTION OF THE TWELVE (MATT. 10)

Matthew 10 begins with Jesus' call of the twelve disciples on a mission parallel to his own. As Jesus was sent originally to Israel, so too his disciples are to minister only to the lost sheep of the house of Israel (Matt. 10:5–15). However, Jesus underscores the provisional nature of the disciples' mission to Israel in 10:23, noting that it will be terminated by the coming of the Son of man at the fall of Jerusalem (cf. 24:30). Thus, the destruction of Jerusalem and the political end of the nation will leave the mission to Israel unfinished. But the emphasis of the chapter is not so much on mission as on Israel's rejection of the disciples (10:21–42). Since the disciples are charged with preaching the gospel (10:7) and since such preaching will provoke persecution (Matt. 5:10–12), the disciples will be received as Jesus will be—with rejection and persecution.

REJECTION OF JESUS (MATT. 11:2–16:12)

From the genealogy in chapter 1 to the mission to Israel in chapter 10, the Gospel of Matthew generates an intense messianism. The focus then shifts in chapters 11–16 to Israel's rejection of Jesus and his proclamation. In chapter 11 alone, Jesus is rejected by John the Baptist (vv. 2–15), the present generation (vv. 16–19), and the cities (vv. 20–24). Of the three, it is perhaps the most surprising that John the Baptist airs concern about the nature of Jesus' ministry, which does not conform to John's expectation of messiahship in action. Since John had taken account only of Jesus' deeds (v. 2), he is not convinced of Jesus' messianic vocation, but the messengers of John are to report what they hear as well as see (v. 4), that is, Jesus' words as well as his deeds. Not only have miracles occurred, but the good news has been preached to the poor (v. 5, perhaps an allusion to the Sermon on the Mount)—signs that indeed Israel's Messiah has come (see Isa. 61:1–3).

Matthew, continuing to refer to Jesus' messiahship, describes conflict between Jesus and the religious authorities in chapter 12. Through the narrative, Matthew affirms Jesus' Davidic messiahship and his lordship of the Sabbath (vv. 1–14). As Lord of the Sabbath, Jesus interprets the true function of the day and thus performs healings on it. His healing of the blind mute in verses 22–23 spurs the astonished crowd to wonder whether Jesus is the Messiah, the son of David. Matthew wants the reader to have no doubt, for he classifies Jesus as greater than the temple (v. 6), Jonah (v. 41), and even Solomon (v. 42). Moreover, Matthew uses a messianic Servant passage from Isaiah to justify the miraculous healings that Jesus performed (Matt. 12:18–21; cf. Isa. 42:1–4). In sharp contrast to the doubters and the revilers is the new family of disciples, who gather around Jesus (vv. 46–50).

Healing, teaching the crowds, feeding Israel, and rejection by Israel are recurrent motifs in Matthew 13–16. To the crowds, as representative of Israel, all things now come in parables (13:1–35), for the kingdom is revealed to only a nucleus of faithful covenant people (13:11, 36–52). Despite Jesus' wisdom and good works, and perhaps even because of them, the crowd of Israel is offended by Jesus (13:57). The next three chapters show Jesus' being rejected by Israel's rulers (cf. 16:1–4), but he continues to manifest his messiahship through feeding (14:13–21; 15:32–39) and healing (14:34–36; 15:29–31). The encounter with the Canaanite woman (15:21–28) is given great prominence, and it, with its messianic emphasis, follows naturally from the discussion of what is clean and unclean (15:1–20), which forms the centerpiece of the unit.

Self-characterization and Public Recognition (Matt. 16)

Through such observable feats as feeding the thousands and healing the sick, Jesus demonstrated his messiahship. Still there was another facet to his ministry, that is, his teaching. We now turn to examine what Jesus taught us about himself and how others perceived him.

In the beginning, middle, and end of Matthew 16 appear allusions or references to the "Son of man" (vv. 4, 13, 27–28), a title that in Matthew only comes from the lips of Jesus. Verse 4 alludes to the Son of man through the reference to "the sign of Jonah," for in 12:38–41 a comparison is made between Jonah and the Son of man. In reply to the Pharisees' and Sadducees' request for a sign, Jesus responds that the only sign given to this corrupt generation will be the death of the Son of man (note there is no allusion to the resurrection; cf. Patte 1987, 226). By naming Jonah, Jesus might also be alluding to a future Gentile mission, since Jonah had been sent on one. The next reference to the Son of man is more explicit. In verse 13 Jesus asks his disciples, "Who do people say the Son of man is?" (Note the difference in Mark 8:27, where Jesus asks, "Who do you say I am?" Also, see Luke 9:18.) For Matthew, the Son of man is a suffering figure (16:21; 20:28) whose function is associated with eschatological judgment against the nation and the world, as was the function of Ezekiel, another figure called the Son of man (Maddox 1968, 45–74). In chapter 16 the judgment is directed towards Israel through the ministry of Jesus, and from this judgment the church will emerge. The disciples reveal various popular opinions about the identity of the Son of man (v. 14), but only one correctly identifies him. Jesus, the Son of man, is Israel's Messiah (v. 16). In the words of Peter, Jesus is "the Christ, the Son of the living God." A messianic reading of the double epithet is warranted, for there is evidence from the Qumran community that "Son of God" was appearing as a messianic title at this time (Beasley-Murray 1986, 56–57).

Upon Peter's confession, Jesus pronounces the formal beginning of his church: "And I tell you that you are Peter, and on this rock I will build my church (*ekklēsia*), and the gates of Hades will not overcome it" (Matt. 16:18). (Note that in the play on Peter's name [*Petros*, "a stone"] and rock [*petra*, "foundation bedrock"] Jesus makes a distinction between the specific example of Peter and the bedrock on which the *ekklēsia* will be built.) The translation of *ekklēsia* as "church" in the English versions of verse 18 is misleading and anachronistic. In the Septuagint, *ekklēsia* is used frequently and naturally to refer to Israel, as is *synagōgē*, which would have been unsuitable in this context. At the turn of the twentieth century, F. J. Hort suggested that in Matthew 16:18 Jesus had in mind the restoration of Israel (1900, 10–17). This suggestion should be adopted as conveying the intention of Jesus, if not the exact sense. What underlies Jesus' statement of the building and durability of the restored Israel is probably an allusion to Isaiah 28:16. If this is the case, then Jesus refers to the messianic building of the new temple, for Isaiah announces God's laying of a foundation stone in Zion or, better, the laying of Zion as a foundation stone, as a touchstone for the faithful in Israel of God's determination to uphold a theology of election based upon the divine purposes for Israel as signified by the existence of the Jerusalem temple. Both Isaiah 28:16 and Matthew 16:18 refer to a building and the laying of a foundation stone; both point to a believing, eschatological community; and both are concerned with protection from evil. The Old Testament background of Matthew 16:18 makes the implications of the text clear. For Isaiah, it is the temple, as signifying the divine presence in Israel, to which faith is to be directed. Israel's later traditions viewed the foundation stone upon which the temple was built as the cosmic rock, the lid over the netherworld, the point of contact with heaven, and the world mountain that offered access to both heaven and Hades (Patai 1947, 54–139). For the rabbis, the cosmic rock on Zion on which the temple had been founded was the site of creation, of Paradise and the tree of life, the source of the world rivers, and the proof against the deluge (Meyer 1979, 185–86; Jeremias 1926, 66–68). Some believed the messiah to be the builder of the new temple (Meyer 1979, 186), while the Septuagint and Targum interpreted the sure foundation in Isaiah 28:16 as the messiah. The popular expectation was that the messiah would choose the foundation stone on which the new temple would be built (Meyer 1979, 197). Once Yahweh had gathered the dispersed of Israel together, then his glorious dwelling place, the temple on Zion, would draw nations from the four quarters of the earth. On that day the Davidic king would be a signal for the nations (Isa. 11:10), and the nations would seek him. The dark world would then raise its eyes to the radiance of Israel. It appears that Jesus identifies the *ekklēsia* as the renewed Israel, the gathered people of God. Significantly, Matthew 16:18 foreshadows the initiation of this Old Testament vision of the future.

Jesus proclaims he will give the keys of the kingdom of heaven to Peter (Matt. 16:19). On the analogy of the keys given to Eliakim as first minister of the royal Zion household (Isa. 22:20–22), we interpret Peter's possession of the keys as signifying authorization and power. Matthew reveals in 23:13 that the Pharisees and the teachers of the law shut the kingdom of heaven in men's faces; therefore, it appears that Peter's power includes the right to teach and to provide access into the kingdom. Peter exercises such a right in the case of Israel at Pentecost (Acts 2), in the case of the Samaritans (Acts 8:14–17), who were remnants of the northern kingdom of Israel, and in the case of the Gentiles (Acts 10). In verse 19 Jesus further describes the authority he gives to Peter and restored Israel, "whatever you bind on earth will be bound in heaven, and whatever you loose on earth will be loosed in heaven." By saying that whatever is condemned by restored Israel on earth will have already been condemned in heaven and that whatever is forgiven by restored Israel on earth will have already been permitted in heaven, Jesus empowers restored Israel to announce previously made heavenly decisions concerning eschatological judgment. Verses 21–23 then show that Peter's representative position is provisional, for he is the rock only when he is the confessor of the true faith. Otherwise, Peter is a snare or stumbling block.

Matthew 16:24–28 returns to the subject of the Son of man, this time adding the elements of suffering and the cross, for it is upon the cross that restored Israel will be built. The cross of the Messiah, which is presented in verses 21–23, points logically in verse 24 to the cross of the disciples. It is a divine necessity that the Son of man suffer since redemption through suffering reaches to the very heart of divine revelation. The Messiah can be the glorious judge of verse 28 only if he first has been the suffering Son of man. It is now understandable why Jesus introduces the title *Son of man* in verse 13 and then reinterprets Peter's confession of Jesus as Christ into terms of the suffering Son of man.

And what of verse 28? Jesus says, "I tell you the truth, some who are standing here will not taste death before they see the Son of man coming in his kingdom." This difficult verse with its reference to Daniel 7:13 most naturally refers to the fall of Jerusalem. What follows in 17:1–8, the report of the transfiguration, at which the details of Jesus' "exodus" were arranged (see Luke 9:31), confirms the message of Matthew 16. Jesus gives to his inner core of disciples a glimpse of the Son of man's heavenly glory of which 16:28 had spoken. The voice from heaven endorsing the sonship of Jesus in 17:5 echoes Jesus' baptismal vocation (cf. 3:17) and points forward to the way in which his commission for ministry will be fulfilled. As the three disciples—Peter, James, and John—descend from the mountain of transfiguration, Jesus commands them to silence about what they have seen for a limited time, that is, "until the Son of Man has been raised from the dead" (17:9).

Entry into Jerusalem (Matt. 21:1–22:14)

In Zechariah 3:7 Joshua, the high priest associated with temple cleansing and rebuilding after the exile, was charged with the tasks of ruling over God's house and keeping watch over God's courts. Bearing the high priest's name, Jesus enters Jerusalem as Israel's King to claim the temple (Matt. 21:1–9). The description of Jesus in Matthew 21:5 basically repeats Zechariah 9:9 but omits a phrase. While the citation of Zechariah underscores the humble nature of the one to enter Jerusalem, the omission of "having salvation" portends ominously for Israel, as does the use of the language of earthquakes to describe the entry, that is, "the whole city was stirred" (v. 10). Jesus' action of cleansing the temple was one traditionally associated with restoring the kingdom (e.g., Hezekiah in 2 Chron. 29–30, Josiah in 2 Kings 22, Ezekiel in Ezek. 40–48, and Judas Maccabeus in 1 Macc. 4:36–59 and 2 Macc. 10:1–8) and with fitting the temple for the blessings of the new age. However, Jesus' use in Matthew 21:13 of the words of Jeremiah that signaled the destruction of the Solomonic temple (see Jer. 7:11) serves to threaten Israel's loss of the temple as well as the Promised Land. Matthew continues this skillful juxtaposition of suggestions of the fulfilment of messianic promises and of hints of destruction and loss. For instance, Jesus' healing of the blind and the lame at the temple indicates realization of promises associated with the messianic age (21:14; cf. Meyer 1979, 200). But the Jerusalem temple had not only failed to be the reality that it symbolized, it also was no longer a point of divine reference, that is, a house of prayer (21:13). Moreover, it had never served as a world center and as a potential rallying point for the nations. Thus, when Jesus alludes in 21:13 to Isaiah 56:7 ("for my house will be called a house of prayer for all nations"), he omits the final phrase. Another example of the juxtaposition of hope and loss occurs in Matthew 21:18–22 (cf. Mark 11:12–14, 20–25) in the story of the destruction of the barren fig tree. Jesus uses a prominent symbol of the security afforded by the messianic age—a time when each man would sit under his fig tree without fear (Mic. 4:4; cf. Zech. 3:10). However, this fig tree is not only barren (reversing the new-age expectation), but it also withers.

Jesus' teaching and healing at the temple caught the attention of the chief priests and elders. When they questioned him about the basis of his authority, Jesus refers to John's ministry (Matt. 21:23–25a). Is Jesus saying that he is the Lord of the covenant who will come suddenly to the temple (Mal. 3:1), the one anticipated by John the Baptist? The reference to John's baptism is quite obviously meant to silence discussion over Jesus' authority to act in the temple (21:25b–27). If the priests and elders admit the authority of John, then they would be forced to recognize John's baptism of Jesus as the means through which the voice from heaven conferred messianic status on Jesus (Wright 1985, 87). It is clear from the parables that follow that disobedience to the final messenger, the Lord of the covenant, will mean Israel's loss of nationhood (see especially 21:33–46). According to verse 43 the kingdom will be taken from Israel and will be given to an *ethnos*, a new community, that will bring forth its fruits. The parable of the wedding feast in Matthew 22:1–14 reinforces the point. Two invitations have gone out to Israel, and they have been refused. Though now the invitation is extended to the Gentiles, there will be no acceptance into the wedding feast until certain conditions are met (see the issue of the wedding garment in vv. 11–14).

Prophecy of the End (Matt. 23:37–25:46)

When Jesus leaves the temple in Matthew 24:1, the presence of God leaves national Israel. The *oikos*, the national house including the temple, is forfeited (23:38; 24:1–2; see Burnett 1981, 112). The pronouncements in chapter 24 that Jesus issues as he sits on the Mount of Olives (v. 3), the place of eschatological judgment from which a processional way is to be leveled for the divine entry into Jerusalem (Zech. 14:4–5), seal the city's fate. Matthew has drawn most of his material for chapter 24 from Mark 13 and has followed Mark's order. But Matthew's account is stamped as his own by some additions. Let's look more closely at selected verses in the chapter.

Jesus describes Jerusalem's destruction in 24:2. In verse 3 the disciples want to know more, precisely when this will occur. Their query refers only to the fall of Jerusalem since "and what will be the sign of your coming and of the end of the age" is explanatory. (Note that the phrase "end of the ages" in Heb. 9:26 refers to the sacrifice of Jesus.) Matthew expands Mark's account through additions in verses 26–28, 29–31, and 37–41. In verses 26–28 the ominous note of the eagles gathered together, presaging the advent of the Son of man, raises the grim specter of Roman eagle standards encircling Jerusalem. Verse 30, referring to "the sign of the Son of Man . . . in heaven" (NRSV) and "the Son of man coming on the clouds of heaven" (NRSV), indicates that the advent is not a physical one of the Son of man but a witness to the Son of man, who is in heaven. That is, the coming is to occur through historical events, for if the coming were to take the form of the Son of man's visible return, then the sign of the fig tree would be superfluous (vv. 32–33; Wright 1988b). Thus, the judgment to be visited upon Jerusalem is a sign that the Son of man is in fact reigning in heaven. Verses 37–41 illustrate the lack of warning that will precede the coming of the Son of man, for everyday life before the destruction will appear utterly normal. In the parable of the wise and foolish virgins in 25:1–13, Matthew reinforces the theme of the uncertain timing of Israel's coming judgment. Both this parable and the parable of the talents in 25:14–30 demonstrate that Jesus requires proper discipleship at all times, not just when the judgment nears.

Matthew concludes his account of Jesus' public ministry by recounting the parable of the sheep and the goats (25:31–46). As the last teaching in Jesus' public ministry, this parable of the judgment has great significance. Though Jesus had previously referred to the judgment (13:37–43), he had not heretofore treated it so expansively. Since the Gospels present the figure of the Son of man basically in terms of prospective judgment, it is not difficult to determine the meaning of the parable. After the gospel mission has been completed, all nations, Christians and non-Christians, will be gathered before the judgment throne for one universal and final judgment. Almost before the very eyes of those assembled, the Son of man will become the King of the ages, that is, Israel's Messiah. Thus, the nations will be, gathered together before the one who is revealed to be what he always was, the vice-regent of the universe.

Seated upon the Mount of Olives (Matt. 24:3), Jesus envisions himself sitting on the great white throne within three days of his death upon the cross. His Jewish audience would have been familiar with the picture Jesus presents—that of the day of the Lord, the final, universal judgment of all. It is Israel's Messiah who judges the multitudes as sheep or goats (25:32–33). The criterion for the judgment is simple: works of human kindness, not as works in themselves but as evidence of belief, identify the faithful. (Specifics will be worked out later by Paul [Rom. 2:12–16].) Jesus' death and resurrection will change the usual conception of this final judgment. As we know from Paul's doctrine of justification by faith, the judgment of the last day occurs in one's present experience. His doctrine of works after justification teaches that works are indicative of one's covenantal status.

The primary disclosure of the parable is that the King, the exalted Judge of the world, has been hidden in "the least (*elachistos*) of these My brethren" (Matt. 25:40 NKJV). Since the parable is painted in bold, inexact strokes, we should not restrict the identity of the least, the little ones (either *mikros* or the superlative *elachistos*), to the disciples (Via 1987, 93). Though *adelphos* (brother) is used as a community term in Matthew (e.g., 5:22, 47) and though "little ones" is used to refer to members of the Christian community, that is, disciples (e.g., 10:42; 18:6, 10, 14), "the least of these My brethren" has a wider reference here (Catchpole 1979, 396). The phrase connotes needy people in general.

Matthew's account of the parable has many similarities with material in 1 Enoch. In both Matthew and Enoch, the elect one is enthroned; and judgment ensues (1 Enoch 62:1). With all the world assembled, the multitudes are divided into two groups—the righteous and the wicked (1 Enoch 62:3, 8, 13). Both Matthew and Enoch picture the Son of man as presiding over a final judgment based on the manner in which those judged treated associates of the Son of man (cf. 1 Enoch 62:1–9, 11). Thus, the picture of Jesus as the eschatological Messiah who will vindicate the defenseless is not a new idea; rather, it is a typical Jewish portrait of messiahship.

The Passion and Commission (Matt. 26–28)

What stands out about the narrative of Jesus' passion is his, the Messiah's, calm demeanor. Matthew adds a detail, not found in Luke or Mark, that casts a unique light on the significance of Jesus' death. After Jesus died, but before he was resurrected, tombs in the city opened, and the Jewish saints entombed therein were raised to life (Matt. 27:50–53). Much earlier Ezekiel had prophesied such an occurrence (Ezek. 37:12–14). Quite notably what permits this renewal of Israel is not the resurrection, which had not yet taken place, but the death of Jesus, as the Messiah, for Israel.

Matthew's Gospel concludes with the Son of man's commission of the disciples on the world mountain (28:16–20). As directed by Jesus (28:10), the disciples had returned to Galilee, the place where the kingdom proclamation had begun (4:12–25). By the resurrection, Jesus had been exalted to God's right hand as the victorious Son of man. Though during Jesus' earthly ministry his authority was limited to the earth, that is no longer the case (28:18). Just as his new authority transcends all the limitations of the historical ministry, his charge to make disciples of all nations revokes the limitations of the mission charge to the disciples in 10:5–6. In verse 20 Jesus refers to "the very end of the age." Since the new age dawned with the resurrection, what does Jesus mean? Now he is looking beyond the fall of Jerusalem to the end of the historical age.

Matthew 28:19–20 is a call to the world to submit to the proclamation of Israel's risen Messiah. Baptism in the name of Jesus will now replace circumcision as the initiation rite for the new community. Jesus' command that the disciples teach the nations all he has commanded is his own recision of the Torah. Jesus is with his disciples as the Immanuel. Thus, we can anticipate fulfilment of the Abrahamic promises of blessing for all nations. Indeed, the universalism incipient in chapter 1 and in 5:13–14, 8:10–12, 10:18, 11:20–24, 12:17–21, 12:41–42, and 15:21–28 is now given full rein. The entire world must come in pilgrimage, not to Jerusalem and to the temple, but to Jesus, the new rallying point through which the continuity of Israel's Old Testament expectations are now expressed.

Jesus as Israel

Through the narrative of the life of Jesus, Matthew demonstrates that Israel's vocation finds its fulfilment in Jesus. And demonstration was necessary, for the fulfilment signifies rejection of national Israel and the realization of various prophecies in quite unexpected ways. For instance, the gifts of the magi in Matthew 2:11 fulfil the Isaianic expectation that Gentiles would bring gold and frankincense to the people of God in Zion (cf. Isa. 60:1–6). Interwoven throughout Matthew's Gospel are threads proclaiming the consummation of Old Testament prophecy, threads portraying Jesus as Israel, and threads demonstrating the rejection of Israel.

For Matthew, the Old Testament points to Jesus, who fulfils the utterances of Isaiah, Daniel, the psalmist, Hosea, and so many others. Jesus is Isaiah's Servant (Matt. 12:15–21; cf. Isa. 42:1–4), Daniel's Son of man (Matt. 26:64; cf. Dan. 7:13), and the rejected stone that has become the capstone (Matt. 21:42; cf. Ps. 118:22). Through signs of miraculous healings and table fellowship with outcasts, Jesus reveals himself as the Messiah (Wright 1985, 85). Jesus is also Israel, an identification Matthew makes by portraying experiences in the life of Jesus as those in the national life of Israel. Both Israel and Jesus go down to Egypt and are called out. Both hunger in the wilderness, though Jesus' success in resisting temptation stands in sharp contrast to Israel's failure. And Jesus appropriates the very words of Israel's national lament (Matt.

27:46; cf. Ps. 22:1). Through the gathering from east and west (Matt. 8:11–12), the gathering of the elect (Matt. 24:31), and the choice of the Twelve, Matthew shows Jesus to be the New Israel.

Jesus comes to Israel in the guise of an end-time prophet, a covenantal disturber of the national conscience. Indeed, so much of Jesus' teaching is devoted to the prospect of Israel's impending judgment, before which the nation stands unconsciously, that his message to his compatriots can be summarized using the words of Amos, "Why do you long for the day of the Lord?" (5:18; Wright 1985, 80). In the ministry of Jesus, Israel's time of crisis arrives. But the generation to whom Jesus speaks exhibits the same recalcitrance to the divine voice as national Israel always had (Matt. 23:29–32). In response to the Jewish leadership's challenge of his authority (Matt. 21:23–22:14), Jesus proclaims that the kingdom of God entrusted to Israel will be taken away from Israel's present leadership and will be given to a new nation. But since Jesus is the fulfilment of Israel, there is also continuity. In Jesus and the men and women he summons to follow him is the reconstituted Israel (Wright 1985, 85). Jesus is also the new temple, the place of reconstituted Israel's worship (Matt. 26:61). While Jesus' ministry fulfils the expectations centered on Israel, it also judges national Israel, separating the wheat from the chaff. Jesus as the eschatological prophet, Messiah, son of David, Son of man, and Son of God both brings and embodies God's final word to Israel.

8

Marcan Eschatology

The Gospel of Mark is distinguished by its Christology, which identifies Jesus as the King of Israel, the Son of man, and the suffering Servant, who ushers in the kingdom of God by his passion, thus fulfilling God's purposes for Israel and enabling the consequent missionary activity to the Gentiles. From the very beginning, the Gospel moves toward the passion of Jesus so that his kingship is cast in its distinctive light. As evident from the Gospel of Mark, the eschatological expectations of the early church were based on Jesus' teaching and his appropriation of concepts from the Old Testament. To understand the eschatology, we will look closely at the titles for Jesus in Mark, their association with Israel's charter, and the concept of the kingdom of God.

Preparation for Jesus' Ministry (Mark 1:1–13)

Mark begins his Gospel with the following words, "The beginning of the gospel of Jesus Christ, the Son of God (1:1 NKJV). In fact, these words are the key to his Gospel since they combine with the Roman centurion's climactic identification of Jesus as the Son of God in 15:39 to form a theological *inclusio* (Guelich 1982, 5–15). Though the word *gospel* may refer to the entire content of Mark, it is best understood as a reference to Jesus' preaching ministry, which commences in verse 14 following the witness of John the Baptist. The Greek allows us to interpret the relationship in verse 1 between Jesus and the gospel in two ways: (1) with Jesus as the author of it ("Jesus Christ's gospel") and (2) with Jesus as the content of it ("the gospel about Jesus Christ"). Another noteworthy relationship is the one between verses 1 and 2, for verse 1 is not a complete sentence and verse 2 begins with the word *kathōs* (even as). Mark begins no other sentence with this word. Furthermore, wherever *kathōs* is used in the New Testament to introduce a quotation from the Old, it almost invariably follows its main clause (Ambrozic 1972, 18). For these reasons, we must link unfinished verse 1 to verse 2. Thus, the beginning of the gospel of Jesus Christ is linked to the prophetic utterance to which Mark refers in verses 2–3.

Mark draws attention to Isaiah by attributing the following words to him:

> "I will send my messenger ahead of you,
>   who will prepare your way" —
> "a voice of one calling in the desert,
> 'Prepare the way for the Lord,
>   make straight paths for him.'"
>
> [1:2–3]

However, these words are drawn from several sources. In Exodus 23:20 God promises to send a messenger, who will precede Israel on the march from Sinai to Canaan. In Malachi 3:1 the promise is of "my messenger," who will prepare the way of the Lord. The ministry of this messenger is later interpreted in terms of Elijah, the covenant-renewal prophet (Mal. 4:5–6). But the primary source, especially of Mark 1:3, is Isaiah 40:3, in which the messenger of consolation, who introduces the new exodus, calls for the way for the Lord to be prepared. Exodus 23:20 represents the first exodus and the promise of the land; Isaiah 40:3, the exile and the return to the land. And Malachi speaks of Elijah's return, which will precede the restitution of all things. Addressed to an Israel which in a sense is still in exile, this chain of Old Testament promises prepares us for the ministry of John the Baptist. The motifs of the new exodus and the march through the wilderness suggest that the way to be prepared will lead to a new covenant, for the one who comes after judgment will bring eschatological salvation to Israel.

In Mark 1:4 John the Baptist appears as the returning Elijah figure. References in verse 6 to John's garb and life-style emphasize his Elijah-like features. Malachi had foreseen the last days as the time when Elijah would reconcile the fathers to the children and the children to the fathers (4:6). The Book of Ecclesiasticus had expected Elijah to restore the tribes of Jacob (48:10). Representatively taking back all Israel to the point of covenant renewal, John calls for Israel's repentance, her return to the covenant, by submitting to the preached word in baptism. (In

Mark's time, the Greek word for repent [*metanoeō*] was equivalent to the Hebrew *šûb*; thus, John was using Old Testament terminology familiar to his audience [Cranfield 1959, 44–45].) Though Mark surely casts John as an Elijah figure, the Gospel writer also subordinates John to the mightier one who is to come (v. 7).

In Mark 1:9 Jesus appears. After being baptized by John, Jesus receives the Spirit and is thus endorsed as Servant and Messiah (vv. 9–11; cf. Ps. 2:7; Isa. 42:1). The opening of the heavens and the descent of the Spirit, which was to be active again only in the last times, in verse 10 and the voice from heaven in verse 11 underscore the advent of the new age. Since Jesus' act of submission is an act of covenant renewal for Israel, the typology of Jesus' wilderness-temptation experience in verses 12–13 is clear. As illuminated by the Spirit, Jesus ushers in the new covenant age and is Israel's representative of it. In the wilderness Jesus, victorious over Satan, lives in harmony with the wild animals. Does this mean that Jesus has reversed the effects of the fall? More likely Mark's presentation of Jesus with the wild beasts depicts him as the victorious Messiah of Israel living in harmony with the animate world in keeping with the promises found in Isaiah (11:6–8; 65:25).

The Ministry of Jesus (Mark 1:14–13:37)

Mark 1:14 both begins the account of Jesus' public ministry and ominously foreshadows its end. The verse opens with these words, "After John was put in prison." The verb used to convey what happened to John is the same one used in chapters 14–15 for the betrayal and handing over of Jesus. Through this repetition, Mark underscores John's role as forerunner, indicating that John and Jesus are bound together by a common fate. The public ministry virtually concludes with the recognition of Jesus as Israel by the blind Bartimaeus, who indicates a perception that "blind" Israel never finds during the ministry's course (10:46–52).

Preaching

After John is arrested, Jesus comes to Galilee preaching the gospel, proclaiming that "the time has come" and "the kingdom of God is near" (Mark 1:14–15). For Mark, now is the time when the expectations of the scriptural prophecies in 1:2–3 converge. The coming of the kingdom is inextricably bound to the preaching of the gospel. Since the time *has* come, the kingdom is a present availability. With the gospel and the kingdom as central motifs, fulfilment is the key note of this beginning message, which is basic to our understanding of eschatology.

THE GOSPEL

The gospel is at the heart of Jesus' first public command as recorded by Mark, for at the end of 1:15 we find the words *pisteuete en tō euangeliō*, "believe the good news." Mark freely uses various prepositions with the verb *believe* in his Gospel. Since he exhibits a tendency to replace *en* (in) with *eis* (into), the use of the former in this construction is noteworthy. Though the use of *en* could be a Semitism, it appears that Mark chose his words carefully to convey this idea—believe *on the basis of* the gospel that the kingdom of God is at hand (Ambrozic 1972, 26). But what is the gospel? Though the noun *euangelion* is not found in the Septuagint, the verb *euangelizō* is used to translate the Hebrew *bāśar* (proclaim, announce), which often appears in contexts signaling Yahweh's universal victory over the world and his consequent kingly rule in a new era (see Ps. 40:9; 68:11; 96:2; Isa. 41:27; 52:7). Particularly significant is the use of *euangelizō* in Isaiah 61:1, where one who appears to be both a prophetic and a royal figure announces, and by his proclamation calls into being, the reality of the New Jerusalem. (Note that Jesus himself makes use of Isaiah 61:1–3 in Luke 4:16–30.) Outside the Scriptures in classical Greek words related to *euangelion* are most often associated with the news of victory, as in the case of *euangelos*, the messenger who brings favorable political news (Keck 1966, 361).

What is the gospel, the basis of faith, of which Jesus speaks in 1:15? Elsewhere in Mark (8:35; 10:29) and in other writings of the New Testament, *gospel* is a technical term to denote the content of the Christian message, often connoting strict judgment rather than divine favor (Rev. 14:6–7). However, the word *gospel* in verse 15 refers back to "the gospel about Jesus Christ" in verse 1, which was expounded upon in verses 2–3 through the series of quotations from the Old Testament. While the quotations introduce the ministry of John, the gospel emerges as the substance of John's preaching. Remember too that Jesus begins his ministry with the same message as the one proclaimed by John (Matt. 3:2; 4:17). Thus, the gospel is John's gospel proclamation, which on the basis of the references in verses 2–3, particularly to Isaiah 40:3, has in mind the coming of the kingdom of God as associated with the ushering in of the new creation. Jesus endorses John's gospel (cf. Matt. 3:1–2; 4:17), and the implications of the proclamation of the kingdom are clear. God will bring about a new order through Israel's Messiah and, as Paul puts it, will reconcile all things to himself in Christ (Col. 1:20). The gospel quite clearly bears a cosmic intention.

THE KINGDOM

"The Kingdom of God is near," proclaims Jesus in his first public teaching recorded in Mark's Gospel (1:15). What does Jesus mean by these words, which are found in both eschatological and apocalyptic speculation? Is the *kingdom* God's reign, or is it his realm? The phrase "kingdom of God" serves not to denote an area over which rule is to be exercised but a conceptual framework within which God reigns as King. But how do we arrive at this understanding of the phrase? We must begin by looking at its use in extrabiblical works.

The eternal kingdom, or reign, of God was a common tenet of Jewish belief. References to the reign appear in the Psalms of Solomon (17:4) and the Wisdom of Solomon (6:4; 10:10), while the kingdom of God is proclaimed in the Testament of Moses (10:1) and the War Scroll (IQM 6:6). It was generally held that the resurrection of the dead would usher in the final demonstration of the kingdom as the age to come (Sib. Or. 3:45–46, 652–54, 767–89; T. Mos. 10:1–10). The phrase "kingdom of God" first appears in works of late Judaism—in the Apocrypha, Pseudepigrapha, the Targums, and Philo. (Sometimes the phrase refers to the present sovereignty of God over Israel and the nations; see Ps. Sol. 5:2; Jub. 12:19; 1 Enoch 84:2–3; T. Reuben 6.) Use of the phrase increases in the rabbinic literature. After the fall of Jerusalem in A.D. 70, the rabbis used the phrase "to take the yoke of the kingdom upon oneself" to signify a commitment to purifying discipline and to living a life carefully insulated from alien influences, that is, a life characterized by submitting to the Torah, reciting the Shema, and becoming a proselyte.

The Qumran community linked kingdom-of-God language to belief in an approaching struggle. The concept of God's rule appears in the War Scroll, where it is associated with conflict brought on by the dominion of Satan. To be a member of the kingdom at Qumran meant to prepare for the coming struggle by which the kingdom would be finally ushered in. Though the final apocalyptic struggle garners less attention in the Community Rule, the concept is clearly present, in this case related to the concept of two messiahs, a priestly one and a kingly one (1 QS 9:11). Regarding God's Kingdom, the Pharisees had two major concerns: (1) the establishment of a sacral realm by punctilious conduct, which sought to preserve the bond between Yahweh and Israel, and (2) the destruction of the wicked and impure within the nation (Riches 1980, 117).

Amid the sectarian expectations of the Pharisees and the Qumran community was an understanding in the literature of the time, which upheld the Old Testament depiction of God as King (Wright 1992, 302–307). From the Old Testament, the people knew full well that God reigned (Exod. 15:17–18; Num. 23:21; 24:7; Ps. 47; 93; Pss. 96–99) and that his kingdom would endure from generation to generation (Dan. 4:34). The people also believed that the reinstitution of the reign of David's great messianic successor would commence the ideal age in

which the Israelite king would be seen as God's operative agent on
earth. The Books of Samuel linked the expectation of the kingdom with
messianism. Remember the picture of David as the divine deliverer of
his people who against Israel's foes fought the battles of the Lord as
messiah (1 Sam. 17:45). The Davidic empire was commonly deemed to
be political confirmation of God's will for Israel and the pattern for the
future (Wright 1983, 364–65), a view arising from the picture in Genesis
1 of the world ruled under the aegis of God through the divinely designated human agent. Israel's ongoing task was popularly conceived in
this way—to rule the world from her sanctuary in Canaan and be a light
to lighten the Gentiles.

The exile somewhat altered the centuries-old hopes, which in some
instances became transcendental. For example, in the Book of Daniel
Israel looks for heavenly intervention since there appeared to be no
hope within the historical realm (2:44) and in the present age. However,
the kingdom for which Daniel yearns is not otherworldly; it is very
much of this world—even though it is a new world. For Daniel, as well
as for others in the postexilic and apocalyptic movements, the kingdom
of God would mean the end of the old, the purgation of all evil through
judgment and destruction, and the re-creation of national Israel; this is
the general tenor of Daniel 7. Indeed, in the popular mind the kingdom
of God became associated with the vindication of Israel and the judgment of the Gentiles and particularly with the destruction of the wicked
and the resurrection of the righteous. The people believed that a remnant Israel would arise from within the nation as a renewed national Israel. Though Isaiah's doctrine of the remnant had been reapplied in
Daniel and associated with the saints, it was still thoroughly national.
Even the doctrine of the resurrection of the righteous (Dan. 12:1–3) was
cast in terms of the servant community of Isaiah 40–55, and thus as
ideal Israel. And what about the Gentiles? They would be saved by incorporation into this still national body.

During Jesus' time, there was no unanimity regarding God's kingdom. The people expected that a Davidic figure, Israel's messiah, would
institute a reign of justice and peace for Israel and the world. Showing
affinity with beliefs of the Qumran community, John the Baptist at the
threshold of the breaking in of God's rule preached a message of repentance and judgment. For John and the pietistic groups of the day (the
Qumran community and the Essenes), what distinguished those whom
God would vindicate from those whom he would destroy was obedience
to the Torah, a concept with wide-ranging implications. As preparation
for Jesus' ministry, John attacked Jewish particularism, warned against
reliance upon physical descent from Abraham, and thus undermined

nationalism. His expectation, then, was that God would reward works of fundamental humanity and would punish those who neglected them.

Jesus retains the traditional conception of the kingdom of God as God's future reign, preaching that the world would experience God's rule over creation, by which the dominion of Satan would be ended, and would see the full manifestation of divine sovereignty. Though Jesus and his audience would have held these beliefs in common, Jesus' teaching goes beyond the traditional view. He preaches that the breaking in of God's kingdom has begun, and he transforms the popular expectation of the kingdom of God, for the type of rule to which Jesus points differs markedly from popular supposition. For Jesus, God's concern for the underprivileged, the distressed, and the handicapped is a mark of the kingdom's entry. To counter the charges that nothing was happening in his ministry and that he was just another prophet, Jesus replies in parables, the hallmark of his preaching. He speaks of the mystery of the kingdom, of the paradox of God's ongoing rule over Israel being demonstrated in his person, and of Israel's new day. When Jesus speaks of God, he does so in personal, as opposed to nationalistic, terms. Such personal reference was unparalleled in Jesus' day, and it pointed to a different type of kingdom—a familial, not a nationalistic, one.

Can there be any doubt that Jesus' proclamation of the advent of the reign of God would have triggered a call for the restoration of Israel (Meyer 1979, 133)? The cry that would usher in the new age was to be "Your God reigns" (Isa. 52:7). In terms of the Old Testament, God's reign would mean a new exodus, a new return to the Promised Land, and a new world. Jerusalem would become the world center, and there would be a consequent ministry to the nations, who would come in pilgrimage, since Yahweh was the God of the Gentiles as well as of Israel. To the popular mind, Jesus' proclamation would have been understood in these terms: All the world will now see the salvation of Israel's God. The twelve tribes will be regathered, and history will be consummated. At the center of this world-reviving movement will stand a remnant of national Israel.

Jesus uses the phrase "kingdom of God" to connect with his Jewish audiences. Unless he had been operating within the same conceptual framework as they had been, his teaching would have been unacceptable, even meaningless (Marshall 1985, 7). On the basis of a small number of so-called genuine sayings of Jesus, some argue that Jesus used "kingdom of God" as a symbol for the saving revelation of God himself (Allison 1985, 107–12). This interpretation, however, means that the kingdom cannot be tied down in time (Chilton 1978, 261–70). Moreover, to spiritualize the meaning of the kingdom of God in this way is to ignore the consistent tie between the kingdom and God's purposes for humankind through creation found in the Bible. When the Jewish people spoke of the age to come, the one that would end the rule of Satan and commence the rule of God, they did not regard this as being beyond history, but as being the next stage of history, brought about by God's action within history. Accordingly they viewed the kingdom of God as the full and powerful manifestation of the sovereignty of God, which God presently exercises over the world.

Jesus refers to the kingdom in what are clearly temporal terms. He regards the kingdom as future (Mark 14:25; cf. Matt. 7:21; Luke 22:16, 18), imminent (Mark 13:32; cf. Matt. 10:23; 25:13; Luke 12:46; 18:8; 21:36), and yet present (Mark 1:15; 9:1; cf. Matt. 10:7; 11:12; 12:28; Luke 10:9; 11:20; 16:16; 17:21; 19:11; 21:31). What would Jesus' contemporaries have made of these teachings? Could they have harmonized the two strands, that is, the present and the future/imminent? Is it possible that the sense of imminence was so strong for Jesus that he could speak of the kingdom as if it were present? An essential and distinctive element in the teaching of Jesus is found in the relationship between Jesus' ministry and the kingdom, for Jesus teaches that the peoples' hoped-for, future kingdom has already come in his person and ministry. This teaching is without parallel. God's purposes, and thus Israel's world rule, were being fulfilled in the strangest of ways—a fact that John the Baptist finds difficult to accept (Matt. 11:2–3).

For Jesus, the kingdom is both now and not yet: God presently acts in power through Jesus' ministry as a demonstration of the presence of the kingdom to construct a bridge between the present and the future. What reinforces the "now and not yet" aspect of Jesus' teaching and activity are two closely associated concepts from the Old Testament— kingdom and Spirit. Look at the connection Mark establishes between Jesus' baptism and his desert preparation, which leads directly to the beginning of his ministry (1:10, 12). The narrative seems to indicate that the working of the Spirit, its authorization and empowerment, enables Jesus to announce that the kingdom has come. (For further links between Spirit and kingdom, see John 3:5; Rom. 14:17; Gal. 5:16–21.) The Spirit, the promised gift of the new age for Israel (Joel 2:28), is now operating through the ministry of Jesus! Elsewhere Jesus claims that the presence of the kingdom of God in his ministry is the visible sign that God through the Spirit is at work in Israel (Matt. 12:28), beginning the process of setting up his rule over Israel through her anointed messianic King.

Jesus views the advent of the kingdom as blessing come for Israel and opens wide the door blocked by officialdom in Judah (Matt. 23:13). The divine reign is God's triumphant consummation of his lordship over events present in Jesus' own ministry. The language that Jesus uses regarding the kingdom (e.g., it comes, it overtakes, one may not be far from it, one expects it or looks for it, one may inherit it, and so on) demonstrates that he sees the kingdom as an approaching order of things for the world (France 1984, 35). Moreover, the kingdom necessitates a revolution of the human value system. But what does this mean? How is the advent of the kingdom to be reflected in human conduct? In rabbinic thought of the time, repentance was regarded as a necessary precursor to the messianic reign, but the question of how repentance relates to redemption remained unanswered. For Jesus, the reign of God is a free gift come at last to Israel, and repentance is, not the precursor to, but the response of acceptance of the gift. Repentance does not bring the reign of God near; rather, the coming of God's reign is the presupposition for it (Meyer 1979, 132). God first gives the gift, but there can be no giving unless there is acceptance—for the gift will not be imposed on Israel. Repentance does not prompt God's mercy, but is the response to it though joy and thanks as well as tears of remorse and resolution. The time of Jesus' presence is the time of the wedding feast, the period when the guest cannot mourn, the day of good things come (Mark 2:19–20; cf. Matt. 11:5–6; Meyer 1979, 131).

Conflict

The context in which the baptism of Jesus takes place can be described as cosmic, for the heavens open, betokening the onset of a new age and new revelation, the voice of God identifying Jesus as Messiah and Servant is heard, and the gift of the Spirit for ministry is received. What follows is the struggle of the temptations (Mark 1:12–13). In a similar cosmic setting, the story of Jesus' victory over Satan in the wilderness is preliminary to a series of encounters with Satan by which Mark's Gospel is distinguished. After proclaiming the good news (1:14–15), Jesus begins his public ministry by calling disciples (1:16–20). But what happens next? At once, at the very commencement of Jesus' public ministry, the kingdom of God is brought by Jesus into contact with the rule of Satan and the domain of evil over which Satan presided. The call of disciples is followed by an exorcism in the synagog (1:21–28). At the time, it was generally supposed that Israel's real enemy was Rome, the oppressing power of foreign control, but this telling account indicates something different.

At the onset of the kingdom, God battles against Satan, who is entrenched within the people of God, but this was not the sort of battle that Judaism expected or wanted to fight (Wright 1988a, 349). Exemplifying the authority of Jesus, the encounter in Mark 1:21–28 highlights his ability to withstand Satan. By his victory, messianic healing is brought to Israel (e.g., see 1:29–34). (Since the Jewish people of Jesus' time attributed various kinds of disease and misfortune to demons, the miracle stories can also be viewed in the context of conflict with Satan.) The Spirit of God working through Jesus casts out Satanic forces (Matt. 12:28; Luke 11:20), for Jesus' operation in the healings and exorcisms is the entrance of the power of the holy to cleanse Israel. In these victories, the presence of the kingdom of God is strikingly revealed, not as an ideal, but as a new physical reality. The dawn of the new creation has begun!

The healings and exorcisms of the early chapters of Mark (e.g., 1:40–42; 3:1–5, 10–11), which are described so as to cast the presence of the Spirit in clear relief, thus appear in the context of continuing cosmic engagement between Satan, under whom all demonic forces are united (3:23, 26; cf. 1:13; 5:2, 12), and Jesus and the Holy Spirit (1:10, 12; 3:29). The conflict would prove to be ministry-long. Jesus is identified as the Holy One of God (1:24), the bearer of the Holy Spirit; thus, the contrast between the combatants is clear, as is the command exercised by Jesus over Satan's world. As a matter of course, Jesus orders or rebukes demons (1:25, 27; 3:12; 9:25), who recognize Jesus' power and fall down before him in servility (3:11; 5:6). The demons confess who Jesus is; quite remarkably they also understand something about his role: "Have you come to destroy us?" (1:24). Indeed Jesus has come to destroy demons—has come from heaven itself (Robinson 1982, 85). And his victories represent the imposition of normalcy, that is, a return to order (5:15).

Conflict for Jesus in Mark's Gospel extends beyond healings and exorcisms. James Robinson views the debates between Jesus and the Jewish authorities in 2:1–3:30 (particularly 3:23–29) as a life-and-death struggle, similar to the one with Satan (1982, 91–97). These debates are the continuation of the cosmic battle, for they are struggles in the mind against Satan, who always attempts to snatch the word away (4:15). Robinson argues that such debates (e.g., 8:11; 10:2; 12:15) can be described as temptations, thus making their diabolical character clear. As Jesus' ministry progresses, even the disciples put conflict, also described as Satanic opposition (Robinson 1982, 51), in his path. By the disciples' attempt to dissuade Jesus from the cross, they reveal their total inability to understand Jesus' role (8:31–9:1; 9:30–50; 10:32–45). Moreover, it is the disciples' affinity with Satan that renders them unable to withstand the temptation in Gethsemane (14:37–42) and that finally makes them unconscious allies of the Jewish authorities in the cosmic struggle with evil, which reaches its climax in the crucifixion and resurrection (Robinson 1982, 51). With their inflexible opposition to messianic suffering betraying their narrow nationalism, the disciples oppose Jesus' eschatological understanding of history. Yet through his death Jesus meets and quashes the ultimate diabolical antagonist and decisively brings in the kingdom of God. Cosmic order is thus potentially reestablished by the cross!

Self-characterization and Public Recognition

The Gospel of Mark records the use of several designations applied to Jesus in the course of his ministry: son of David, Son of God, Son of man, and Messiah. "Son of David" appears only once in Mark's Gospel—near the end of the narrative of the public ministry in the identification of Jesus by Bartimaeus (10:47–48). In the narratives of Jesus' ministry, Mark uses "Son of God" in the sense of "Messiah." "Son of man" and "Messiah" are the most frequent designations. Of these, the former is the more important for our purposes, for it is Jesus' self-designation. Though it is applied to Jesus just once beyond the Gospels (Acts 7:56: cf. Heb. 2:6; Rev. 1:13; 14:14), it is the appropriate term to sum up Jesus' ministry and its aims. Mark uses "Messiah" sparingly, and usually only editorially. When it is applied to Jesus, he normally translates it into Son-of-man terms (e.g.., 8:28–31).

SON OF MAN

The process of Jesus' redefinition of the kingdom of God brings us to the first occurrence and use by Jesus in Mark's Gospel of the title *Son of man*: "But that you may know that the Son of Man has authority on earth to forgive sins" (2:10). Though Daniel 7:13 certainly emerges as background for this title, it is generally agreed that the phrase *Son of man* was undefined in Jesus' day and did not signal expectation (Fitzmyer 1979, 147, 153; Vermes 1973, 163, 188). For generation of the significance and function of the title, many look to the later church (Bultmann 1952, 1:28–32; Hahn 1969, 15–53). But how does Jesus use the phrase? Some point to Jesus' use of it as an instrument of vivid self-reference or to the supposed distinction he makes between himself and the coming Son of man (passages cited include Mark 8:38; Luke 9:26; 12:8; Lindars 1983, 17–24). Indeed, the so-called Son-of-man sayings have been classified in the past according to the following categories: future (e.g., 13:26), suffering (e.g., 8:31), and personal (e.g., 2:10). Of these, only the future sayings were accepted as genuine. According to this view, the future sayings referred originally to some figure other than Jesus; however, the church subsequently identified the Son of man with Jesus. Such classification of the sayings has now been largely rejected since the categories overlap and cannot be maintained. Other issues arising from the classification further question its legitimacy. Proponents of classification argue as to which sayings group was original. But there are difficulties here. If the title was first used in contexts of future glorification, how would its use have been extended to include personal and suffering sayings? On the other hand, if the title arose out of personal contexts of self-deprecation, how could its use have been extended to Jesus' prophesies about the future glorification of the Son of man? Even if the suffering claims were self-deprecating, why were they made? How did Jesus' conviction that the Son of man must suffer, which appears in Mark's prediction of the passion (8:31; 9:31), arise? The statements concerning the Son of man's suffering varied so much from messianic expectation that they could not have been linked with the personal and future sayings, which were reconcilable with messianic claims, unless Jesus himself had supplied the link. If, as is claimed, Jesus distinguished between himself and the Son of man, why did the church equate the two? Finally, why did the church create the sayings on the Son of man used in the synoptic Gospels when it did not include Son of man as a title in its basic gospel proclamation (Kim 1983, 10)? These various questions indicate the inadequacy of previous attempts to categorize and interpret the Son-of-man sayings. If we are to understand them, we must take a different approach.

Let's begin by examining the background for the title *Son of man*. Daniel 7:13 is the commonly accepted antecedent, a determination based on two lines of evidence. The first focuses on the use of the definite article with the title in the synoptic Gospels; that is, we find "*the* Son of man" (emphasis added), as referring to the well-known Son of man (Moule 1974, 419–21). The second focuses on allusions to, or quotations from, Daniel 7 in Mark 8:38, 13:26, and 14:62 and on Jesus' implicit identification with the Danielic figure (Matt. 10:23; 13:37, 41; 16:28; 19:28; 24:27, 37, 39, 44; 25:31; Luke 12:40; 17:24, 26, 30; 18:8; 21:36). Though some argue against Daniel 7 on the grounds that the Son of man therein is not a judgment figure (Tödt 1965, 44), as he often is in the Gospels, judgment is implicit in Daniel 7:13–14 (Kim 1983, 65). Moreover, judgment is associated with the dominion and authority with which the Son of man is equipped in vindication of Israel since the exercising of judicial authority was a crucial element of a Semitic king's function. Thus, the context allows that "one like a son of man" in Daniel 7 would receive the same power as given to Nebuchadnezzar in Daniel 2:37 and 5:18 (Schaberg 1982, 160). If, as suggested, the background to Daniel 7's use of the term is to be sought in Ezekiel and Psalm 8, there are undoubtedly representative Israelite notions in the term as there seem to be from the context of Daniel 7 since Ezekiel as Israel's representative is addressed as son of man and since Psalm 8:5 has Israel's role in mind. Dated to the last third of the last century B.C., a fragment of Daniel from Qumran may identify the Son of man with the Son of God and the messiah (4Qps Dan Aa; Kim 1983, 21). Such an identification would prove that linking the messiah and the Son of man was coming into vogue in Jesus' time, a link taken further by 4 Ezra and by the Similitudes (where in 37–71 the Son of man is preexistent and is identified with the messiah and the Servant). However, these theological extensions represent movement beyond the strict sense of Daniel 7. Unlike these examples, Jesus' use of "Son of man" seems not to have been provocative in any way and seems to have called forth no Jewish expectations or reactions (Vermes 1973, 161).

As reported by Mark, when Jesus first uses "Son of man" in 2:10, its use does not affect the scribes. They are alarmed by Jesus' claim to forgive sins (2:7), but not by his use of the title. Nor do the disciples or crowds ever make the title a matter of inquiry. Though Jesus refers to himself by the expression, no one else ever does. Nor is his use of the title a matter of accusation at his trial. Quite simply, it never seems to cause concern. Perhaps the explanation for the indifference is ambiguity. We know that the corresponding Palestinian Aramaic phrase for "Son of man" could mean "human being" or could substitute for the indefinite pronoun, thus meaning "anyone" or "one." It is possible, though not certain, that the phrase was used in Jesus' time as a circumlocution for "I" (see, e.g., Matt. 11:19; 12:32; 13:37; 16:13). The meaning of Son of man may have been just ambiguous enough to allow Jesus to use it to identify himself as the carrier of Israel's hopes without doing so in explicit messianic terms. Thus, the title may have been a perfect self-designation, an enigmatic expression that Jesus fills with his own particular content.

The use of the title *Son of man* does not extend beyond the ministry of Jesus, meaning that it is important for the ministry but not later. If Jesus uses the title to refer to a heavenly being or divine status, would not its use extend beyond his ministry? If Jesus uses it to refer to his humiliation, then perhaps its disuse after the resurrection is comprehensible. How does Jesus use the title? N. T. Wright suggests that Jesus uses it as a corporate figure for the saints of Daniel 7 and thus for Israel to indicate that he himself will experience Israel's classic destiny of being cast away and restored after suffering (Matt. 12:40; 26:2; Mark 8:31; 9:12, 31; 10:33, 45; 14:21; 1988a, 350). If Wright's suggestion is correct, the title then connotes innocent suffering and vindication after the fashion of ideal Israel's. In the vindication, Jesus will be given authority to judge, as is clearly indicated by the future glorification prophecies regarding the Son of man. Yet for Jesus, this authority for the future has somehow already arrived and is manifest in his ministry. The following suppositions seem quite reasonable: (1) that the title grows out of Israel's experience and (2) that in the Gospels the title is specially applied to Jesus' mission and carries undertones of messiahship. Yet in describing a future figure, the title is more extensive and more authoritative than "Messiah," which is always this-worldly in the Old Testament. By using Son-of-man language, on the analogy of Daniel 7, Jesus says that Israel's destiny is reaching its climax in his person. Once again, the ambiguity is crucial. On the one hand, Jesus uses the language to convey that the kingdom had arrived; on the other hand, Jesus uses it to defy cherished Jewish expectations.

Let's return to Mark 2:10: "But that you may know that the Son of Man has authority on earth to forgive sins." In this context, Son of man cannot be an oblique figure of speech for "a man" since the idea of a man's forgiving sins would have greatly offended Jewish orthodoxy (Hooker 1967, 81–93). Also, the logic of the passage does not allow us to interpret Son of man in the general sense of "humankind" since at issue is Jesus' authority to forgive sins, not humankind's as such (Tuckett 1982, 66). Moreover, if Son of man means "humankind," then "on earth" is redundant. (Note that the phrase never occurs as a periphrasis for "man" elsewhere in the New Testament.) If Mark 2:10 is an editorial aside by Mark, then this is the only instance in the New Testament in which someone other than Jesus uses the phrase. The reaction of the crowd in Matthew 9:8 is sometimes cited (Hooker 1967, 94–95) as support for the interpretation of *Son of man* as "humankind": "they praised God, who had given such authority to men." However, doing no more than pointing to the popular reaction to Jesus' miracle, Matthew 9:8 does not provide a comment on Jesus' use of the phrase. Matthew himself would not have intended such an interpretation, for the notion of humankind's forgiving sins was as unacceptable then as it is now.

Synoptic parallels to Mark 2:10 appear in Matthew 9:6 and Luke 5:24. Comparing the parallels with 2:10 reveals a position-related emphasis on the phrase "on earth" in Mark. If the Son of man was perceived as part of the adjudicating heavenly council, then perhaps Jesus is intending a contrast with what might have been expected "in heaven." That the Son of man possesses "authority on earth" is news to Mark's readers, and possibly to Jesus' audience. In this new age there is not only forgiveness of sins in heaven but now also on earth because the authoritative Son of man has come! Jesus claims divine authority to forgive sins, not necessarily deity. Why does Jesus introduce the title at this point in his response to the scribes? It seems from Mark 2:10 that there is a natural relationship between the Son of man and the forgiveness of sins. If Jesus is associating his own role with that of the figure in Daniel 7:13, then he is revealing that the last judgment is now taking place on earth in his ministry and that he is exercising his dominion.

Indeed, this association of the Son of man, forgiveness, and judgment is in fact characteristic of the majority of Son-of-man sayings in the Gospels (Maddox 1968, 45–74).

Mark refers to the Son of man yet another time in chapter 2: "The Sabbath was made for man, not man for the Sabbath. So the Son of Man is Lord even of the Sabbath" (vv. 27–28). It seems natural to use verse 27 as evidence for defining Son of man as "humankind" in verse 28 (Beasley-Murray 1986, 231). Taking this further, let's consider C. H. Dodd's suggestion that verse 28 refers to humankind's appointment to rule over the earth, an appointment now demonstrated in the ministry of Jesus, in whose ministry the potential of Genesis 1:26–28 is being exhibited (cited by Beasley-Murray 1986, 233). The Sabbath was made for humankind, the crown of God's creation, and the sovereignty over the Sabbath that belonged to humankind is now exercised by the Son of man, who is the representative and mediator of divine rule and so is the one through whom the many may experience divine rule (Beasley-Murray 1986, 233). The narrative thus indicates that the destiny of humankind to rule is now being exercised by Jesus, the Son of man.

Mark 2:27–28 and 2:10 both emphasize the judgment and lordship roles of the Son of man, who as representative of humankind assumes the roles of Adam and of Israel. Subsequent references in Mark to the Son of man as a suffering figure (e.g., 8:31; 9:31; 10:33–34) simply elaborate upon the manner in which judgment will come. At Caesarea Philippi, Jesus interprets Peter's messianic confession (8:29) in terms that stress the necessity of the Son of man's suffering and resurrection (8:31). The messianic goals of Jesus' ministry, the overcoming of Israel's enemies, will be achieved through suffering. God will deliver the suffering Son of man (9:31), who should be feted but will be crucified (10:33–34). And his cross is the standard by which all humankind will be judged. Beyond the suffering lies the vindication of the Son of man, for the future sayings point to his role as final Judge and Lord (14:62).

MESSIAH

Jesus virtually refuses the title of Messiah, "Christ," until he appears before the high priest at his trial (Mark 14:62). Though the title is applied directly or indirectly to Jesus several times in Mark's Gospel (1:1; 8:29; 14:61; 15:32), Jesus uses "Christ" only once (9:41). The literature between the Testaments exhibits little interest in such a figure. In the apocalyptic literature, the emphasis is on something different—on the direct breaking in of the kingdom of God. But in the Pharisaic Psalms of Solomon, from about 50 B.C., a messianic figure is present. A nationalistic victor over the Gentiles, a son of David appears as the savior and restorer of Israel, a view influenced without doubt by the Pharisees' re-

jection of the Judean Hasmonean kings. This Pharisaic view of a purely
earthly messiah seems to have been the representative one at the time
(Vermes 1973, 133). No mention of a messiah is found in some prominent intertestamental books, namely, Jubilees, 1 Enoch (1–36; 91–104),
Testament of Moses, 1 Baruch, 2 Enoch, 1 and 2 Maccabees, Tobit,
Wisdom of Solomon, Judith, and Ecclesiasticus (Beasley-Murray 1986,
52). At Qumran the sect interpreted Genesis 49:10 in conventional messianic terms (see pp. 36–37), as it did in Isaiah 11:1–9. Speculation from
that community, however, went beyond the traditional view to also include a priestly and a prophetic messiah (e.g., T. Levi 17–18; T. Judah
17:5–6; 24:5–6; T. Reuben 6:12; T. Joseph 19:8–12; T. Simeon 7:1–2;
T. Dan 5:10–13). Qumran's Rule of the Community speaks of the messiahs of Aaron and Israel (IQS 9:10–11), anticipates the coming of an
eschatological prophet (1QS 9–11), and links the messiah's precursor
with two messianic figures—priest and king (1QS 9:11). Two documents from the sect equate the messiah and the Son of God; for example, consider these words from the Rule of the Community, "in the
event of God begetting the Messiah to be with them" (1QS 2:11; cf.
4QFlor 1:6–7; Beasley–Murray 1986, 54–56). In writings from the first
and second centuries A.D., the messiah surfaces as a purely human but
nationalistic figure, as in 2 Baruch and 4 Ezra. Though there is little evidence of messianic speculation before the second century A.D., what exists varies widely. In ordinary use during the time between the Testaments, however, the title *Messiah* refers to a Davidic redeemer king.

Jesus' assertion that in his person the kingdom of God has come is
quite naturally associated with claims of his messiahship. It is possible
that Jesus himself did not use the title *Messiah* because of its limitations; instead he used the phrase "kingdom of God" to redefine *messiah*
as a concept. Surely "kingdom" is comprehensive enough to embrace
the implications of rule by Yahweh through his designated representative. Since Jesus contemplated a kingship different from traditional expectation, perhaps he viewed Messiah as a title open to misunderstanding. The burden of much of Jesus' preaching involved conveying his
redefinitions to an Israel in danger of being rejected. In fact, almost by
necessity Jesus redefined Israel, for his conceptions of the kingdom and
of Israel's future are so intricately intertwined (Meyer 1979, 134). This
certainly wasn't the first time that Israel was redefined. What did this
redefinition mean? Jesus implies that national Israel was not essential
to the purposes of the new kingdom, an implication that his audiences
would have found very difficult to accept. Moreover, the disciples, as
the nucleus of the New Israel, are privileged to judge national Israel
(Matt. 19:28; Luke 22:29–30). Yet this privilege does not signify the disciples' elevation as much as it does Israel's rejection (Meyer 1979, 185–

97). Beyond the Gospels lies a different outlook, a reduced emphasis, on the kingdom of God, an outlook intimately tied to Jesus' proclamation and to the public's recognition of him. In his ministry Jesus indirectly announces his messiahship, but after the resurrection he is openly proclaimed to be Israel's Messiah, the Christ and King. Since the Holy Spirit ushers in the kingdom age in the postresurrection period, the kingdom is no longer a matter of expectation, for it comes to power in the life of the early church. As a new society, the early church is constituted as Israel of old had been, bound together not merely by bonds of brotherly love, secular considerations, or ethics, but of a common headship with God as King and Jesus as his vice-regent.

Something about Jesus fostered the impression of him as a messianic candidate, for during the course of his ministry people recognized him as son of David (Matt. 1:1; 9:27; 12:23; 15:22; 20:30–31; 21:9, 15; 22:42), a title Jesus found unsatisfactory (Mark 12:35–37). At the beginning of the twentieth century, the Dutch scholar William Wrede argued that Mark's Gospel presents Jesus as having attempted to keep his messianic identity a secret. This portrayal, suggested Wrede, was a theological invention by the early church to project back into the ministry of Jesus an office to which Jesus never laid claim, for Jesus never believed himself to be the Messiah. But what are the facts? Jesus is confessed or implied to be the Messiah, but does not publicly claim the role. As described in the temptation narratives, Jesus rejects the invitation to adopt Satan's methods for attaining messiahship. When demons and demoniacs recognize Jesus' messiahship, he rebukes them (1:25, 34; 3:12; 9:25). Though Jesus' miracles of healing are confessedly messianic in character, he enjoins silence (1:44; 5:43; 7:36; 8:26, 30). On occasion Jesus retires from public view as though to avoid notoriety (1:35–38; 7:24). It is possible that none of these incidents is a conscious attempt by Jesus to avoid the issue of messiahship, for he directly claims it in other ways, such as in his role as shepherd (Mark 6:34). Perhaps Jesus' apparent rejection of the title is necessitated by the various circumstances. For instance, Jesus' rebuke of the demons' confessions may have served to bring the demons under control and to silence them. Jesus may have commanded those healed to silence because he recognized that miracles alone would not produce saving faith, but would give rise to improper nationalistic expectations for his ministry. In other words, Jesus operated under the conviction that he could not be truly confessed and understood except by faith. In this sense the messiahship of Jesus is always a secret to outsiders. Like the secret of the kingdom itself (Mark 4:10–12), his messiahship is there, but only for those with eyes to see it.

Jesus does not outrightly reject the title *Messiah*, but his attitude to it throughout the Gospel is ambivalent (Mark 8:27–33; 11:1–11; 14:62). He takes the view that people must find out for themselves. The claims he makes for himself are of the parabolic kind, but all people can pierce through to the truth if they try hard enough. Jesus' indifference to the title suggests that he has another concept of the office. Thus, in cases where misunderstanding could arise he counsels silence. The messianic secret is, therefore, dependent upon the type of Messiah that Jesus is (Martin 1972; 209). Mark well knew the Jewish objection to a suffering Messiah, but the Gospel writer retained both the direct and indirect assertions to suffering. Moreover, Mark doubtlessly would have argued that it is precisely the suffering that makes Jesus the Messiah. Few really perceive the nature of Jesus' person during his ministry. It is the fringe of Israel—the outcasts, the deaf, and the blind—and the Gentiles who do. Those close to him, the disciples and his family fail to understand. Throughout Jesus' public ministry, Israel continues to reject his teaching, but at the end of his ministry, as a judgment upon Israel, blind Bartimaeus clearly sees the truth and for the only time in the Gospel confesses Jesus as son of David (Mark 10:46–52).

Teaching in Parables (Mark 4)

Consideration of the hidden character of Jesus' messianic claims brings us to his teaching in parables and, thus, to Jesus' concept of Israel, which is crucial for our study of eschatology. Before we look at Jesus' concept of Israel, however, we should examine what he says about family in Mark 3:31–35, for the two are closely related. Verses 34–35 reveal that the family of Jesus is no longer to be constructed by natural ties of birth and family relationships, but by ties of belief. Whoever does the will of God is henceforth considered to be a member of the new Jesus family. The seed parables, which follow in chapter 4, redefine Israel as a saved remnant, as the citation from Isaiah implies (Mark 4:12; cf. Isa. 6:9–10). Following upon Jesus' redefinition of the family in 3:31–35, the seed parables serve to equate this new family with Israel.

Otherwise often taciturn, Jesus delivers two major eschatological pronouncements in the Gospel of Mark. Chapter 4 deals with the nature of the kingdom, while chapter 13 focuses on its coming. However, chapter 4 is no ordinary speech. Verse 2 reveals that Jesus taught the crowd of people "many things by parables." For the meaning of the first parable in Mark, the parable of the sower (4:3–9), an understanding of which is fundamental for all parables (v. 13), we are dependent upon Jesus' explanation in 4:14–20. The focus of the parable is upon the hearing of the Word. The sower scattered seed, that is, the Word of God, the

Word about the kingdom (v. 14). A threefold pattern of failure (vv. 15–19) is offset by the threefold success of the seed as the Word (v. 20). This is the mysterious way, the mystery of the kingdom, the way in which the kingdom works, the law of the eventual success of the word built upon repeated and public failures. Seeds also function prominently in the two other parables of chapter 4. The parable of the secretly growing seed (4:26–29) illustrates the manner in which the final harvest will come. Underscored by the almost automatic way in which the seed progresses from stage to stage of growth (vv. 27–28), the harvest is certain, assured because the seed contains a power in itself (v. 29). The third parable of the chapter uses the image of the mustard seed (vv. 30–32). Like the mustard seed, the kingdom at its beginning may seem small and obscure (v. 31), but the ending will be great—a great tree in which the birds of the air will nest (v. 32). Through the image of the tree, Jesus alludes to the great tree of Nebuchadnezzar under which the world seeks shelter in Daniel 4 (vv. 10–12, 20–22), the tree that provides protection for all who seek its shelter. Jesus uses the image to reveal that no matter how humble and insignificant a beginning the kingdom may have, the end destined for it will finally come. Then all nations will be gathered into one kingdom, and God's plan will have reached its completion.

The primary message of the three seed parables concerns the hidden kingdom of God. Though now concealed, the kingdom is waiting to manifest itself with power (Ambrozic 1972, 91), as the Messiah of the kingdom is hidden but visible to those of faith. The mystery—the outworking of the kingdom—is that the kingdom will be born when Jesus goes to the cross and, like the seed growing secretly, falls into the ground and dies (Ambrozic 1972, 99). The mystery Jesus reveals is the eschatological power of the divine plan, which is already at work in the world. The kingdom is gathering the elect into one family of Jesus, giving them insight into God's purposes for humankind, and causing them to participate in the power that is carrying out those plans. The irrevocable division of the end time is being formed in this way every day. The teaching of Jesus creates the community, setting the ultimate destiny before its eyes. For the key to interpreting the parable of the sower, John Bowker looks to Mark 4:12, an adaptation of Isaiah 6:9–10 (1974, 311). These verses are also instructive for understanding Jesus' redefinition of Israel. Remember that in 6:9–13 Isaiah prophesies the rejection and exile of the kingdom of Judah and the emergence of a remnant as a holy seed. The sower parable depicts a similar paradoxical situation: most of the seed seems wasted, but nevertheless the few produce a good harvest. Here, then, is the mystery of the kingdom. Those outside, that is, Judaism at large (Mark 4:11), exclude themselves by their nationalism, their preconceived notions of the kingdom, and above all by their failure to believe in Jesus. Israel will thus be judged and rejected. However, for the insiders, for those around Jesus as in 3:34–35, a new messianic family is being created, the product of the holy seed. The analogy with Isaiah 6 makes the message clear. After judgment upon Israel, whereby the national tree will be felled, a remnant of faith will emerge. This still-hidden mystery of the kingdom is now taking place through the ministry of Jesus. As stories, these parables that had grave implications for Israel were not difficult to understand, but the audiences found themselves unable to accept them and what they foretold regarding Israel.

Teaching the Disciples (Mark 8:27–13:37)

Mark 8:27 represents a turning point in the Gospel. With Jesus' arrival in Caesarea Philippi, the direction of his ministry shifts. Before this, Jesus taught the crowds and performed miracles. From this time onwards, he concentrates his teaching upon the disciples, and miracles virtually cease. The narrative also marks a change in Jesus' messianic stance, but in what way? Peter confesses Jesus as the Christ in 8:29. In verse 30 Jesus commands Peter to silence, just as he commanded demons and demoniacs before (see, e.g., 1:25; 3:12). What has changed? Why would Jesus silence one of his disciples? Was it not the appropriate time to reveal Jesus' messiahship by open proclamation? Was Jesus concerned that a popular, but false, impression of him as a wonder-worker would be taken messianically? Was the truth to be revealed to initiates only? The reason for Jesus' command emerges in verse 31. By immediately linking Peter's declaration of messiahship with necessary suffering, Jesus reveals the real nature of his office. The Messiah must die for Israel, for he is Israel's suffering Servant, who reveals the essential nature of what it means to be Israel (Wright 1988a, 350–51). Only by way of the cross can a public declaration of Jesus' messiahship be made (Luke 24:26) since the nature of his messiahship can only be understood by the crucifixion. Any declaration before Jesus' suffering would be prematurely, and wrongly interpreted in terms of existing presuppositions.

Following Peter's messianic confession at Caesarea Philippi, Jesus reveals the nature and cost of discipleship, that is, the persecution and trials the disciples must bear (Mark 8:34–38). Then he assures his disciples that some of them will "see the kingdom of God come with power" (9:1) in their lifetime, though he gives no guarantee that they will understand what they see. To what is Jesus referring? The time frame implied by the flourish of "some who are standing here will not taste death" indicates an event later than the transfiguration, which occurs just six days hence (9:2). Note the words "the kingdom of God come with power" in 9:1, which refer to an event that will occur after the death of Jesus but in the lifetime of the disciples. The coming with power must refer to the destruction of Jerusalem (France 1971, 140, 233–35), the end of the Jewish state, and the end of national Israel, which the cross will accomplish.

After six days, Jesus, Peter, James, and John ascend the mountain of transfiguration (Mark 9:2). Similarities with God's establishing a covenant with Moses at Sinai frame this event as a new covenant. The three disciples who accompany Jesus remind us of the three men who ascended Sinai with Moses (Exod. 24:1). And Jesus alone is transfigured, just as Moses alone saw the glory of Yahweh (Exod. 24:2) and bore the mark of a transfigured face (Exod. 34:29–35). The divine presence shining through Jesus evokes Peter's somewhat lame suggestion to build three tents (Mark 9:5), perhaps recalling the Mosaic tent of Exodus 33:7–11. Since Jesus cannot be equated, as Peter tries to do, with Moses and Elijah, Peter's suggestion is rejected. The cloud and voice from the cloud of Mark 9:7 echo Exodus 24:16, but divine revelation, which shines solely through Jesus, is now direct, not mediated as it was at Sinai. The divine command that Peter, James, and John hear Jesus only legitimates the passion prediction of Mark 8:31 and establishes Jesus' uniqueness.

The transfiguration operates as an endorsement of Jesus' suffering messiahship. During the event, plans for his death are finalized (see Luke 9:31). It is not surprising, therefore, that the next, and final, major address by Jesus in the Gospel (chap. 13) serves as his last will and testament (Hooker 1982, 81–83). Between the transfiguration and the occasion of the address in Mark 13, Jesus is acknowledged as King on entry into Jerusalem (11:9–10), whereupon he challenges the religious authorities to accept him (11:15–19, 27–33; 12:1–40). Their refusal leads to his death; however, the quotation of Psalm 118:22–23 at the end of the parable about the tenants indicates that Jesus will be vindicated (see Mark 12:10–11). Moreover, Israel's rejection of Jesus leads to God's rejection of Israel. Mark 13:2 specifies her punishment: Jerusalem and the temple will be destroyed.

Jesus' address (Mark 13:5–37) follows soon after his prediction of the destruction of Jerusalem. What prompts it are two questions asked by the disciples: "Tell us, when will these things happen? And what will be the sign that they are all about to be fulfilled?" (13:4). He begins by addressing the last question first. In his exposition, Jesus forecasts the fall of Jerusalem as the herald of the end-time judgment. Verses 5–13 describe what will happen before the catastrophe: false Christs will rise up

(vv. 5–6); upheavals and wars will break out (vv. 7–8); and the disciples will be persecuted (vv. 9, 11–13). In addition to all these events, one other is preliminary to the fall: "And the gospel must first be preached to all nations" (v. 10). If preaching to all nations *representatively* satisfies the sense of verse 10, then there is evidence of its accomplishment within the New Testament itself (Acts 2:5–11; cf. Rom. 15:19).

In Mark 13:14 Jesus identifies a sign of the approaching destruction—Roman armies will surround Jerusalem (cf. Luke 21:20). In verses 15–23 he then describes various disastrous circumstances associated with the siege and fall. Though verses 24–27 are often treated as referring to the parousia (Wenham 1984, 358), the organization of the entire chapter and the use of Old Testament theophanic language, particularly in verses 24–25, indicate that these verses also refer to the fall of Jerusalem (cf. Tasker 1961, 225–28; Kik 1948, 69–77). The language Jesus uses in verses 24–25 is virtually identical to that used by Isaiah to predict the fall of Babylon (Isa. 13:10; cf. Isa. 34:4; cf. Ezek. 32:7–8; Joel 2:10; 3:15; cf. Amos 8:9). Jerusalem's fall will thus be the attestation of Jesus' authority to act as judge of those who presumed to judge him (Mark 13:26–27). Using theophanic language of judgment (Dan. 7:13; cf. Isa. 19:1), verse 26 describes the theological significance of the destruction of Jerusalem. In the next verse Jesus says that the Son of man "will send his angels." This could refer either to consolation offered to believers during the fall or to the Christian community in mission after A.D. 70 (since "angels" can also be translated as "messengers"; cf. Matt. 11:10; Mark 1:2; Luke 7:24; 9:52).

When will Jerusalem fall? the disciples had asked Jesus. He responds to their query in Mark 13:28–37. Verses 28–31 create a sense of historical immediacy through the image of the fig tree (v. 28) and the plain sense of "this generation will certainly not pass away until all these things have happened" (v. 30, where "generation" should not be adulterated to mean "race" or "age"). Verses 32–34 demonstrate and support the need for constant vigilance, and verses 35–37 are an admonition controlling the chapter as a whole. A logical sequence of thought structures this chapter. Jesus spells out for Israel the prospective fall of Jerusalem and the end of the Jewish nation. The enormity of the destruction, brought on by the crucifixion, of the symbols of Jewish faith—city and temple—is plain. As history has unfolded, the consequence of this destruction, another exile, seems to have no end.

The Trial and Passion (Mark 14–15)

Withheld by Jesus during his public ministry, the secret of his messiahship, his kingship over Israel, is about to be revealed. Jesus' arrest and trial are at hand. Having stirred up the people against Jesus, the chief priests arrange for his arrest (Mark 14:10–11). At the trial before Caiaphas, Jesus stands condemned as a confessed messiah (14:53–65; cf. Matt. 26:57). Though the Pharisaic bias of later Mishnaic evidence makes it difficult to question the legality of Jesus' trial, the court clearly is predisposed to a guilty verdict (Juel 1977, 63). Earlier Jesus had predicted that the trial would indeed be a miscarriage of justice (8:31). The high priest presses Jesus with this question in 14:61, "Are you the Christ, the Son of the Blessed One?" Jesus responds, "I am" (v. 62). Jesus' answer is a clear acceptance of his messianic status (cf. 13:6 for evidence of "I am" as a messianic claim formula). The appropriate time for public disclosure of Jesus' office has now come! To Israel's representative Jesus reveals the true nature of his messiahship.

As recorded by Mark (see also Matt. 26:59–68), the trial proceedings indicate that the high priest's question to Jesus in 14:61 is not idly put. Rather, it is prompted by the charge in verse 58 that Jesus claimed he would rebuild the temple after its destruction. Such a building task was traditionally deemed a messianic one, as is evident from the Targums. In a Targum of Isaiah 53:5 the messiah is called upon to rebuild the temple, for it had been profaned by the guilt of the people (Stenning 1947, 180; Juel 1977, 183). Targums of 1 Chronicles 17:12 and Zechariah 6:12 charge the future king with building the temple. During Jesus' time, moreover, 2 Samuel 7:13 and Exodus 15:17, which refer respectively to building the temple and establishing the sanctuary, were interpreted eschatologically (Juel 1977, 178). Jesus' cleansing of the temple soon after he entered Jerusalem (Mark 11:15–19) also signified rejection of the temple's keepers, the officialdom of Israel. They retaliated by fabricating a charge against Jesus and voicing it at the trial: "We have heard him say, 'I will destroy this man-made temple and in three days will build another, not made by man'" (14:58). Comprising various elements of Jesus' predictions, this charge accuses Jesus of claiming his messiahship. The high priest's use of "again" in verse 61, where the question of messiahship is asked directly, supports our viewing the charge this way. The charge against Jesus also refers to the eschatological replacement of the *naos*. Though *naos* is translated as "temple," it actually refers to the temple building itself, the shrine (see also 15:29, 38), rather than the whole temple complex (*hieron*). The new shrine will not be made by man—literally "not made with hands." What does this mean? In the Old Testament what is made with hands is deemed idolatrous. By describing the existing temple as "man-made," Jesus lays bare its character and rejects it. By contrast, the new shrine will be heavenly and spiritual. Jesus is simultaneously the builder of the new temple and the building itself, which is to be constructed by his resurrection, that is, "in three days" (v. 58). Since temple imagery and symbolism can be used to connote "community," Mark 14:58 may refer to the incorporation of the new community into the Messiah (Juel 1977, 167–68).

In questioning Jesus about his messiahship, the high priest asks if he is "the Christ, the Son of the Blessed One" (Mark 14:61). Used in apposition in verse 61, "Son of the Blessed One" is a way of saying "Son of God" that reverentially avoids the divine title. Jesus accepts the designations, but goes on to say, "And you will see the Son of Man sitting at the right hand of the Mighty One and coming on the clouds of heaven" (v. 62; cf. Ps. 110:1; Dan. 7:13). By using "Son of man," Jesus is not merely substituting a preferred title; rather, he is making a claim that is far more authoritative and extensive than messiahship. The tenor of his statement makes clear that Israel's judgment is at stake. By using the language of Psalm 110:1 and Daniel 7:13, Jesus combines two facets of Old Testament expectations of vindication, that is, judgment ("sitting at the right hand of the Mighty One") and implementation ("coming on the clouds of heaven"; Robinson 1956, 336–40). But Israel will not be vindicated! Jesus pronounces judgment upon Israel—Jerusalem will be destroyed at the hands of the Son of man. Moreover, his visitation upon Israel in Jerusalem's fall will be witnessed by Israel's enemies, her own hierarchy. The coming vindication will belong not to Israel but to Jesus.

What is the reaction to Jesus' messianic claim and prediction? Mark records in 14:63 that the high priest tore his robe, an act understood as a legal response to blasphemy, that is, an infringement of divine prerogatives (Juel 1977, 97). Thus, the high priest represents the official reaction. How do the others hearing the testimony react? The seeming absurdity of his prediction in 14:62 has little effect on them, for they mock Jesus as a prophet without credibility (v. 65).

Bitter irony emerges in the account of the passion of Jesus in Mark 15. As the truth of Jesus' kingship over Israel becomes more and more clear, so does the realization that this kingship means the end of the nation. Upon having led Jesus into the Praetorium, the soldiers dress him in a royal robe (vv. 16–17) and mockingly hail him as the king of the Jews (v. 18). Three times Jesus is identified by Pilate the same way (vv. 2, 9, 12). On the basis of Jesus' supposed kingship, chief priests, scribes, and criminals taunt Jesus as he hangs (vv. 31–32). Verse 26 records the words inscribed on the cross: "The King of the Jews." What a paradox this Roman title represents, for the Jews never used it to refer to the messiah (Meeks 1967, 79 n. 1). Jesus dies as a common felon, a nationalist messiah convicted by Rome of the political charge of sedition and sentenced to the punishment meted out to any insurrectionist (cf. Luke 23:2; Wright 1985, 86). Upon the drawing of Jesus' last breath, the temple veil is torn in two (vv. 37–38). By the death of Jesus, the earthly Jerusalem temple had been profaned. No further use existed for the temple or the nation.

Mark's Gospel fulfils its christological purpose, proclaiming the messiahship of Jesus as one quite different from Jewish expectations. But in the end, Jesus as Israel's King embodies all of Israel's hopes. The words of the Roman centurion who witnessed Jesus' death encapsulate the special emphasis of Mark: "Surely this man was the Son of God" (15:39). In claiming to be Israel, Jesus is given up to death by Israel and thus dies the death that is rebellious Israel's (Wright 1985, 89–90). In dying as Israel and for Israel, Jesus as the Servant of Yahweh atones for Israel's sinfulness by taking upon himself the judgment he had pronounced against the nation (Wright 1985, 90–93). By in dying as Israel, Jesus dies representatively for the world, whom Israel had represented by her call. The fulfilment of Israel's role to be a light to lighten the Gentiles is now possible for restored Israel. So for Mark the victory of the cross is a cosmic one: the powers of evil have been defeated, and God's rule has been established. In Jesus we clearly see God's ruling activity, for Jesus fulfils the mandate of Genesis 1:26–28 and reconciles the world as Israel's Messiah.

9

Lucan Eschatology
in His Gospel and Acts

The Gospel of Luke and the Acts of the Apostles form a two-part work with a unified eschatological view. Like Matthew and Mark, this Gospel tells the story of Jesus and his salvation. Unlike any other New Testament writing, Acts traces the movement of Jesus' salvation to the Gentiles. The Gospel begins with a summary of what had been promised to Israel and an assurance that these promises are now to be fulfilled, even if paradoxically by the rejection of national Israel. Thus, the Gospel sets the stage for what we find at the beginning of Acts—the regathering of Israel and her mission as a light to the nations.

Two crucial strands emerge from the eschatological base of Luke-Acts. One, the theology of the redemption of Israel, is conveyed by the infancy narratives of Luke 1–2. The other, the messiahship of Jesus, is finally authenticated at the end of the Gospel by the ascension. Both strands warrant close scrutiny, but before doing so, we must note a charge often leveled at Luke. That is, because Luke abandoned any hope of Jesus' early return, Luke replaced eschatology with a salvation history extended into the church age. Is the only eschatology in Luke a realized one with a transcendent kingdom? No. Though we grant that Luke disavows an imminent end (17:20–22; 19:11; 20:9), his eschatology emerges from the entire gospel, not from select verses that deal, questionably, with the second coming.

Fulfilment, Promise, and the Infancy Narratives (Luke 1–2)

The infancy narratives of Luke's Gospel establish continuity with the Old Testament and at the same time not only survey what will happen in the course of Luke-Acts but also provide a framework of interpretation for the subsequent events. It is generally agreed that the hymns of the infancy narratives function in much the same way as the speeches in Acts: to introduce the main figures and anticipate their ministries while simultaneously interpreting the course of events. The hymns of Luke 1–2 thus demonstrate that God continues to intervene in the history of Israel as the pious await fulfilment of Israel's hopes (Carroll 1988, 39). God has helped Israel (Luke 1:54) and has visited and redeemed his people (1:68). The present salvation will be for the glory of his people Israel (2:32); indeed, all of Israel's history has pointed forward to his coming salvation. The events described by the infancy hymns are in keeping with and are a continuation of Old Testament expectation.

The events of the new age begin with Gabriel's revelation to Zechariah, a pious priest with impeccable credentials, that his prayer has been heard (Luke 1:13). Elizabeth, Zechariah's wife, will give birth to a son, who will be the Elijah figure charged with preparing the people for the coming of Yahweh (1:17). Gabriel's further announcement to Mary concerns the Messiah: God will send to Israel a Davidic savior who will reign forever (1:30–35), thus fulfilling the expectations of Nathan's prophecy in 2 Samuel 7:12–13. The child is to be named Jesus, a name foreshadowing his salvific role (1:31; cf. Matt. 1:21). Climaxing the visitation theme of Luke 1 is the Song of Mary (vv. 46–55), a hymn of praise for the gift of a son whose birth will restore Israel in fulfilment of the promises to Abraham. Thus, at the beginning of his Gospel Luke introduces the concept of universal eschatology based on Israel—God's presence will be with his people permanently. Hints of conflict arise in the song from the reversal-of-fortunes motif. From the reversal, however, will emerge the restoration of Israel (v. 54), which is not to be equated with the nation that bears the name (vv. 50–53). In this paradoxical way, the Abrahamic promises to Israel will be fulfilled (v. 55).

The Song of Zechariah in Luke 1:67–79 elaborates on the significance of the births of John and Jesus. Beginning with a blessing formula that often ends psalms of praise in the Old Testament (e.g., Ps. 41:13; 72:18; 106:48; 135:21), the song hails the intervention of God whose visitation in the incarnation signifies that the day of Israel's redemption had arrived, thus confirming the Abrahamic covenantal oaths. The two-part song celebrates the arrival of the Davidic Messiah

(vv. 68–75) and describes John's role as forerunner (vv. 76–79). Since John's father is on the temple staff and his birth is announced during sacrificial requirements of the old covenant, John is certainly part of Old Testament history. Though he will restore Israel to her covenantal vocation, his role as the prophet of the Most High (v. 76) is preliminary to that of Jesus, the Son of the Most High, the Messiah of the house of David (v. 69). The mighty savior Jesus will repeat the triumphs of the exodus in fulfilment of the Abrahamic promises (vv. 71–73). The theme of salvation for Israel is raised in verse 69, cast as a future prospect in verse 71 and as an accomplished feat in verses 74–75, and interiorized in terms of the forgiveness of sins in verse 77. According to verse 78, the messianic light is about to dawn: "the rising sun (*anatolē*) will come to us from heaven." Since *anatolē* is used for the messianic term *branch* in the Septuagint of Jeremiah 23:5 and Zechariah 3:8 and 6:12, the messianic interpretation of Luke 1:78 is certain (Brown 1977, 373). The ultimate goal of the Messiah's coming will be to fulfil Israel's vocation of serving God in holiness and righteousness (vv. 74–75). Here at the beginning of his Gospel Luke commences to redefine the salvation that the Davidic king is expected to bring, for Luke presents it not as political salvation but as a release from sins that produces freedom to serve (Carroll 1988, 46). What Luke anticipates is not a typical restoration of Israel with a return to the Davidic borders; in fact, in his Gospel no physical restoration of Israel is expected.

The Song of Simeon (Luke 2:29–32) represents the theological climax of the infancy account. The fulfilment of God's promises brings peace to Simeon, God's servant, who has been waiting for proclamation of the good news of peace, the consolation of Israel (2:25), that is, proclamation of the salvation from God, which is prepared for the world through Israel. Coming in the person of Jesus, this salvation is in fact for the glory of Israel, God's chosen people (v. 32). Thus, the advent of the Messiah to Israel is in accordance with the Abrahamic promises. Though salvation will eventually come to the Gentiles, they will witness it (v. 31) before they share it (v. 32; Johnson 1977, 86–91). And thus Israel is the destined light to the Gentiles, who are still differentiated from Israel (v. 32). Simeon's prophecy to Mary in verse 34 reveals something else about the ministry of Jesus—not all Israel will accept the salvation he offers (cf. v. 32). Jesus as the Lord's Christ is destined to cause a division between the people (v. 34), a schism that is part of God's predetermined plan. Despite the promised opposition, God's plan of salvation for Israel and her world will not fail but will redound to Israel's glory. This plan, which God has prepared in the history of all Israel, will be declared "in the sight of all people" (v. 31). What a fitting capstone to the infancy narratives is Simeon's song with the promises contained therein.

The infancy narratives, functioning as a prolog to Luke-Acts, embody a value judgment upon the ministry of Jesus (Franklin 1975, 81). The canticles, the three hymns in Luke 1–2, disclose the theme of the two books: the promise of Israel's restoration is fulfilled in Jesus, the consummation of Old Testament expectations. Israel's hopes of a Davidic savior are about to be fulfilled. Indeed, this present salvation has its roots in Israel's history—in Abraham, the exodus, and David. Nothing less will accrue from the Savior's birth than the realization of the Abrahamic promises by which Israel is to be a world blessing. What we learn from chapters 1–2 is that the old covenant leads to Jesus (Franklin 1975, 85). The hymns and the narratives of circumcision and presentation in the temple indicate that Jesus is fulfilling his expected role in the covenantal community. The activity of the Spirit (1:41, 67; 2:25–27), the awakening of prophecy, which according to tradition had ceased at the close of the Old Testament period until its revival in the messianic age, and the outbursts of joy combine to give these narratives an eschatological flavor. In the temple, Jewish prophecy, represented by Simeon, and piety, represented by Anna, pass favorable judgment upon Jesus. Temple, law, and prophecy all see Jesus as the consolation of Israel (Franklin 1975, 82).

The Ministry of Jesus (Luke 4:14–21:38)

Luke records various events preceding the beginning of Jesus' ministry in 4:14. His birth stands poised between the mighty and the lowly—the mighty Augustus Caesar whose decree prompts Joseph and Mary to go to Bethlehem (2:1–5) and the lowly shepherds who recognize the child's stature (2:8–20). As in Matthew and Mark, Luke follows his account of Jesus' baptism (3:21–22) with one of his temptation (4:1–13). The verse that ends the temptation narrative, and hence the account of Jesus' preparation for ministry, is notable. Luke 4:13 reads, "When the devil had finished all this tempting, he left him [Jesus] until an opportune time." What does this mean? Some suppose incorrectly that Jesus' ministry was free of temptation until the passion, when the activity of Satan is explicitly pronounced (22:3, 31–32). Though after 4:13 the next direct reference to Satan's temptation of Jesus occurs during the Last Supper, "you are those who have stood by me in my trials" (22:28) implies that the temptations have been ministry-long. Thus, the temptations of 4:1–13 are only the beginning of the struggle between Jesus and Satan, and the passion continues Satan's ongoing assault. Equipped with the Spirit, Jesus travels throughout Galilee (4:14) and goes to Nazareth (v. 16), where his public ministry begins.

Self-characterization and Public Recognition

Jesus goes to the synagog in Nazareth on the Sabbath and stands up to read from the prophet Isaiah (Luke 4:16–17). Who is this man? Though in time Jesus will be recognized as a prophet, the Messiah, and the Son, Luke makes sure we do not miss one essential aspect of his identity at the beginning of his ministry. Luke refers to the activity of the Holy Spirit in the account of Jesus' baptism (3:22), temptation (4:1), and travels (4:14). And the account of Jesus' reading in the synagog includes yet another reference to the Spirit (4:18). It is the Spirit's messianic activity that is determinative for the ministry that follows.

Through the receipt of the Holy Spirit at the baptism, Jesus was messianically anointed, that is, empowered for ministry. This empowering was a necessary prelude to Jesus' application of Isaiah 61:1–2 to himself (Luke 4:18–19; Brawley 1987, 7). By omitting "to bind up the brokenhearted" from Isaiah 61:1 and in a different place adding "to release the oppressed" from Isaiah 58:6, Jesus indicates the care with which he chose the words from Isaiah (Luke 4:17–19). When Jesus rolls up the scroll and appropriates its message, he ascribes to himself its reference to the anointing of the Spirit (vv. 20–21), thus alluding to his baptism and his conquest of temptation. Since there are few references to the Spirit in Luke's Gospel after this point (10:21; 11:13; 12:10, 12), this one is important. Jesus' claim regarding the Spirit and his anointing is presented with resounding messianic overtones, indicating that Luke understood anointing in messianic terms. Jesus thus proclaims himself the anointed Messiah.

Jesus also presents himself as the eschatological prophet who will pronounce the ultimate jubilee: "to proclaim the year of the Lord's favor" (Luke 4:19; cf. Lev. 25:8–10). By ending his reading with this phrase, which appears in the middle of Isaiah's sentence, Jesus emphasizes it. His audience would thus have understood his announcement that "today this scripture is fulfilled in your hearing" (v. 21) to mean that the eschatological jubilee year had arrived. But what does this mean? We know that rabbinic traditions linked Isaiah 61:1–3 with the eschaton. The Qumran community also understood Isaiah 61:1–2 as a proclamation of the advent of the kingdom of God in terms of the final jubilee (Brawley 1987, 13). In citing passages that refer to the jubilee year, the Melchizedek text from Qumran (11QMelch) interprets them in light of Isaiah 61:1–2. Melchizedek, who will appear in the tenth jubilee year to proclaim liberty to the captives (Isa. 52:7; 61:1–2; Turner 1981, 19), is represented as the supramundane messiah carrying out the will of God for salvation and judgment and thus bringing the Gentiles' time to an end. Despite the intriguing correspondences, we must not make too much of this reference to the jubilee in Luke, for none other appears in Jesus' ministry. Moreover, in Luke 4:16–30 it is not the *time* that is fulfilled but the Scriptures, the messianic portrait of the advent of the kingdom. Since the last days had arrived, the gift of the last days—the universal outpouring of the Spirit on Israel—could now be expected (Isa. 32:15; 44:3–5; Ezek. 18:31; 36:26–27; 37:14; 39:29; Joel 2:28–29). Jesus had received power to promulgate the messianic forgiveness; this power, the Spirit, is a concomitant of life for those in the kingdom in the new age (Turner 1981, 22).

In Luke 4:18 Jesus identifies one of his tasks as "to preach good news to the poor." How should we define "the poor"? Poverty in the Psalms is generally ascribed to those of inferior position or to the humble. By the exilic period "the poor" is extended metaphorically to designate the great need into which the nation had fallen as a result of the exile (Seccombe 1982, 26). In Isaiah 49:13 the poor ("afflicted ones") seem to be those returning from captivity, and in Isaiah 41:17–20 the poor and the needy seem to be Jacob/Israel. Isaiah 61 supposes that, while the return from exile is imminent, those returning to Jerusalem will be depressed and awaiting God's salvation. Thus, in Isaiah 61 the poor are a particular eschatological community—the suffering exiles, that is, the faithful of Israel who have been spiritually oppressed (Seccombe 1982, 36–39). As evident from Acts 10:34–38, Luke understood the healing of the oppressed to be the result of Jesus' conflict with and victory over demonic forces that hold people in captivity. That the Nazareth sermon in Luke 4:16–30 falls between two encounters with Satan (vv. 1–13, 31–37) is further evidence of Luke's view. Jesus' omission in 4:18 of the words "to bind up the brokenhearted" from Isaiah 61:1 has the effect of emphasizing the good news of release. God grants freedom to the prisoners! From what sort of bondage will the prisoners be released? Since Jesus follows his message of release with an exorcism, it seems clear he means the bondage of Satan.

Luke follows his account of Jesus' reading in the synagog with the reaction of those who heard his words—they "were amazed at the gracious words that came from his lips" (4:22). But is this reaction positive or negative? Many expositors interpret verse 22 positively, suggesting that the crowd turns against Jesus as he reveals the possibility of a Gentile mission (vv. 23–27; Nolland 1989, 198). If verse 22 is approving, however, the statements in verses 23–24 follow strangely. John Nolland suggests that verse 22 is an authorial aside by Luke to explain the synagog congregation's amazement at Jesus' rhetoric (1979, 226–29). At the very least, the possibility exists that Jesus met the unacceptance of his townspeople at once. After establishing the people's incredulity (v. 22), Luke reports the retort of Jesus in verse 23 and the proverb of verse

24, that no prophet is accepted in his own country, that is, Israel. These verses suggest that Jesus' having come from Nazareth, from the people's midst, caused the problem. In verses 25–27 Jesus warns his hearers that the nation is at risk of losing God's blessings, as in the time of Elijah and Elisha, who were also unaccepted at home. These verses serve to sanction Jesus' ministry in the face of rejection. Judged as Elijah and Elisha on the basis of unacceptability, Jesus emerges as a true prophet in Israel!

Jesus clearly does not meet the people's preconceived eschatological expectations! Moreover, his prophecy is unacceptable since he omits the promise of vengeance upon Israel's enemies (Luke 4:18–19; cf. Isa. 61:2b), a preconception of true prophecy that the people would have applauded. In rejecting Jesus, however, his townsfolk reveal his identity as the Messiah and Servant. The pattern of initial acceptance followed by rejection evident in Luke 4 is worked out in the remainder of the Gospel. After chapter 4 Jesus' messianic identity is muted and alluded to rarely. Though the demons know him as the Messiah (4:41), Jesus does not make a direct messianic claim until after the cross (24:26). More prominent in Luke's Gospel is the presentation of Jesus as a prophet. (The issue of Jesus' prophetic identity is taken further and provided with an eschatological setting in Acts.) See, for example, 7:1–8:3, in which the acts of Jesus bear close resemblance to those of Elisha (7:1–10; cf. 2 Kings 5) and Elijah (7:11–16; cf. 1 Kings 17:17–24). After Jesus restores the life of the widow's son (7:14–15), the people claim Jesus as a great prophet (v. 16), thus taking us back to 4:25–26 (Johnson 1977, 98). The miracles to which Jesus refers the messengers of John the Baptist in 7:22 remind us of the warrant of 4:18 and of the deeds that signify the mission of the Messiah as the anointed prophet in Israel. And what of John? He is labeled a prophet in 7:26. Despite his greatness, however, John is preparatory, a forerunner to the great prophet whose coming effects God's visitation. In 7:36–50 Jesus' role as a prophet is evaluated once again. This time Simon rejects Jesus on the basis of his attitude toward the woman of the narrative. What Simon forgets is Israel's history, for the prophetic movement had always posed radical challenges to many of Israel's carefully nurtured positions. In evaluating Jesus' behavior, Simon fails to apply the right criteria. The Book of Acts will later verify that Jesus was not only a prophet, a challenger of popular conventions, but he was the great prophet, even greater than Moses.

The transfiguration in Luke 9:28–36 reveals the nature of Jesus as the Son, who will be rejected. Speaking of his death as an exodus (9:31), Jesus signifies that his departure provides continuity with the history of Israel. The transfiguration itself anticipates the glory into which Jesus would enter after his death (cf. 24:26). Verse 36, the last verse of the account, indicates that only later did the disciples realize the significance of what they had seen—that in Jesus the kingdom of God had come.

As we have seen, Jesus is variously denominated in Luke—as prophet, as Messiah, and as Son of man. "Prophet" was a most useful public affirmation applied to Jesus, since he spoke to the historical circumstances of the day with a peculiar authority as a judgment on the present and future circumstances of Israel (Harvey 1982, 52–63). However, Jesus' claims to authority always took him beyond the narrow prophetic identification. Thus, "prophet" was too limited a title, so much so that the disciples at Caesarea Philippi, while acknowledging the use of such a popular designation, felt constrained to go beyond it. Jesus identified himself as "Messiah" after the crucifixion, when the work of the Messiah had been done (24:26). But above all, it is another title that captures the salvific and eschatological character of Jesus' ministry— Jesus, the Son of man.

Preaching (Luke 9:51–19:27)

More than one third of Luke's Gospel is devoted to the predominantly Lucan material known as the travel narrative (9:51–19:27). It is connected with the ongoing purpose of the Gospel by the pregnant use of the word *analēmpsis*, "ascension," in 9:51: "As the time approached for him to be taken up to heaven." Ambiguity in Luke's text allows us to see herein a possible reference to the cross (cf. the passion prediction in v. 22). But the Gospel of Luke will conclude with the true ascension of Jesus into heaven. Thus, the long approach to Jerusalem will be completed by a quite different "going up." All along the way to the city, Jesus preaches. Though Jerusalem will not recognize Jesus' visitation (19:44), what takes place will climax God's relationship with Israel.

Jesus "set his face to go to Jerusalem" (Luke 9:51 NRSV), an expression echoing previous prophetic encounters with that city (e.g., Jer. 21:10; cf. Ezek. 6:2; 13:17; 15:7). Luke's report of the mission of the seventy (10:1–16), which probably alludes to the table of the nations in Genesis 10, prefigures the universal mission of the church. Chapter 13 stresses the necessity of Israel's repentance or her doom. Verses 22–30 predict unrepentant national Israel's exclusion from salvation and the entry of the Gentiles after Jesus' death. In verses 31–35, which represent the midpiece of the entire travel narrative, Jesus discloses that the prophet must perish in Jerusalem by divine necessity. Indeed, Jesus' death will be brought about, not by Herod, but by Jesus' encounter with Jerusalem (Maddox 1982, 48). And what will be the result? In verse 35 Jesus laments, "Look, your house [Israel's leadership] is left to you desolate."

The parable of the great feast, which addresses entry into the kingdom, throws open the door to the Gentiles, indicating that Israel has rejected the ministry of Jesus and his representatives (14:15–24). By redefining the kingdom and offering it to outsiders, Jesus challenges the privileged and powerful. Luke 16:16 comments further upon entering the kingdom, "everyone tries to enter it by force *(biazetai)*" (NRSV). Though *biazetai* can be translated as either the passive "is taken by force" or the middle "exercises force," the context of the parable, that of the shrewd manager, suggests a middle reading as in "everyone is forcing his way into it" (NIV). Jesus is saying that the old legalistic gates that barred the way to the kingdom are being brought down. Though every risk must be taken to get in, people are trying to force their way in on their own terms.

Eschatological issues emerge in a long discourse on faith that begins in Luke 17:5 and climaxes in 18:8 (Franklin 1975, 16). It is within this discourse that Jesus enigmatically proclaims, "The kingdom of God is within you" (17:21). What does this mean? Since Jesus is addressing the Pharisees, he cannot be speaking of an inward spiritual reality. The statement must mean something like "the kingdom of God is with you, but you must make a personal response." The kingdom will not visibly come, for it is a spiritual reality; signs are useless (v. 20). The kingdom will also not come by rigorous personal legalism, as Pharisaic groups had hoped. What follows in 17:22–37 is an exposition of the coming kingdom in terms of swift judgment (v. 34) to fall upon Jerusalem, the day of the Son of man. Since in verses 22–37 Jesus describes a national, not individual, judgment, he is not referring to the parousia. The bird imagery (vultures or eagles) in verse 37 clearly alludes to the threat that Roman standards pose to Jerusalem (Gaston 1970, 352–53).

The crowd associates Jesus' entry into Jerusalem with the appearance of the kingdom of God (Luke 19:11). By the parable of the ten minas, which follows, Jesus indicates there will be a postponement before an intervention of a kind quite different from what the crowd expects. The parable refers, not to the parousia, but to the return in the hearers' lifetime of the now-acclaimed king, who will bring judgment. Placed where it is, the parable illustrates and interprets Jesus' passion, resurrection, and ascension and prefigures the fall of Jerusalem and the loss of national leadership in A.D. 70 (Johnson 1982, 153–58).

Entry into Jerusalem (Luke 19:28–44)

The three-stage description of Jesus' drawing near to Jerusalem (Luke 19:29–36, 37–40, 41–44), demonstrates the imminence of his encounter with the city. The first stage deals with the acquisition of a colt and the disciples' enthronement of Jesus. When the disciples unloose the colt (19:33), they signify Jesus' appropriation of Judah's blessings from Genesis 49:11. The act of impressment discloses the stature of Jesus, for the impressment of animals was a royal privilege (1 Sam. 8:16). What should we make of the colt? The selection of an unused animal is characteristic of the offerings to be made to the Lord (Giblin 1985, 49). Jesus' mounting the colt in verse 35 recalls the coronation of Solomon (1 Kings 1:33). And the peoples' placing garments on the road (v. 36) indicates a royal progress (2 Kings 9:13). The stage is thus set for the entry of the Messiah!

The second stage records the disciples' messianic acclamation of Jesus and the opposition of the Pharisees. Verses 37–40 resume the movement towards Jerusalem, specifically toward the Mount of Olives. The praise with which the disciples greet Jesus is associated in the context of verse 38 with messianic designation. We know the disciples' response, but what about Jerusalem's? Jerusalem had not recognized the terms for peace on earth (see v. 42). Thus, the Pharisees urge Jesus to silence his disciples (v. 39). In refusing to grant their request, Jesus says, "If they keep quiet, the stones will cry out " (v. 40). This image of the crying stones derives from a context of woes proclaimed against an unjust nation (Hab. 2:11; Giblin 1985, 55).

Luke 19:41, which inaugurates the third stage of the journey, depicts Jesus as weeping over Jerusalem. The time of the visitation, which Jerusalem does not recognize (v. 44), is the day on which God makes known the truth about his relationship to his people (Luke 1:78–79; Giblin 1985, 56). Since Jerusalem does not and will not acknowledge Jesus as the Messiah, the city will be destroyed. Jesus depicts his prophecy of the destruction not in terms of a Roman campaign against Jerusalem but of a divine assault upon Israel in the manner of Psalm 137:9, Isaiah 3:26, and Ezekiel 4:1–2 (Giblin 1985, 56).

Teaching in Jerusalem and Prophecy of the End (Luke 19:45–21:38)

Upon Jesus' arrival in Jerusalem, he teaches in the temple every day (Luke 19:47a). His marked polemic against the high priests and scribes precipitates division between the authorities and the people (19:47b–48; 20:1–44). The central episode of the confrontation with the authorities is Jesus' telling of the parable of the tenants (20:9–19), which prefigures messianic rejection. In 20:1–21:36 Luke presents a sample of Jesus' teaching. Jesus addresses the people but principally the disciples in a major section that extends from 20:45–21:36. Of these verses 21:5–36 is an eschatological discourse. Verses 5–6 provide prediction and verse 7, transition, as the disciples ask Jesus *when* his prediction will be fulfilled and *what* sign will precede it.

Jesus' response is made in three stages. In verses 8–9 Jesus begins to answer their questions. His hearers are not to be deceived by false prophets, wars, and tumults. Though these are part of God's plan for the last days, they are not in themselves an indication that the time is close at hand. Verses 10–28 represent the second stage of Jesus' response. Jesus describes an end-of-this-age scenario in verses 10–11. The signs of verse 11, which are general and typically apocalyptic, recur in Revelation 6 (e.g., vv. 6, 12; Marshall 1978, 765). In verses 12–19 Jesus proclaims the necessity of the disciples' suffering prior to the end, and in verses 20–24 he pronounces judgment on Jerusalem, thereby developing and clarifying verses 10–11a. Though Jesus' description of Jerusalem appears to relate to the Roman siege of A.D. 66–70, some believe he is describing a time that antedates Jerusalem's fall (e.g., Gaston 1970, 358–65). Verses 25–28 develop verse 11b, setting forth concomitants of the siege. Joel 2 is the primary source of the graphic language: the darkening of the sun, moon, and stars (21:25; cf. Joel 2:10); the anguish of men (21:26; cf. Joel 2:6); and cosmic disturbances (21:26; cf. Joel 2:10). The third stage of Jesus' response appears in verses 29–36, in which he proclaims the paradoxical proximity of the kingdom (vv. 29–33) and then concludes with an exhortation (vv. 34–36).

Jesus carefully chose the background for his discourse so as to relate the accompanying cosmological signs to the destruction of Jerusalem. Thus, he uses Old Testament day-of-the-Lord language to describe the coming retribution. Israel must pass through a time of the Gentiles; this has long since been God's way. Divine vengeance, however, leads to divine retribution (Luke 21:31; cf. Zech. 12:3; 1 Macc. 3; 2 Bar. 67; Tiede 1980, 93). The same vengeance that punishes Israel for unfaithfulness will require vindication from the punisher for the sake of God's name in the presence of the Gentiles (Deut. 32:35–36, 39; Tiede 1980, 94).

The Passion, Resurrection, and Ascension (Luke 22–24)

In the Lucan narratives, attacks by Satan frame the beginning (4:1–13) and end of Jesus' ministry. Satan is present at the passion (Luke 22:3, 31, 53; note v. 53, where "the power of darkness" [NRSV] connotes the realm of Satan), indicating that this is a time of eschatological crisis when Satan's activity within Jesus' ministry is brought to a climax. In this war between two kingdoms, Jesus' role has been to despoil Satan and rescue prisoners (11:22). There is absolutely no uncertainty about the outcome of this conflict (10:18), for victory is achieved by the progress of the gospel, which necessitates vindication through suffering.

Jesus bids farewell to his disciples in the context of the Last Supper (Luke 22:7–38). As a Passover supper, the meal proclaims divine covenantal protection, communion, and atonement. At the trial before Caiaphas in 22:54–71, Jesus responds as the Son of man (v. 69), the one rejected on earth but vindicated in heaven (Neyrey 1985, 74), the formal witness in Israel's assembly. Bearing witness to God, Jesus speaks as the Christ, the Son of God, and the Son of man. Thus, he serves as a model for the apostles. Once his testimony is rejected by Israel, the trial of Jesus becomes the trial of Israel. In judging Jesus, Israel judges herself. In verse 69 Jesus prophesies his vindication. Jesus acts as the Davidic king, who as ruler of God's covenant is obligated to exercise judgment (3:17; 10:13–15; 13:27; 19:27; 23:27–31).

In addition to suffering and judging, another act is associated with the passion—the act of saving (Luke 23:35, 39–43). But even salvific activity creates division within Israel, as illustrated by the two crucified criminals. The remarks of the repentant criminal in verses 40–42 constitute a model of faith in Jesus as ruler of God's covenant people and indicates the manner in which messianic blessings are to be conferred. In recognizing Jesus as the Davidic king, the thief is neither deterred nor scandalized by the cross. To the contrary, he petitions for blessing on the basis of it (Neyrey 1985, 140). Accordingly, Jesus promises the criminal forgiveness and eternal life (v. 43), since the Paradise to which he is directed is the abode of the righteous. Jesus thus assumes his kingly reign, not by a return at the parousia, but on the cross. Since Jesus dies as the Christ, he cannot save himself (9:22; 17:25; 24:7). At the end of his life, he cries what every pious Jew uttered at the end of every day, "Father, into your hands I commit my spirit" (23:46; Marshall 1978, 876). This is the moment Jesus knew he must experience when he set out for Jerusalem in 9:51. Indeed from that verse forward the focus of the narrative is on Jerusalem, the city which represents the classic pattern of hostility to God, the city where God's Word is always spurned, and the center where God redeems but is always rejected.

The story of Jesus in Luke's Gospel doesn't end with the crucifixion. Luke tells us of Jesus' burial, resurrection, postresurrection appearances, commissioning of the disciples, and ascension. The Evangelist mentions no appearance in Galilee, but does cite appearances in Jerusalem and the surrounding area. One is on the road to Emmaus. In Luke 24:21 Cleopas's wistful hope of Israel's redemption revives the tenor of Zechariah's benediction (1:68) and of Anna's word in the temple (2:38), but it is Jesus himself who supplies the credal formulary of the early church. Appealing to no particular Old Testament passage but to the general tone of Old Testament messianic expectation, Jesus asks the travelers, "Did not the Christ have to suffer these things and then enter his glory?" (24:26). Christ died for our sins according to the Scriptures! After completing the Emmaus walk, Jesus commissions the disciples to go forth in mission and foretells the gift of the Spirit (24:44–49). In this episode Luke summarizes the teaching of the resurrection appearances (Marshall 1978, 904).

Luke's Gospel reaches its climax with the ascension (24:50–53). Verse 53 is set where the Gospel began—in the temple. In verse 52 Luke refers to worship being offered to Jesus for the first time. Just as the narrative had begun, it ends with pious people blessing Jesus in the house of God. In 9:51 Jesus had set out for Jerusalem "to be received up" (RSV). Yet even after the resurrection this had not yet been accomplished, and we find Jesus still journeying. At last in 24:51 the journey ceases. The significance of the ascension and its meaning for a divine Christology of expectation are taken up at the beginning of the Acts of the Apostles. Luke's Gospel ends with Israel's hopes having been paradoxically fulfilled, with redemption for Israel having been provided (24:21), and with the messianship of Jesus authenticated by his resurrection and exaltation. The stage is set for the advance of the gospel to the Gentiles.

The Bridge to the Acts of the Apostles (Acts 1:1–5)

The beginning verses of Acts link the volume with the Gospel of Luke in various ways. Acts 1:1–5 recapitulates Luke 24:49–53. Verses 1–2 summarize the entire Gospel and link the two volumes by the activity of the Holy Spirit, the mention of which in effect summarizes Acts. Verses 3–4 add information about the period before the ascension—when Jesus appeared to his disciples for forty days, thus establishing them as his successors. The city of Jerusalem provides a further link between the volumes. The very last verse of the Gospel is set in Jerusalem, in the temple. In Acts 1:4–5 Luke reports that Jesus charged the disciples with waiting in Jerusalem for the ministry of the Holy Spirit. This link indicates that the new Christian group, not non-Christian Judaism, carries the blessings and promises formerly given to Israel.

The Acts of the Apostles continues the story of the Messiah and Israel. Indeed, the book reports the consequence of Israel's rejection of her Messiah and the ensuing ministry to the Gentiles. Throughout the book, the ministry to Israel continues, as indicated by references to the kingdom of God, the divine plan for the Messiah's world rule through restored Israel (1:3, 6; 8:12; 14:22; 19:8; 20:25; 28:23, 31). At the beginning of Acts, Jesus speaks to the disciples of the kingdom (1:3); at the end, Paul openly proclaims the kingdom and teaches about the Lord Jesus (28:31). Since the kingdom is so closely related to Spirit, it is not surprising to find references to the Holy Spirit at the beginning (1:2) and end (28:25) of Acts. Through the Spirit, Jesus is closely linked in mission with his disciples, and their acts represent the continuation through the Spirit of his ministry.

The Promise of the Spirit (Acts 1:6–11)

During one of the postresurrection meetings between Jesus and his disciples, he reminds them of the gift promised by God—that of the Holy Spirit (Acts 1:4–5). Verse 6 next records a question they ask of him, "Lord, are you at this time going to restore the kingdom to Israel?" The position of the question between two sayings of Jesus dealing with the gift of the Holy Spirit indicates that the disciples believed the gift would effect the restoration. But what are they asking? Since the disciples had spent much time over the past forty days being taught by Jesus about the kingdom, it is unlikely they are asking a nationalistic question. Quite possibly, the disciples are inquiring about the manner of the restoration as well as about the time. Given the command to remain in Jerusalem and to wait the reception of the Spirit, do the disciples interpret this order as a sure sign of the onset of the last days (Joel 2:28–32)? Is now the time when Jerusalem becomes the world city to which the Gentiles will journey? Is the timetable of Israel's mission to the world now in effect? Is this not the time when divine rule from Jerusalem will proceed? Thus, when told about the Holy Spirit's coming, the disciples naturally and logically think of what constitutes the last days since the coming of the Holy Spirit reinaugurates the prophetic role of Israel as world witness (Tiede 1986, 286). It appears that the disciples simply want to know, When the Spirit comes, will the end come too? (The suggestion that the Spirit is the substitute in Acts for the imminent expectation of the parousia in the Gospels cannot be correct in view of the disciples' question in v. 6.)

Jesus' response to the disciples' query is noncommittal (Acts 1:7–8). He gives no direct answer to the question, though he does correct the disciples' desire to know the times and the seasons. The disciples are not to know the details (v. 7); theirs is the ministry of witness to the widening world (v. 8). As Israel was before (Isa. 43:10), the new community is to be a witness to divine revelation. If perchance the question in 1:6 is evidence of some lingering nationalistic hopes, since restoration often meant a reconstitution of Israel in her own land (as in Jer. 16:15; 24:6; 50:19), the saying in 1:8 would serve to be totally corrective: "You will be my witnesses in Jerusalem, and in all Judea and Samaria, and to the ends of the earth." In Acts 13:47 (cf. Isa. 49:6) the phrase "the ends of the earth" means the Gentile world; presumably it has a similar meaning in 1:8. From this verse emerges the missionary theme to the Jew first and then to the Gentile as a method to be followed, and Luke casts Gentile incorporation into restored Israel as an indication of the arrival of the last days. In Acts the witness begins in Israel (chaps. 2–7), proceeds to Samaria (chaps. 8–11), and then breaks loose from its Palestinian habitation, moving finally to Rome. Though this movement is to the center of the empire, not the ends of the earth, the ending of Acts leaves open the possibility of further movement.

Luke never uses the missionary commission of Acts 1:8 as a measure by which to judge the apostle's activity among the Gentiles, though Paul uses Israel's commission (Acts 13:47; cf. Isa. 49:6) to justify his work among them. In keeping with his own commission (Acts 9:15), Paul witnesses to Gentiles (chaps. 13–20), before kings (chaps. 21–26), and then finally to the people of Israel (chap. 28). Worldwide mission thus appears at the beginning and end of the Book of Acts (1:8; 28:28–31). At the beginning the disciples are not expected to know the times or seasons, but at the end the Jews are expected "to know that God's salvation had been sent to the Gentiles" (28:28), indicating the successful progress of restored Israel's witness.

But what does Luke tell us about the mission to the Gentiles? The reference to it in Luke 24:47 allows no doubt regarding Jesus' intention in Acts 1, and yet in chapter 10 Peter is reluctant to go to the Gentiles. Luke's report thus indicates a historical tension between what ought to have been done and what actually came to pass. That the apostles have to be "sold" on the concept of a Gentile mission after experiencing Pentecost is both extraordinary and indicative of the factuality of the account. By the guidance of God (10:9–16) and by the enterprise of others (8:4–8; 11:19–21; 15:12–21), restored Israel eventually goes out in mission (Wilson 1973, 92). This missionary activity of Israel, a departure from the centripetal program of the Old Testament, was necessitated by national Israel's end as the geographical center for divine revelation. Moreover, after the formal end of the nation in A.D. 70, there was no Promised Land into which converts could come! When the mission finally goes out, who participates? Luke reveals that the Twelve, apart from Peter, are nonparticipants and are reluctant to get involved. They lead and guide the Jerusalem community but are not active in missionary enterprise even in Judea. The Twelve remain in Jerusalem, even when the church is scattered by persecution. What this reveals is striking. The mission activity was not an organizational response by the early Christians to the supposed delay of the parousia; on the contrary, it emerged from the direct involvement of the Spirit of Jesus in the life of restored Israel, just as Jesus proclaims in 1:8.

In Acts 1:9 Luke reveals what happened to Jesus after meeting with his disciples: "He was taken up before their very eyes, and a cloud hid him from their sight." That Luke considers the ascension in both his Gospel and Acts signals its theological importance. Though the accounts are similar, they are not identical. However, the differences are capable of being harmonized as they arise out of their respective narrative contexts. Let's briefly examine where the accounts coincide and differ. There is correspondence regarding the command to wait for the Spirit (Acts 1:4; cf. Luke 24:49), the witness to all nations (Acts 1:8; cf. Luke 24:47–48), the departure of Jesus (Acts 1:9; cf. Luke 24:51), and the disciples' return to Jerusalem (Acts 1:12; cf. Luke 24:52). Though apparent chronological differences emerge regarding the postresurrection appearances (Acts 1:3–11; cf. Luke 24:36–49), the Gospel account should be viewed as a summary of such appearances (Marshall 1978, 904). There is no dialog between Jesus and the disciples in Luke (24:36–49; cf. Acts 1:6–8). And the raising of the hands and the blessing at the end of Luke (24:50) are missing from Acts. In Luke Jesus "left them" at Bethany "and was taken up into heaven" (24:50–51); in Acts Jesus "was taken up" from the Mount of Olives (1:9, 12). The mention of the cloud and the two heavenly messengers in Acts 1:9–10 is missing from Luke. In Luke the disciples return to the temple (24:53), and in Acts to the upper room (1:13). Despite the differences, in both accounts Luke casts the ascension as an event that fulfils the heart of Israel's expectations (Franklin 1975, 41).

What is significant about Luke's account of the ascension in Acts 1:9–11 is its particular presentation. The Son of man ascends in a cloud to the right hand of the Father. This exaltation completes his ministry and ushers in the new era, in which the hopes of Israel will be realized. Indeed, the exaltation appears to enact the scenario of Daniel 7:13–14: The books will be opened. Based on response to the gospel, judgment will be passed, and the verdict of the high court of heaven will be handed down in individual cases. In Acts 1:10–11 two angels then appear to help the disciples grasp what they have seen and to announce for the first time that Jesus, the Son of man, will return to inaugurate the messianic reign at his parousia. The importance of this announcement of the parousia is evidenced by the presence of the two angels, which links the return of Jesus and the resurrection (cf. Luke 24:4).

The Gift of the Spirit (Acts 2)

With the election of a twelfth disciple to replace Judas (Acts 1:15–26), the nucleus of restored Israel is reconstituted, and the mission to Israel beginning from Jerusalem is yet another step closer. Soon thereafter about 120 followers of Jesus (1:15), including the Twelve, meet together on Pentecost (2:1). Originally a harvest festival, Pentecost came to be a celebration of the giving of the law. It is not surprising, therefore, to find Sinai and Pentecost connected in various intertestamental texts (e.g., Jub. 1:1, 5; 6:1–21; 15:1–24). Thus, the group gathers to celebrate the anniversary of Yahweh's revelation of law to Israel. What happens next is surely a divine act, as revealed by language of wind and fire that was integral to Old Testament theophanies (Lincoln 1985, 204–5)—"a violent wind came from heaven" (2:2) and "tongues of fire" (v. 3). The Spirit of God descends on the group.

Pentecost represents the miracle that effects a repentant and reestablished Israel, adding it to the existing nucleus. All 120 Jews (Acts 2:5, 14, 22) in the group, not just the Twelve, receive the Spirit, for the promise as stated by Peter is to *all* (2:38–39). (Gentiles receive the Spirit for the first time in Acts 10:45.) The outpouring of the Spirit is associated with the gift of prophecy, and the repetition of "will prophesy" in verses 17–18, as Peter interprets the event in terms of Joel 2:28–32, underscores this. The expected restoration of Israel to her prophetic vocation as proclaimed in Isaiah 49:6 thus is effected by this spiritual endowment (Tiede 1986, 286). All in the house and all of Israel are to hear and proclaim the basic message of renewal and eschatological blessing.

What happened at Pentecost does not reverse Babel (Gen. 11:1–9), for the confusion of tongues is not remedied. But what happened does appear to shift the emphasis from law to Spirit in the life of restored Israel, and the Spirit becomes the replacement for Jewish law. Moreover, the world will be universally affected by the Pentecost event because "Jews from every nation under heaven" (Acts 2:5) are represented and what has happened now to Israel is a paradigm for the Spirit of prophecy to descend in these last days "on all people" (v. 17). The event sets the character of the new age, prescribing the way in which God will meet the new people of God, that is, in mission led by the Spirit. In Acts there are additional accounts of the bestowal of the Spirit (4:23–31; 8:14–17; 10:44–48; 11:15–18; 19:1–7); these "mini-Pentecosts" occur at crucial stages of missionary expansion. And the Spirit intervenes at other critical points (e.g., 8:29, 39; 10:19–20; 11:12; 13:2, 4; 16:6–7; 20:22–23). Indeed, it is the gift of the Holy Spirit that initiates the mission at Pentecost and gives the mission shape. Through this gift, Jesus will direct the work of the churches. Not so much a personal gift to believers, the Spirit is the link between Jesus and his disciples and the means by which Jesus is able to continue his messianic forgiveness (Turner 1982, 180–81).

The evidence of the working of the Spirit, the paradoxical force of the presence of God in history, leads at Pentecost to the mocking, amazement, and perplexity of the crowd (Acts 2:12–13). Their reaction, however, doesn't alter the circumstance that is described clearly by Peter—the eschaton has arrived. In the manner of Jesus' programmatic speech at Nazareth (Luke 4:16–19), which introduced and anticipated the character of his ministry and interpreted the coming of the Spirit upon him in terms of messianic activity in Israel, Peter's speech in Acts 2:14–39 foreshadows the missionary expansion to occur through the preaching ministry of the disciples. He begins by announcing that the Pentecost gift fulfils Joel 2:28–32. The charter of Israel to be a prophetic witnessing community, which was anticipated by Joel, is thus also fulfilled. While Judaism would have been acquainted with the concept of a messiah who receives the Spirit, Peter speaks of something unparalleled in Jewish experience, that is, the Messiah who directs the work of the Spirit (Turner 1982, 182–83).

Peter's use and revision of Joel tell us much about the apostle's understanding. By adding "in the last days" at 2:17 (cf. Joel 2:28), Peter demonstrates that he has perceived the eschatological character of the outpouring of the Spirit and that he has responded to the postresurrection teaching on the kingdom of God, which he received from Jesus. The manifestation of the Spirit is the climactic event for which the prophetic Moses had wished (Num. 11:29), and Peter recognizes the outpouring as the sign by which the appearance of the last days can be gauged. Thus, the repeated manifestations of the Spirit and the subsequent witnessing in the Book of Acts are expressions of the eschatological character of the Christian movement. Peter makes two other significant alterations to Joel. In verse 18 Peter adds the words "and they will prophesy" to Joel 2:29. By doing so, Peter defines the Spirit as the eschatological gift of prophecy given to what is now the new prophetic community. Thus, the gift of prophecy equips the people of God for ministry, for their prior conversion is presupposed. In verse 19 Peter adds "and signs" to Joel 2:30 so that the verse reads, "I will show wonders in the heaven above and signs on the earth below." This "signs and wonder" terminology is used commonly in the Septuagint in descriptions of the efficacy of the Word of God in the exodus. From this revision of Joel, Peter's understanding emerges clearly: Once again the people of God, the possessors of a new covenant, are on the move. The promised Spirit will lead Christians forward into a New Canaan. Israel may once again lay claim to the blessing of rest in God's presence, the onset of which this time will signify creation renewed. Verse 21 reads, "And everyone who calls on the name of the Lord will be saved" (cf. Joel 2:32a). Since salvation in Christ sums up all that this great development in eschatological reality means for the new community, Peter concludes his citation of Joel at this point.

Calling on the name of the Lord signifies faith in Jesus, who has been raised (Acts 2:24) and who is, therefore, the eschatological son of David of Psalm 16:8–11 (cf. Acts 2:25–28). Jesus has been given dominion as Messiah in accord with Psalm 110:1 (v. 25) and reigns in this new age, fulfilling the mandate of Genesis 1:26–28. The Spirit, available to all Israel, is now the means of Jesus' presence and activity. Peter thus proclaims a divine Christology as he depicts Jesus as the messianic ruler under whose feet God subjugates all Jesus' enemies (2:34–36), thus completing the work of the messianic age. Established conclusively by the ascension, the divinity of Jesus is the foundation upon which are built the theological conclusions of the early preaching in Acts. On the basis of the ascension all the house of Israel is to recognize this paradox—that the crucified Jesus is now Lord (the word used in the LXX for "Yahweh") and Christ, that is, God and yet Messiah (v. 36).

Peter concludes his speech by reiterating the promise of the gift of the Holy Spirit (Acts 2:39). Let's put the promise in context before looking at it. Christians were convinced that God's promises to Israel were fulfilled through the resurrection of Jesus. The promise of an eternal kingdom and a Davidic king to sit upon the Davidic throne (Luke 1:32–33, 69) had been fulfilled through the ascension. However, the promises and blessings to Israel can be traced back further than to David. The blessing in Luke 1:68–79, for example, is a remembrance of the oath sworn to Abraham (see Luke 1:72–73). Indeed, all the messianic promises to Israel stem from the basic promise to Abraham (Acts 13:32–33; cf. Luke 19:9). Evidence of this promise to Abraham emerges in the Pentecost event, which lays the foundation for the apostolic ministry to the Gentiles. Recalling the terms of the Abrahamic covenant, Peter concludes his speech in Acts 2 with these words: "The promise is for you and your children and for all who are far off—for all whom the Lord our God will call " (v. 39). The promise, that is, the gift of the Holy Spirit, goes first to Israel, but since reconstituted Israel is missionary Israel, the promise extends beyond Israel "to all that are far off" (Parker 1978, 57–58). In process of restoration, Israel is called to come out of her "corrupt generation" (v. 40), out from bankrupt national Israel. And these converted Jews will provide the nucleus of the new theocratic community.

Witness in Jerusalem (Acts 3:1–8:1a)

God's promises to Abraham and to the patriarchs is a motif that runs through Luke-Acts. In keeping with the promises, the early Christian movement first offers salvation to Israel. Accordingly Acts 3:1-8:1a records activity of the Jerusalem church. The accounts of the miracle at the gate (3:1–10) and of Peter's teaching in the temple complex (3:11–26) demonstrate the desire of the early church to maintain continuity with Israel. After the death of Stephen and the ensuing persecution (7:60–8:1), salvation is offered to the Gentiles, enabling them to call upon the name of Israel's Lord (11:17–18; 20:21; 26:20).

Peter at Solomon's Colonnade (Acts 3:11–26)

Peter's sermon underscores the Abrahamic origins of the gospel, for the disciple seizes the opportunity provided by the miraculous healing of the lame man to speak of the return of Christ as the time for Israel's restoration of all that God had promised the patriarchs and had spoken through the mouths of his holy prophets. Converted Jews, repentant Israel, form the nucleus of the church (v. 19). And it is their repentance, and later the repentance of others, that brings about the time of refreshing, which lasts until Jesus comes at the full restoration: "Repent, then, and turn to God, so that your sins may be wiped out, that times of refreshing may come from the Lord, and that he may send the Christ, who has been appointed for you—even Jesus. He must remain in heaven until the time comes for God to restore everything, as he promised long ago through his holy prophets" (vv. 19–21). What does this Scripture mean? Misunderstanding verses 20–21 and thereby labeling them "the most primitive Christology of all," some interpret them to mean that Jesus becomes the Christ, the Messiah, only at the parousia (Robinson 1961, 146–47). However, a statement of Christ's suffering (v. 18) precedes verses 20–21, indicating that Jesus' messiahship was endorsed by his suffering (cf. Luke 24:26). Verses 20–21, therefore, represent "the most primitive eschatology of all" (Bruce 1974, 68). Looking to the future, Peter reveals that heaven will retain the exalted Jesus until the time of the end, that is, the restoration of all things (v. 21).

What is to be restored, and when will the restoration take place? Jacob Jervell claims that Israel *had* been restored by the gift of the end-time Spirit in the early chapters of Acts (1972, 53), which we can accept as true but only in a proleptic sense when we consider the theological potential of the events in Acts 1–2. Among others, Arthur Wainwright argues that the full restoration of Israel could hardly have preceded the destruction of Jerusalem, which according to Luke meant the end of the nation (1977, 77). The restoration contemplated in Acts 3:21 is broader than the restoration of Israel and must refer to the parousia. However, the choice of the Twelve and the new community's reception of the end-time Spirit brought into being the form that restored Israel would take. Though restoration has begun, the final restoration of the true Israel lies ahead, as confirmed by the Old Testament expectation that the last times will be consummated by the restoration of Jerusalem and the world's recognition of it as the city of God (Isa. 65:17–19; Dan. 8:9–14; cf. Rev. 21:1–22:5). Times of refreshing for Israel and her world have commenced through the apostolic mission and will continue until the full restoration takes place with the return of Jesus.

In Jewish thought, restoration went hand in hand with expectation of an eschatological prophet. Peter's reference to restoration in Acts 3:21 leads quite naturally then to his contention that Jesus is the end-time prophet (v. 22). Though in the Gospel of Luke the title *prophet* is freely applied to Jesus, it is done so only by Jesus himself (4:24; 13:33) and by nonbelievers and the unenlightened (7:16, 39; 9:8, 19; 24:19). And the transfiguration narrative in Luke magnifies Jesus over two Old Testament prophetic representatives, namely, Moses and Elijah (9:35, with allusions to Deut. 18:15). But the risen Jesus of Acts 3 is no mere prophetic representative. Jesus is more than a prophet, more than a proclaimer of judgment to the nation, for he is the end-time prophet, the final divine representative with a ministry to Israel, who was antic-ipated by Moses in Deuteronomy 18:15, and the climax of God's saving activity through the prophetic line. In verse 26 Peter extends his por-trayal of Jesus to include the title *Servant* (cf. 3:13; 4:27). (Philip applies the title to Jesus in his exposition of Isaiah in Acts 8:32–35.) The refer-ence to the Servant in Acts 3:13 alludes to the suffering Servant. Refer-ences in Acts 4 allude to the Davidic king (vv. 25, 27). Although in 3:26 Peter most likely alludes to the suffering Servant, the royal connota-tions may be present as well. In Acts, therefore, Luke describes a royal but suffering Servant, an image that first emerges in Isaiah 40–55. And the paradoxical success of the Servant's mission has led to the inclusion of the Gentiles and to universal restoration. At the end of her history, Israel disowned and killed the Servant (Acts. 3:13), but he had been ap-pointed a portion with the great (Isa. 53:12), had seen the travail of his soul, and had been satisfied. Now resurrected, the Servant speaks as prophet and Messiah through his apostles in the climax of prophetic forgiveness.

Stephen's Defense and Death (Acts 7:1–8:1a)

In Acts 7:2–53 Stephen's speech, a defense against the twofold charge of denigrating the temple and the law, marks the turning point in the ministry to national Israel and prepares us for the Christian commu-nity's decisive break with Judaism. By its tenor and images, the speech betrays Stephen's knowledge of Israel's relationship with God. The bur-den the speech bears, however, is Stephen's conviction that Israel has consistently rejected God's will and his messengers and has constantly broken the law. Thus, Stephen sets forth Israel's history as a tragedy of lost opportunities.

The bulk of Stephen's speech focuses on preconquest Israel, from which we can infer that Israel's national character had been formed before entry into the Promised Land. A promising start had been made with Abraham. God gave him "a covenant of circumcision" (Acts 7:8) with the intended goal of Israel's worship of God in the Promised Land—they will "serve me in this place" (v. 7 KJV). That is, Abraham's call, which culminated in the exodus, was meant to have been consummated by the building of the temple in Canaan (Tannehill 1985, 80). Though God had given Abraham a covenant of circumcision, Israel would prove to be uncircumcised in heart (v. 51). Stephen describes Israel's remarkable preservation in spite of her blatant idolatry, reminding his Jewish prosecutors how God had acted outside of Palestine in remarkable ways for Abraham (vv. 2–8), Joseph (vv. 9–14), and Moses (vv. 20–41). It was in Egypt where Israel multiplied (v. 17) and experienced God's deliverance (v. 36). Indeed, not even Israel's famed law had been given to her in the Promised Land (v. 38). In regard to Moses, Stephen refers to the building of the tabernacle, the pattern of worship that God gave to Israel (v. 44), even though on Sinai Israel had succumbed to idolatry. By the time Solomon built the temple, national patterns had become fixed, which leads to Stephen's appraisal that Israel simply looked upon the temple as a house, a purely human edifice (v. 47). The flagrant desert idolatry and the sophisticated temple apostasy differed thus only in degree. Stephen uses these various examples to make his point that neither the Promised Land nor the institutions Israel developed in it were constitutive of the true Israel. Israel, her institution, her place in history, and the land were all the result of divine election outside the land. Moreover, neither the land nor the temple could account for God's presence among his people. The problem was not the temple, but Israel's failure to understand the nature of God's presence and the factors that conditioned it. Without such understanding the temple was simply a human artifact exposed to the depredations of history (v. 48).

What is required of Israel, Stephen sees so clearly, is a pattern of worship not "made with hands" (Acts 7:48 KJV). Jesus is the new temple to whom the dying Stephen looks. His assertion that Jesus now occupies the place of power at God's right hand in heaven and is now the vindicated Son of man to whom universal dominion has been given, not his critique of the temple, leads to Stephen's death. The belief that the glory of God cannot be confined to a house (vv. 48–49) is confirmed in Stephen's martyrdom. Before his death, Stephen looks through the open heavens and sees the presence of the glorified Son of man himself standing where Daniel prophesied he would be (vv. 55–56; cf. Dan. 7:13–14). At God's right hand, Jesus has been entrusted with dominion, a kingdom, and vindication of his saints.

Witness beyond Jerusalem (Acts 8:1b–28:31)

The persecution that follows upon the death of Stephen moves Christians out of Jerusalem (Acts 8:1b). Then through the Spirit, the old breach between north and south is healed, and the Samaritans are incorporated by Peter and John into the new people of God, the messianic people (8:14–25). Saul's conversion then occurs between this phase of the ministry to Samaria and the beginning of the Gentile mission (9:1–22). The ministry to the Gentiles proper begins with the episode of Cornelius in 10:1–48, sometimes called the Gentile Pentecost. Here at the beginning of the Gentile mission, Peter's apostolic ministry finds its climax. Thus, Peter, who moves the gospel witness beyond Jerusalem to Samaria, Judea, and Phoenicia, dominates the first half of Acts (chaps. 1–12).

In the second half of Acts Paul becomes the elect witness, and thus the ideal Israelite whose story has been prepared for by Barnabas and Stephen. Throughout the Gentile mission, Jewish rejection of the gospel is clear, but in Acts Paul never absolutely rejects the Jews. Nor does Christianity reject the law, though it is critical of it. Luke pictures Christianity as standing on the shoulders of Judaism, and the myriads of Jews who were converted early attest to the truth of the gospel and its compatibility with the religion of Israel. Indeed Paul's initial missionary sermon in the synagog at Pisidian Antioch (Acts 13:16–41) emphasizes the continuity between Christianity and the salvation history of Israel, and this becomes Paul's consistent missionary stance. However, Paul's conception of the sure blessings of David (v. 34) is not a restored Davidic kingdom with its center in Jerusalem but an eschatological kingdom based on Christ's resurrection and enthronement as the Son of God (Krodel 1986, 244). For Paul, the marks of Jesus' universal reign as Messiah are found in the message of salvation (vv. 32–34); they are equality in faith for Jew and Gentile and the forgiveness of sins (vv. 38–39).

The early Christians broke with Jerusalem during the time represented between Acts 12:25 and 13:1. Chapters 13–14 record events of Paul's first missionary journey, the results of which provoke the crisis meeting of chapter 15. Paul's Gentile mission generates controversy, for some Christian Pharisees (15:5) challenge the salvation of the uncircumcised Gentiles. That is, these challengers view Jesus as the Messiah of a circumcised people. Paul and Barnabas are sent to Jerusalem in response.

Acts 15 does not legitimate a Gentile mission; however, it does defend Paul against opposition generated by his mission. Results of the proceedings are summed up in the speeches of Peter and James. In his speech (15:7b–11), Peter proclaims that the law of Moses, even though it is a burden gladly accepted by the Jews (Nolland 1980, 110), is not and never had been the basis of salvation (v. 10). Salvation for all is by that grace in which Jewish Christians and Gentiles alike believe (v. 11), that is, the grace that had also come to Cornelius. Peter's reference to the Holy Spirit's earlier legitimation of the Gentiles silences the opposition (vv. 8, 12a). What follows in verses 13–21 constitutes the high point of the chapter. For James, the problem to be resolved is, How do the Gentile converts relate to Israel? That is, can they in fact continue as redeemed without a change in life-style? His basic point appears in verse 14—God had taken to himself a people (*laos*) from the Gentiles who now belong to him as does Israel (Dahl 1958, 326). By using *laos*, a word customarily used for Israel, James links the new people, the Gentiles, to Israel. This means that believing Gentiles now have a share of Israel's hope. James then uses Amos to further his argument (Acts 15:16–18; cf. Amos 9:11–12). Arguing that the kingdom of the Messiah ("David's fallen tent" in v. 16) presently being established is clearly not national in character, James identifies two groups within the kingdom: (1) "the remnant of men" (v. 17) and (2) "all the Gentiles who bear my name" (v. 17). (The word *kai* [and] in v. 17 is not epexegetical and two groups are identified. The soteriological concept of the remnant is limited in the Old Testament to an Israelite group within Israel, a group in which Gentiles do not figure. (In the Old Testament, the word *remnant* is used in connection with the Gentiles only in contexts of judgment [Braun 1977, 120].) To this nucleus of the restored Israel, the Gentiles are added.

James fully recognizes the emergence of a new people in full continuity with the remnant of Israel. Aware of the possible problems when the groups join in fellowship, James proposes that the observance of certain regulations be required of Gentile converts (Acts 15:20). These regulations concern the problem of ritual defilement, as the Jews would perceive it, and not the invoking of the resident-alien prohibitions of Leviticus 17, as some have argued (Wilson 1983, 75). As far as we know, the regulations of verse 20 were never required of proselytes to Judaism in the first century A.D.; so, James is not promoting the application of existing strictures (Wilson 1983, 86). Moreover, this sole obligation required of the Gentiles, that is, the regulations, does not address any question regarding the Gentiles' relationship to the law; it is simply an attempt to prevent problems of Christian fellowship. Remember that in an earlier episode with Cornelius Peter had pronounced salvation as not dependent on the law (10:34–35, 43). And the apostolic council recognized the Gentiles, apart from the law, as full heirs of salvation and as members of the people of God (Wilson 1973, 193). James ends his speech with these words, "For Moses has been preached in every city from the earliest times and is read in the synagogues on every Sabbath" (v. 21), which possibly means that Moses has enough preachers and there is no need to preach him and the law. If this is the case, then James recognizes, as Peter already had, that only Jesus, not Jesus *and* the law, has to be preached to the Gentiles, for the messianic reign transcends law, and nowhere in Acts is the Spirit said to enforce the law.

After the council at Jerusalem, the Christian mission extends to western Asia and Europe (Acts 15:36–19:41). The call of Paul is to both Jews and Gentiles (9:15; 22:21; 26:17–18, 23), and he, too, witnesses to the Jews first. And we surmise from Acts that Luke knows nothing of an independent Gentile mission disassociated from Israel, for he depicts Paul's missionary enterprise as one to the Jewish Diaspora which also reaches out to Gentiles. In 21:15–28:31 Paul witnesses in Jerusalem, Caesarea, and Rome. Brought to trial on political and religious charges, Paul defends his orthodoxy, and his life bears out the claim. Indeed, the Bible portrays him as an exemplary Jew who takes a vow (Acts 18:18), is purified (Acts 21:26), takes alms to his people (Rom. 15:25–27), and apologizes for speaking against the high priest (Acts 23:5). Charges against Paul's orthodoxy are easily rebutted. Paul even upholds the Pharisaic belief in the resurrection of the dead as the basis of Jewish hope, but he recognizes that hope as fulfilled by the resurrection of Jesus the Messiah (23:6; 24:15; 26:8). What happened to Paul, of course, is his conversion. He narrates it in Acts 22. The crowd listens until Paul recounts his being sent to the Gentiles; then the people revolt (vv. 21–23). Trial narratives in 23:1–25 and chapters 25–26 follow the same pattern (O'Toole 1978, 155). Like Christ before him, Paul is led before officialdom, suffers, and announces salvation for Israel and then for the Gentiles (O'Toole 1978, 157). According to Paul, the reason for his arraignment is his hope for Israel (23:6), which is sustained by the Messiah's resurrection from the dead; virtually the same reason appears in the trial before Agrippa (26:6–7). In his preaching, Paul always makes it clear that the resurrection of Jesus fulfilled the promises to Israel, was prophesied in the Old Testament, and was part of the Davidic messianic promise (13:33) as well as a precursor of the general resurrection (26:23).

The gospel precedes Paul to Rome; so, Acts is concerned, not with its movement to Rome, but with the circumstances that take Paul there. Despite the journey to Rome, Jerusalem remains the center for Paul (Acts 9:26–29; 11:27–30; chap. 15; 21:15), even when he is in Rome

(28:17). Paul's arrival in Rome caps his role as God's chosen instrument to testify before Gentiles and kings and the people of Israel. And Luke demonstrates how Paul executes God's plan without forsaking Judaism, for Paul's defense emphasizes his Jewishness (24:5, 14–15) and his loyalty as a Jew (26:4–7, 22). Jewish opposition simply furthers the purposes of God for Paul, who stands as the legitimate heir of the hope of the patriarchs (26:6, 22).

Salvation and the Jews in Luke-Acts

We may now summarize the theological movement in Luke's two volumes. The Gospel relates the story of the salvation brought by Jesus, and Acts traces its progress to the Gentiles. Another current also runs through the two-volume work, that is, the story of the offering of salvation to the Jews. As early as the Song of Simeon (Luke 2:29–32), the missions to the restored kingdom of Israel and the nations are interrelated. The familiar pattern of mission emerges from the Nazareth episode in Luke 4:16–30, with the main characteristics being proclamation in the temple or synagog, division among the Jews, rejection, and withdrawal, but progress for the gospel (Krodel 1986, 245). In the synagog of Nazareth, Jesus uses the Old Testament stories of the widow of Zarephath and Naaman the Syrian to indict his Jewish audience and indicate salvation is sent to the Gentiles. Thus, Luke's theological understanding of Jew and Gentile is fully developed in Luke 4: God's salvation will enrich the Gentiles but not the Jews, because of Jewish unbelief. The travel narrative of Luke 9:51–19:27 is framed by Samaritan unbelief at the beginning (9:52–56), which is excusable, and Jewish unbelief at the end (19:11–27), which is not. The journey leads to Jerusalem, where Jesus dies as Israel for Israel. At the end of the Gospel Jesus proclaims that the way is now clear for the forgiveness of sins to go from Jerusalem to all the Gentiles (24:44–49).

At the beginning of Acts, the apostles question Jesus about the restoration of Israel. His response in 1:7–8 does not mean that Israel is *beyond* restoration, but that the matter should not concern the apostles, for the timing is in the hands of God and the Messiah (cf. 3:19–21). The biblical witness reveals that the gospel was first preached to the Jews; after all, they had the prophecies by which the Christian claims could be tested and interpreted. Jervell's suggestion that there was no period in which the gospel was offered to Jews alone, because from the beginning Gentiles were part of renewed Israel and shared in the blessings of salvation, is not supported by Luke's record (1972, 43, 61). Indeed, Jesus' first followers are Jews (2:5, 11, 14). As the mass conversions in chapters 1–9 illustrate (2:41, 47; 4:4; 5:14; 6:1, 7; 9:42), myriads of them do convert. Moreover, as Christianity emerges out of Judaism in Acts 6–12, Jewish opposition to the gospel gradually grows.

An early Jewish openness to the message of Jesus is replaced by apostasy and infidelity. Jervell's depiction of a divided Israel is correct (1972, 61). In the early chapters of Acts, the opposition is generously called ignorance (3:17). By Stephen's period, however, the Jews are denounced as incorrigible (7:51). Conflicts between Jews and Christians increase. Chapters 12–28 depict the pervasive hostility of the Jews to the gospel and how this forces Paul to turn to the Gentiles. But the turning is not a rejection of the Jews, for it is part of the divine plan to reach the Gentiles. Consider the synagog rejection that appears in 13:46–51, 18:6, and 19:9. This is not an absolute rejection of Israel that results in the Gentile mission, for the turn to the Gentiles had already begun, was part of a decided missionary strategy, and was temporary, that is, lasted until another city was reached and the proclamation order of to the Jew first was resumed (Krodel 1986, 248). Moreover, the rejection scenes in 13:1–19:10 do not indicate that Judaism was rejected once and for all (Richard 1984, 198). For example, Paul's rejection of the Jews and turn to the Gentiles in 13:46, 18:6, and 19:9 appear to be customary forms of his missionary preaching. To be sure, the Jewish response was disappointing, for the witness reveals that the Jews were resistant (Sanders 1984, 109). The only certain references to Jewish conversions beyond chapter 9 appear in 14:1, 17:11–12, and 18:8. Though Jervell argues that "persuading the Jews" (13:43; 17:4; 18:4; 19:26; 28:23–24; 1972, 71) refers to conversion, this is not Paul's usual way of expressing it (Sanders 1984, 108). Also, it is not clear that 12:24 and 19:20 refer to the conversion of Jews—they note the growth and multiplication of the Word; and 21:20, which refers to Jewish converts previously made, appears to be a recapitulation of the successes recorded in chapters 1–9 (Parsons 1987, 164).

The disappointing failure to win converts would certainly have justified the content of Paul's closing speech to the Jews in Rome (Acts 28:25–29), but the shift from Israel to the Gentiles does not mean that Paul's openness to Israel has been withdrawn or that Israel is excluded from subsequent missions. As one might expect, interpretations of that final speech vary widely. Jervell argues that the speech leaves room for hope (1972, 63), while Parsons sees none, for "despite the bright happiness of the early chapter, it is the end of the story which is most impressive" (1987, 169; also see Tyson 1992, 176–78). David Moessner cites the use of Isaiah 6:9–10 in Acts 28:26–27 as evidence of final judgment on Israel (1988, 96–104). However, for Paul, the believing Jews and unbelieving Jews are still Israel at the end of Acts. The believing ones form the eschatological remnant designed to provoke Israel to repentance, and some still respond. What, then, is the point of citing Isaiah 6:9–10? It is not an isolated statement but the third in a chain of similar statements (13:46; 18:6). Paul uses Isaiah in Acts 28 because he recognizes that the days of fulfilment and the fall of Jerusalem are coming swiftly and that disobedient Judaism will soon experience disaster, but Paul has hope for an obedient remnant (see Gal. 6:16). As a whole, Israel had always been disobedient, but God continued to send prophets to plead with the people. Though Israel rejects Jesus, the crowning point, she is still a people (*laos*) in verses 26–27. Yes, there still is hope. In chapter 28 Judaism is not rejected for all time, and there could still be repentance and forgiveness (cf. 5:31). The stage is set at the end of Acts for the fulfilment of Luke 19:44, the chastisement of Jerusalem as God had done in 587/586 B.C., for Israel as a whole has failed to recognize the moment of her visitation. Yet, Paul is still concerned for the nation at 28:17, and Christianity is still the hope of Israel at 28:20. Luke leaves the matter of mission to Israel open-ended. Though the ears of national Israel and her leadership seem closed and their eyes blind, mission to Israel is possible as long as they have Moses and the prophets (Richard 1984, 199).

In keeping with prophetic expectations for the eschaton, Gentiles were entering the reconstituted Israel. The expectation of a pilgrimage to Jerusalem was observed in spirit by means of the collection for the city (Rom. 15:16, 25; 1 Cor. 16:1–4), since the dissolution of Israel as a geographical entity made physical compliance with the prophetic hopes impossible. And Simeon's hope that Israel would be a light to lighten the Gentiles (Luke 2:32) became and continued to be the guiding principle of the apostolic missions.

10

Johannine Eschatology

Everything found in the Gospel of John has been recorded for a single purpose—"that you may believe that Jesus is the Christ, the Son of God, and that by believing you may have life in his name" (John 20:31). That is, upon finishing the Gospel, the reader will recognize Jesus of Nazareth as Israel's divine Messiah, "for salvation is," as Jesus remarks to the Samaritan woman, "from the Jews" (4:22). Those who believe in Jesus' name, those whose lives are profoundly changed by receiving him, are given the "power to become children of God" (1:12 NRSV; Vellanickal 1977, 120). In this way, Israel is both restored and transformed.

The Logos and the New Israel (John 1:1–18)

The prolog, the lengthy theological introduction to John's Gospel, begins by introducing Jesus as the divine, preexistent Logos (v. 1) and ends by identifying him as the incarnate "only begotten God" (v. 18, the most probable textual reading). Thus, the statement of Jesus' deity introduces the Gospel and effects the transition between the prolog and the narration of the earthly ministry, which begins in 1:19.

Within the prolog, the focus shifts from the role of Jesus in creation (vv. 1–3), to his gifts to us through the incarnation (vv. 4–5), to the witness of John the Baptist (vv. 6–8), to Jesus' entry into the world (vv. 9–11). After the summary statement of verses 12–13, the Evangelist reverses his reflection, moving from the incarnation (v. 14), to the witness of John (v. 15), to Jesus' gifts to us (v. 16), to Jesus' role and his relationship to the Father (vv. 17–18; Vellanickal 1977, 132–36). What the prolog provides is a context for reading about the events of the life of Jesus—that being a postresurrection understanding of Jesus as the divine Messiah of Israel.

Entry into the World (John 1:1, 10–13)

John 1:1 proclaims Jesus as transcendent, powerful, permanent, and unchanging: "In the beginning was the Word (*logos*), and the Word was with God, and the Word was God." The Logos appears four times in the New Testament, always in Johannine literature. In verse 1 the Logos is preexistent; in verse 14 the Logos is incarnate. One John 1:1–3 describes the early community's encounter with the earthly life and ministry of the Logos, and Revelation 19:13 depicts the Logos as the victorious Messiah. As a religious/philosophical concept, *logos* has roots in a number of traditions. To the Stoics, *logos* was the cosmic reason, the mind at the center of the universe. And they believed a fragment of the *logos* resides in every human being. In the Old Testament, the Word (*dābār* in the Hebrew Bible; *logos* in the LXX) of God brings everything into being. In later thought, Wisdom is the personification of one of the attributes of God and is identified with the Word of God (Wis. 9:1–2) Thus, the Word is the revelation of God, which as divine Wisdom enlightens. Identified as the Logos, Jesus is the embodiment of divine revelation, the creative Word of God, the divine Wisdom come into the world to bring life. The Evangelist, by introducing the Logos in the prolog, sets before us the parameters of a new creation. A new revelation of God, as that which came through the Word in Genesis 1:1, is come in the person of Jesus.

Verses 10–11 of the prolog describe the result of the entry of the Logos into the world: neither it (v. 10) nor his own (v. 11) would receive him. A broad term, *kosmos* (world) refers to the human sphere. Elsewhere in the Gospel John uses *world* for those opposing Jesus—the Jews, as representatives of the larger world, who hate him (cf. 7:1, 7; see also 8:22–23; 14:17; 15:18–19; 16:20). In verse 11 we learn that Jesus went "to his own home" (*eis ta idia*; cf. 16:32; 19:27; Acts 21:6), which connotes Israel (Pryor 1990, 217), and the ones there, his own people, would not receive him.

The entry of the Logos meant division within Israel, however, for some did receive Jesus and believe in his name (John 1:12). Mainly found in the Johannine writings, the phrase "believe in his name" means to acknowledge Jesus as the Son of God, the bearer of the divine name, that is, the revealer of the divine character. What the phrase conveys is the continual need to direct one's faith to Jesus. To those who did believe, Jesus gave authority (*exousia*) to become children of God. While the meaning of *exousia* is not always easy to discern in John, the word conveys the right to do something, or dispose of something, *and* the ability to do it. In verse 12 the right is both the enabling and the empowering to become *tekna theou* (children of God), a change that requires not merely a change in status but also in nature. The technical term *children of God* that John uses to describe the new community is derived from descriptions of Israel in the Old Testament. Though the phrase per se does not appear there, divine beings and Israelite kings are called "sons of God" (Gen. 6:2; 2 Sam. 7:14; Job 1:6; 2:1; 38:7; Ps. 2:7; 29:1; 82:6; 89:6). And references to Israel's sonship appear in Exodus 4:22 and Isaiah 1:2. "Children of God" appears one other time in the Gospel of John. In 11:52 John comments upon Caiphas's ironic prophetic utterance that Jesus would not merely die for the people because in addition the nation would not perish (see v. 50). The Evangelist then distinguishes between the nation and the people, who are "the scattered children of God." In 8:39 "Abraham's children (*tekna*)," that is, his true descendants, are the possessors of true freedom, the believers, and not the Jews whom Jesus is rebuffing (Culpepper 1980, 27). In light of 8:39 and 11:52, "children of God" in 1:12 refers to the new community, which is called into being by the ministry of the Logos and which serves as a replacement for Israel.

Verse 13 defines in both positive and negative terms what causes the change in status to children of God: "who were born, not of blood or of the will of the flesh or of the will of man, but of God" (NRSV). Quite clearly, the status of sonship or daughtership does not arise as a result of dormant or latent potential within the believer. Those who receive the Logos are born, not by bloods (the singular "blood" seems to be a doctrinal replacement for the plural; Schnackenburg 1968, 1:264–65) and not by human decision or will. John excludes every natural relationship before moving to the positive force behind the new birth, which is, of course, God.

Ministry of the Logos (John 1:14–18)

The word *Logos* in verse 14 of the prolog signals the beginning of a new section, the focus of which comes into view by comparing verses 1–6 with verses 14–18. In verses 1–6 John considers the metaphysical dimensions of the incarnation, revealing the transcendence and permanence of Jesus. But verse 14 proclaims that "the Word became flesh (*sarx*)." Thus, John turns to the incarnation—the limited, restricted, impeded, and impermanent part of the life of Jesus—reminding us that the Logos did not only enter the human sphere but took on human limitations and burst them asunder. What John considers in verses 14–18 is the character of Jesus' ministry and of the inner life of the new community. In the second section are striking parallels, which will be noted where applicable, to the account of Israel's national beginning in Exodus, including such motifs as rebellious Israel and the role of Moses in securing the covenant. By casting the beginning of the new community in terms from Israel's inception, John indicates that the new community replaces the old one, that is, Israel.

After the incarnation, the Logos "dwelt (*skēnoō*) among us, and we beheld His glory (*doxa*)" (John 1:14 NKJV). Though the verb *skēnoō* occurs only in the Johannine writings, verse 14 does echo a biblical text, the Old Testament account of the giving of the tabernacle, for in both the concepts of tabernacling and glory are related closely. The goal of the exodus was the identification of the Promised Land as a sanctuary (Exod. 15:17), of which the building of the tabernacle was to be the most prominent symbol. That immediately following the ratification of the covenant (Exod. 24) God gave Moses the blueprint for the tabernacle is, therefore, significant. Interrupted by the episode of the golden calf, the construction of the tabernacle was delayed until after the second giving of the law in Exodus 34. But the exodus account concludes with the finishing of the tabernacle and its being filled with the glory cloud (40:34).

Biblical accounts of the exodus depict Israel as a worshiping community. The construction of the tabernacle symbolized Israel's implementation of the Sinai covenant, for when this covenant operated, God tabernacled with Israel. If we can infer the significance of the tabernacle from that of the later temple, we recognize the tabernacle as a symbol of God's presence and final authority in Israel. Both the tabernacle and the temple served as expressions of Yahweh's kingship exercised over Israel, and both pointed to the final locus of Israel's political authority vested in Yahweh's sovereignty. Thus, the tabernacle and temple were kingdom-of-God governmental models. Associated with Old Testament covenantal beginnings, the reference to tabernacling in John 1:14 casts an important light on the matter of the divine authority of Jesus, who operates within a new covenant and under the divine government of a renewed Israel.

John's reference to "his name" in 1:12 and "his glory" in 1:14 echoes another account from Exodus—that of the exchange between Yahweh and Moses in chapter 33. After the incident of the golden calf, Yahweh saw fit to change his manner of associating with this sinful people, apostate Israel. God appeared disposed to relate solely to Moses and to reject Israel by constructing a new people around Moses. Verse 14 proclaims that God's presence will go with Moses only and that only Moses will obtain rest, that is, enter the Promised Land. By the intercession of Moses, however, Israel's place within the divine economy was temporarily retained (v. 17). Seeking confirmation of Yahweh's intent, Moses asked for his own personal theophany, which would be analogous to the confirmation Israel received in chapters 19–20: "Now show me your glory" (33:18). Moses' request is denied in verse 20; however, he learned he would receive God's name (v. 19) in continuity with the revelation to Israel in Exodus 3:14. The glory represents the uniqueness of the divine majesty irrupting into history, appearing episodically, and then being withdrawn, but the name signifies accessibility, availability, and approachability in worship. The name provides the content of ongoing revelation; it may be freely used in worship; and on it one may continually call.

For John, the name is determinative for faith, for believers are those who believe in Jesus' name (1:12). The Evangelist further makes clear that a change has taken place since the time of Moses. Under the old dispensation the glory was hidden from Moses and Israel, but now "we have seen his glory" (1:14), that is, the nature of God has been completely manifested to the New Israel. In becoming flesh, the Logos made the divine *doxa*, the manifestation of the divine nature, readily available in the person of Jesus Christ. Moreover, the Logos "dwelt [tabernacled] among us" (v. 14 NKJV). John thus depicts Jesus as the embodiment of the rule of God, as the replacement for the tabernacle of the exodus, as the true temple, that is, the new focus of true worship. No more would worship be directed to Jerusalem or engaged in on Mount Gerizim (4:21); the new humanity would worship God through Jesus by rebirth by the Spirit. The person Jesus was the unveiled manifestation of the divine nature; those who saw him in the days of his flesh could properly describe themselves as eyewitnesses of his majesty.

Verse 14 pivots on *doxa*, the repeated word that translates the substance of the first half of the verse into understandable Old Testament terms. "Glory" also unites the two halves—the human and the divine, the incarnation and the preexistence. Without question, the concept of the glory was significant for John, but what does it convey? The glory of the incarnate Logos was in fact the glory of a unique Son, who was especially commissioned and who enjoyed the immediacy of the divine presence. The personal character of the relationship between Father and Son is underscored in verse 14 by the proposition *para* (from the side of) in "who came from (*para*) the Father." The Logos, however, was not endowed with glory from the Father by virtue of having been begotten, but in tabernacling among us the Logos reveals the eternal nature of his relationship as the unique ("One and Only") Son of the Father. In the Old Testament, one and only children were the recipients of sincere affection and were precious but under threat (Gen. 22:2, 16; Judg. 11:34; cf. Jer. 6:26; Amos 8:10; Zech. 12:10). We can assume that John meant no less regarding Jesus; yet, John's focus seems to go beyond Jesus' filial relationship to God. The correspondences between the prolog and Exodus 33–34 suggest that what was true of the Father in relation to Israel in Exodus is now true of Jesus in relation to the new community.

What does the sonship of Jesus mean for the renewed Israel? Verses 16–18 supply an answer, while noting a contrast with Israel's national experience. To receive the fulness of the Logos is to receive grace instead of grace (v. 16, "one blessing after another" NIV). John then uses a contrast to explain what this means: "For the law was given through Moses; grace and truth came through Jesus Christ" (v. 17). In other words, the revelation that came through Moses—the law of Moses and the covenant—is now subordinate to the new revelation and new covenant that comes through Jesus Christ. But perhaps John is saying even more. Consider his use of law and truth. Beyond the prolog John's use of law (*nomos*) is always depreciatory and national. *Nomos* is the comprehensive term he gives to the oral and written tradition that was passed on from Sinai through Moses (Pancaro 1975a, 517–22). Truth (*alētheia*) is a comprehensive term John uses for revelation (Schnackenburg 1980, 2:238). When John proclaims that the full revelation of divine grace came through Jesus, is he denying that it had once come through Moses? Looking at the background to verse 17a provides a clue to John's meaning. The background appears to be the second giving of the law and the renewal of the covenant in Exodus 34. Earlier, in chapter 20, the covenant had come unmediated, and the law had come to all Israel directly. But after the episode of the golden calf, revelation for Israel comes mediated through Moses (chap. 34). After Sinai, Israel depended upon the activity of mediators, a succession of priests and prophets through whom Israel was addressed. Never again was Israel personally addressed as she was at Sinai. Furthermore, it was never possible for the nation to rise to her vocation as a kingdom of priests and a holy nation (Exod. 19:6). Perhaps in verse 17 John is expressing a thought similar to Paul's in 2 Corinthians 3:13–16—that Israel's experience of the covenant was always veiled. Only in Christ, to whom Christians had turned, could there be direct experience of the covenant and fulfilment of Israel's vocation.

John 1:17 serves to resolve the tension between Israel's eschatology and her history. Through Jesus the divine intention for Israel becomes clear once again, but Israel as members of the new community who through the new exodus of the cross and resurrection have recovered national Israel's status as "sons." The grace that restores the true Israel had come through Jesus. Having drawn the community into the life of the New Israel, this grace was manifested in the life of the Logos in whom the glory of God had become visible. The fulness of the revelation offered by Jesus first to Israel and then to the world had been this new understanding of sonship. However, Judaism, wishing to rely on its written and oral traditions alone, refused to receive Jesus. Those who did receive him became the continuing people of God, who would not be the recipients of a new law, but who would see the Sinai commandments brought to their fullest expression. What God had planned for Israel had been again revealed in Jesus, the new tabernacle, the new point of divine authority. Around him, the new community of John 1:12–13 had been formed.

Early Witnesses (John 1:19–51)

John the Baptist and the first disciples provide the early witness to Jesus found in John 1:19–51. In verses 19–34 John proclaims Jesus as the Lamb of God and the preexistent one. In verses 35–51 the disciples recognize Jesus as the Messiah and the King of Israel.

John the Baptist is a witness to Israel (John 1:31), and indeed there is a close connection between his baptism and the reconstitution of Israel. Through a series of negations, John delimits his role: he is neither the Christ (v. 20), nor Elijah (v. 21a), nor the end-time prophet (v. 21b). John is only a voice announcing the new exodus to a generation still in the wilderness (v. 23), and his baptism is only preliminary (vv. 24–28). These various negations and qualifications are a fitting backdrop to John's bold identification of Jesus as the Lamb of God (v. 29), the preexistent one (v. 30), and the Son of God, that is, the Messiah (v. 34). But what do these identifications mean? In view of the synoptic evidence regarding the Baptist's evaluation of Jesus, it is unlikely that at this point John the Baptist recognizes Jesus' deity. Indeed, the climax, and virtual conclusion, of John's Gospel is Thomas's recognition of the deity of Jesus in 20:28. In verse 30 perhaps John the Baptist views Jesus as the expected figure of Elijah. The Baptist's identification of Jesus as the Lamb is often identified as a reference to the Servant of Isaiah 53 or to the Passover lamb. For Christian readers with the benefit of looking back on the life, death, and resurrection of Christ, these references seem clear. But what about John the Baptist? Since in the Synoptics he is pictured as uncertain regarding Jesus' messiahship (Matt. 11:2–3), he could hardly have intended to identify Jesus as the Servant or the Passover lamb. C. H. Dodd plausibly suggests that the Lamb refers to the victorious ram of the animal apocalypse of 1 Enoch (1954, 230–32) as the leader of Israel. In verse 32 John designates Jesus as the Spirit-bearer, since the Spirit, which descends as a dove, remains on him. The dove was a prominent rabbinic symbol for Israel; therefore, the descent of the dove marks Jesus as the representative of the New Israel.

In the remaining verses of John 1, disciples identify Jesus in ascending order of veneration as the Christ (v. 41), the eschatological prophet (v. 45), the Son of God (v. 49), and the King of Israel (v. 49). The exchange between Jesus and Nathanael is noteworthy. Recognizing Nathanael as an Israelite without any trace of Jacob's guile (v. 47; cf. Gen. 27:35), Jesus refers to Nathanael in terms applied to Israel in Old Testament times (see Hos. 9:10, where God speaks of finding Israel as "the early fruit on the fig tree"). Nathanael spontaneously proclaims faith in Jesus as the Messiah by using appellations of messianic address—Son of God and King of Israel (v. 49). Though a reader of John's Gospel would recognize a deeper divine truth behind Nathanael's words, those who ministered with and for Jesus would only recognize his divinity after the resurrection (20:28). Thus, Nathanael represents messianically expectant and perceptive true Israel, who acknowledges that the Messiah has come in the person of Jesus. Nathanael is in step with Philip, who recognized Jesus as the one about whom Moses wrote (v. 45; Pancaro 1975b, 399), and Nathanael's confession marks the continuity between the old and the New Israel. As Jesus will later argue (5:46), those who believe in Moses should believe in Jesus, and those who follow Jesus are the true followers of Moses. Those unworthy to be called Israelites are the ones who refuse to believe (Pancaro 1975b, 399). John the Baptist had come to manifest Jesus to Israel and to associate him with current messianic speculation. Representing the renewed Israel, Nathanael is brought by John's witness to Jesus and acknowledges him.

Prefaced by words of great solemnity, Jesus' remark to Nathanael in John 1:51 climaxes the christological themes of the chapter: "You shall see heaven open, and the angels of God ascending and descending on the Son of Man." This angelic progression is in the same order as in the famous vision to Jacob at Bethel (Gen. 28:12), in which angels ascended and descended a ladder that reached from earth to heaven. In verse 51, however, the angels will ascend and descend on the Son of man, the present means of heavenly communication, and the disciples as Jacob/ Israel will receive the vision. What is Jesus promising Nathanael and the others? In John, as in the Synoptics, the Son of man is a human figure who is to be rejected and killed but who will be the end-time judge. By coming into the world, the Son of man assumes a human role, but prior to this he was preexistent as the Logos in heaven (3:13). Is Jesus, therefore, promising vindication delivered by the Son of man (Acts 7:56), and is he assuring the disciples of his own vindication, which they will "see" after the resurrection? The syntactical construction permits two interpretations of verse 51: (1) that the demonstration of the heavenly background of the Son of man will follow in the course of his ministry and (2) that the demonstration is something the disciples will perceive only after the ministry has been completed and they have reflected on the cross and resurrection. Since John characteristically insists on the need of help beyond the course of Jesus' ministry to understand his nature, perhaps the latter interpretation is the more apt. In any event, the chapter concludes in verse 51 with a demonstration of Jesus' heavenly connection, which was also proclaimed in verse 1 (de Jonge 1973, 168–69).

Jews, Samaritans, and Jesus (John 3:1–4:42)

Upon reading John 1, we begin to recognize that Jesus' heavenly nature sets him on a collision course with the world, which is structured in complete hostility to God. Such hostility pervades the public ministry of Jesus and arises from within the ranks of the Jews. John's account of the public ministry of Jesus deals with the matter raised in John 1:11, namely, that when Jesus came into his own, his own would not receive him. Through the story of Nicodemus in 3:1–21, John explores one of Judaism's inadequate approaches to Jesus. In contrast to this approach is that of the Samaritan woman, whose story John tells in 4:1–42.

An Encounter in Jerusalem (John 3:1–21, 31–36)

In Jerusalem, Jesus encounters Nicodemus, "a member of the Jewish ruling council" (John 3:1). The dialog between the two is crucial to an understanding of the eschatological emphasis of Jesus' rejection of national Israel in the Gospel. Verse 2 divulges the key to the encounter— what Nicodemus, as the representative of Judaism, knows about Jesus: "Rabbi, we know you are a teacher who has come from God." In what amounts to a christological statement, the Pharisee pronounces Jesus an acceptable teacher. But in what sense has Jesus come from God? The dialog, which consists of three exchanges between Nicodemus and Jesus, reveals the total inadequacy of the knowledge that Nicodemus is bold enough to assert (Neyrey 1981, 118–19). A counter christological statement is Jesus' reply: "I tell you the truth, no one can see the kingdom of God unless he is born again [from above]." This statement about Jesus himself, the only one who possesses the credentials for understanding the kingdom of God, is progressively clarified in the ensuing exchange.

Nicodemus questions Jesus regarding the *how* of being born again (John 3:4). Though the concept in itself is not beyond the Pharisee's comprehension, his question reveals the limitations of his professed knowledge: "How can a man be born when he is old?" Complicating the matter is the meaning of *anōthen* in verse 3. Though Jesus uses *anōthen* as "from above" (cf. v. 31), Nicodemus understands it as "anew," thus indicating a second human birth. The Pharisee's very human understanding demonstrates clearly that he is from below (Nicholson 1982, 84). Jesus clarifies the issue in verse 5, for his demand for rebirth by water and Spirit goes beyond the realm of human birth. Moreover, since Jesus did not universally practice or require baptism, he cannot be demanding that Nicodemus be baptized. Jesus then explains this matter of spiritual cleansing (vv. 6–8). He seems to refer to the spiritual cleansing of Israel, which Ezekiel had identified as a sign of the last days, that is, when the new covenant would be conferred on Israel (36:24–26). Ezekiel continues in chapter 37 with the recognition that God is promising nothing less than life from the dead, which Israel would receive in quite the same way as life had been given to Adam (Niditch 1986, 223). Such spiritual cleansing of Israel means birth from above—spiritual rebirth for the nation and its individuals. As a leader and teacher in Israel, Nicodemus represents a test case. To enter the kingdom, he must experience what has been prescribed for corporate Israel. At issue in the debate between Jesus and Nicodemus are the two types of knowledge: the earthly and the heavenly. Earthly knowledge cannot give understanding of the process to which Jesus refers in verse 5, nor is it able to give a real comprehension of the mysterious origin of the life from above (vv. 6–7). In fact, this new life, mysterious and spiritually enduced as it is, cannot be understood; it must be experienced (v. 8). It will turn out that the whence and the whither of the birth from above are identical with the whence and whither of the origin and destination of the Son of man. By another question in verse 9, Nicodemus further betrays his ignorance: "How can this be?" His question had already been answered in verse 8. We can feel the Spirit just as we can feel the wind, but the Spirit's source and destination are hidden. If Nicodemus cannot feel the force of Jesus' analogy, then the Pharisee is flesh and is from below (v. 6). Jesus admonishes him, for Nicodemus, as "the teacher of Israel," should have known about the necessity of spiritual rebirth.

With verse 11, the discourse shifts from dialog to monolog. Forming a bridge between verses 1–10 and 13–15 is the recapitulation of verses 11–12. Jesus reveals that the possessor of heavenly knowledge is the Son of man, who alone has personal knowledge of heavenly things and who alone is the one born from above (John 3:13; with the NIV and NRSV we omit from consideration in v. 13 the early textual addition "who is in heaven"). Unlike every other man before him, the Son of man understands heavenly things. And the Son of man is destined for lifting up (v. 14). The distinct impression one gets from reading the monolog is that Jesus uses the title *Son of man* as a convenient periphrasis for speaking about himself. Thus, the *whence* of the discussion is from God, and the *whither* to which the Son of man will move is to the cross! Jesus' identification of himself with the Son of man is not taken beyond its implications for Nicodemus in John 3, but it will certainly be made clear during the course of Jesus' ministry. The Son of man is the preexistent Logos, who has descended as man in the incarnation.

The heavenly things which Nicodemus has found bewildering but ought to understand turn out to be the revelation of the need for Jesus' death as the supreme manifestation of God's love for the world (John 3:16). As "from above," the Son of man manifests a new revelation. Because he is the unique revelation of God, he *must* be lifted up, which refers in the Gospel to Jesus' death (3:14; 8:28; 12:32). Beyond the fitting- ness conveyed by "must" is the necessity because only by being lifted up can Jesus demonstrate the qualities of which he speaks. Verse 14 reveals the manner of the lifting up; verse 15, its purpose; and verses 16–21, its consequences. (Note the use of the titles *Son of man* and *Son* in the passage, the former being used to underscore the function of Jesus as the bearer of heavenly revelation [vv. 13–14] and the latter being used to indicate the closeness of the relationship between Jesus and the Father [vv. 16–18].) Though God sent the Son on an errand of mercy (v. 17), unbelief brings judgment (vv. 18–21). To believe on Jesus is to believe on the Word authenticated by him and thus to pass beyond judgment. The monolog resumes in verses 31–36. The Son of man is the one from above (v. 31) and is privy to the heavenly secrets (v. 32). Verse 34 adds to the thought of Jesus' saving mission, and verse 36 restates the judgment of verses 18–21.

As in John 1:1–18, chapter 3 presents Jesus as a heavenly being come into the world to his own and rejected by them. Those who believe on him are born of God, for Jesus, as the heavenly revealer, admits them into his confidence. Thus, the nature of his ministry may be understood (cf. 1:14). The muted polemical differences between Nicodemus and Jesus cast their crucial meeting as the first major confrontation between Judaism and the Son of man. By using the language of judgment in this chapter, John demonstrates that this confrontation is already viewed as a trial.

An Encounter in Samaria (John 4:1–42)

From Jesus' discussion with Nicodemus, the teacher of Israel, John's Gospel moves to Jesus' encounter with the woman at the well in Samaria. Jesus identifies himself to the woman as the source of living water (John 4:10) and with uncanny prescience reveals facts about her personal life (v. 18). She identifies Jesus as a prophet (v. 19) and puts before him the old problem of the religious division between Judah and Samaria (v. 20). Refusing to accept these divisions, Jesus indicates that in eschatological worship Israel will be one (v. 21) on the basis of a unity of salvation in the Messiah—a salvation stemming from the Jews (vv. 22–23; Schnackenburg 1980, 2:435). God transcends all material issues such as those the woman raises, and worship of God must be by divine revelation (spirit and truth), not by human adjudication (v. 24). The Samaritan woman confesses in verse 25 that such worship will result from the coming of the Messiah (called the *Restorer* in Samaria), who will restore the kingdom and institute true worship in Israel. What Jesus demands of the woman is her entrance into the true Israel, which would cut across the old national boundaries. Her apparent belief in verses 28–29 indicates her assent.

The narrative of Jesus' Galilean ministry ends with the healing of the official's son (John 4:46–54). Note that verse 54 returns us to John 2:1–11 and so completes the complex. In this section Jesus has called for a number of replacements—the new wine of the Gospel for Jewish law (2:1–11), a replacement for the present physical temple (2:13–22), a new nonnational method of entry into the kingdom of God (3:1–10), and a new focus of worship (4:21–24). Having laid down a considerable challenge to the Jewish nation, Jesus will enter into serious controversy with crowds and leaders alike, leading to his final rejection of the nation in 12:37–50.

Conflict and the Journey to Jerusalem (John 5–12)

Chapters 5–12 of John's Gospel record three journeys to Jerusalem made by Jesus (5:1–47; 7:1–10:39; 11:1–53), which are followed by three retreats or withdrawals (6:1–71; 10:40–42; 11:54–57), and a final journey from which there can be no withdrawal (12:1–50; Nicholson 1982, 64). As the trips progress, so does the hostility. During the first visit emerges the initial attempt to kill Jesus (5:16–18). There are two attempts to kill Jesus on the second visit (8:59; 10:39), and the Jewish council decides officially to have Jesus put to death during the third (11:46–53; Nicholson 1982, 48–49). In the face of such hostility, Jesus ends his ministry to his own (*ta idia;* cf. 1:11) and holds them up to judgment (12:48). Beginning in chapter 13, John records the ministry of Jesus to those who received him. Thus, the structure of John's work echoes the pattern of rejection and acceptance found in 1:11–12.

The Gift of Eschatological Life (John 5–6)

Chapters 5–6 constitute the introduction to the "great controversy" of chapters 7–12, in which Israel is arraigned by Jesus (Trites 1977, 103). In chapter 5 Jesus uses the controversy over his Sabbath healing to pronounce the promise of eternal life. Chapter 6 then focuses on the means by which this life is made accessible.

A controversy between Jesus and the Jews arises in John 5:1–18 when Jesus heals a lame man on the Sabbath day (vv. 8–9) and the Jews allege that Jesus has made himself equal to God (v. 18). Jesus himself investigates the messianic claims, as he puts the nation on trial (vv. 19–30). Jesus interprets the charge of equality with God as power to judge and the power to confer eternal life, both of which are activities associated in Jewish thought with the end. One's reaction to Jesus' word brings present judgment (v. 24)—condemnation or eternal life. Within this context and generally in John, eternal life is not endless life, but the life of the age to come, life in the presence of God experienced now (17:3), the eschatological life drawn with anticipation into the present age (3:15–16; 5:40; 6:40, 47, 53, 68; 10:10). And condemnation is the anticipation of the exclusion of the last judgment, that is, exclusion from fellowship with God, in this present life and eternally. In verses 25–30 Jesus refers to the future resurrection from the dead, which will be the consequence of this present appropriation of eternal life. The thought in the passage thus moves from present belief and its hope to the future resurrection, as a consequence of that belief. Verses 31–40 underscore the validity of Jesus' words in verses 19–30 by pointing to his function as a reliable revealer of the messianic truth supported by four compelling witnesses. Jesus reveals yet another messianic truth at the end of chapter 5—that the only activity we engage in worthy of praise is belief in him (vv. 41–44). The controversy between Jesus and the authorities will be carried further in chapters 6–11. Though no ground will be given on either side, the enmity generated against Jesus will paradoxically ensure his "lifting up" and the completion of his saving work.

In chapter 6 Jesus refuses the popular move to make him king (6:15) and feeds Israel with "manna" in the wilderness, thereby drawing attention to the significance of the parallels with Moses to which his miracle points. Moreover, Jesus offers further and decisive evidence to support his messianic claims and discloses what will make the gift of eternal life possible. The Son of man will give life by the giving of himself (John 6:51). In an explanation of the feeding motif of verses 35–51, verses 52–59 point to Jesus' voluntary death. Indeed each use of the title *Son of man* in the chapter (vv. 27, 53, 62) refers obliquely to the cross (cf. 3:14).

Though the humanity of the Son of man is subject to death, he will be resurrected.

The Messiah (John 7:1–11:44)

Through the recounting of various events in the life of Jesus, John considers the issue of Jesus' messiahship in chapters 7–11. Initially the issue of Jesus' precise identification and mission is framed by secrecy (John 7:4; 8:59), but with chapter 9 it bursts out into the open. The Jews have many questions about Jesus: Where does he come from? Where is he going? Who is he? What is the basis of his authority? The public debate about him thrives. However, what becomes clear is that Jesus cannot be molded to fit the titles and expectations of the Jews.

Chapter 7 begins with Jesus in Galilee because of threats against his life made by the Jewish leaders (v. 1). When Jesus ventures into Judea, specifically to Jerusalem, for the Feast of Tabernacles, three groups debate his claims of messiahship. In verses 14–24 the Jews puzzle over Jesus' authority to teach given his lack of rabbinical education. In verses 25–31 some of the inhabitants of Jerusalem debate whether Jesus is in fact the Christ. And in verses 32–36 the Pharisees and chief priests continue their hard-core opposition. In responding to all the talk about him, Jesus refers to his origin in verse 29 and to his return to the Father in verse 33. Then on the last and greatest day of the feast, Jesus makes the decisive announcement that in him the promises of God to Israel are to be fulfilled (vv. 37–39), for he is the holy rock, the new temple from which rivers of living waters will flow, springing up more richly and lastingly than the rivers of Paradise from Ezekiel's new temple (Ezek. 47:1–12; Schnackenburg 1980, 2:156). As the chapter ends (vv. 40–52), the Jews are divided on whether Jesus is a prophet or Christ or neither, but the issue is clear: the true Messiah comes not from Galilee or Judea but from heaven.

Public debate at the Feast of Tabernacles on Jesus' messianic claims continues in John 8:12–58. During the festival, light played an important role, as great lamps were lit, thus illuminating the courtyard of the temple. Jesus uses this prominent symbol by declaring himself the Light of the World (v. 12). Jesus does not illumine merely the temple or the city, but he is the universal light, that is, salvation, for the world and the light to lighten the Gentiles. Such light is nothing less than the liberating truth that Jesus brings. In verses 13–24 Jesus answers the question of his authority by pointing out that he alone of all human beings knows from where he comes and where he is going.

Despite all that Jesus has told the Jews about himself, they still do not know who he is. Their question "Who are you?" in John 8:25 is the basic christological question of the Gospel. Jesus' response is one that occurs nine times in John—"I am" (*egō eimi* without predication to complete the meaning; v. 28). In the Old Testament, a similar self-predication appears when Yahweh speaks as Creator, Redeemer, and Lord of history (e.g., Isa. 43:10). In John, the expression serves as an object of belief and underscores the unity between the Father and the Son (8:24, 28, 58; 13:19). By the time Jesus, the Son of man, is "lifted up," that is, crucified and ascended, the Jews will know that he is the "I am," that his claim to deity has been vindicated. The significance of Jesus' claim to be "I am" is not lost on the Jews. In 8:59 they pick up stones to stone him. Note a similar incident in chapter 10. After Jesus openly declares that he and the Father are one (v. 30), the Jews stone him for blasphemy by claiming to be God (vv. 31, 33).

In John 9–10 the discussion over Jesus' person is clarified by a number of declarations by Jesus himself regarding his person and his aims (9:35–37; 10:11, 18, 27–29, 38). In chapter 9 Jesus demonstrates the claim made in 8:12 that he is the Light of the World, for he heals a man born blind (v. 7). As the man regains his sight, so too does he grow spiritually. That growth climaxes in 9:38 with the man's expression of faith in Jesus as the Son of man. Since judgment is a strong motif in the chapter, the title *Son of man* is appropriate, for it is he who came into the world for judgment (v. 39), that is, for a judicial separation between believers and unbelievers. Jesus affirms his messianic claims by healing the blind because such acts were expected signs of the new age (see Isa. 29:18; 35:5; 42:7).

Jesus, the Light of the World, moves to other self-predications in chapter 10 to convey his identity to those who hear him. In verse 7 he is "the gate for the sheep," and in verse 11, "the good shepherd." Behind these images stands Ezekiel 34, in which God rejects the shepherds of Israel in favor of a Davidic shepherd to watch over the sheep. In 10:1–18 Jesus shows us how to distinguish between good and bad shepherds by assessing their claims to messiahship in terms of their means of entry into Israel and their actions during a crisis. Jesus proclaims himself to be the gate, the messianic way to salvation (v. 7). The gate by which Jesus enters (vv. 1–2) is the right means of access to Israel and poignantly anticipates Jesus' death, by which his messiahship will be validated. There is no other means of approach. Jesus who enters through the door becomes the door himself (vv. 7–10); that is to say, the cross, which provides for Jesus the means of entry to the kingdom, also becomes the means of approach for Israel. There can be no other. The truth is now inescapable—Jesus' claims to messiahship will be vindicated by his death. Others who came before Jesus were thieves and robbers (v. 8), and indeed Israel would later prefer a robber to the Good

Shepherd, who lays down his life for the sheep (18:39–40). Jesus becomes much more explicit in verses 11–18, demonstrating that he is the
Good Shepherd, not a hireling or false messiah, by his willingness to die
for the sheep. In this and no other way does he demonstrate his ownership of God's flock. Thereafter the Jews ask Jesus to state plainly
whether or not he is the Christ (v. 24). Jesus' reply in verses 25–30 says
in effect that his works, not titles, indicate his relationship with God
and that he is to be known from them (Michaels 1984, 174). Since Jesus
does not fit into Israel's developed categories, he cannot use their titles.
Moreover, the question of titles is irrelevant (vv. 31–39). To support this
claim, Jesus quotes from Psalm 82:6. His point in verses 34–36 is not
that he is the Son of God rather than God, not that he is God in the sense
the word is used in Psalm 82, but that titles are irrelevant in his revelation of himself to the world. Titles do not matter; only the works are important. Though one may call Jesus "Christ" (v. 24), "God's Son" (v. 36),
or even "God" (v. 33), what ultimately matters is the relationship between Jesus and the Father.

In John 7–10 Jesus clearly defines the various issues of messiahship
and proclaims the inescapable truth that messiahship means death.
Chapter 11 goes on to reveal that death is not the end. Jesus is summoned to the bedside of Lazarus, but he defers because the sickness is
to the glory of God (vv. 1–4). When Jesus finally goes to Bethany, he
finds that Lazarus has been dead four days (v. 17). Jesus then reassures
Martha that Lazarus will rise (v. 23), which she interprets in terms of
the orthodox Jewish belief in the general resurrection of the righteous
at the last day (v. 24). In the next verse Jesus puts himself at the center
of resurrection faith: "I am the resurrection and the life" (v. 25a). The
two conditional statements that follow explain what Jesus means by
resurrection and life, respectively. If it is true that "he who believes in
me will live, even though he dies" (v. 25b), then it is also true that "whoever lives and believes in me will never die" (v. 26). The veracity of the
second statement depends upon first establishing that not death but
eternal life is the prospect for the believer. Since life is a relationship to
Jesus, there is life as long as he is present with the believer through faith
(Michaels 1984, 188).

In John 11:27 Martha confesses her faith, acknowledging that Jesus
is the Messiah and that a believer has life in his name. This open confession of Jesus as the Christ exactly fits what John spells out as the aim
of his Gospel (20:31) as well as climaxes the movement from 7:1–4 and
the call therein for Jesus to look for public endorsement. Jesus is se-
quentially recognized as a prophet, the Christ, the Light of the World,
the door to life, and the resurrection and the life. The astounding claim

by Jesus at 11:25 anticipates his own resurrection and ensures ours, but it also precipitates a reaction by the Jews.

The Plot and the Anointing (John 11:45–12:11)

Jesus' demonstration of his lordship over death through the raising of Lazarus spurs the Jewish leadership to plot against Jesus. At a session of the Sanhedrin, the Jewish ruling council in Palestine in postexilic times, Jesus is presented as a political messiah; thus, popular support for him could mean Rome's putting an end to the temple and the Jewish state (John 11:48). In an unconscious witness to Jesus, the high priest Caiaphas offers ironic counsel: Jesus must die to save the people (*laos*) so that the nation (*ethnos*) does not perish (vv. 49–50). He equates people and nation, but let us look at the words. A word often reserved for the Gentile world, *ethnos* can simply mean the Jewish nation as a political entity without theological significance. However, *laos* is a theologically sensitive word, which to the Jews would mean the people of Israel and which to the Christian reader would mean the people of God. Caiaphas unwittingly says that Jesus, while dying for national Israel, will save the people of God. By virtue of Jesus' crucifixion, national Israel will become simply another nation. As a result of this expedient course urged by Caiaphas, the death of Jesus will paradoxically bring an end to Jewish self-rule and relative freedom and will yield the emergence of the true people of God. In verse 52 John summarizes the aim of Jesus—the construction of the one flock of the people of God. Not only will Jesus die for the nation, not only will his be a death for national Israel, but it will be a death for the wider family of God, a death to bring into being the church!

The scene is set for confrontation—the Jews plot to kill Jesus (John 11:53) as Passover approaches (11:55; 12:1). From Ephraim (11:54), Jesus returns to Bethany (12:1), where he had raised Lazarus and where Mary now anoints Jesus as a royal figure in the manner of Old Testament authorizations (12:3). Jesus, however, views Mary's act as pointing in another direction. In response to criticism by Judas of Mary's use of the costly ointment (12:4–5), Jesus prophesies his own burial (12:7) and a time when he will not be with them (12:8). Though John portrays Jesus as looking forward to his death, the presence of Lazarus in 12:2 points beyond the death to the triumph after the cross.

The Messiah in Jerusalem (John 12:12–50)

The day after the anointing Jesus enters Jerusalem for the last time (John 12:12). The crowds acclaim him as the Messiah, the national one they expected (v. 13). By strewing palm branches, as the Jews had done for the Hasmonean Simon (1 Macc. 13:51), the people demonstrate their homage to the victorious ruler. John's use of Zechariah 9:9 in verse 15 indicates how the crowd received Jesus, but the significance of the crowd's acclamation was lost on the disciples (v. 16), who needed a later postresurrection interpretation. What is striking in the midst of the crush of people and the noise is the manner of Jesus' entry, which surely signals the peaceful nature of his rule.

Among the many who had journeyed to Jerusalem for Passover were Gentiles from the Greek-speaking world (John 12:20). Their desire to see Jesus signifies that "the hour has come for the Son of Man to be glorified" (v. 23). In John's Gospel the completion of Jesus' mission is characteristically identified with the verbs *lift up* and *glorify* (e.g., see 12:23, 32). Both connote the return to the Father by way of the cross. In 7:39 the Spirit has not yet come because Jesus' work is not completed and he has "not yet been glorified." In 12:16 the disciples cannot understand the significance of Jesus' entry into Jerusalem before the completion of his ministry. When the Greeks, a token of the later Gentiles who are to come into Israel, ask to *see* Jesus, Jesus associates the request with the time come for his glorification. If they are to see him, it must be in his death, as the illustration about the grain of wheat in verse 24 makes plain. The concept of glorification appears again in the prayer Jesus utters and God's response in verses 27–28. Jesus prays not for salvation from the hour but for the glorification of the name of God in the hour, to which God responds with these words: "I have glorified it, and will glorify it again" (v. 28b). The past glorification may well refer to Jesus' ministry, in which his divine sonship has been revealed in a messiahship devoid of political content and linked to service as well as to the cross, where in the death of Jesus the nature of God will be more clearly seen. This is the glory that Isaiah saw when he prophesied Israel's rejection of the truth (John 12:40–41; cf. Isa. 6:10). In the course of Jesus' ministry, the glorification has been his performance of the task that God had assigned him (17:4). Jesus' obedience unto death, his return to the Father, will lead to the resumption of the glory Jesus had in the presence of the Father "before the world began" (17:5).

The other concept associated in John's Gospel with the completion of Jesus' mission is that of lifting up. It first occurs in John 3:14 in a comparison between Moses' elevation of the wilderness serpent as salvation for Israel and Jesus' elevation, or lifting up, by crucifixion. References to lifting up in John correspond to the predictions of death and resurrection in the synoptic Gospels; however the lifting up of the cross is but the first step in the process of exaltation which is completed when Jesus returns by the ascension to the Father. Jesus associates the concepts of lifting up and deity in his assertion of the necessity of the Son of man's being lifted up (8:28). By dying a death for which the Jews are instrumental, Jesus will attest his deity. The cross alone will prove that Jesus is God's fully authorized agent. Though the lifting up means glorification for Jesus, there are other effects as well. By being lifted up, Jesus will draw all humankind unto himself (12:32). And the passion will mean the defeat of Satan, now cast out from heaven (12:31; cf. 16:11; Rev. 12:7). Thus, the inner meaning of the cross is the *possibility* of freedom from Satan's rule. Paradoxically, the cross will prove to be the judgment bar before which all the world will be drawn (12:31–32).

The crowds remain puzzled by Jesus' prophecies (John 12:34). The questions they ask reveal their inability to integrate Jesus' words in verse 23 with their understanding of messiahship. What sort of Messiah is it, they ask, who can be identified with the Son of man? Jesus gives no answers to the crowds' questions, but it is clear from the context of verses 35–36 that the cross will be the place of victory where the nature of God in Jesus will be revealed. If Greeks or any others are to see Jesus, as the Greeks wish in verse 21, then they must see him in death, for there is no other way. Despite Jesus' teachings, miracles, and signs, the people do not believe in him (v. 37). When Jesus departs and hides (v. 36b), his public ministry concludes. John uses Isaiah in verses 38 and 40 (cf. Isa. 6:9–10; 53:1) to signify that the ministry of the Servant was and is a judgment upon Israel and that Jesus came into the world to bring out Israel's blindness. John then summarizes Jesus' ministry in verses 44–50. Jesus had come into the world as Light and as Judge, and now all people are judged by his words. However, the delivery of the individual sentences will occur on the last day (v. 48). The public ministry is over. Jesus had come unto his own, but they received him not.

In his Gospel, John presents the ministry of Jesus as a cosmic lawsuit by which the world is called to account before God. Jesus speaks of the universal and fundamental changes that will take place with the lifting up of the Son of man, which will be his vindication and on which the decision in the case rests. Jesus uses the title *Son of man* to speak of his humanity (cf. Blank 1964, 288); indeed, it is the title to which he resorts in 12:23 to correct the expectation of those who had proclaimed him "King" as he entered Jerusalem. John's Gospel makes clear that the work of the Son of man is the revelation of God (3:13–14; 6:27; 8:28; 12:23). We shall now see the supreme revelation in the death of the Son of man (13:31–32).

Fellowship in Jerusalem (John 13–17)

In chapters 1–12 the Evangelist focuses on Jesus' ministry to those who did not receive him, that is, to his own, to national Israel. Thereafter John shifts his view to focus on Jesus' ministry to those who did receive him. In chapters 13–17 Jesus reveals the meaning of his ministry to his disciples.

The ascent of Jesus to the right hand of God begins with chapter 13. Verses 1–3 represent a minor prolog, one displaying many of the themes and motifs found in 1:1–18: love, life through death, going to the Father, foreknowledge, willingness to suffer, and the work of the prince of the world. On the eve of the Passover (v. 1), according to the custom of the day, Jesus receives his disciples as guests in his Father's house (14:2; Hultgren 1982, 542). Jesus, the servant of a rich and generous host in heaven, welcomes them and serves them in the most concrete of ways by washing their feet (vv. 4–12). By laying aside his garments, which anticipates the crucifixion, and by washing the disciples' feet, Jesus demonstrates what supreme authority will do—it will serve by dying. So the death of Jesus will wash clean those who believe (Moloney 1978, 195).

Departure is a repeated motif in chapter 13, occurring in verse 1 and again in verses 31–38. Indeed, it is such a part of what takes place in the upper room that portions of the text are traditionally referred to as farewell discourses. When Jesus departs, he is to go to his Father's house to prepare spiritual lodging (*monē*) for his disciples within his own person (John 14:1–3; Gundry 1967, 70). The word *monē*, often translated in 14:2 as "rooms," is also used in 14:23 to refer to the spiritual lodgment of the Father and Son with the believer. As shown in verse 23, a major theme of the discourses is the disciples' and believers' being "in Christ." In 14:1–3 Jesus' remarks about preparing a lodgment for his disciples by going away seem to refer to Christ's spiritual cleansing and his incorporation of the believers after the resurrection. There is no evidence that these verses suggest a glorious parousia. Since the concept of the parousia is not found elsewhere in John, a reference to it here would be too allusive without further elaboration (Schnackenburg 1982, 3:62). Neither is there any indication that the reference is to the later resurrection appearances of Jesus, to the individual deaths of the disciples, or to the end of the world (Forestell 1974, 93). Elsewhere in the narrative Jesus tells his disciples that he will come to them and they will see him again (14:18–19, 21; 16:16, 22) and that his departure is for the glorification of the Father (14:28) and for the coming of the Paraclete (16:7). Jesus will return by the coming of the Spirit and will make his home with the disciples (14:18–24). The character and function of the disciples will then be identical with the character and function of Jesus (Woll 1980, 235), for Jesus will return to dwell in his successors.

After Jesus departs, another will come—the Paraclete—whose coming is a major feature of John 14–16. Indeed, Paraclete (*paraklētos*) is found only in these chapters (14:16, 26; 15:26; 16:7) and in 1 John 2:1. Several passages identify, or imply the identification of, the Paraclete with the Holy Spirit (14:26; 15:26; 16:8–11, 13). Though *paraklētos* has been translated in various ways (e.g., Counselor, Advocate, Helper), it is perhaps best to leave it untranslated and focus on the function of the one that will come.

In 14:16 Jesus tells the disciples that the Father will give them another Paraclete. Since the first Paraclete was Jesus, the coming of the Holy Spirit in this guise is designed to continue the work of Jesus through the apostles. The Father will send the Paraclete, according to Jesus in 14:26, "in my name." Thus, the Paraclete will bear Jesus' name, thereby replacing him. The same verse identifies the Paraclete's didactic function: The Paraclete will teach the disciples by reminding them of the revelation of Jesus. References to the Paraclete in 15:26 and 16:7 occur within text that deals with the world's persecution of the disciples and the witness of the Paraclete against the world. In 15:26 Jesus refers to the Paraclete as the Spirit of truth. (Note that Jesus characterizes himself in 14:6 as the truth.) Thus, the Spirit will be dependent upon truth and will communicate truth. The major task of the Paraclete, however, is to put the world on trial through the ministry of the disciples (16:7–11), as Jesus had done in his public ministry to Israel. The Paraclete will testify against (*elenchō*) the world "in regard to sin and righteousness and judgment" (v. 8). "Sin" refers to the people's unbelief (v. 9). "Righteousness" involves the rightness of Jesus in the matter of his lawsuit against the world (v. 10), since his going to the Father is his vindication. And finally, "judgment" refers to the world's false assessment of Jesus, whereby it is now under judgment (v. 11). Guiding the disciples "into all truth," the Paraclete will make fully clear Jesus' revelation to them and will glorify Jesus, that is, declare the heavenly origin and power of Jesus (vv. 13–14). The world in which the Paraclete operates is hostile, for the world can neither receive him (14:17) nor give peace (14:27).

There is not the slightest indication that the Paraclete's function is to defend the apostles in the world; rather, the Paraclete will enable them to bring the world to the judgment bar. Not a spokesman *for* the disciples, the Paraclete is a spokesman *through* them (Brown 1967, 117). As such, the Paraclete's function is bound to the apostolic ministry after the resurrection. Note also the tandem relationship between Jesus and the Paraclete. The Paraclete comes from the Father, as did Jesus, is the Spirit of truth, as Jesus was truth, abides with the disciples, as did Jesus, announces the things to come, as did Jesus, and reminds them of what Jesus taught. Even though the Paraclete will be at the side of the disciples, the world will not believe them, because it cannot accept the Paraclete, as it could not accept Jesus.

The great news for the disciples is that the ministry of Jesus will continue in them by his Spirit-presence. In fact, their ministry will be his ministry. As Jesus' continued ministry, however, the ministry of the disciples will be subject to all the trials and difficulties that beset his, for the gift of the Paraclete is, in effect, the laying of his cross upon them. In the disciples' witness to the world, they may expect tribulation, but this tribulation will be within the context of the deep peace that Jesus will leave with them.

The Passion and Commission (John 18–20)

After Jesus' fellowship with the disciples, his time has truly come. His arrest, trial, and crucifixion are imminent. In the passion narrative that follows, John presents Jesus as King, but not as king of the Jews, a title which John uses pejoratively for the most part. When Pilate asks Jesus, "Are you the king of the Jews?" (John 18:33), Jesus indicates that his kingdom "is not of this world" (v. 36), that is, his kingdom is not given by this world but is heavenly in origin. Refusing Jesus' kingship, the Jews transform themselves into just another kingdom, not the kingdom of God, when they accept Caesar as their king (19:12–16; Meeks 1967, 76). Rather than save Jesus, the King, the Jews save a *lēstēs*, an insurrectionist (18:40). Nevertheless, despite Israel's rejection, the Divine King reigns from the cross (Meeks 1967, 80). John presents the crucifixion as an enthronement. And even though the public roars, Jesus, who was proclaimed King at the beginning (1:49) and the end (12:13) of his public ministry, bears in death the title *King of the Jews* (19:19–22). When the new family of mother, son, and true disciples is constituted at the foot of the cross (19:25–27; Forestell 1974, 87–88), Jesus can then die (v. 28).

The continuation of Jesus' ministry through the disciples, as foreshadowed in John 14–16, is the logical outcome of the resurrection of Jesus. Thus, on the first evening of the resurrection, Jesus commissions his disciples in the upper room (John 20:19–23). The form of the commissioning narrative is quite similar indeed to narratives of prophetic commissions in the Old Testament. The shared elements include the introduction (v. 19), confrontation by the deity (v. 20a), reaction usually of fear or unworthiness, here, of course, of joy (v. 20b), and act of commissioning (vv. 21–23). Only two elements generally found in prophetic commissions are missing here: the individual's protest of inability and the divine reassurance. Jesus' repetition of the greeting in verse 21a underscores the importance of what he is about to do. The language of the commissioning itself is extraordinary and revealing. Jesus will send (*pempō*) the disciples as agents of himself into a hostile world, as he had been sent (*apostellō*) by the Father (v. 21b). The force of *apostellō* in "as the Father has sent me" cannot be missed—Jesus has completed his personal mission. However, his ministry will be continued in the mission of the disciples. In the sending, the disciples are to know the Father, to share the life of the Father, to be one in nature with Jesus (17:21) and bound by the same Spirit, to do the will of the Father, and to reflect the teaching of Jesus.

After announcing the sending, Jesus breathes on (*emphysaō*) the disciples, thus infusing them with the Holy Spirit (John 20:22). The verb *emphysaō* recalls Genesis 2:7 and the breathing into the man. Jesus' act is hardly the baptism of the Spirit to which John refers in 1:33 because the gift in chapter 20 is restricted to the forgiveness of sins: "If you forgive anyone his sins, they are forgiven; if you do not forgive them, they are not forgiven" (v. 23). The breathing seems not to refer to the gift of 7:39 since Jesus has not yet been fully glorified and the ascension still awaits. Though John 20:19–23 is often regarded as an anticipation of Pentecost, the imperative "receive the Holy Spirit" in verse 22 rules out any notion of a promise to be fulfilled later. Also, there is little correspondence between verses 19–23 and the promises concerning the coming of the Paraclete, which takes place on Pentecost. Note that chapter 21 witnesses to further appearances by Jesus, whose ministry the Paraclete is to continue. Since Jesus still appears, the Paraclete has obviously not yet come. Only after Jesus has gone away and been glorified would the Father send the Paraclete. Finally, the event in verses 19–23 does not seem to refer to Pentecost itself because the gift is received on the spot without the disciples' waiting in Jerusalem as they were bidden (Acts 1:4–5).

How should we interpret the breathing and the gift in John 20:22–23? We agree with B. F. Westcott that it is unnatural to regard the words and the act of Jesus only as promise (1958, 295). John Calvin suggested that they were an earnest of the Pentecost to come (1949, 269). Others suggest that Jesus inaugurated or empowered the disciples for mission. All these suggestions, however, are too general. The commission is not specifically apostolic, for it is not confined to the apostles but given to all in the upper room. Moreover, the authority to bind and loose, which is associated with verse 23, is elsewhere in the New Testament given to the community as a whole (e.g., Matt. 18:18). By the exercise of this authority, the community will perpetuate the division by judgment which brought Jesus into the world, since to forgive, or remit, sins implicitly means to pronounce salvation or judgment. The apportionment of the gift of forgiveness speaks of the consequence of a witness to Christ. Westcott spoke of the paschal gift of new life to the community, that is, of that regeneration which was necessary before Pentecost, but the Synoptics presume regeneration for the disciples prior to the passion. Furthermore, similar wording between verse 21 and 17:18 indicates that the Spirit had been active in the disciples before the ascension.

Perhaps a verse in Ezekiel holds a clue to the understanding of John. In the Septuagint of Ezekiel 37:9 are two words found in John 20:22—*pneuma* (spirit) and *emphysaō* (breathe on). Ezekiel refers to the breathing of new life into Israel after the climatic effect of the word of judgment he pronounces on Israel when she was dead in exile. In the episode the prophet is taken to the valley where he had received his commission (cf. Ezek. 3:22) to see the effect of the prophetic word of judgment. The prophet then breathes into lifeless Israel, who then rises as a mighty army (37:10). The reception of the Spirit is thus the means by which Israel is revived for ministry. Now let us turn to John. By chapter 20 Jesus' public ministry has ended, and Israel has been rejected. John has already used the experience of Isaiah to describe Israel's unbelief (12:38, 40; cf. Isa. 6:9–10; 53:1; Lindars 1972, 437) and makes clear that the ministry of Jesus, after the rejection of the nation, had in mind the creation of remnant Israel in true prophetic continuity. Though Pentecost would direct the new community into prophetic mission, John reveals that before Pentecost an alternative Israel is called into being, which the Gospel had long envisaged (see 1:10–12, 31 and the replacement claims that Jesus makes as the true Israel in chaps. 2–4). Christians are to proclaim sins as having been forgiven, and what Jesus transfers in verse 23 is the ability to provide assurance for the forgiveness. In verse 23 Jesus does not transfer to the disciples the power to forgive; rather, they can pronounce on divine forgiveness as having been given or withheld.

When the Gospel of John ends, the new community foreshadowed in 1:12 has been called into being. And the disciples are poised to go out in mission to the Jews first and then to the Gentiles. John's eschatology has focused on the construction of this restored community of Israel, brought into being by the nucleus of "as many as received him" (1:12 KJV). This restored Israel is a community established by the forgiveness of sins, in which Jew and Gentile alike are joined by a membership of grace, not race. At the head of the community is the one responsible for its form and function, that is, Jesus of Nazareth, the divine Messiah of Israel. Questions of *whence* and *whither* regarding Jesus' origin and destination have now been resolved, as the Gospel ends with the resurrection and the impending ascension of the divine Son of God.

11

Pauline Eschatology

The call of Paul as apostle to the Gentiles surfaces as a major determining factor of his eschatology. Whereas the ministry of Jesus ushered in the end, Paul's function was to facilitate the implementation of the divine plan that was enabled by the crucifixion and resurrection. Indeed, Paul identifies his function with the messianic events that ushered in the final day of salvation (Bowers 1976, 172). Conscious of his eschatological function and mission, Paul was driven to minister by his conviction that the Gentiles must now unite with Israel. His soteriology is thus based on his eschatological understanding of the implications of the Christ event as it completes Israel's expectations. In Jesus, Israel's Messiah, the expectations for humanity at the end had now been drawn into the present in terms of judgment and salvation with, in both cases, interim verdicts requiring final confirmation. The Jewish doctrine of two sequential ages, this age and the age to come, is modified by Paul. He taught that the two overlapped, and that through the Spirit of Christ believers could partially and presently experience the blessings at the end. In ecclesiological terms, this Pauline soteriology reaches its corporate conclusion when Jew and Gentile become a third factor (see Eph.). They are spiritually integrated in Christ into one new man that requires continual growth and development until the fullness of the one new man is achieved at the eschaton.

The Context of Paul's Eschatology:
The Overlap of the Ages

Characteristic of Paul's eschatology, as of Jewish eschatology, is a dualistic doctrine of the two ages, two worlds in conflict with one another. In Paul's writings, *aiōn* (age) connotes a temporal view of the situation; and *kosmos* (world) connotes a spatial view. (The Jews conceived of "this age" and "the age to come.") Paul regards this age as being in the hands of the evil powers that had come to rule over it, creating cosmic disorder as they did. Though the present age is a time of overlap, it will be replaced by the coming age. At the end of the present age will be a final judgment, when the sway of the powers, which had in fact been defeated by the work of the cross, will finally be abrogated and when all humanity will appear at the judgment bar: the righteous to receive their reward of eternal life in consequence of their covenant membership and their careful safeguarding of covenant demands and the wicked to receive eternal punishment.

The present eon, under the rule of its god Satan (2 Cor. 4:4), is an age characterized by sinfulness, rebellion, and unrighteousness. The principalities and powers of the age are opposed to Christ and to believers (Rom. 8:37–39). The word *kosmos* connotes the life-style of this age, which is antithetical towards God. Paul never uses the word in a positive sense to refer to the future eon. Though the *kosmos* is evil and God will destroy it, it is still the arena of God's saving work. Indeed, God is presently at work reconciling the *kosmos* through Jesus Christ to himself (2 Cor. 5:19).

Paul's experience on the Damascus road revealed to him that the age to come, by means of the death and resurrection of Jesus the Messiah, had obtruded into the present evil age. Through the person of Jesus, the last age of salvation had come into the world. Though believers are still members of the present evil age, they are also members of the new people of God, looking forward to the advent of the new world (Eph. 1:20–21), the foretaste of which they are now experiencing. Thus, in Paul's view, the death, resurrection, and ascension of Christ represent the breaking in of the new age into the present, by which the future has become a present reality. Having died in Christ, believers are now members of the new age.

Paul uses distinctive terminology to express the dualism of this age and the age to come (cf. Eph. 1:21; 2:7) and to connote a bridge between the old and new, terminology such as the first and Last Adam, the old and new man, and the flesh and the spirit. The final eschatological movement towards a new age had come in Jesus Christ. He is the first born of this new age in both time and rank. He is the inaugurator of the new age, the one who has ushered in the new world. Envisioning two orbs of power, Paul calls on us to indicate by our actions to which sphere of power we belong (Duff 1989, 280). For Ernst Käsemann, the fundamental question of apocalyptic is, "To whom does the sovereignty of the world belong?" (1969, 135). Indeed, Paul's theology incorporates such dualism, though limited, in which principalities and powers vie for lordship over creation (Duff 1989, 282). An individual's choice for Lord is either the demonic powers or Jesus. Either we are in bondage to sin, or Christ has made us free as his bondslaves. According to Käsemann's interpretation of Paul, however, we are never solely on our own. We are always specific pieces of the world, and we become in the last resort what we are by determination from outside. Käsemann is correct that each individual life mirrors the cosmic contention for the lordship of this world. For Paul, sin is no longer a list of wrong acts but a cosmic influence, a personified power. Sin is not something we do, but a power come into the world that claims us (Rom. 5:12). It enslaves us (Rom. 6:16) and demands its wages (Rom. 6:23). Thus, the self always acts in relation to a power beyond itself. I, but not I, commits sins. And Paul has the same understanding of grace. Though Paul or any other person may work hard, it is God who has worked in him to produce the result.

Paul stands among those upon whom the end of the ages has come (1 Cor. 10:11) and among those aware that the form of this world is passing away (1 Cor. 7:31). Standing at the turn of the age, Paul speaks of a new way of knowing that is ours, not by nature, but by the gift of the Spirit (Duff 1989, 286). Our new vision enables us to realize that there is a war being waged in our world between God and the powers of sin and death. But in the resurrection of Christ we see the outcome of the battle.

Prophetic Call and Eschatological Function

In Galatians 1:15–16 Paul refers to the decisive event of his life—the one that took place on the Damascus road. However, the images Paul uses are not predominantly ones of conversion but of prophetic commission. He expresses his experience in language similar to that of the Servant's call in Isaiah 49:1. Both the Servant and Paul had been set aside before birth with a mission to the nations to fulfil Israel's Sinaitic vocation as a divine witness. The textual correspondences between the verses in Galatians and the verse in Isaiah (also see Acts 13:47; cf. Isa. 49:6; and Acts 26:16–18; cf. Isa. 42:1–4) do not signify that Paul saw himself as the Isaianic Servant, but do indicate that Paul viewed his mission as arising from the ministry of Jesus, the Servant: "Paul understood his mission as an element of the eschatological events previewed in Isaiah 40–66 and fulfilled in Christ" (Bowers 1976, 143).

Paul worshiped the same God both before and after his call, but the call led him to reconsider and, indeed, reverse some fundamental convictions. Consider his persecution of Christians. It is apparent that before his call Paul was aware of and most resolutely rejected the basic Christian claim that Jesus was the Messiah of Israel, had been raised from the dead, and had been exalted to be Lord (Acts 2:36). Further, Paul's persecution reveals that he regarded the emerging Christian group as a pernicious and deviant form of Judaism, and his role in the death of Stephen indicates that Paul believed the new sect to devalue the law of Moses.

According to Paul, his authority as an apostle stems from his encounter with the risen Jesus on the Damascus road. Jesus approached Paul with one end in mind—to make him an apostle to the Gentiles. Note that each of the three accounts of Paul's conversion in Acts mentions his commission to the Gentiles (9:15; 22:21; 26:17–18). It is not likely that Paul viewed himself as being called to be an apostle and then later narrowed his mission to the Gentiles (Dunn 1987, 252). No, Paul's commission was specific, for Jesus revealed a great mystery to him—that by the death of Christ the Gentiles had become fellow heirs and members of the one body of the people of God (Eph. 3:6).

Paul's understanding of his mission appears to have been clear; yet, is there a sufficient explanation to account for it? We suggest there is— Paul's recognition of Jesus' messiahship. Though some would challenge this view (Dunn 1987, 256–57), the nature of Jesus' messiahship as Israel's King determined the mission of Paul to the Gentiles. As Christian preaching had claimed, the advent of Jesus as Servant-Messiah made possible the fulfilment of Israel's traditional eschatological role as a light to the Gentiles (Acts 13:47; cf. Isa. 49:6). Indeed, Paul's christological and soteriological emphases were derived from his enlightenment on the Damascus road (Kim 1982, 267, 329), for he understood that the salvation of the Gentiles had been rendered possible by their incorporation with believing Israel into the risen Jesus, Israel's Messiah and now Lord of all.

God revealed his Son, whose followers Paul had previously persecuted, to the Jew from Tarsus. The call to preach the Jewish Messiah to the Gentiles necessarily caused Paul to reevaluate Mosaic law and Jewish tradition, since these along with circumcision had been the great factors separating Jew from Gentile. In speaking of his former life in Judaism, as in Galatians 1:13–14, Paul does not say that he cut the ties with his religious past. Rather, Paul indicates that the call radically changed his practice of Judaism. And what of the Gentiles—were they to practice Judaism? The issue of Paul's understanding of the relationship between Mosaic law and Gentiles and Christians is one of several we will consider before addressing each Pauline epistle.

Regarding Gentiles, Christians, and Mosaic Law

Paul's vocational understanding, a major tenet of his theology, appeared in the form of a commitment to missionary activity that included the Gentiles in a new people of God. From his experience on the way to Damascus, Paul received a new comprehension of Israel's role under her Messiah as well as other theological insights for the emerging new people of God, itself to be the mark of the eschaton come. Paul henceforth saw that Jew and Gentile are related as one people of God under the primacy of the Abrahamic covenant.

To be sure, Paul's ministry to the Gentiles evoked opposition, for how were they to be admitted into a group that after the resurrection was essentially a saved Jewish community? Through the years, Christian traditions have variously defined the opposition facing Paul as well as his response. For example, the traditional Protestant view has cast the opposition to Paul as Jews or Jewish Christians who argued that circumcision was necessary for entrance into the covenant and that obedience to Jewish law was necessary for salvation after entrance. In response, Paul preached that salvation in Christ derived solely from the grace of God and presented Judaism as a religion of works, for God had given Israel the Torah so that Judaism might earn salvation by fulfilling it (Watson 1986, 1–19). According to this traditional Protestant view, the issue that stood between Paul and his opponents was the question of how one obtained and retained God's acceptance. But does this particular formulation of the issue take into account the historical context of Paul's day? Ever since the publication of Krister Stendahl's provocative essay on Paul in 1963, some have suggested that Pauline studies since the Reformation have been dominated by the personal historical concerns of Martin Luther, who, taking a cue from Augustine's application of Pauline teaching on justification to timeless human problems, brought to the Pauline Epistles a very different personal agenda from that which had prompted their writing.

Modern Pauline studies began with Luther. His interpretation of Paul was dominated by a presupposition that the attempt of sinful human beings to earn salvation by merit is a terrible misuse of the law. In his 1535 lectures on Galatians he noted in regard to 3:10 that to be justified by the works of the law is to deny the righteousness that is by faith. Here and elsewhere Luther refuted the traditional conception of sin as the transgression of particular commandments, asserting that those who keep the commandments manifest the essence of sin since they rely on themselves and reject the grace of God. When Paul condemned works, argued Luther, he meant moral activity in general and not just Jewish ceremonies, which were abolished by the coming of Christ. Such moral performance was for Luther the essential Jewish misuse of the law, for the law was given to teach us about Christ so as to enable us to recognize our inability to do good, since the demands of the law must be fulfilled. Otherwise humanity would be condemned without hope. Luther identified two additional purposes for the law. It was given to reveal sin and provoke despair, thereby causing us to flee to Christ for mercy, and it was given to guide the earthly lives of those who are justified by faith.

Stendahl and others argue that Luther missed the point of the historical context of the Pauline correspondence. Thus, as a result of Protestant incorporation of Luther's experience and interpretation into Paul's theology of justification by faith, we think too much about Paul's conversion in psychological terms and consequently provide models for a theology of personal justification by faith that ignore the Pauline context. Indeed, even the word *conversion*, while a correct expression of the reality, focuses too much on Paul as a personality. Consider Paul's account of his encounter on the Damascus road. It is not likely that Paul viewed this as a conversion, for Paul, unlike Luther, never seems to have labored under a burden of personal guilt. Paul appears to have been a fulfilled Jew confident in the credal basis on which his faith had rested (Phil. 3:6). He seems to have experienced no troubles, no qualms of conscience, no feelings of shortcomings. Nowhere in Paul's writings is there any indication of spiritual difficulties suffered by Saint Paul in his pre-Christian life. According to Stendahl and others, the Christian apostle Paul set behind him, not a series of shortcomings the recall of which was agonizing, but a wealth of past achievements in which, as a loyal Jew, he took justifiable pride (Phil. 3:13). Though the fact that such past glories, including his persecution of the church, caused Paul some remorse, it came after his call. Moreover, there is no indication in Paul's letters of such remorse or doubts prior to his call to mission. That the persecutor became the apostle only gave more glory to God. The only identifiable sin that Paul recalls is his persecution of the church, and to recognize that sort of sin does not require, Stendahl argued, an "introspective conscience" (1963, 199). In 1 Corinthians 15:10 Paul implies that he had in fact atoned by working harder than all, seemingly confident that before the judgment seat of Christ he would be cleared. Thus for Paul the law had not been a tyrant but a benign tutor.

The modern debate begun by Stendahl was carried further in 1977 by E. P. Sanders, who examined Jewish writings relating to the early

Christian period. He asserts that the long-held view that Paul's objection was to Judaism's use of the law to gain acceptance with Christ misrepresents Palestinian Judaism, for it did not teach that human beings must earn salvation by their own efforts. Consider Sanders's summary of his understanding of rabbinic religion:

> God has chosen Israel and Israel has accepted the election. In his role as king God gave Israel commandments which they are to obey as best as they can. Obedience is rewarded and disobedience is punished. In the case of failure to obey, however, man has recourse to divinely ordained means of atonement, in all of which repentance is required. As long as he maintains his desire to stay in the covenant, he has a share in God's covenantal promises, including life in the world to come. The intention and effort to be obedient constitute the condition for remaining in the covenant but they do not earn it. (p. 180)

Thus, Judaism was based on covenantal election by grace and the use of the law to maintain election. For Paul, salvation is by Christ alone, and Judaism is not so much wrong as it is inadequate. Nevertheless, Paul's view of the rights of Gentiles would mean the ultimate separation of emerging Christianity from Judaism. Sanders frames the debate in the early development of Christianity as whether Christians should continue as a reform movement within Judaism or separate from it. The difference between Paul and the Judaism of his day, reasons Sanders, lay in the realm of salvation history. The Jews depended on their status as God's covenant people who possessed the law; as a result, they missed out on a better righteousness that is based solely on the new status of being found in Christ. Thus, the difference between the Jews and Paul was not merit versus grace but a difference between two dispensations. Sanders's argument rests on his analysis of rabbinic materials, an analysis which is consistent with the work of G. F. Moore published in 1932 and with continued Jewish criticism of the traditional Protestant view of Rabbinic Judaism. The essential thrust of the argument is sound. Thus, sanctification emerges as the difference between Judaism and Saint Paul. That is, Judaism recognized the role of grace in covenant acceptance (Christian *justification*) but viewed subsequent acceptance by God and spiritual growth (Christian *sanctification*) as dependent upon allegiance to the Torah. According to Paul, both justification and sanctification are dependent upon faith. Human effort is the effect and not the cause of the better righteousness, which means covenant incorporation in Christ.

When Saul the Pharisee was confronted by Christianity, he saw problems regarding messianism and the law. Christianity had unacceptably and blasphemously proclaimed a crucified Messiah. As the antithesis of what was expected, Jesus had died the death of a pretender. The law contained God's will for Israel. Jesus, and later Stephen, had questioned its role. No loyal Jew would have dared to do this! But from Acts 9 onward the converted Paul comes to see the Christians as the new people of God. For him questions regarding the Messiah and the Torah had been resolved on the Damascus road. No longer would he view national Israel as the inheritor of the promises, and no longer would the Torah provide a barrier between Jew and Gentile.

When Paul refers to the law (*nomos*) in his letters, as he does over one hundred times, his remarks are in regard to the Torah, the Mosaic law. In each case, Paul uses the singular *nomos*, never the plural, indicating his view of the law as a single entity, a body of legal corpora. Expositors seeking to analyze Paul's use of *nomos* have claimed the existence of distinctions in his use of the word. For instance, some claim that when Paul uses *nomos* with the article, he refers to the Mosaic law. But when he uses it without the article, Paul refers to a body of legal principles or to law in general. Such distinctions, however, cannot be carried through consistently and are usually abandoned. Even in such contested passages as Romans 3:27, 7:21, and 8:3, the connotation of Israel's Torah can be maintained. To the Greeks *nomos* referred to a system of customs or rules, whereas to the Jews *tôrâ* was direction for life within the covenant, not an absolute code. Even so Paul argues that the era of the Mosaic Torah is now over (Gal. 3). He replaces the demand for Torah performance with direction now offered to the believer through the work of the Holy Spirit by which the will of God, generally manifested in the Torah, is expressed. Though the emphasis on conduct in Paul loses its Jewishness, the expected results are basically the same as those anticipated by the Jews.

Regarding the Church

The correspondence of Paul found in the New Testament is addressed not to individuals but to groups of the faithful, that is, to congregations or churches. The word *ekklēsia* (assembly, but often translated as "church") occurs almost sixty times in Paul's writings. Outside of the New Testament, *ekklēsia* commonly refers to the town assemblies of the Greek city-state (also in Acts 19:39, 41). In the Septuagint, *ekklēsia* appears as the translation for *qāhāl*, which signifies the congregation of Israel gathered before Yahweh.

What does Paul mean when he uses the word *ekklēsia*? Consider his first epistle to the Thessalonians, which was sent to "the church (*ekklēsia*) of the Thessalonians in God the Father and the Lord Jesus Christ" (1:1). Paul addresses a specific assembly, one distinguished from secular assemblies and guilds by "in God the Father" and from the Jewish synagogs by "and the Lord Jesus Christ." In other early epistles, Paul uses *ekklēsia* in a similar way, such as in Galatians 1:13, where the "church of God" probably refers to the Jerusalem church. Paul also addressed correspondence to the faithful in cities that would have had more than one church, as to those in Corinth or Rome. Here Paul, sometimes using the plural *ekklēsiai* (Rom. 16:4, 16), speaks to those in house churches. The idea of a national or universal church, which is so common to us, would have been foreign to Paul (see, for example, 1 Cor. 11:18, "when you come together as a church").

In the later epistles to the Colossians and the Ephesians, despite some variation and perhaps development in Paul's use of *ekklēsia*, it is still doubtful whether Paul moves much beyond the concept of a local church. For instance, Colossians 4:15 indicates clearly that the church at Colossae was a local church. In Colossians 1:18–23 Paul introduces the notion of a nonlocal church of which Christ is the head, but this is not a reference to a universal church but to a supranatural, heavenly phenomenon, the evidence for which is manifested in the local body. To discern what this means, consider the context in Colossians. In 1:9–2:7 Paul refers to the victorious Christ and the kingdom of light, which believers have entered (Banks 1979, 54). In 3:3 we learn that believers already dwell with Christ in the heavenlies. Perhaps Paul was influenced by the concept of the heavenly Jerusalem (Tob. 13:16) or of Christians as citizens of the heavenly commonwealth (2 Esd. 7:26) in order to picture Christians as enrolled and already assembled as citizens of heaven. Thus, in Colossians and Ephesians Paul depicts a heavenly assembly in which Christians, as members of the body of Christ, are now participating (Eph. 2:5–6). Though the assembly's culmination will take place on the last day, its earmarks are presently expressed through local Christian churches.

In Paul's now and not-yet schema, believers are now metaphorically with Christ enjoying fellowship with him in the heavenlies. Enriched by this present fellowship, Christians are to look forward to its eschatological consummation (Eph. 1:14; 2:7). In Ephesians 3:10 Paul refers to the wisdom of God as manifested in the existence of local churches, which are visible to the world. The thought most likely shifts to the heavenly and eschatological church, which is gathered at worship as the local church is gathered, in Ephesians 3:21. References to the *ekklē-sia* in chapter 5 also refer to the end-time assembly, for it is to be presented to God as a glorious church, not having spot or wrinkle (vv. 23, 25, 29, 32).

In summary, Paul uses *ekklēsia* to denote a local body of believers in which the present tensions of reconciliation are exhibited. *Ekklēsia* also represents a divine conception for which Christ died (Eph. 5:25) and which is presently gathered around Christ in the heavenlies. Finally, Paul uses *ekklēsia* for the final assembly of the redeemed, the new man fully composed (Eph. 2:15), the body perfectly expressed, the fulness of believers constituted as a continuously worshiping assembly. In Paul's view, Christians belong both to the heavenly church, which perpetually worships, as well as to the local church, which meets intermittently. Not merely part of the heavenly church, the local gatherings manifest the principles and essentials of the heavenly one while emphasizing the completed action of Christ and its heavenly implications.

Epistle to the Romans

What lay before Paul as he wrote the Epistle to the Romans exemplifies the international character of his ministry. Consider the following scenario: Paul, in Corinth (Rom. 15:26), is planning to take a collection to the Christian poor in Jerusalem (15:25–26). Thereafter, his destination is Spain, though he hopes to stop in Rome on the way (15:24). In one sense, the letter is a substitute for Paul's once again deferred visit, but, as we shall see, it does much more as well.

Paul's understanding of the time in which he lived is clear—the reign of God had come, and the people of God are in the process of reestablishment. In the early years of Paul's ministry, the issue on which he focused was the admission of the Gentiles into the believing community by faith alone and their perseverance by the same doctrine. While upholding Abraham as the one father of God's people, Paul also used Abraham's example to demonstrate that all blessing from God comes through faith. Thus, when Paul writes to believers in Rome, his mind and heart are heavy with the great problem of finding compatibility between Jews and Gentiles in the growing churches. Indeed, what he writes will become a theological exposition of the basis for reconciliation between the races.

The Epistle to the Romans seems a surrogate for Paul's contemplated but postponed visit (1:13; 15:22–23; Elliott 1990, 84). In it Paul explores virtually every major tenet of his theology as he expounds the nature of his gospel. The main theme of the early chapters (1:18–3:20) is human accountability, that is, the equal status of Jew and Gentile in judgment. The argument continues (3:21–4:25) with the question of the equal status of Jew and Gentile in salvation, under the Abrahamic covenant (4:1–25).

For there is only one people of God, and the partition between Jew and Gentile has been broken down (Eph. 2:11–22). While Christians are the continuation of the believing Israel of the Old Testament, Christians are also a new creation, one new man in Christ incorporating the Gentiles. As demonstrated in Acts, the Christian break with Judaism was real, indeed inevitable once the crucified Jesus was confessed as Lord and Christ (Acts 2:36). Church and synagog come to be distinct groups within the society. Thus, the Gentiles enter the new people of God, which both continues and replaces the believing Israel of the Old Testament as well as appropriates Israel's privileges.

In the nineteenth century, Ferdinand Baur with some correctness argued that the purpose of Romans was to do away with Jewish exclusivism, contending further that early church history was dominated by a struggle between the Pauline, universalist wing and the Jewish, particularist wing, which was represented by Peter and James and was identified with Jerusalem (1873, 322). Paul, according to Baur, did not regard the Jew/Gentile problem impersonally, that is, as a generally applicable paradigm illustrating the human plight and its resolution, for the problem was much more immediate than that. As apostle to the Gentiles, Paul realized that if righteousness and salvation could be obtained only by the works of the law, then Jews alone would possess them. Baur correctly perceived Paul's universalist emphasis.

The Epistle to the Romans helps us understand Paul's state of mind as he was about to undertake a journey to Jerusalem, where he would be required to show the compatibility of his gospel with the purposes of God for Israel. After establishing that justification by faith is open to all (chaps. 1–8), Paul demonstrates in the climax of the letter that Jew and Gentile are now incorporated into a new people of God, built upon the promises given to Abraham and continued through historic Israel (chaps. 9–11). What follows (chaps. 13–16) is ethical instruction based upon the resolution of the Jew-Gentile controversy. While seizing the opportunity to proclaim the significance of the death, resurrection, and present enthronement of Jesus, the Christ, Israel's Messiah, Paul attempts in the letter to reconcile the Christian and Jewish factions in Rome (Donfried 1970, 449).

Ancient Promises (Rom. 1:1–17)

After Paul's call, his focus was to share his faith with the Gentiles. Such inclusion had been anticipated by prophetic eschatology as a characteristic of the arrival of the last days and thus the advent of the new creation and new covenant. Paul himself operated under the assumption that the present possibility of incorporation into Christ is the hallmark of the advent of the last days. Indeed, the major mark of Pauline theology is the present eschatological oneness of humankind in Christ, which has been made possible by the universality of the gospel, which obliterates all distinctions. As he begins his letter to the Romans, Paul notes that the gospel had first been formulated and announced by the Old Testament prophets (1:2) and stands in theological continuity with Israel's faith. The gospel concerns the messianic sonship of Jesus, whose deity had now been attested by the resurrection (v. 4). Paul argues that the concept of messiahship he preaches is advocated or implied in the Old Testament and is thus clearly congruent with Old Testament expectations. After stating his gratefulness for the believers in Rome and his desire to visit them, Paul moves in verses 16–17 to the theme of his writing, which is a further definition of the gospel. This gospel concerns God's righteousness and manifests the power of God leading to final salvation (v. 16). (Note that the preposition *eis* in the phrase "for the salvation" directs attention to the goal [Williams 1980, 255].) In short, this gospel brings to fulfilment in this new age all the hopes bound with Jewish expectations of the end. God is presently allowing his righteousness to be revealed through this gospel on the basis of faith, and this revelation leads to the exercise of further faith (v. 17).

What is God's righteousness? Paul does not explain precisely what his understanding of God's righteousness is. Presumably his readers would have been familiar with the concept; however, we are dependent upon the context of verses 16–17 and upon Paul's use of similar phrases in other writings. Among the many suggestions offered as to Paul's meaning, three stand out as the most favored: God's righteousness is (1) what God requires in terms of human conduct, (2) God's gift effected through justification, and (3) God's powerful saving activity. The first suggestion is contextually inappropriate since in verse 17 the righteousness is a divine, not human, property and is not a divine demand. Though the second suggestion is a possibility, Paul could have expressed the idea unambiguously, as he does in Philippians 3:9 ("the righteousness that comes from God"). Moreover, the notion of God's righteousness as something that God gives is problematic in the context of verse 17, for the parallel in verse 18 is God's wrath, something that belongs to and is intrinsic to God (Williams 1980, 259). The third suggestion has been strongly presented in recent years (Williams 1980, 242–43), but contrary to it is the precise language of verse 16. The *righteousness* of God is not "the power of God unto salvation" (KJV); rather, the *gospel* demonstrates the power of God, for through the gospel God's righteousness is presently being revealed.

Any determination of the meaning of God's righteousness must take into account two factors, the first of which is often overlooked, namely, (1) the parallel established between God's righteousness and God's wrath (Rom. 1:17–18) and (2) the association of the righteousness of God in verse 17 with the quotation from Habakkuk 2:4. Since God's wrath is an intrinsic characteristic of God, a fixed attitude against sin that issues appropriate punishment, it follows that God's righteousness must also be an intrinsic divine characteristic. As the polar opposite of God's wrath, God's righteousness must be God's fixed and manifested readiness to save his people. The quotation from Habakkuk is found again in Galatians 3:11, in a context that identifies the gospel with God's adherence to his intention to bring both Jews and Gentiles within the framework of his promises to Abraham (Gal. 3:6–18). Since Paul quotes Habakkuk 2:4 only in Galatians 3:11 and Romans 1:17, it is quite likely that Paul understands God's righteousness in Romans 1 as divine faithfulness to the promises made to Abraham (Williams 1980, 263–64).

The Ages (Rom. 3:21–5:11)

Paul's theme as stated in Romans 1:16–17 is the base on which the remainder of the letter rests. Romans 1:18–3:20 demonstrates the accountability of all humankind before an impartial God (Bassler 1982, 164–70) who demands righteousness. Redemption for all is thus required; even Jews have no excuse but are united with Gentiles in subservience to sin (Elliott 1990, 135–46). The focus then shifts in 3:21–31 to the way in which God has met our basic need. As God's response, the death of Christ ushers in the Christian's experience of the last days. Given an eschatological setting, Jesus' death constitutes the decisive eon-changing event within the Pauline apocalyptic framework (Beker 1980, 205).

THE EON-CHANGING EVENT AND THE LAW (ROM. 3:21–31)

With the advent of the new age, Jew and Gentile (note the "all" of Rom. 3:22–23) are now reconciled. Divine fidelity to the Abrahamic promises, God's desire for salvation for all, has thus been manifested apart from the law (v. 21), since both Jew and Gentile must be included in this new forgiveness and since Jews may make no particular claim and the law would exclude the Gentiles (Elliott 1990, 145). Moreover, it has been manifested as the Old Testament promised it would be. God bypassed the law in this new eschatological demonstration of his righteousness (v. 21), which has been mediated by faith in Christ and is universally applicable (v. 22). Obliterating present distinctions, this faith produces the one new family of God (vv. 22–24). All sinned in Adam, resulting in a loss of glory (v. 23), a typical Jewish reference to the fate of Adam by which the distinctive divine gift to humankind in the creation narratives was forfeited (Dunn 1980, 102). But God accepts and restores sinners to a right relationship in the covenant, that is, justifies them, taking the initiative to do so on the basis of Christ's death (v. 24). God does this unconditionally, with no reference to human performance (cf. v. 23), by the gift of grace whereby a new action had been taken to free humanity, just as in Israel's exodus. Not merely a general message of forgiveness, the redemption of verse 24 points toward a change of ownership, a transfer of lordships, characteristic of the new age which Jesus' death has ushered in (Ziesler 1981–82, 356–59). Christ, who opened up a new mode of existence, is the eschatological breakthrough of God into a new reality of human existence in which all may participate.

In verse 25 Paul refers to what God has done in Christ in sacrificial terms: "God presented him as a sacrifice of atonement (*hilastērion*) through faith in his blood." God was appeased, propitiated by the death of Christ. The word *hilastērion* is used invariably in the Septuagint for the lid of the ark, the mercy seat which played such a crucial role in ceremonies on the Day of Atonement. On that day, the priestly representative of Israel and Israel's God would meet at the mercy seat; therefore, atonement would be made at the place of atonement. It is likely that Paul uses *hilastērion* to refer to Christ as the new mercy seat, as both the place and yet the means of atonement offered sacrificially. The place is the blood-spattered Messiah, whose offering needs to be received by personal faith in its efficacy (v. 25), just as in Old Testament times when believers approached God by faith in the God-given sacrificial system. God has graciously provided what his righteous attitude towards sin demanded, but that provision is so different from the hidden transaction within the veil of the tabernacle on the Day of Atonement. God displayed Christ publicly to show his justice and to put in the right those who have faith in Jesus (v. 26) for the remission of sins formerly committed (v. 25). This propitiation in Christ is God's final declaration against sin. By this, all Jewish boasting is excluded since law-keeping, and thus Jewish particularism, has played no part in the transaction (v. 27). God has gained the eschatological victory by the sacrifice of Christ. Both Jew and Gentile are justified only by faith (vv. 28–30).

The essence of Paul's doctrine of soteriology is based on the sacrificial death of Christ. Even beyond Romans 3:25–26 this is the central message of the Pauline gospel (see, e.g., 1 Cor. 2:2; 1 Thess. 5:9–10). Since the message involved an unthinkable doctrine of a crucified God, it was not generally acceptable to the Gentiles. The Jews could not associate the cross with their messiah. Thus, the cross was a scandal, an insult to messianic hopes as it was foolishness to the Greeks (1 Cor. 1:23). Yet Paul shows the cross to be part of the divine plan to rescue humankind from the present age, lying in the hands of the evil one (Gal. 1:4). Using the traditional Jewish concept of the two ages, Paul customarily contrasts this present age with "the age to come" (Eph. 1:21 NRSV) and recognizes the tension between these two ages being brought to bear upon Christians as the good fight of faith is fought in present experience. The new age will be formally completed with the eschatological return of Christ, but, according to Paul, this new age is presently overlapping with the age of evil.

For Paul, the turning point of the ages, the critical moment in history, was the death of Christ. The death also occasioned the cosmic eschatological battle preceding the end, called *Armageddon* in Jewish theology. As the beginning of the end, Jesus' death delivers the world from cosmic powers, which are overcome and defeated by the cross (Rom. 8:38; Eph. 6:12; Col. 2:15). This salvific interpretation of the Messiah's death constitutes the gospel that Paul received (cf. 1 Cor. 15:1–5).

ABRAHAMIC FRAMEWORK (ROM. 4)

In chapter 4 Paul explores in Jewish terms the implications of the soteriology set forth at the end of chapter 3. That is, God's covenant faithfulness, demonstrated through the salvific death of Christ, makes all believers one in Christ Jesus and of the family of Abraham. The verdict of the last days has been anticipated in Jesus, and the particularism of the Sinai covenant has gone. Covenant acceptance is now available to all, not on the basis of the Torah, but by belief in God's steadfast maintenance of the Abrahamic promises in spite of human sin and transgression and in God's provision for forgiveness of sins in the death of Jesus Christ. This does not mean, however, that Gentiles are to become Jews (Rom. 4:1–4, 9–12). Consider the rhetorical questions in verse 1, "What shall we say? That we have found Abraham as our forefather according to the flesh?" (Hays 1985, 81). These questions suggest what Paul states clearly in verse 13—faith, not physical descent, makes all in the world legatees of the Abrahamic promises.

RECONCILIATION AND JUSTIFICATION (ROM. 5:1–11)

Paul uses various concepts to describe God's soteriological movement toward us. One such concept found in Romans 5 is reconciliation, which is drawn from the sphere of human relations. Though reconciliation holds a vital position in his theology, Paul uses the language of reconciliation infrequently. For instance, the verb *to reconcile* (*katallassō*) appears just five times in Paul's writings (once in a secular context, see 1 Cor. 7:11). Apart from Romans 5, the other principal context in which Paul addresses the concept is 2 Corinthians 5 (see p. 292).

Reconciliation is the cessation of human-initiated hostilities against God (cf. Col. 1:20–22), but it is based upon the action of God's love in Christ's death. This eschatological act of salvation has made possible a new way to live, that is, we have the possibility of being accepted by God and living at peace with God (Rom. 5:1). Reconciliation's eschatological character is seen most clearly in Colossians 1:20, where Paul describes reconciliation as the achievement within the cosmic order of harmony and peace, brought about by Christ's dethronement of the powers of evil.

Paul's conception of reconciliation reveals his eschatology to be a partially realized one, as do other aspects of Pauline theology. On the one hand, reconciliation has happened (Rom. 5:8–11; 2 Cor. 5:18–21; Eph. 2:11–19; Col. 1:20–22), having become the foundation for the new creation, the "now" of the day of salvation and the acceptable time (Ridderbos 1975, 183). On the other hand, reconciliation points to a final end, when the "new creation" (2 Cor. 5:17) finds final fulfilment in the descent of the New Jerusalem (Rev. 21:2). Though reconciled, the present creation waits with eager longing for its final liberation (Rom. 8:18–25). Though reconciliation has been accomplished by Christ's victory, we await the full and total restoration. Thus, Paul's eschatology is both realized and future.

In Romans 5:1–11 Paul also summarizes his thoughts on another important aspect of his theology—justification—the discussion of which began in 3:20. A concept drawn from legal proceedings, justification is another way, along with having peace with God (Rom. 5:1), of describing the present state of humankind's potential as a result of God's intervention in Christ. Since justification deals with the basic issue of entering into a right covenantal relationship with God, it is foundational (Wright 1980, 15). Both attesting salvation from the past and securing it for the future, justification looks forward as well as backward, but the movement is basically eschatological since justification is, as it is in Jewish terms, evidence of the judgment of the last day having been drawn into the present. Justification focuses on Christ's saving work for humankind and speaks to humankind's basic need of a right relationship with God (Rom. 1:16–18). In addition to justification, Paul refers to a future judgment according to works, which is associated with the last day (among others, see Rom. 2:14–16; 14:10–12; 1 Cor. 3:13–15; Snodgrass 1986, 85–87; Travis 1986, 61–64). Such judgment indicates the need for faithfulness to the revelation personally received, thereby revealing justification to be an anticipation of the final judgment. By insisting upon conduct appropriate to one's newly received status as the means of personal assurance of salvation, Paul does not espouse a doctrine of sanctification by works righteousness, but rather provides a description of those for whom the justifying grace of God has become real (Snodgrass 1986, 85–87).

Since Paul claims that demonstration of his righteousness has revealed a new eschatological horizon, it would follow that salvation is essentially an eschatological prospect. Consider what Paul writes in Romans 5:9: "Since we have now been justified by his blood, how much more shall we be saved from God's wrath through him!" Indeed, Paul conceives of salvation in Christ as fully achievable only in the age to come. Though the death and resurrection of Christ brought the advent of the new age, completion of the age must wait until Christ's return at the parousia (1 Cor. 15:22–28). Christians now enjoy the blessings of the end time, but there are still greater blessings to be enjoyed. True to his Jewish heritage, Paul speaks of salvation as basically future (Rom. 13:11; 1 Thess. 5:8), for Christians are presently in the process of being saved (1 Cor. 1:18; 15:2; 2 Cor. 2:15; 6:2). Rarely does Paul use the verb *save* in the past tense. When he does, it is qualified by some future note, as in the hope of Romans 8:24–25.

The World Groans (Rom. 5:12–21; 8:18–23)

According to Paul, the need for salvation can be traced all the way back to Adam (Rom. 5:12)—when humankind and the rest of the created world began to groan. Thereafter, the historical people of Abraham became God's intended answer to the problems raised by Adam's sin. Thus, Genesis 12 is a sequel to Genesis 1–11. Israel and her call to the Promised Land were to be the answers to Adam's expulsion from the garden, but Israel's failure meant that the task of being a light to lighten the Gentiles fell to Israel's representative, the Servant of Isaiah 40–55, and then to Israel's final representative, Jesus Christ. Since Israel could not receive the promises carried by her institutions, she also could not be God's new humanity. Though she was meant to be the remedy for Adam's sin, Israel became involved in the sin. In the Old Testament Israel provides not light but darkness; from the incident of the golden calf onwards (Exod. 32), the nation is always a clear failure. The Second Adam, Jesus, provides the salvation that humans, indeed the entire created world, so desperately need.

THE SECOND ADAM (ROM. 5:12–21)

Paul's Adam Christology as expressed in Romans 5:12–21 (cf. 1 Cor. 15:20–28; Col. 1:15–20) can best be understood in light of speculation regarding Adam during the intertestamental period. Such speculation focused on Adam as Israel, rather than Adam as a representative of humankind (Wright 1983, 363). The transfer of the original command to be fruitful and multiply from Adam to Abraham and his descendants (Gen. 12:2; 17:2, 7; 22:17–18; 28:3; 35:11–12; 47:27; 48:4) suggests that Abraham and his family would inherit the role of Adam. Indeed, God's purpose for the human race as expressed in Adam had devolved upon Israel. But Israel's possession of the land, the New Eden where Abraham's children were the new humanity, only multiplied Adam's sin.

Through the fall of Jerusalem and the exile in the sixth century B.C., Israel was expelled from the "Eden" into which she had been put. Associating Adam with Israel continued throughout the intertestamental period. By appropriating the status of Adam, the Qumran community thus claimed to be the New Israel (Wright 1983, 364). According to Jewish eschatology of the period, Adam, whose glory will be restored, incorporated the whole eschatological people of God.

Paul takes the speculation regarding Adam as Israel one step further by adding Jesus to the equation. In Romans 5:12–21 Paul contrasts human origin in Adam with human origin in Jesus, the Second Adam. Yet, Jesus is not a mere replacement for Adam, for Christ first had to deal with the trouble created by the old Adam. The regime of death prevailed from Adam to Moses, even upon those who had not sinned as Adam had done by disobeying a direct divine command (v. 14). In other words, death is universal because all have sinned in Adam (v. 12). The absence of law in the period between Adam and Moses serves to emphasize the direct connection between sin and death (Byrne 1981, 561). The entrance of Israel and her means of blessing for the world, the Torah, should have changed human history in a positive way; however, in Romans 9:30–10:4 Paul claims that Israel's misuse of the Torah was responsible for her fall. Elsewhere, in Galatians 3:19, Paul argues that the law had not helped Israel but had exacerbated her transgressions. Somehow Jesus had to undo what had been done; only then could Israel be given new life (Rom. 5:18–19). In verse 15 Paul contrasts the dire consequences induced by Adam's fall with the salvific results for humankind stemming from Christ's death. To atone for Adam's sin, the Last Adam obediently went to Calvary so that grace might abound where sin once had (Wright 1983, 372). By entering the human sphere at the point of "many trespasses" (v. 16), Jesus thus began where Adam had ended (Wright 1983, 371).

The Hope of Creation (Rom. 8:18–23)

Paul addresses the effect of Adam's sin on the created world in Romans 8:18–23. Verses 19–21 clearly imply that the frustration to which the creation has been subjected is linked to the fall since the revealing of the sons of God, that is, the full redemption of humankind, will reverse the process: "The creation waits in eager expectation for the sons of God to be revealed. For the creation was subjected to frustration [absence of purpose], not by its own choice, but by the will of the one who subjected it, in hope that the creation itself will be liberated from its bondage to decay and brought into the glorious freedom of the children of God." Though traditionally Adam has been identified as the implied subject of the passive "was subjected" in verse 20 (Cranfield 1975, 414–

15), the phrase "not by its own choice" excludes the human pair of Genesis 3. Rather, the created world was subjected by God to the curse upon the ground that resulted from the fall (Gen. 3:17–19).

Paul's references to the created world remind us of the very intimate connection between humankind and the world, for humankind is the reason for creation's subjection. Indeed, traditional Jewish exegesis binds the fate of the two together (see Isa. 2:19–21; 13:9–11). Paul emphasizes that humankind's fall is evident from the transmitted effects of the fall through humankind to the natural world. That is, the natural role of creation had been perverted by humankind's exploitation of it and inability to work fully with it. Yet, Paul recognizes an eschatological perspective regarding the world's subjection, for it was done "in hope" (Rom. 8:20). Thus when humankind finally enjoys the full experience of the final blessings of salvation, when the eschaton has arrived and the bodily resurrection of humankind will provide visible evidence of the new age, the natural world will also experience a release.

God had given humankind dominion over a world that needed care, a world in which chaos was a present reality. Yet, at the center God had also constructed an ideal, a model. The garden of God, the sanctuary at the center, manifested the potential for the world as a whole. In this sense, the garden served as a witness to the full purposes of God for humankind and the world. But what about the world as Paul knows it? It groans in travail (Rom. 8:22) until the time when with humankind it is released from the bondage into which the fall had brought it. In the meantime, our personal redemption requires that we assume the mantel of complete stewardship to which we were called in Genesis 1–2. God put us in the world for our development and for its care, and we are to serve one another by a rightful use of it.

Israel and Salvation (Rom. 9–11)

In Paul's view, believers and the created world will reap the benefits of Christ's having bypassed the failings of Israel to become the Second Adam. However, where does Israel now fit in the divine plan? What is the position of national Israel in this new era of salvation? According to Romans 1:16, the gospel is for the Jews first. Yet, should this be interpreted exclusively to mean that only some Jews will be saved or inclusively to mean that the nation as a whole will be brought into blessing? Paul addresses such questions and wrestles with the problem of Jewish unbelief in chapters 9–11.

Throughout Paul's early ministry, his main focus was the admission of the Gentiles into the believing community by faith alone. The apostle argues that salvation and sanctification are both by faith since there is only one people of God and that the true descendant of Abraham is the Christian. Christianity is thus the continuation of believing Israel of the Old Testament, the ideal worshiping community that lived on after all the political externals by which national Israel had been defined were gone. At the same time, Christians are also a new creation, one new man in Christ (Eph. 2:15; cf. Eph. 4:24; Col. 3:10). However, Paul emphasizes continuity between Israel and the new people, taking the view that one does not convert from Judaism but in Christ finds the fulfilment of the promises to Israel. Throughout Acts and the Pauline correspondence, Paul show a continued commitment to Israel. In Romans 9–11 this commitment is tempered by Israel's unbelief and the challenge of reconciliation.

After affirming his sorrow over national Israel (Rom. 9:1–5), Paul proclaims that Israel's unbelief does not mean that the Word of God has failed, for there is and always has been two Israels (v. 6). Yes, the rejection of Jesus by many Jews has drawn attention to the ambiguity of the term *Israel*, but the salvation of every Israelite was never guaranteed (vv. 6b–13). An individual's salvation depends on God's election, argues Paul. Those upon whom God has shown mercy are thus identified as Jew and Gentile, and not Jew alone (vv. 25–29). By quoting Isaiah 10:22 in verse 27, Paul attempts to prove that theological Israel had always been believing Israel, not national Israel. Moreover, believing Israel now includes the Gentiles who find a faith they did not seek and excludes those Jews who seek to confirm faith by works righteousness (v. 32). The Torah, or Christ, is the stone in Israel's midst over which she stumbles (v. 33). Israel's problem is similar to Paul's before his conversion, namely, zeal without knowledge (10:2). Ignorant of God's faithfulness, the Jews do not submit to Christ, who embodied God's faithfulness (v. 3). They must recognize that Christ, having brought the period of the law to an end, is thus now the one basis of salvation for all (v. 4).

Throughout Romans 11 Paul describes his own ministry (Robinson 1967, 81–96). In verses 1–24, which serve as a rebuke to the Gentile majority in Rome, Paul insists upon Israel's priority in the gospel. His interest is the Jews, not the Gentiles, who are drawn in only incidentally. Offering himself as living proof, Paul proclaims that Israel as a whole has not been cut off (vv. 1–10). Indeed, he is the Jew through whom God is now calling Israel. There is and will be a remnant of Israel into whose faith the Gentiles are now coming. However, this remnant of Israel differs from the traditional Jewish notion of a national entity, for this remnant will be by grace, not race. National Israel's transgression in filling out the sin of Adam has meant good news for the world (v. 11). Using the metaphor of the olive tree, Paul admonishes the Gentiles to recognize that they are dependent upon God's choice of Israel (vv. 17–24).

But though the Gentiles become partners with Israel, they are not part of Israel (Robinson 1967, 89). At the same time, Paul makes clear that God has not reserved a special way for the Jews to enter the new covenant. As do the Gentiles, the Jews must enter by faith alone.

In verses 25–32 Paul averts any criticism of Israel's unbelief by casting their hardening in terms of the divine plan. The Jews will remain hardened until the gospel has been dispensed, that is, "until the full number of the Gentiles has come in" (v. 25). The fulness of the Gentiles and the salvation of all Israel correspond "to the two arms of the divine purpose to be achieved through the Servant of the Lord as foretold in Isaiah 49:6" (Robinson 1967, 88), whereby the Servant's mission is to restore the tribes of Jacob and raise up the preserved of Israel but also to be a light to lighten the Gentiles to carry the divine plan of salvation to the ends of the earth. Those Jews whom God has elected will be saved in the way that Jews are saved by the Pauline missions—by ministries presenting the Christian gospel. In this way and no other, all of Israel who are to be saved are being saved and will be saved (v. 26). There can be no other special way. The mystery to which Paul refers in verse 25 is "that the Gentiles are both the beneficiaries of the Israelites' lapse and also the means of the salvation of those very Israelites" (Robinson 1967, 93).

Paul uses but also significantly alters Isaiah 59:20 in verse 26: "The deliverer will come *from* Zion" (emphasis added). In the Hebrew Bible and the Septuagint we find the phrase "*to* Zion" (emphasis added). It appears that Paul intentionally alters Isaiah's words so as to refer to the work and ministry of Jesus for Israel, and thus representatively for the world. But Paul does not equate Israel and Christianity and does not use the term *Israel* to describe the new people of God. The historic promises given to Israel are still Israel's (9:4–5). Gentiles are children of Abraham, but not sons of Israel. Though there is presently a remnant of Israel, the gospel era will close with Israel's fulness as the Gentiles' fulness, being gathered. Christianity is simultaneously a matter of provocation for national Israel and the means by which Israel is addressed by God. It follows from Paul's argument that "both the 'remnant' and 'the rest' will remain integral to the nation Israel until the end" (Robinson 1967, 87). Verses 28–32 continue with the point that there is only one family of God. At the moment, the Jews are enemies so that they may obtain mercy. Indeed, God has made both Jews and Gentiles disobedient so that the mercy of the gospel might be extended to all and so that the one family of God might arise.

Though the dogmatic arguments of Paul's letter virtually cease after chapter 11, there is a clear statement of Paul's perception of his ministry in 15:15–29. The context of the chapter concerns the collection undertaken in Pauline churches for the Christian poor in Jerusalem, the city that remained theologically critical for Paul to the end of his ministry as an acknowledgment of the order of salvation to the Jews first and then to the Gentiles. This voluntary financial contribution from the Gentiles for Jerusalem in one way represents the major offering of the gospel triumph, that of the Gentiles themselves to the God of Israel (v. 16).

In his letter to a predominantly Gentile community, while recognizing the primacy of the promises made to Israel and insisting on the gospel's proclamation to the Jews first, Paul preaches a gospel that creates a new eschatological family of God, the spiritual descendants of Abraham. With the onset of God's reign, the people of God find themselves in the process of reestablishment in a new arena, for the gospel has burst asunder the bonds of privilege, race, and creed. All are now one in Christ, Israel's Messiah.

Epistles to the Corinthians

In his letters to the house churches in Corinth, Paul addresses specific concerns affecting the life of the Corinthian congregation. The nature of the correspondence thus determines Paul's major foci. For instance, since he is interacting with a congregation in a city composed of house churches, one focus is the church and what it means to be "in Christ." Among the various issues confronting the congregation at Corinth is, in Paul's view, an overrealized eschatological position, which has wide-ranging manifestations in the life of the church. To counter those who believe they are presently reigning with Christ and thus see no need for human leaders, Paul takes a futurist stance, pointing to a future resurrection and affirming the overlap in his two-age scheme (see pp. 260–61). An overemphasis on the priority of Israel in the new dispensation is an issue Paul addresses in 2 Corinthians, where he looks to the resurrection and transformation of the believer as the great eschatological climax. Without doubt, the Corinthian correspondence demonstrates how the believers' eschatological tenets affect daily church life.

Sanctified in Christ (1 Cor. 1:2)

Paul addresses his first letter to the Corinthian congregation with these words: "To the church of God in Corinth, to those sanctified in Christ Jesus and called to be holy, together with all those everywhere who call on the name of our Lord Jesus Christ—their Lord and ours"

(1:2). What does it mean to be "in Christ"? Though the phrase may not seem to impart any eschatological meaning, we shall see that it does.

Sometimes Paul uses the phrase *in Christ* to simply mean "Christian" (e.g., Rom. 16:3), and sometimes he uses it on a soteriological level to indicate that salvation is available through a relationship to Christ. For instance, in Romans 6:11 the phrase relates to the saving events of the redemption. In Galatians 3:28, where Paul uses "in Christ" to signify incorporation into the body of Christ, the church, the phrase takes on an ecclesiological bent. In other instances Paul uses "in Christ" to refer to the new level of fellowship a believer has with the exalted Lord (Kourie 1987, 34). Here is where Paul's use of the phrase is distinctively eschatological (Parsons 1988, 28). (Note that Paul reserves "with Christ" for a future level of fellowship, as in Col. 3:3.)

The genesis of Paul's eschatological use of "in Christ" is to be found in his experience on the Damascus road, when he himself entered into a new, dynamic relationship with Israel's Messiah (Kourie 1987, 34). Through the phrase Paul conveys the idea that believers now share the eternal existence that Christ has with the Father and proclaims that the end time has broken into the present (2 Cor. 5:17). Indeed, union with Christ is the very core of what the phrase connotes. Since the phrase signifies participation in the new age instituted by Christ's work (Eph. 2:6), then the various nuances may be subsumed under one general meaning, that is, incorporation into Christ and not merely belonging to Christ in the sense of "Christian." In 1931 Albert Schweitzer suggested that Paul uses "in Christ" to signify incorporation into Israel's Messiah (110–18). This interpretation seems essentially correct since Christ's role was to begin again as a corporate figure representing Israel, on the one hand, and Adam, on the other. By using the images of Adam and Christ, Paul brings together two great periods of history, each with a leader whose people share in his fate.

Wherever, as in 1 Corinthians 1:2, Paul uses "in Christ" to connote incorporation into the Messiah, he applies it to all believers and not just to a privileged group. One comes to be *in* Christ by being baptized *into* Christ, whether that baptism is interpreted as metaphorical or physical. The phrase "dead in Christ" in 1 Thessalonians 4:16 prevents restricting the incorporation to this lifetime; thus, believers are in Christ until the consummation. On a personal level, the phrase indicates that individuals die and rise with Christ. On a corporate level, "in Christ" conveys the concept of inclusion in the body of Christ. Recent exposition tends to regard "in Christ" as a phrase pointing to participation in a reality that was determined historically by the Christ event, that occurred or existed outside of and prior to the believer, and that has individual implications. Insofar as "in Christ" refers to the salvation of the individual by incorporation into the expected Messiah of Israel, realized by the historical objectivity of the cross, the tenor of this recent exposition seems correct. By being incorporated into the Jewish Messiah, Jew and Gentile become in him members of the one new man—with previous differences obliterated.

The Body of Christ (1 Cor. 6:15; 10:16b–17; 12:27)

Paul expresses his theology using a varied diction that includes both abstract words and concrete images. One such concrete image is the "body of Christ." The phrase bears ecclesiological connotations (see pp. 266–68), for it is identified with the local *ekklēsia* in 1 Corinthians 12:27 and the heavenly *ekklēsia* in Ephesians 1:22–23. Paul's use of the image demonstrates that the body overarches and connects the earthly and heavenly manifestations of the church. Such movement beyond an earthly church reveals eschatological connotations as well.

In 1 Corinthians Paul appears to conceptualize the image of Christ's body before he actually uses the phrase. The words that convey the idea appear in 6:15 as "members of Christ." In the passage Paul contrasts two unions—the material union that results when one engages in sexual activity with a prostitute (v. 16) and the spiritual union that is possible for the believer in Christ (v. 17). It appears that Paul uses "members of Christ" in verse 15 to refer to the wider Corinthian community as a corporate and spiritual fellowship; if so, the verse anticipates Paul's later use of "body of Christ."

The phrase *body of Christ* appears for the first time in 1 Corinthians in a context that suggests the origin of the image of the physical body. Paul uses the analogy of the Lord's Supper in 10:14–22 to caution fellow believers against pagan worship. In verses 16b–17 Paul argues, "And is not the bread that we break a participation in the body of Christ? Because there is one loaf, we, who are many, are one body, for we all partake of the one loaf." The one loaf of the supper becomes the basis for viewing the group of believers as one, unified spiritual body. Indeed, since the supper as instituted by Jesus stresses the unity of the new community and its new covenant oneness with him as sovereign Lord, it is possible that the Lord's Supper is the origin of the body imagery found in Paul. The fellowship of the supper expresses the believers' dependence upon God's gift of Christ and an interdependence upon one another. Such interdependence and unity were apparently lacking in the congregation at Corinth. In 11:17–34 Paul offers very careful instruction regarding the observance of the Lord's Supper, pointing out that if there is no real unity of believer with believer, that is, no recognition of the body (v. 29), then there can be no Lord's Supper, since it represents believers in unity. The disunity at Corinth manifests the lack of consideration of believer for believer, which thus evacuates the meal of content and destroys the bodily oneness.

In chapter 12 Paul addresses the matter of spiritual gifts, which provides the occasion for the further development of the image of the body of Christ. Though there is a variety of spiritual gifts, says Paul in verse 4, there is a mutual relationship among those who possess them, for all gifts are given by the one Spirit in response to the acknowledged lordship of Christ. Stressing diversity in unity, the fact that many members make up one body, Paul argues that "the body is a unit, though it is made up of many parts; and though all its parts are many, they form one body. So it is with Christ," where "Christ" is probably elliptical for "body of Christ" (v. 12). In other words, Christians have been brought by redemption into relationship with each other and Christ so perfectly that they have become one body in Christ. The local gathering is in fact the person of Christ manifested through the fellowship of the Spirit, which ensures oneness in the local meetings. Paul exhorts the Corinthians in 12:27 with the following proclamation: "Now you are the body of Christ." The implication is that Christ is fully manifested when Christians gather. Thus, the image of the body stresses that the unity of the new social form, the Christian *ekklēsia*, emerges from the Spirit through the sharing of Christian experience.

There is consistency in Paul's use of the image of the body: (1) the image always stresses the relationship of members to one another in Christ and (2) it never refers to the relationship of the church to the world. Note that in the passages we have examined Paul addresses only the Corinthians. Moreover, he uses the image of the body in connection with local problems. Paul's use of the image in Romans is similar, though in 12:4–5 there may be evidence of some development since Paul appears to include himself in the Roman body. If this is so, there is a progression in Paul's use of the image of the body in which Romans is intermediate between Corinthians and Ephesians/Colossians (see pp. 301–3, 307–8). The body is the image found in both Corinthians and Romans to depict the ongoing continuous entity of the people of God, whereas *ekklēsia* is restricted by Paul to refer to intermittent local assemblies as they meet. In other words, the body that is manifested in any *ekklēsia* is the body of Christ, for the assembly, or congregation, has no life of its own that is not derived from its members, who are all interrelated by one Spirit. As Ephesians and Colossians will attest, Christ is the heavenly, exalted head of the body, while the *ekklēsia* is the local, temporal existent. However, Christ is not in the body but in the members who compose the body and whose unity is constituted by their sharing a common life and a common experience.

The concept of the body of Christ underscores the eschatological significance of the people of God, who now constitute a heavenly unity. This unity will be manifest at the parousia, when the perfections of life in Christ, now available to the members, will be fully understood and expressed. Furthermore, as the body of Christ, Christians presently have a corporate identity, the aim of which is to demonstrate more and more fully the presence of the life of Christ in the local fellowships.

The Not-Yet (1 Cor. 15)

Near the beginning of Paul's first epistle to Corinth, it is clear that the apostle is concerned to redirect the church's overdeveloped eschatological position. Thus, Paul's description of Christians as those who *wait* for the revealing of the Lord (1 Cor. 1:7) seems to be a corrective against that which is pictured in 1 Corinthians 15 as a spiritualized, overrealized eschatology in Corinth. The Christ party (see 1:12) seems to have been superspiritualists who saw no need of a human leader since the future had already been ushered in. Against these tendencies Paul's basically futurist stance is revealed in 4:5, where he insists that nothing be judged before the time. It appears that the self-styled spiritual men at Corinth wished to parade their newly found freedom in libertarianism and that they regarded themselves as presently reigning with Christ (4:8). Conscious of their spiritual attainments, these Corinthians were boastful (1:29, 31; 4:7; 5:6) and proud and arrogant (4:6, 18–19; 5:2; 8:1; 13:4). And they believed themselves to be the possessors of wisdom (1:19–27; 3:18–23) and knowledge (8:1–3, 7; 15:34), judging that for themselves "all things are lawful" (6:12 NRSV; De Boer 1988, 103) and delighting in a libertarianism that denigrated the physical and the material (6:13, 15). To this situation Paul brings into play in 6:14 the thought framework of a future resurrection in order to counter such excesses.

Besides countering excesses in life-style, Paul also makes corrections to the theology of those in Corinth. Many seemed to think that they had reached "the goal" through baptism, which they viewed as the medium of spiritual transfer (1 Cor. 1:16–17; 15:29) and perhaps as a prerequisite for salvation. Some in the congregation viewed the Lord's Supper as offering spiritual food and drink (10:3–4). In Paul's mind, the Corinthians placed an unhealthy emphasis on Christian sacramentalism. Pointing out that they, as all Christians, are still sinners, Paul urges the Corinthians to examine themselves. Chapters 12–14 indicate another area in which Paul believes the Corinthians had gone astray, that is, in the area of pneumatic giftedness. The Corinthians assumed they lived a quality of life appropriate to angels (13:1; Lincoln 1981, 34). Indeed, by speaking in tongues, they used the language of angels. Since the Corinthians considered their present pneumatic experience to be a sacramental and spiritual resurrection, they saw no need for and did not recognize a resurrection of the dead (15:12). Not expecting death, they were troubled when it occurred in the community (Lincoln 1981, 35). It is under all these circumstances that Paul began his corrective exposition in chapter 15, a chapter that fully details Paul's eschatological expectations.

In 15:1–11 Paul restates the gospel he had already proclaimed to the Corinthians, whose "exalted Lord" Christology had led to a triumphalist understanding of the new life in Christ. Verses 3b–5 represent a most primitive tradition. This early credal statement sets forth the essentials of the kerygma: that Christ died for our sins, was buried, was raised, and appeared. Note in verses 5–8 Paul's emphasis on the appearances—to Peter, to the Twelve, to five hundred, to James, to all the apostles, and to Paul himself. Paul uses the continuity of Christ's person as attested by the appearances to prove the corporeal resurrection of Jesus.

Having set forth the basic gospel message, Paul summarizes it in verse 12a: Jesus has been demonstrably raised from the ranks of the dead and buried! In verse 12b Paul begins his argument by asking, "How can some of you say that there is no resurrection of the dead?" As a result of the common experience of death between Christ and humanity, Paul claims there is a real connection between Christ's resurrection and that of Christians (vv. 13–19). Christ's resurrection was not a special case that rendered theirs unnecessary. The argument, as Paul voices it, runs two ways. If Christ has been raised, then we will rise, for Christ has experienced what saved humanity is to experience. But if there is no resurrection of the dead, then Christ has not been raised (v. 13). Moreover, the new life all believers experience is a gift of the resurrection. To deny Christ's resurrection is to deny that new life and to evacuate the gospel of content.

As Paul continues the argument in verses 20–28, he insists that the connection between Christ's resurrection and ours is not logical but causal. Verse 20 contains the central thesis of the chapter (De Boer 1988, 109): "But Christ has indeed been raised from the dead, the firstfruits of those who have fallen asleep." That is, the resurrection of Christ has done more than raise the possibility that others can rise after him, for Christ was so one with humanity as to be the firstfruits of them that slept and the solution to the problem of those in the faith who have died.

The resurrection of the Christian dead is guaranteed by Christ's resurrection since his was not the resurrection of an individual but of the leader of the people of the new age (1 Cor. 15:21–22). As Paul explains in verse 21, death and resurrection come alike by a human agency. Verse 22 elaborates upon this idea in terms of the two great figures of sin and salvation—Adam and Christ. Christ's role in salvation of ensuring life through resurrection corresponds to Adam's role of ensuring death. Indeed, it appears that Paul recognized Adam's role as having been transferred to Christ. All life in Adam, in whom all humanity is included, leads to death; all life "in the Christ" (*en tō Christō*), that is, in Israel's Messiah, leads to resurrected life (v. 22; Hill 1988, 304). Remember, however, that Paul was addressing believers in response to the problem raised in verse 18 of the Christian dead in Corinth. The contemplated resurrection is not the lot of all humankind, only of those who by faith are incorporated in Israel's Messiah.

In verses 23–28 Paul's argument regarding the future resurrection turns from the identification of the firstfruits to the notion of order. The two stages defined in verse 23 grow naturally out of the concept of the firstfruits as the guarantee of the final harvest to follow at the parousia (Hill 1988, 308): "Christ, the firstfruits; then, when he comes, those who belong to him." Verse 24 does not identify yet another stage, for the sense of "then" seems to be a logical sequence of thought rather than of time. Paul writes, "Then the end will come," but he is not contemplating a general resurrection of the unjust to follow the parousia. In effect, the parousia is the end, the time when the Messiah will surrender the kingdom to God. The subjection of Christ to the Father in verses 24a and 28 assumes the prior subjection of all things to Christ. This prior subjection climaxes in the parousia, by which the last enemy, death, is destroyed (v. 26). Note that verses 24–25 (cf. Ps. 110:1) correspond structurally to verses 27–28 (cf. Ps. 8:6; Hill 1988, 300). Through such correspondence, Paul draws together the subjection of verses 27–28 and the reign at the right hand of verses 24b–25 (cf. Rom. 8:34, 38–39; Eph. 1:20–2:10; Phil. 3:20–21; Heb. 1–2; Hill 1988, 313) to depict the heavenly reign of Christ in the present era. Thus, Paul views the present reign of the Messiah as the fulfilment of Psalm 8:6–8 as well as of the purposes for humankind as expressed in Genesis 1:26–28. At the end, Christ hands the peaceful realm over to the Father "so that God may be all in all" (v. 28), which represents the very goal of creation.

In verses 29–57 Paul focuses on specifics regarding a bodily resurrection. Verses 29–34 reveal a Corinthian baptismal practice for those who died without having previously been baptized. This practice stemmed from a highly sacramental view that baptism by water was so effective that it did not matter which body underwent it. In verse 29 Paul points out the inconsistency between the Corinthians' theology and their practice. Though the Corinthians did not expect a bodily resurrection, they baptized dead people. Paul challenges the members in Corinth to explain why.

In verses 35–57 Paul discusses the nature of the resurrection body. As he makes known in verse 35, the Corinthians' difficulty in accepting a resurrection can be summarized by two questions: "How are the dead raised? With what kind of body will they come?" To affirm the fact of the resurrection, Paul uses the analogy of seed (vv. 36–37). Every time you sow seed, says Paul to the Corinthians, a sort of death and resurrection ensues, and you answer your own objections. Extending the analogy and beginning the discussion of the nature of the resurrected body, Paul then points in verse 37 to the great difference between the physical manifestation of the sown seed and that of the emerging plant. What matters is not the seed, the before, argues Paul in verses 38–41, for all earthly and heavenly bodies have their own special worth. Thus, we should not be anxious to free ourselves of our bodies. What really matters is what happens as a result of the death/resurrection transformation, the after.

In verses 42–49 Paul applies the seed analogy to the future resurrection body (Wright 1983, 367). Verse 42 suggests that the transformation at the resurrection entails both a physical and a moral change. Indeed, verse 43 indicates the inner ethical change of the resurrected body's freedom from sin. The Corinthians, however, had failed to reckon with the physical change, that is, the disappearance of the corruptible body (Fee 1987, 785). But, as Paul explains, the present body is a natural one (*psychikos*)—appropriate to its earthly sphere and, therefore, subject to death (v. 44). By transformation, not by development of spiritual powers, the natural body will become a spiritual body (*pneumatikos*)—controlled by the Spirit, free from sin, and truly conformed to Christ (v. 44). There seems to be no question that the Corinthians would recognize the distinction between *psychikos* and *pneumatikos* (Lincoln 1981, 40), for some in the congregation considered themselves to be *pneumatikoi* (3:1; 12:1; 14:37). Indeed, that was the problem, for the truly spiritual state, the era fully controlled by the Spirit, must wait until the parousia. Those at Corinth who regarded themselves as possessors of heavenly blessing and superior spiritual wisdom were, however, subject to ordinary human existence and prone to Adamic sin. Though certain Corinthians claimed to be spiritual, the state relates only to the age to come.

In verse 45 Paul draws a distinction between the concepts *natural* and *spiritual* in terms of the Adam and Christ parallels introduced in verse 22 (cf. Gen. 2:7): "'The first man Adam became a living being'; the last Adam, a life-giving spirit." This is not a christological aside, however, but an anthropological assertion, for Paul continues to speak of the nature of the resurrection body. Thus, all in Adam are subject to death and decay (v. 22). All in Christ, who by his incarnation became the Second Adam, will become a living spirit through incorporation into him (v. 22). Paul argues that there is a direct connection between the natural body and the spiritual body; that is, the "first" Adam presupposes a "second." Moreover, Paul implies that from the outset God had made provision for a higher body. In other words, the created form of Adam necessarily pointed forward to a higher form. The first Adam thus prefigured the Last Adam.

In the intertestamental period, Jewish speculation over Adam's role focused on Israel's, not humankind's, claim to the restored honor and glory which had been projected for Adam. Pointing us back to the analogy drawn in verse 22, Paul indicates that inclusion in Israel's Messiah is necessary for redemption. As the first Adam included fallen humanity, the Last Adam represents the new and true humanity. Two conclusions can be drawn from Paul's argument: "There was an inherent eschatological structure to creation and . . . the eschatological prospect held out to the first Adam which he had forfeited by his disobedience had been realized by the last Adam" (Lincoln 1981, 43). The first man had become a living soul with an appropriate body (v. 46); he was of the earth (v. 47). But the story does not end here. The Last Adam by incarnation completed the obedience required of Israel for her world and thus by the resurrection entered for Israel a new mode of being, a higher quality of life. Paul does not suppose that believers will become life-giving spirits like Christ, for Christ is the unique source of new life as a spiritual body (Wright 1983, 368). But though Christ is exalted (v. 47), Paul still focuses on Christ's humanity as the source of and model for the new eschatological humanity. Jewish tradition had envisioned that Adam would be returned to Paradise by a general resurrection and would possess the eschatological glory which was to be shared with the righteous in the age to come (Lincoln 1981, 49). Paul's view is in keeping with the tradition, for he sees the return as having been accomplished by Christ.

Paul continues the argument in 1 Corinthians 15:48–49 by focusing on Adam's and Christ's representative character. By his inclusion of the redeemed, Christ is the prototype for the resurrection body of believers, just as Adam had determined the bodily fate of earthly humanity (v. 48). Believers who share the earthly humanity will certainly share the heavenly spirituality (v. 49). Though complete conformity to Christ awaits the granting of the heavenly body, the process of transformation has already begun (cf. 2 Cor. 3:18). Paul's exhortation in verse 49, which is based upon our present incorporation into Christ, thus presumes this ongoing change: "So let us bear the likeness of the man from heaven" (the preferred reading; Lincoln 1981, 50). From the preceding argument Paul deduces that flesh and blood, the perishable, cannot inherit the kingdom (v. 50). Christ's disclosure, the mystery, solves the predicament (v. 51). Not all will die, but all will be transformed at the parousia (v. 52). Humankind, as we now are, cannot enter the kingdom. But when the herald of the new age will sound, all Christians dead or alive will be transformed instantaneously. The sign of death's defeat will be that corruption will put on incorruption and the mortal will put on immortality (vv. 53–54). And with this Paul answers the question posed in verse 35 regarding the *how* and the *what* of bodily resurrection.

The Two Covenants (2 Cor. 3:7–18)

Paul's conciliation toward the Corinthians through his first epistle and through a severe epistle, which remains unknown, had apparently been undone by renewed opposition to Paul's apostleship and life-style. When these opponents, probably Jewish Christians from Jerusalem, arrived in Corinth, they brought with them letters of recommendation from Jerusalem, letters that overemphasized the Mosaic dispensation and the primacy of Israel in the new dispensation (2 Cor. 3:1). In 2 Corinthians 3:7–18 Paul corrects the undue attention given to the Mosaic covenant by comparing it with the new covenant.

Paul's description of the Mosaic covenant is dependent upon the story of the veiling of Moses in Exodus 34:29–35, which examines Moses' and Israel's quite different experiences of the covenant. As Paul thinks of the covenant within the context of Israel's history, he views it as glorious, but also destructive, for it condemns (2 Cor. 3:9). Since the new covenant does not condemn, the ministry of the Spirit in the new covenant will be even more glorious than in the old.

In verses 12–18 Paul examines the covenants from the standpoint of access. Whereas the new covenant is accessible through the Spirit (v. 17), Moses could not share the full blessing of the Sinai covenant with Israel (v. 13). Though God had intended that the Mosaic covenant would reveal, not conceal, a veil stood between Israel and the old covenant (v. 14). Moreover, Moses' veil might have suggested to the participating Israelites that there was a covenant dimension in which they were not sharing, but the Israelites perceived none of this, for the work of hardening in their hearts was already complete. Paul notes that until this very day a veil of the same character rests on Jewish minds during the reading of Exodus 19–34 (v. 14). Now we are in a new age. The access that the Sinai covenant should have provided is available now through Jesus. When Judaism turns to Jesus, who takes the place in the covenant occupied by Yahweh in the Old Testament, the veil is removed (v. 16), as it was when Moses turned to Yahweh in his Sinai experience.

As a representative Israelite, Moses could experience the intimacy of full covenant fellowship. This is now possible for all Israel through the Spirit, who makes Christ available. Even the glory that Moses experienced is available through the Spirit (v. 18). No longer to be associated with a remote mountaintop, Yahweh now dwells in the heart of each believer. But how is this possible? In verse 18 Paul speaks of a necessary transformation. All within the new domain of the Spirit, Jew and Gentile alike, "are being transformed into his likeness [the same image]" (v. 18). With unveiled faces, that is, with unrestricted access, all believers now behold the glory of God revealed in the gospel. The goal that God had in mind for humanity is being reached.

Sharing in Death and Resurrection (2 Cor. 4:7–5:21)

In 2 Corinthians 4:7–15 Paul identifies suffering as a necessary component of the personal transformation to which he referred in 3:18. Indeed, such personal suffering and difficulty, which accredit his apostleship, cause him to reaffirm the transformation as a characteristic of the parousia. With his focus firmly set on eternal realities (4:18), Paul looks beyond the destruction of a believer's earthly tent, the earthly body, to the heavenly body given by God at the parousia (5:1). While not providing new information, this introductory and general statement reasserts what Paul had previously written to the Corinthians in chapter 15 of his first letter. What follows in 2 Corinthians 5 spells out details regarding our future life.

Two certainties emerge from 2 Corinthians 5:1: the certainty of the termination of earthly life at death and the certainty of transformation at the parousia (Gillman 1988, 446). Paul uses the tent metaphor in verse 1a to emphasize the transitoriness of earthly life. In contrast to the tent is the "building from God" (*oikodomē ek theou*), the resurrection/transformation body of the end time (cf. 1 Cor. 15:47–49). This building is an eternal house; it belongs to the coming age in which the experience of the believer will be totally controlled by the Spirit. That the building is "not built by human hands" indicates the reality of the spiritual, or heavenly, order (v. 1b; cf. Acts 7:48; 17:24; Col. 2:11; Heb. 9:11, 24). Writing to believers in Corinth, Paul teaches that the heavenly house is permanent through transformation; however, it is neither ours nor does it exist until the tent of the earthly body is dismantled by death. Only at the second coming is the resurrection body received.

Given Paul's certainty about the resurrection life and his experience with affliction, rejection, and suffering, the apostle groans for his heavenly body (2 Cor. 5:2). By wishing to put on the body as one would put on clothing, Paul reveals the manner in which the transformation at the parousia will take place. (Note the presence of the double compound *ependyō* [to put on over] in verses 2 and 4 and the single compound *endyō* [to put on] in verse 3. Despite the difference, it appears that in each verse Paul is referring to the putting on of the resurrection body [Harris 1983, 223].) The "putting on over" is clearly distinct from death, which is a "putting off." The seeming aside in verse 3 reinforces the thought of the preceding verse: "because when we are clothed, we will not be found naked." Though the word *naked* has a variety of meanings, in this context it best refers to alienation from Christ at the parousia (cf. Gillman 1988, 447). Does Paul hereby refer to some intermediate state between death and final transformation, which is attested in contemporaneous Jewish apocalyptic literature but is otherwise unknown in the New Testament? The text allows such a supposition, although Paul does not teach it explicitly. Paul's concern in this context is the end; thus, verse 3 is a strong statement of Paul's assurance of embodiment by transformation, that is, of the resurrection body. Moreover, in the verse Paul rejects the view of some Corinthians that disembodiment is the ideal and future state. Verse 4 restates the thought of verse 2 while adding "so that what is mortal may be swallowed up by life." In verse 4, as a contrast to "mortal," Paul notably uses "life" rather than the expected *immortality*, indicating that for Paul immortality is inconceivable without the associated view of a bodily resurrection (Harris 1990, 263–69). In verse 5 Paul introduces the Spirit as the link between the renewal, which is presently taking place (4:16), and the final transformation. While believers are being transformed from glory into glory (3:18), there is a consummation yet to be expected. Though we will die and be absent from the body, eventually we will be with the Lord (5:8). In light of this prospect, Paul is able to face the future.

The plain sense of 2 Corinthians 5:1–10 does not go beyond what Paul wrote in 1 Corinthians 15. As noted heretofore, there is no explicit teaching in the passage of an intermediate state after death. But what are we to think about the time between one's physical death and the final transformation at the parousia? We concur with the suggestion made by F. F. Bruce that the interval between death and resurrection is not an interval in the consciousness of the believer, no matter how long it might be measured chronologically (1977, 312 n. 40).

For Paul, the death and resurrection transformation of Christ was the turning point of the two ages and the great moment of Christian hope. All Paul's expectations about the future are based on the hope of sharing in Christ's experience. The resurrection and transformation of the believer is thus the great eschatological climax. Though death leads to disembodiment for a time, in the end the glorious transformation will take place. Paul identifies with certainty the source of our transformation and thus of our reconciliation: "All this is from God, who reconciled us to himself through Christ and gave us the ministry of reconciliation" (2 Cor. 5:18). As Paul explains in verse 19, God's wrath against human transgression was exhausted by the death of Christ, which God was using to reconcile the totality of humankind, the world, to himself. The divine action thus becomes the basis for Paul's exhortation to humankind in verse 20: "Be reconciled to God." Paul speaks of reconciliation as something humankind has received (v. 18), but reconciliation is only complete when there is a human response to the initiative (v. 20).

It is often argued that the implication of a time lapse between death and resurrection in 2 Corinthians 5 represents a development in Paul's thought beyond that found in 1 Corinthians 15 (Harris 1990, 207–12). We have argued, however, that the two chapters demonstrate continuity in Paul's thinking. Moreover, if Paul in 2 Corinthians 5 was contemplating his own death before the parousia, this possibility was scouted as early as 1 Thessalonians 5:10. In his first epistle to the Corinthians Paul confronted the problem of a realized eschatology, which reasoned that a spiritual resurrection for the believer was presently available since Christ had already risen. Not only did Paul challenge the dangerous ethical stance accompanying the Corinthians' judgment, but he argued forcefully in 1 Corinthians 15 that a passage of time must take place between Christ's resurrection as the firstfruits and that of the believers as the final harvest.

Epistle to the Galatians

In the Epistle to the Galatians Paul above all considers the Jew Gentile relationship and the place of the Mosaic covenant in the Christian dispensation. In examining the relationship of Christians to the Mosaic law and the Sinai covenant, Paul broaches matters basic to life in the new age. Paul's letter to the churches in Galatia also reveals his intent to resolve any question regarding his apostolic authority. In chapters 1–2 Paul establishes his credentials as an apostle, independent of Jerusalem and the Twelve, who has been called to preach the Jewish Messiah to the Gentiles. Beginning in chapter 3 Paul considers the issues of access to grace and the place of the law in this pursuit.

Life in the New Age (Gal. 3)

In Galatians 3:1–5 Paul appeals to the circumstances of the Galatians' faith: Through hearing the gospel message, which had generated faith, and receiving the Spirit, the Galatians had become Christians. Afterward, however, they attempted to make the covenantal membership more secure by adding the Jewish law. But what ensures Abrahamic covenantal membership? Since all believers in the gospel of the crucified Messiah are members of the Abrahamic covenant (vv. 6–7), faith alone, not additions to it, ensures membership in the covenant. Extending the argument in verses 8–9, Paul explains how Abraham's call in Genesis 12:1–3 had foreshadowed the inclusion of the Gentiles. Thus, Paul implies that the period of the Mosaic covenant, by which Israel was set apart, is now over.

Paul looks to Abraham for evidence that God had intended Mosaic law and the Sinai covenant, to which the law was attached, to be in force only for a defined period of salvation history (Gal. 3:15–25; Schreiner 1989, 50). Salvation was possible within the promise structure given to Abraham and then to Israel, but the law as it was given in Exodus 20–23 was an inner Israelite development designed to indicate what it meant to be national Israel and how, therefore, national Israel could function vocationally as a light to lighten the Gentiles. Meant to be a help to Israel, to reflect the nature of the true people of God, the law became a curse, for Israel came to require observation of the law as the means of retaining covenant membership. But, as Paul argues in verses 10–11, righteousness cannot be obtained by the keeping of the law. Thus, the law can be neither the means of entry to the covenant nor the method of its retention. It is by faith alone that the Abrahamic covenant, on which Christian salvation is dependent, is entered and kept (v. 11). What is the status of the curse under which Israel labored under the law? It has been swept aside by Israel's Messiah, who on the one hand has fulfilled the law by keeping it for Israel, that is, by succeeding where Israel had failed, and who on the other hand has absorbed the curse of the law directed against Israel for her failure by becoming a curse for Israel (v. 13). Though the law has proven itself unable to convey blessing, the way to blessing is open because of the work of Jesus.

The superiority of promise to law is made plain, according to Paul, by the fact that the law was added to the original Abrahamic covenant some four hundred years after its conclusion (Gal. 3:17). Since the law was not intrinsic to the covenant, it cannot determine the way of salvation (vv. 15–18). So what was the point of the law (v. 19)? The law was added for a period in salvation history merely to produce transgressions, that is, to define the character of Israel's sin. As the privileged people of God and possessors of the law, the Jews unwittingly demonstrated that even the chosen people of God are sinful and thus cannot be saved by the law. If this is so, the implied argument continues, how much less can the Gentiles be saved by the law! Neither Jews nor Gentiles, however, need to rely on the law, for the promises given to Abraham and the full operation of the Abrahamic covenant, which was prior to and wider than the Sinai covenant, have devolved upon Abraham's true descendant—Israel's Messiah—through whom Jews and Gentiles are now blessed.

In Galatians 3:21–22 Paul somewhat tempers his portrayal of the law by reiterating its role in the divine plan. If the law could have given life, salvation would have come by law and not, as it has, by promise. Since the law could not give life, God enclosed first the Jews, the possessors of the law, and then the rest of the world, in other words all the world, under sin (v. 22). Therefore, the salvation produced by the faithfulness of Jesus to the covenantal demands, and thus to the Abrahamic relationship, must be given to all who believe, not merely to one chosen race that may have seemed meritorious. Temporary in duration, the role of the law was to bring Jews to Christ through whom alone the promise can be obtained (vv. 23–24). Christ's death had brought the rule of law to an end and yet ironically had fulfilled it. Does this mean, however, that the law has been abolished? For Paul, the law is never anything more than the expectation of the way in which the covenant of promise is to be reflected by covenant members. Moreover, every facet of Christian experience, sanctification as well as justification, is by faith. Human effort is the effect, not the cause, of the better righteousness which signifies covenant incorporation in Christ. Nowhere, however, does Paul depreciate law in itself. When Paul refers to Christians as not being under the law (Gal. 3:23–25; 4:4–5; cf. Rom. 6:14; 1 Cor. 9:20) or as having been released from the law by the death of Christ (Rom. 7:1–6), his understanding is that law in terms of the Mosaic covenant has ceased (2 Cor. 3:7–11; Schreiner 1989, 50). Since in salvation history the period of the Mosaic covenant has passed, specific strictures regarding food (Gal. 2:11–14; cf. Rom. 14–15), the observance of special days (Gal. 4:10; cf. Rom. 14:5; Col. 2:16), and circumcision (identified by Judaism with the Mosaic covenant but in fact connected with Abraham) have also ceased to apply. That is, ritual law has been dissolved (Schreiner 1989, 56). All that separates Jew from Gentile, and which has hindered the full operation of the Abrahamic covenant welding Jew and Gentile together, has been abrogated by the coming of the Messiah.

Paul identifies the problem with the law, not as the law in itself, but as its misuse by sin and the flesh (Rom. 7:8, 11, 14). In fact, Paul does not imply that law, as such, has been abrogated; rather he presupposes that the commandments are still operative (Rom. 13:8–10). As the center of the Christian ethic, love does not exclude reference to commandments, for love and obedience cannot be separated (John 15:10). The enabling factor in the new age, as it was in the old, is the Spirit, which displays in conduct the fruitfulness of the new relationship of being in

Christ. Where norms of conduct in the New Testament age are clearly universal (e.g., 1 Cor. 5–6), Paul does not appeal to Old Testament Scriptures. Still he does not hesitate to do so when he needs a warrant for conduct (e.g., 1 Cor. 10:7–8).

For Paul, the Jewish hope that the Messiah would come and perfectly express the law and that messianic fulfilment of the law would bring grace was realized in Jesus Christ. The purpose of the law to produce an Israel based on faith had been achieved through Christ; now in Christ, by incorporation into Israel's Messiah, the essential principles of the law are mysteriously being fulfilled through the gift of the Spirit. Remember that the Ten Commandments as the heart of the Jewish Torah had expressed the basic relationship between man and God that had come into being with creation itself; thus, both the Abrahamic and Sinaitic covenants presuppose the Decalogue. Since God's will for human conduct had been expressed through the Decalogue, for Paul the fruits of the Spirit, which could be summarized by the one word *love*, would mean the keeping of its principles. That the new covenant is a morality of love (Gal. 5:22) does not signify the absence of obligation and thus law, for love requires guidelines for its exercise, which Paul saw clearly. In Christian experience under the new covenant, however, the total demand of the law is brought to a fulfilment in *agape* (Deidun 1981, 153). In the new covenant the external biblical word of command that the New Testament imposes or continues from the Old combines with the inner illumination of the Spirit to produce transforming Christian character. Though the Spirit is the guide in the general orientation of conduct, the need for the external word remains, as Paul's continued exhortations to his converts make clear (Deidun 1981, 186–87).

The Heavenly Jerusalem (Gal. 4:26)

Paul's relationship to the city of Jerusalem is complex. In Romans 15:19 Paul identifies Jerusalem as the site from which the gospel proclamation began. Moreover, we learn in Romans that the fruits of Paul's Gentile ministry would be brought in pilgrimage to the city (Rom. 15:27–28). Paul's arrest in Jerusalem while he was on this mission of charity prompted Luke to dismiss the earthly Jerusalem and replace it with Rome as Paul's final focal point. In the Epistle to the Galatians Paul accepts the centrality of Jerusalem for his message; yet, he did not go to Jerusalem immediately following his call on the Damascus road (1:17). Paul in fact waited three years before he journeyed there (1:18). Still, he is eager to help the poor in Jerusalem (2:10). And he wants the Gentiles to recognize the city's spiritual centrality.

In Galatians 4:26 appears an interesting and unique phrase regarding Jerusalem: "the Jerusalem that is above." While the notion of a restored Jerusalem in the eschaton is a commonplace of Old Testament eschatology (see pp. 81–85, 105–8, 121–25, 127–30), this concept of the heavenly Jerusalem is not prominent in either the literature of the intertestamental period or of late Judaism. It does not appear in Jewish literature until the second century A.D. (Lincoln 1981, 19–20). However, the concept becomes particularly important in the later Revelation of Saint John. Paul seems to use the heavenly Jerusalem, which has biblical roots in Isaiah (see 54:1–18; cf. Gal. 4:27; Heb. 12:18–24), in response to his opponents who have concentrated their attention upon the centrality of geographical Jerusalem. Indeed, his argument, which contrasts the Sinai covenant with the new covenant, appears to be aimed toward Jews, not Gentiles (Robinson 1965, 41). After turning the issue of physical descent from Abraham against his Jewish opponents (chap. 3), Paul denounces the present Jerusalem (4:25) in favor of the heavenly one. But what is this heavenly city? Since in verse 26 the believers are still on earth, the heavenly Jerusalem is not the church but "rather . . . the new age depicted in spatial terms and the anticipation of the full life of this new age now present in the church" (Lincoln 1981, 25).

In the Epistle to the Galatians Paul preaches the unity of the people of God in salvation, declaring that no longer do Gentile converts need to become Jewish proselytes. Having recognized the passing of the Mosaic covenant with its Jewish particularity, Paul proclaims that the wider benefits of the Abrahamic covenant by which all are one in Christ Jesus are now operating.

Epistle to the Ephesians

The reconciliation of Jews and Gentiles in one body, the church, as revealed in Christ is the basic theme of Ephesians as well as a typical Pauline concern. The eschatology of the letter, however, is often cited among the features evidencing non-Pauline authorship. In the Epistle to the Ephesians, believers are described as already having been made alive and elevated into the heavenly places (2:5–6; cf. Col. 2:12; 3:1–3). Thus, this realized eschatology is said to contrast with that in the undisputed Pauline letters, in which the heavenly exaltation does not take place until the parousia.

But is the eschatology in Ephesians so different? In Ephesians and in Colossians Christians are viewed as already risen with Christ and tasting the good things of the age to come. This, however, is not new for Paul, for he is ever aware of a present dimension of salvation, which he expresses principally through metaphors of liberation and adoption. Thus, the language in Ephesians, and also in Colossians, of being made alive and sitting in heavenly places means no more than justification and its consequences—present blessing in Christ. Note, for instance, the explanation that "it is by grace you have been saved" following Paul's declaration that we have been made alive in Ephesians 2:5 (see similar explanations in Col. 2:13; 3:1). Through such declarations and explanations, Paul conveys the believers' present position of living in two ages, which is a customary feature of the gospel he proclaims. In Ephesians the language functions to explain the present aspect of salvation without denying the future, for Paul faces a local context in which the present dimension of the work of Christ needs to be made plain.

The Mystery of God (Eph. 1:3–14; 3:1–13)

Serving as an introduction to and summary of the epistle, Ephesians 1:3–14 is a eulogy to God, which states that God is blessed and then identifies what God has done as the grounds for blessing him. The five acts, which begin and end in eternity, are election (Eph. 1:4), predestination (v. 5), redemption (v. 7), the giving of wisdom (v. 8), and the revelation of his mystery to gather together all things in Christ (vv. 9–10). Starting in heaven with election, we come down to earth with the shedding of blood and redemption and are taken back to heaven with the bringing together of all things (Caragounis 1977, 49). What is emphasized about the divine acts is God's grace (vv. 6–7), which can now be readily seen through the revelation of the mystery, once concealed, but now clear in Christ. Moving from what God has done to that which we have experienced, verses 11–14 deal with the unfolding of the mystery of redemption and reconstitution, which reached Jew first (as indicated by "we" in v. 11 since Paul writes from a Jewish vantage point) before being extended, as was always intended through Israel, to the Gentiles. The focus of the eulogy is thus the cosmic Christ, who sums up all things, and the mystery of verse 9 concerns the final restoration of order in the universe, the reconstitution of creation under Christ.

The key word *mystery* appears again in chapter 3, this time as an aspect of the bringing together—in particular the acceptance of Gentiles into the one people of God on the same basis as Jews. With the removal of the old distinction between Jews and Gentiles, the church presents a new harmony between the races and thus exhibits God's many-sided wisdom. God's mystery as defined in Ephesians is thus the general, all-inclusive plan of God running through the ages relating to the unity of humankind and having as its eschatological goal the reconstitution of everything under Christ. The prerequisite for fulfilment of the goal, and its guarantee, is the unity in the church of Jews and Gentiles, for such unity foreshadows the harmony of the end (Eph. 3:10). Paul's eschatology will be consummated, and the goal of Genesis will be reached, when Jews and Gentiles lose their distinctiveness in the one new man (2:14–15), when all differences are obliterated. This, the supreme end of all things, is to the praise of the glory of God, for what is the ultimate intention of eschatology but the self-glorification of the divine? The pivotal point in the divine plan was the death of Christ. Before the death there was darkness, ignorance, and hopelessness, but the picture has changed completely. All past formal differences between Jew and Gentile have been swept away. The revelation of the mystery that the Gentiles are heirs together with Israel has dealt the deathblow to Jewish pride (3:4–6) and has confounded the powers (vv. 9–11). These had been totally outwitted by God's counsel, as the Jews had been (1 Cor. 2:8), but the powers continue their rebellion and steer humankind toward the same course (Eph. 2:2–3).

Cosmic Struggle and Spiritual Warfare (Eph. 1:20–2:10; 3:10; 4:8–10; 6:10–20)

Christ came to break the nexus between the powers and sin. But what are these powers to which Paul refers? To signify the phenomenon of the powers, Paul uses various interchangeable words in Ephesians as well as in Colossians—powers, principalities, rulers, authorities, and thrones (Yates 1980, 102). The terminology, which probably originated in the Old Testament concepts of the angels of the nations, the hosts of heaven, and the sons of God, reflects Judaism's influence (see, e.g., 1 Kings 22:19; Job 2:1; 38:7; Dan. 10:13, 19–21). Consider, for instance, terminology in the Book of Daniel. In 7:27 we find that "all *rulers* will worship and obey" (emphasis added) the Son of man, in whom "the authority, glory and sovereign power" (7:14) taken from the defeated kingdoms had been invested. *Archontes* (rulers) appears in the Greek translation of Daniel 10:13 to signify the angelic princes with whom Michael fights. First Enoch 61:10 offers a listing of the heavenly powers. Paul's use of the various terms without explanation suggests they were commonly used and understood in his day. Judaism's well-documented interest, at the time of the Christian era, in spiritual and angelic forces indicates a continuity in thought that in the intertestamental period interacted with the ideas of the Greek world, as seen in the Septuagint and the works of Philo. People of the day considered themselves to be subject to a cosmic totalitarianism of evil forces that had to be placated. Such belief in supernatural cosmic forces, angels and demonic beings who potentially could enslave humankind beneath a cosmic totalitarianism, was part of the Jewish apocalyptic and of the New Testament milieu.

The New Testament bears witness to a variety of evil forces, under a unified head, that exhibit their power through human nature and institutions. These forces were created; they fell; and they were defeated by Christ in his death. The defeat, however, will remain hidden from the present world until its manifestation at the second coming. Though the warfare conducted between God and the powers took place in the unseen world of spiritual reality, the heavenly places, there will be no cessation of hostilities until our departure to be with Christ at his return, for the defeated powers continue to exist. However, they cannot harm the believer in Christ, and their ultimate overthrow is certain (1 Cor. 15:24–28).

Paul views the powers as part of the created order subject to Christ. He speaks of the various cultural, social, and religious pressures brought to bear upon believers as manifestations of the powers of evil, which were unmasked and unarmed by the cross and resurrection (Eph. 1:21; cf. Col. 2:10, 15). And the powers fit into Paul's now and not-yet eschatological framework. Though the powers have been defeated and deprived of their influence (Eph. 1:20–21; cf. Col. 1:16; 2:14–15), their hostility continues. Through baptism, the believer has died to the influence of these powers and has been raised by Christ to be outside of their control (see Col. 2:20; 3:1). Not until the full work of the cross is revealed at the parousia, however, will the subjugation of the powers be complete (Eph. 6:12; cf. 1 Cor. 15:24).

As Paul describes in Ephesians 1:20–21, Christ has been exalted above every name that can be named, that is, above anything or anyone to which we could appeal for assistance and for access to power. That God has exalted Christ to his right hand in heavenly places far above the domain of the powers indicates that the powers, as Paul conceives them, are not primarily earthly authorities. Any doubts about this interpretation of 1:20–21 are put to rest by Paul's statement in 6:12: "For our struggle is not against flesh and blood, but against the rulers, against the authorities, against the powers of this dark world and against the spiritual forces of evil in the heavenly realms." Over all these evil powers Christ has been exalted. Furthermore, Christ's exaltation indicates that there is no other name under heaven whereby humankind must be saved (Acts 4:12). The invocation of Christ's name alone, not his name in addition to others, is sufficient for a successful confrontation of the powers. Paul attempts neither to demythologize the powers nor to cast them as earthly authorities or some sort of spiritual atmosphere. The reader is to know the power of God in Christ, who has promised believers their ability to withstand these spiritual threats. The divine power needed to transform these promises into reality is made available in the resurrection and the exaltation of Christ, whose position at the right hand of God makes him superior to every imaginable power.

Paul gives us another glimpse of the powers in Ephesians 4:8–10, which depicts Christ as leading the captives, that is, the powers, he had taken. Paul's use of Psalm 68:18 in verse 8 is instructive, for in the psalm God leads a band of prisoners up to his holy mountain as a sign of his triumph. In Ephesians 4:9 Paul infers that Christ's triumph and ascent were necessarily preceded by his descent "to the lower, earthly regions." To interpret the descent as the incarnation or the gift of the Holy Spirit at Pentecost requires a strained reading of "lower, earthly regions." Verse 9 more appropriately refers to Christ's descent to hell itself in order to proclaim his triumph. Thus, the message Paul conveys is Christ's superiority to divine beings, to powers, both above and below the earth.

In Jewish apocalypticism, the cosmic struggle with the evil heavenly powers will take place in the future. In Ephesians 6:10–20 Paul expands the scope of the struggle to include the present. Yes, Christ has won the decisive victory at the cross, and the powers, which inhabit the unseen world of spiritual reality as a manifestation of the devil's power, have bowed to his cosmic lordship. However, in 6:10–11 Paul bids believers to prepare for a war they must still conduct with these powers. Indeed, the image of the Christian life as a battle is common in the writings of Paul (Rom. 13:12; 2 Cor. 6:7; 10:3–5; 1 Thess. 5:8; Lincoln 1981, 164). The Qumran community also expected to fight against the forces of evil, but they anticipated a war fought with physical weapons. Paul bids the use of spiritual weapons alone (6:13–18). Exhorting believers to put on God's armor *now,* Paul fixes the time for the battle as on "the day of evil" (v. 13), which refers to the intensification of evil, prior to the powers' complete destruction at the parousia (cf. 1 Enoch 50:2; 63:8; 96:2). Verse 13 exemplifies Paul's now and not-yet schema, for the church is conducting spiritual warfare in two ages and in two spheres of power, the heavenly and the earthly.

The Ephesian believers would have been well aware of and concerned about vicious attacks by powers in the present world, but Paul refutes their supposition that they are fighting their way through a heavenly cordon of powers that deny them access to God. Since the heavenlies are under Christ's control, they no longer pose a threat. To prepare for the battle, Paul urges believers to appropriate the benefits that have become available to them through Christ's victory. Thus, the armor of God enables believers to fulfil their cosmic role. It is from a position of strength that the church now fights the evil in its midst. Though Paul describes salvation already interiorized as deliverance from the powers (Eph. 2:1–10), he also knows of a future fulfilment (1:10) and redemption (4:30). Salvation has not been fully realized, for believers have not yet attained perfect knowledge (4:13) and have not experientially reached the fulness of God (3:19). Now, the present era, is a time of spiritual warfare.

Final Salvation (Eph. 1:22–23; 2:11–22; 4:1–16; 5:22–33)

Though the parenesis in the letter to the Ephesians applies to the now, Paul looks forward to the not-yet—the time of final salvation and cosmic redemption. In his attempt to describe the end to the Ephesian believers, Paul uses four recurrent images: the body of Christ, the church (*ekklēsia*), the new man, and the temple. These images are inter-related, and some have applications in the present as well as the future, clearly reflecting the now but not-yet time in which the Ephesians lived and in which we now live.

As defined in Ephesians 1:10, God's ultimate purpose is to bring to-gether all things of heaven and of earth under one head, that is, under Christ. All things have been summed up in Christ, but the historical manifestation of this is presently taking place. Consider what 1:22–23 describes as the work Christ is doing now: "And God placed all things under his [Christ's] feet and appointed him to be head over everything for the church, which is his body, the fullness of him who fills every-thing in every way." Christ is now filling all things (see also 4:10) includ-ing the *ekklēsia*, where the process can most readily be seen. His role is active, whereas that of the church is passive, for it is filled. (The notion of the church as active, that is, of filling up or completing Christ, is for-eign in the New Testament.) And it is through Christ's activity that the saints share in the divine power, in God's inheritance. The sharing oc-curs as Christ dynamically fills all things, all creation, by assuming his function as ruler.

All that Christ is, is presently being achieved through the church, the body of Christ. In Ephesians Paul attempts to reveal the position of the church in the scheme of God's purpose of cosmic redemption. Though Paul writes a circular letter to local churches in Asia Minor, his focus is the total *ekklēsia*. Yet, what is the local church? Ephesians 1:22–23 in-dicates what Paul means. In the passage the referent of "fullness" is the church; thus, the church represents the eschatological totality of the re-deemed not the present universal fellowship of believers. To connote the ongoing fellowship, Paul uses the word *body*. In the eschaton, how-ever, the body and the *ekklēsia* will coalesce.

Paul's proclamation of reconciliation as found in Ephesians 2:11–22 has implications for both the body and the church. In these verses Christ is depicted as the harbinger of cosmic peace through a ministry that reconciles the universe and thus removes barriers between heaven and earth, and thus between Jew and Gentile (Lincoln 1981, 150). Dominating this section is the language of access and citizenry in the new commonwealth (cf. Phil. 3:20). Divisions have been broken down (Eph. 2:14–16, 18), and a new unity, a body, is being created. Past ethnic and physical distinctions are gone (vv. 11–13), and Israel's former advantages have been extended to the new people of God, the fully grown being into which the new man is developing (4:13). The divisive old order, in which Israel possessed the Torah, has been replaced by a redeemed humanity incorporated into Israel's Messiah. Reconciled through the cross, both Jews and Gentiles have access to God through the one Spirit and are members of the new community, which is a legatee of the promises given to Israel.

Paul describes God's purpose in the reconciliation of Jews and Gentiles in Ephesians 2:15: "His purpose was to create in himself one new man out of the two, thus making peace." This new humanity is produced in believers by the operation of the representative life of the risen Christ. The new man, the new humanity so achieved, is in fact the corporate life of Christ manifested in all believers.

In 2:21 another image connotes reconciled humanity—a holy temple with Christ as the cornerstone, the link between heaven and earth (Jeremias 1967, 275). Built upon the foundation of New Testament apostles whose ministry is also prophetic (Grudem 1982, 93–105), the new commonwealth is presented as a household that grows into a temple, that is, a community finally indwelt by God that operates as a temple. Paul had previously applied the image of the temple to individual believers, or perhaps to a congregation (see 1 Cor. 6:19). The image of the temple, which is a clear mark of God's lordship (2 Cor. 6:16–7:1), maintains the nexus between Spirit and kingdom as it appears in both the Old and New Testaments. The indwelling of the Spirit makes the believer a temple, and thus God's rule is spiritually manifested in him or her. The imagery of growth, of the temple under construction, in 2:21 gives the highest expression to the spiritual aspirations of believers, since the temple symbolized the ultimate kingdom-of-God authority over Israel, and thus defined Israel as the people of God. What in the Old Testament was to be the world's focal point, the Jerusalem temple, becomes in Ephesians a symbol of the destiny of the new people of God.

The new unity, which provides the sense of oneness felt by the congregations of the Lycus valley, is a major focus in 4:1–16. Finding expression through fellowship in the one body, the unity was produced by one Spirit (v. 4), enjoys one common hope (v. 5), and is experienced by one means of entry into the faith, that is, one baptism (v. 5). Verses 1–6 state the principles of unity that determine the structure of the body; verses 7–11 identify the gifts that will maintain the unity; and verses 12–16 describe the relation of these gifts to the growth of the body. In verse 13 is revealed the eschatological goal of this growth—a threefold expectation of maturity, not size, to be realized at the parousia: "until we all reach unity in the faith and in the knowledge of the Son of God and become mature, attaining to the whole measure of the fullness of Christ." Though Christ is one aspect of the goal, he is also the source of growth (v. 16), the origin of the whole process who alone engenders harmony among members. Thus, the finally assembled new humanity is to perfectly reflect the nature of Christ in a transformed universe. Yes, this goal is a hope, an eschatological article of faith, but Paul's parenesis makes clear that this goal is to provide the basis of present striving toward holiness.

In the parenesis of 5:22–33 Paul joins the images of the body and the bride. In verse 23 one of the fundamental images pertaining to historical Israel is transferred to the church: "For the husband is the head of the wife as Christ is the head of the church, his body, of which he is the Savior" (cf. Isa. 54:5; Jer. 3:8; Ezek. 16; Hos. 1–3). Christ is the head of the church and hence its cause as its Savior, distinct from it and yet one with it. Christ loves and cherishes the *ekklēsia* because "we are members of his body" (v. 30). Through the image of the bride, Paul casts the church as an eschatological entity that is pure, perfected without spot or wrinkle. It is the essential notion of fellowship in unity between Christ and believers that the body and bride images have in common. The metaphor of marriage points to the identity and yet the distinctiveness of those engaged in it, and the related images are consistent with Paul's now and not-yet schema. The *ekklēsia* is now the body of Christ but not yet the bride, for the *ekklēsia* is being prepared for what she ultimately will be (cf. 2 Cor. 11:2 where the marriage is future). The awaited consummation is clearly a future prospect.

The Epistle to the Ephesians represents a heightened development and, indeed, the summit of Pauline eschatological thought. The apostle proclaims that God's purpose to sum up all things in Christ is presently being furthered through the local assemblies, wherein the former divisions have been surmounted. The Jew and Gentile question so prominent in Paul's earlier letters has given way in Ephesians to the emergence of the new reconciled humanity in Christ, in itself a witness that demonstrates the finality of the cosmic victory of the cross. But the church, in which the fruits of Christ's victory are revealed, is but the local anticipation of the great company of believers already enrolled as citizens of heaven, a reality to be manifested at the return of Christ. What presently remains for the believer is this now and not-yet situation is to take on the whole of God's armor to protect one's faith.

Epistle to the Philippians

Paul's letter to Christians in the Macedonian city of Philippi combines thanksgiving and parenesis. Though the main thrust of the letter is christological, we are also introduced to the call for Christian constancy by perseverance in the race of faith (Phil. 3:12–16) in light of the assured future for the Christian (1:21; 3:20–21). Aspects of Paul's eschatology emerge in both the thanksgiving and the parenesis, particularly in the hymn of 2:6–11 and the warning in chapter 3.

Philippians 2:6–11 extols in hymnic form the sacrificial ministry of Christ. Referring to the preexistent Christ, verses 6–7a describe Christ as one who shares God's nature and is eternally equal with God, but who did not regard his divine status as something to be used for his own advantage. Unlike Adam, who snatched at equality with God to which he had no right, Jesus gladly renounced his dignity. Divine equality for him did not mean *getting* but *giving* (Moule 1970, 267). Rather than excusing Christ from redemptive suffering, divine equality preeminently fitted him for the task. That Christ "emptied himself" does not point to the loss of divine attributes but to their amazing reinterpretation (v. 7a; Wright 1983, 381). Verses 7b–8 describe Christ Jesus' incarnation, that is, his humbling through the assumption of human nature. Though equal with God, Christ became fully human, assuming all human limitations by being born into a world dominated by evil and accepting involvement in the common life of sinful humanity (Caird 1969, 122). Manifesting the form of God in the body of a servant, Jesus was obedient unto death upon a degraded cross. Verses 9–11 describe God's decisive intervention and exaltation of Jesus to the highest station, for God bestowed on Jesus his own name of Lord with all that gives substance and meaning to the name. Worldwide homage to Jesus as Lord is now to be offered by all—by the angelic hosts, by the principalities and powers, and by humanity both living and dead. Jesus now exercises universal lordship, and to this lordship believers respond as they realize the blessings of the new age.

In chapter 3 Paul warns the Philippians about opposition to his ministry from apparently the same Judaistic emissaries he had previously encountered (Gal. 2:11–13; cf. 2 Cor. 3:1–6; 11:13). In verses 3–6 the apostle cites the advantages of his Jewish background. In verses 7–14, however, he explains how the benefits of his new life far outweigh any advantage of the past. On the basis of the benefits of his new life in Christ, Paul appeals to the Philippians for unity (1:27–2:4; Caird 1969, 114). Does this new life intimate a realized eschatology? No, it does not, for in verse 12 the image of the Christian race takes over. No matter the amount of ground covered, the believer always has the distance ahead in mind (Caird 1969, 141). Christian perfection is the goal for which we press on, not something we already possess. But the Philippians must be careful whom they model. Enemies of the cross of Christ abound (vv. 17–18), and Paul is moved to tears as he recalls the frustrations caused by opposition to his teaching. In running the race, believers are not to develop the mind-set of the flesh, for there are false teachers and what they glory in, apparently their Jewish heritage with its emphasis on obedience to the food laws, will turn into their shame at the judgment (vv. 17–19). As a Roman citizen writing to members of a Roman colony at Philippi, Paul reminds them of their ultimate political affiliation as members of the colony of heaven, where Christ now is (v. 20a). But even this citizenship should not be taken as evidence of a completely realized eschatology. Paul's outlook is still future, as in the expectation of verse 20b: "And we eagerly await a Savior from there, the Lord Jesus Christ." Moreover, he anticipates a transformation of the present circumstance of our bodies, which is characterized by weakness. What he expects is a transformation of what we presently have, not an entirely new state (Lincoln 1981, 103). There is no Paradise now, but it will surely come.

Paul's letter to the Philippians moves to a close with thanks by Paul for their support for his ministry and with final instructions. We leave the letter with a strong consciousness of the role of Jesus as the Second Adam who makes available to us membership in the heavenly community. Mindful of Jesus as well as of the joy that is set before us, we have the impetus to run with patience the Christian race, looking unto Jesus, the author and finisher of our faith (Heb. 12:1–2).

Epistle to the Colossians

The Epistle to the Colossians addresses and attempts to counteract a heresy that arose in the fertile soil of the many religious movements in Asia Minor. Evidencing both Jewish and Hellenistic elements, which is not surprising since the cultures so thoroughly permeated each other, the heresy involved cosmology and Christology, specifically the relationship of Jesus to God and to the other powers and principalities of the world. Some Colossians believed that communication between humankind and God was controlled by principalities and powers, that is, the angels through whom the law had been given. Though the Colossians recognized forgiveness in Jesus, they believed it applied to the material world only, for between the material creation and God were unreconciled elemental spirits who shared in the *plērōma* (fulness) of the Godhead. Jesus was most certainly in the hierarchy, but he was only one of many other beings. Thus, humankind, it was believed, must give all the spirits their due, acknowledge their hierarchy, and placate them by a personal asceticism that included the observation of Jewish laws. One's participation in Jesus' death and resurrection was necessary, but so were these various other requirements. For the Colossians, the believer's journey toward redemption began with baptism, but an ascetic regimen was needed for the journey to progress, by which the material world would be shaken off and one would make the transition from darkness to light.

The Supremacy of Christ (Col. 1:15–20)

Realizing that a false Christology was to blame for the Colossians' dependence on the observation of regulations, Paul begins by using a christological hymn in 1:15–20 to point out Christ's supreme role in creation, redemption, and the new creation. He wants the Colossians to recognize that through Christ are available "all the treasures of wisdom and knowledge" (2:3). Moreover, not only have the principalities and powers, the very ones that filled the Colossians with awe, been overcome by the death of Christ, but his death has made possible a great creative harmony in which all things will be reconciled to him. The ravages of the fall have been repaired in Christ, and the way has been cleared for the eschatological realization in the new creation of all that God had intended for humanity. Christ, through whom the world has been made, is now the facilitator of humanity's place in the new creation (Col. 1:15–20). C. F. Burney has plausibly suggested that in 1:15–20 Paul is directing attention to Genesis 1:1 ("In the beginning"; cf. Prov. 8:22) by playing on the four meanings of the Hebrew *beginning* (i.e., beginning, sum total, head, and firstfruits) and on the three possible meanings of the Hebrew preposition *in* (i.e., in, by, and for; 1925–26, 160–77). Burney's suggestion draws added attention to the basic creation/new creation contrasts of the passage.

Verses 15–16 deal with the role of Christ in creation. The exalted Jesus is presented through the timelessness of the verb *is* in verse 15 as the eternal image of God. Though Jesus did not preexist as a human being, he has from all eternity held the same relationship to the Father that was intended for humanity by creation (Gen. 1:26–27). Thus, only in the incarnate Christ have we seen humanity presenting the perfect self-expression of God. While humankind was made *in* the image, Christ alone *is* the image!

The incarnate Christ perfectly represented humanity but also pointed to the new humanity to ensue from his death. As man, Christ was the embodiment of God but was also the Second Adam into whose image we must necessarily be transformed. Paul presents Christ as preeminent—"the firstborn over all creation" (Col. 1:15). Referring to Christ's priority in both time, as divinely preexisting before creation (as was Wisdom; cf. Prov. 8:27–31), and rank, as in his position in redemption and the new creation, this title of preeminence is the one given in the Old Testament to Israel (Exod. 4:22; Jer. 31:9) and to Israel's representative, that is, the Davidic king, the messiah (Ps. 89:27). Thus, in Colossians 1:15 Paul depicts Christ as all that Adam and Israel were meant to be. Christ undoes the sin of Adam and reconciles the world to himself. Both the place set aside for humankind in creation and the role assigned to Israel are appropriate vehicles for the self-expression of the one true man—Jesus, the Second Adam.

By having brought creation into being, Christ is preeminent in creation (Col. 1:16). Moreover, through his work of redemption, Christ is also the goal of all creation: "All things were created by him and for him" (v. 16b). He is thus the Lord of all, even the refractory demonic powers of whom the Colossians stood in awe. However, Christ's victory over them is to be realized in the new community, not in isolation, since the headship of Christ is to be seen in the church (v. 18). Indeed, the very existence of the church is evidence of their defeat (cf. Eph. 3:10).

Verses 17–18a recapitulate the role of Christ in creation and introduce his role in redemption. By depicting Christ in verse 17 as the sustainer of all creation, Paul transfers to him yet another aspect of Wisdom (cf. Prov. 8:22; Sir. 24:8; Wis. 6:22), which in turn evokes the concept of God's wise purpose for creation. In verse 18a the thought moves to the new creation, of which the church is representative: "And he [Christ] is the head of the body, the church." The word *head* does not convey any organic unity between Christ and the body. As verse 18b reveals, Christ's headship arises because of his priority and preeminence over believers who share in their risen life with him to become his spiritual body.

The motifs of verses 15–18a—creation, redemption, and the church—are drawn together in verses 18b–20. The word *beginning* in verse 18b, which alludes to creation in Genesis 1:1, casts Jesus as the new beginning. By the repetition of "firstborn" in verse 18b (cf. v. 15), Paul points to the continuity through Christ from the old to the new creation. Also, as "the firstborn from among the dead," Christ is the foundation of the coming resurrection, the first of many believers to be resurrected. Verse 18 also proclaims Christ's supremacy. As the head of the body, by virtue of his priority and preeminence, Christ has supremacy over the new fellowship, the church, to which the Colossians belong. The reason for his preeminence in the new creation is provided in verse 19: the fulness of God, divinity in all its completeness, took residence in Christ.

Paul reveals the purpose of God's residing in Christ in verse 20a: "and through him to reconcile to himself all things." Verse 20b describes the nature of the reconciliation as cosmic, that is, the reconciliation involves the whole universe. Note the repeated motifs of things in heaven and things on earth in verses 16a and 20b. Through such repetition, Paul signifies that creation and redemption share a common goal. Whatever barriers came to exist between God and the created world have been broken down on the cross. With the effects of the fall reversed, the universe may now look forward to its ultimate reconstitution (cf. Rom. 8:18–23). Human restoration is now available in the church, and this human reconstitution will lead to the parousia and universal harmony.

Paul wants the Colossian converts to recognize the achievements of Christ and to know that they may safely look to him. Christ's redemptive work has brought the body, the church, into being. Thus the body cannot live without Christ, though Christ can, and in fact did, live without the church. A witness to the work of creation and redemption, the body is at once a new creation and a saved entity. Paul's use of the hymn in Colossians 1:15–20 strongly suggests that believers do not need the Jewish appendages of Torah and Wisdom to escape the threatening powers, for Christ embodies both Torah and Wisdom and has overcome whatever threatens (Col. 2:15). After all, Christ is the full embodiment of the one true God. We find in Colossians 1:15–20 the most exalted Christology in all the New Testament.

The Source of Grace (Col. 3:1–4)

After expounding the nature of his ministry (Col. 1:24–2:5) and emphasizing in his response to false teaching the complete victory of Christ over all sinful hostility (2:6–23), Paul turns in 3:1–4 to the source of grace by which the Christian life is maintained and encouraged. In Christ, Christians are already risen with him and are members of the new and renewed humanity, the true image of God (3:10). With the change from "your life" in 3:3 to "our life" in verse 4, the corporate character of this new relationship becomes clear, as does its anticipation of the glory to be ours at the final manifestation of Christ. Our Christian hope, however, is set not merely on the return of Christ, but on the personal transformation of the believer within a transformed universe, which will then take place (v. 4; Wright 1986, 133). After drawing out the implications of 3:1–4 in verses 5–11 and 12–17, Paul closes the letter with final ethical instructions and directions.

In the Epistle to the Colossians Paul seems to have been combating the penetration of Jewish Christian teaching into the Lycus valley area. Paul's message is clear. Every human spiritual need is satisfied in Christ, for whom there can be no alternative. In this letter, as in Philippians, Christians are directed to live motivated by the forward look, for to be in Christ means present citizenship in heaven. It means also that the ethical stance of the Christian life is determined by the transformation of ourselves and of our world expected at the parousia.

Epistles to the Thessalonians

Paul's two letters to Christians in Thessalonica reveal much about the young congregation. The believers had been encouraged by Paul's earlier preaching there about Jesus and the coming parousia, so much so that some were leaving their employment in anticipation of an imminent end (1 Thess. 4:11; 5:14; 2 Thess. 3:6–15). Paul attempts to correct the excesses of the Thessalonians' eschatological enthusiasm and to answer their various questions about the parousia, those believers who died before it, and the day of the Lord.

To Serve and to Wait (1 Thess. 1:9b–10)

Paul summarizes the effect that hearing and accepting the gospel had upon the Thessalonians: "They tell how you turned to God from idols to serve the living and true God, and to wait for his Son from heaven, whom he raised from the dead—Jesus, who rescues us from the coming wrath" (1 Thess. 1:9b–10). In describing the believers, Paul incorporates the essentials of the gospel message, depicting Christ as the historical person named Jesus, as the royal Messiah, as the Son of God, as the present and eschatological Lord, and as judge and Savior. Though this Christology clearly subordinates Jesus to God, it identifies the work of Jesus as that which will save us from the coming judgment. It seems clear that Paul expects some delay in Jesus' return, for the apostle describes the Thessalonians as waiting and the wrath as coming. What is this wrath? It is not an impersonal process that works itself out in history, but is God's eschatological judgment at the end of history. However, deliverance is available even now, for the future acquittal at the last judgment has been drawn into the present. Thus, Paul's eschatology is partially, though not totally, realized. The parousia will complete what has begun; total salvation lies in the future.

The Coming of the Lord (1 Thess. 4:13–5:11)

The now but not-yet eschatology preached by Paul to believers in Thessalonica apparently raised some questions, ones he attempts to answer in 1 Thessalonians 4:13–5:11. The first concern to which he responds has generally been interpreted in two ways. Some suggest that the Thessalonians questioned the nonarrival of the expected parousia (Best 1972, 183). A more likely question, however, pertains to those in the Christian community who died subsequent to Paul's visit. That is, the remaining believers wondered whether their dead brothers and sisters would share in the blessings of the coming kingdom. The second concern, which Paul addresses in 5:1–11, involves the timing of Christ's second coming.

Verse 13 identifies the topic and in so doing suggests that the apostle's pronouncement is in response to questions Paul received from Thessalonica: "We do not want you to be ignorant about those who fall asleep, or to grieve like the rest of men, who have no hope." Note the way in which verses 13 and 18 frame Paul's response and reveal his intention. He wants them not to grieve (v. 13), but to encourage one another (v. 18). What he writes in verses 14–17 is the basis of the encouragement. Verse 14 states the kerygma and its implications: Jesus died and rose, and thus God will lead the dead in Christ with him. In regard to the dead, Paul emphasizes their being with Christ, not their resurrection. The emphasis, however, logically follows from verse 14a and does not signify that Paul's notion of an imminent parousia overshadowed the hope of a future resurrection. If the Thessalonians believed that Jesus died and rose, then they would believe that the future of the deceased believers in Jesus would be secure. Moreover, Paul does indeed make a connection between the resurrection of Jesus and that of believers. Not only does the apostle use the same verb to denote the rising of Christ and the rising of the Christian dead (*anistēmi*; vv. 14a, 16b), but he assumes in verse 14 that the resurrection of Christ integrally affects Christians. The brevity of Paul's simple and unelaborated statement on the future of the dead in verse 14b indicates that Paul has already spoken to the Thessalonians on this subject. Further support that Paul had preached the resurrection of believers to the Thessalonians is found in the detail of a future universal judgment, which appears in 1:10.

Based on the word of the Lord, verses 15–17 represent a three-part explanation about the parousia, the resurrection of the dead, and the assumption of the living at the parousia. In verse 15 Paul reassures the

Thessalonians by proclaiming that "we who are still alive, who are left till the coming (*parousia*) of the Lord, will certainly not precede those who have fallen asleep." The word *parousia* seems to have been understood by the Thessalonians as part of Paul's kerygma. In the Hellenistic world, a parousia could denote the arrival of a king, a god, an emperor, and angel, or even troops, while connoting help or assistance at the arrival (Ware 1979, 110). Consistent with this is the occurrence in 3:13, where Jesus is to be accompanied by his heavenly retinue or army. Such an arrival in the Hellenistic world would be associated with the fanfare of greeting, acclamation by the crowds, the wearing of bright clothing, and the presentation of crowns. In like manner, Paul anticipates Jesus' parousia as a joyous event designed to rescue believers from the wrath associated with the last judgment (1:10).

Verse 15 is often cited (Best 1972, 194–96) as evidence that Paul thought he would still be alive at the second coming: "We who are still alive, who are left till the coming of the Lord." But is this what Paul means? It seems likely that Paul uses "we" in verse 15 to connote the church and thus does not necessarily count himself among those who will still be alive. Furthermore, the focus in verse 15 is not upon the timing of the second coming, which Paul does address in 1 Thessalonians 5:1–11 (cf. 2 Thess. 2:3).

Paul describes the descent of Jesus at the parousia in 1 Thessalonians 4:16: "For the Lord (*kyrios*) himself will come down from heaven, with a loud command, with the voice of the archangel and with the trumpet call of God." By using the word *kyrios*, Paul emphasizes Jesus' role in the parousia, in effect contrasting it with his role as the Messiah, who had no similar role in Jewish expectation (Best 1972, 196). During the time of Paul, *kyrios* was used increasingly in circles of emperor worship. Thus, by using the word, Paul makes a claim about the person of Jesus.

The descent of the Lord together with the command, the archangel's voice, and God's trumpet call will announce the beginning of the kingdom of God (Plevnik 1975, 246). Since in the Hellenistic period visiting emperors were generally accompanied by their armies, Paul's apocalyptic imagery in verse 16 is appropriate. Moreover, the imagery is widely attested. The cloud, the trumpet, and the Lord's descent bear sure overtones of the Sinai covenant (Exod. 19:10–18). Various biblical passages associate the sound of the trumpet with the end (Isa. 27:13; Zeph. 1:14–16; Matt. 24:31; 1 Cor. 15:52) and with the beginning of holy war (Judg. 3:27; 6:34; 1 Sam. 13:3). The prophets had taken the concept of holy war against Israel's enemies and reinterpreted it to mean a day of judgment against Israel. In the Qumran community, the sounding of the trumpet was a prominent symbol of the beginning of eschatological war, that is, of God's powerful intervention for the purpose of enforcing divine rule (Plevnik 1975, 248–49). The voice of the heralding archangel is associated in Daniel 12:1–2 with the resurrection of the righteous. Angelic accompaniment, which is typical in Old Testament theophanies, is linked with the coming of the Messiah in the New Testament (Matt. 25:31). In Revelation the voice of an angel accompanies judgment (6:1, 3, 5, 7), but the motif of judgment is absent from 1 Thessalonians 4:16, where Paul focuses on the gathering of the elect at the parousia.

In verses 16–17 Paul describes the Lord's descent from heaven and the believers' transportation in the clouds. Both heaven and clouds are symbols of power and glory in theophanies in the Old and New Testaments. But what are we to make of this? Is Paul describing the heavenly assumption of the saints who will meet Christ in the air and their final gathering to Christ, as found in Revelation 11:11–12? It appears that Paul's description of the descent of Christ simply recalls the words in Acts 1:11 of the two angels at the ascension: Jesus is to return as he had gone. Though in Acts the cloud conceals the departing Jesus and serves as the vehicle by which Jesus was transported, here the cloud will transport the believers who by divine action are suddenly taken upwards into the same sphere as Christ to an unspecified final destination (Foerster 1964, 472–74). Paul does not say whether the believers will remain in the air, but analogous Hellenistic literature suggests that they will function as a meeting party whose task is to escort Christ to earth. If they are to continue up to heaven, why would Christ have to come so far down (Best 1972, 200)?

Those who died as Christians will rise first. Since Paul's task is to reassure the Thessalonians, there is no need for him to consider the fate of the wicked. Furthermore, he does not specify the nature of the transformation of the risen believers, but that one will occur is implicit. The oblique reference to rising in verse 16 refers to a general doctrine of the resurrection of Christians and does not appear to be a doctrine that Paul is formulating for the first time. Once again, Paul is reassuring the Thessalonians. Why they needed such reaffirmation is unclear, though biblical scholars have offered many suggestions, such as their expectation of an imminent parousia or their concern over their own future. The most plausible cites the Thessalonians' distress as emerging from their belief that deceased Christians were at a relative disadvantage since they would not participate in the joys of the coming parousia.

In 1 Thessalonians 5:1–11 Paul addresses a question about the timing of the day of the Lord. Emphasizing the seriousness of the event and exhorting the faithful to be ready, Paul at the same time reassures them of salvation. His teaching, which is in keeping with Christian tradition, identifies the parousia, the day of the Lord, as the day of God's decisive intervention for the people of God. This day of judgment will come as a thief at a time of ease and security (1 Thess. 5:2–3). Though believers will be protected from this judgment, they are expected to be watchful for it (vv. 4–5, 9–11) and to put on Christian armor (v. 8; Gundry 1987, 170). These exhortations for watchfulness and preparedness would be quite unnecessary if Paul believed the faithful would rise before the coming of the day. Thus, faithfulness in all things is incumbent upon those who wait for the coming.

Signs of the Coming (2 Thess. 2:1–12)

The community of Thessalonica sent a further inquiry to Paul regarding matters of eschatology; the Second Epistle to the Thessalonians represents his response. In 2 Thessalonians 2:1–2 Paul identifies the issue: "Concerning the coming of our Lord Jesus Christ and our being gathered to him, we ask you, brothers, not to become easily unsettled or alarmed by some prophecy, report or letter supposed to have come from us, saying that the day of the Lord has already come (*enestēken*)." Though various biblical versions translate *enestēken* as "has already come," the word can also be rendered as "present" (cf. Rom. 8:38; 1 Cor. 3:22; Gal. 1:4; Heb. 9:9) or "at hand" or "is come" (cf. 1 Cor. 7:26; 2 Tim. 3:1). (For a discussion of the translation of *enestēken*, see Bruce 1982, 165.) It appears that the inquiry was prompted not by sorrow over the missed rapture, but by agitation over the nearness of the Lord's coming, agitation which had led to fanatical excitement and disorders.

Paul's response to the inquiry in verses 3–12 appears to be a summary of what he shared with them more fully at an earlier time (v. 5). Since we do not know what was originally communicated, it is extremely difficult to identify the substance of Paul's recollection. What is clear is thus—a sequence of events involving an individual must first occur (v. 3). Paul denies that the coming is imminent, supporting his contention with the observation that their situation is not one of tribulation (cf. 3:6–15) and with the reminder that a particular disorder must occur before the parousia: "That day will not come until the rebellion (*apostasia*) occurs and the man of lawlessness is revealed, the man doomed to destruction" (v. 3). A religious term, not a political one, *apostasia* is found here and in Acts 21:21, where it means "apostasy." Since the two events that must precede the parousia have not occurred, Paul points to the necessary delay in the Lord's coming. Paul's manner of presenting his teaching on the *apostasia* and the man of lawlessness may indicate his expectation that the Thessalonians will recognize these signs when they occur. Indeed, the identity of the man of lawlessness involves what is presently happening in a disguised way, that is, as a mystery (cf. Robinson 1964, 636). The image of the man of lawlessness, which is perhaps modeled on Antiochus Epiphanes and his actions in 167 B.C. (Dan. 11:31–32), point to an Antichrist figure who will have his own revelation (*apokalupsis;* 2 Thess. 2:3), his own parousia (v. 9), his own signs and wonders like those of a false prophet or a false Messiah (v. 9) as well as his own mystery (v. 7).

In 2 Thessalonians 2:5–6 Paul reminds the faithful that they know the factor that restrains the man of sin. Many identify the restrainer (*to katechon,* which is from *katechō*) as the Holy Spirit and suggest that the tribulational events cannot occur until the Holy Spirit, who is now operating through the church, is taken away (Williams 1991, 126). However, there is no Pauline precedent for the use of the neuter participle in verse 6 to refer to the Holy Spirit; neither is there any parallel in the New Testament for the taking away of the Holy Spirit. Others identify the restrainer with the work of the Gentile mission or the preaching of the gospel (Mearns 1981, 154–57). However, if these identifications are apt, would Paul be so vague and secretive?

Let's look at another possibility. If we take the restraining force (*to katechon* in v. 6) as the principle of law and order, then the removal of the one exercising it (*ho katechōn* in v. 7) could point to the disruption and chaos in Jerusalem in A.D. 66–70 at the time of the Jewish rebellion occasioned by the withdrawal of Roman control. In a manner similar to Mark 13, verses 8–10 could refer to the disordered conditions in Jerusalem under the leadership of the day. The lawless one would then indicate the directive spirit behind the Jewish leadership of the period—when even the priestly leadership was effected (v. 4) and when unconverted Jews were consequently being led astray (v. 10). Whether the activity of Jesus in verse 8 points to his warning issued about the fall of Jerusalem (Luke 21:20–28) or whether the verse refers to the destruction of evil at the second coming remain open questions. However, either would fit the context. Finally, the terrible truth will emerge—that the delusion, which has ended in the overthrow of the Jewish nation, has been sent from God (v. 11).

When the eschatological method in both 1 and 2 Thessalonians is concluded, Paul continues with ethical instruction (1 Thess. 5:6–11, 12–22; 2 Thess. 3:1–5, 6:15). If the Thessalonian correspondence is the earliest we have from Saint Paul, we find in the two letters a graphic but developed eschatology from which the later letters do not vary. The two epistles to the Thessalonians also remind us that the real purpose of eschatological teaching is not to propose a harried watching for the signs of the times but to inculcate in us so great a hope regarding the end that we live at peace with one another and abstain from every form of evil (1 Thess. 5:12–22; 2 Thess. 3:6–15).

Pauline eschatology has been "now" and "not yet." Now the judgment of the last day has been drawn back into the present and God's verdict has been pronounced in favor of the believer, who experiences the blessings of the end time in the midst of the difficulties of the present sinful age. Now Israel's Old Testament commission of being a light to the Gentiles has been fulfilled in Christ, in whom the two peoples, Israel and the Gentiles, have become one new man. The new Christian group receives the promises intended for national Israel, who still, however, remains; and the Christian gospel must continually be addressed to Israelites so that more believers may be called forth. Now the worship of the present churches is an anticipation of the ongoing worship of the new age.

But there are also "not yets." Salvation, Paul taught, is proceeding. We are saved, we are being saved, but we will finally be saved. Final judgment will pronounce for faithful believers the reality of the verdict presently anticipated in justification. The transformation into the image, Christ (a transformation presently proceeding), will finally change us into the likeness of what he really is. Now the receipt of the Spirit as an earnest will give way to the full control of the Spirit over our glorious resurrection bodies, which is not yet. The existential conflicts of the present age will give way to the perfections of the age to come.

So Paul's eschatology is one of contrast, present conflict, future joy. But eschatology is ethically rooted, for from the indicative of what we are will emerge the imperative of what we need to become.

Pastoral Epistles (1–2 Tim.; Titus)

The fundamental Pauline tension between the now and the not-yet controls the eschatological thought of the pastoral Epistles (see, e.g., Titus 2:12–13). It is often suggested that these letters represent a time when the eschatological fervor of the early church had subsided (Wilson 1979, 13). However, the continued danger of apostasy under the influence of false teaching, both signs of the last days, is referred to in 1 Timothy 4:1–5, and the commendation of right teaching (4:6) with the need to reject what is false indicates that Paul is speaking about his own period.

Paul's charge to Timothy to keep himself above reproach until the coming of our Lord Jesus Christ may point to an expectation of an imminent coming (1 Tim. 6:14–15), but the text probably goes no further than the assertion of the end, not its precise timing. The subject of 1 Timothy 4:1–5 is taken up again in 2 Timothy 3:1–9 with the same conclusion. The distortions of the last days is discussed with a clear warning to avoid them (v. 5), indicating further the common Pauline emphasis of the current church era as the last days—the "now" of the eschatological tension. The primitive church's expectation of the second coming is underscored in Titus 2:13 (Kelly 1963, 15), where Paul points out that the coming eschatology is bound up with the manifestation of our great God and Savior Jesus Christ. There is no indication here that the parousia is imminent.

The pastoral Epistles evidence a clear belief in the second coming of Jesus without any evidence of its imminence. Eschatology remains peripheral, however, to the purpose of the letters, which is to establish a proper basis for the continued growth of the early Christian church.

12

Other Eschatological
Voices

The eschatological appears in the New Testament writings of Hebrews, James, 1–2 Peter, and Jude. The Epistle to the Hebrews portrays Christians as on a pilgrimage to the new promised land of Canaan and as equipped with better promises and a better covenant than Israel had been. Addressing a divided community of Jewish Christians, James examines Christian suffering and testing and the joy with which these are to be faced since the end, the inbreaking of the new age, is imminent (James 5:7). If eschatology is not the burden of the book, eschatology is certainly the context (Davids 1982, 39). Through reaffirmation of the believers' hope in heaven, 1 Peter encourages resistance to the persecutions experienced by scattered congregations in Asia Minor. While judgment is about to begin at the house of God, the prospect for those who persevere will be the crown of glory at the manifestation of Christ. Facing the problem of false prophets and teachers, Second Peter offers words of encouragement coupled with warnings and reminders. Though the letter confronts errors concerning the timing of the Lord's coming, it is not altogether clear whether Peter refers to the fall of Jerusalem, as we judge, or to the second coming. The Letter of Jude is full of allusions to the apocryphal books of 1 Enoch and the Testament of Moses, indicating the strongly apocalyptic outlook of the author, who holds that false teaching incurs divine judgment and that such judgment impends.

Epistle to the Hebrews

Through proclamation and exhortation, the writer of the Epistle to the Hebrews urges believers, perhaps those in a Jewish house church in Rome, to maintain their pilgrimage and to persevere so that the promise of rest in the presence of God might finally be theirs. As observed by C K. Barrett, the epistle witnesses a consistency in thought, which is determined by the eschatological (1956, 366). What dominates the epistle is the concept of eschatological fulfilment effected by the ministry of Jesus. Though the writer characterizes the time as the last days (Heb. 1:2), the epistle manifests a consistent futurist eschatology, for the pilgrims in this new exodus have drawn near to the heavenly realities of the last days but have not yet actually entered them.

An underlying theme of Hebrews is the true worship of God and what makes such worship possible. Not surprisingly, then, the epistle considers the perfection of the people of God and their fitness for heavenly worship in the redeemed congregation of believers. The writer conceives of perfection as the reaching of the goal ordained. Thus, Christ, who has been perfected since he reached the end that God had set for him, is the pioneer and "perfecter of our faith" (Heb. 12:2). For pilgrims, perfection is both a present accomplishment and an eschatological reality, though neither is attained by human effort. That is, Christ and believers have been perfected by the historical effect of the cross, by the activity of God. Believers will only be completely and finally perfected when they reach their heavenly rest by entering the heavenly sanctuary of God's eternal presence (Pfitzner 1983, 100).

Chapters 1–7 of the Epistle to the Hebrews focus on the person of Jesus, the one who proved his superiority by his session at the right hand of God after his atonement for human sins; chapters 8–10 consider Christ's work. At the same time, the letter attempts to relate the new people of God to Judaism and its institutions. The writer thus depicts Jesus as bringing into being the eschatological covenant promised by Jeremiah (Heb. 7:22; 8:6–13; 10:16–18), and destroying the power of death (2:14). And the believers are pilgrims pursuing their own exodus on their way to rest in the new Promised Land (4:1, 11). In covenantal terms the letter proleptically brings together the full significance of what has been done by Christ and the expectation given to believers (12:18–24). The death of Jesus has brought believers into the sphere of eschatological existence (Hughes 1979, 67).

The Identity of Jesus
(Heb. 1; 2:5–18; 3:1–6; 4:14–5:10; 7:1–18)

Some problem or crisis of faith prompted the writing of the Epistle to the Hebrews. As chapters 1–7 disclose, the writer aimed to sustain belief in Christ's absolute transcendence. To that end, the author identifies the relationship between Jesus and the Father and explains Jesus' roles as Messiah, as Son, as heir, as apostle, and as High Priest.

Through seven predications, the writer of Hebrews highlights Christ's eschatological rule in 1:1–4. Though in the past God has spoken to us in quite divergent ways (Heb. 1:1–2a), God now speaks through a Son. Jesus is

- the heir who rules over all things—the old world, which is doomed to pass away, and the heavenly world, which lies before redeemed humankind as the goal of its pilgrimage (v. 2b),
- the agent of creation (v. 2c),
- the radiance and the perfect representation of the divine essence of God (v. 3a),
- the sustainer of the universe (v. 3b),
- the provider of atonement (v. 3c),
- the Messiah at the right hand of God (v. 3c; cf. Ps. 110:1),
- a being superior to the angels (v. 4).

By his sacrificial death, Christ—the heir of all things—entered once and for all upon the heavenly inheritance and thus opened the kingdom of heaven to all believers.

In Hebrews 1:5–13 the writer grounds the christological sequence of verses 2b–4 in seven citations from the Old Testament that deal with the supreme dignity of Christ as Son. Angels are called sons of God in the Old Testament, but the writer underscores Christ's superiority over them. The two quotations in verse 5 establish the uniqueness of the Messiah as the enthroned King and his relationship to his Father (cf. Ps. 2:7; 2 Sam. 7:14; Thompson 1976, 355). Since the angels are mutable and since they worship Jesus, he is superior to them (vv. 6–7; cf. Ps. 97:7; Deut. 32:43 LXX; Ps. 104:4). Moreover, Jesus' reign is permanent (vv. 8, 10–12; cf. Ps. 45:6–7; 102:25–27). In verse 13 the author directs our attention to the Messiah's present role in the heavenly session as he awaits the ushering in of the new age (cf. Ps. 110:1).

As the solidarity of Christ with the Deity is emphasized in chapter 1, the solidarity of Jesus as exalted man with humankind is highlighted in chapter 2. In verses 5–18 the writer considers Christ's suffering and humiliation. For a little while Jesus had been subjected to, and was thus inferior to, the angels (vv. 5–9; cf. Ps. 8:4–6). But Jesus has fulfilled humankind's destiny as God's vice-regent. Having received the kingdom as a man, Jesus has fulfilled the intention of God for humankind as expressed in Genesis 1:26–27. Verses 10–16 consider the outworking of

Christ's humiliation, his incarnation. Christ's perfection is his fitness to act as Savior and High Priest (v. 10), as the pioneer or file leader ("author" in NIV) of salvation. Christ's role as pioneer suggests a destination to which believers are heading (cf. 13:14); that is, Jesus brings believers in him, with whom he is not ashamed to be identified, to glory (2:11–12). As the eschatological assembly pictured as gathered in heaven in 12:18–24, these believers reverse the sequence described in Genesis 2–3 (Peterson 1982, 62). Though eternal, Christ became our brother and our helper.

The next step in the developing Christology of the Epistle to the Hebrews is to recognize Jesus the man as High Priest (2:17), a cultic depiction that carries the development of the epistle's thesis. The author's comment in 2:17 sums up the argument of chapters 1–2. These chapters are not about Christ's superiority to the angels but about the exaltation (chap. 1) and the humiliation (chap. 2) of the Son who is now our great High Priest enthroned at the right hand of God (Attridge 1989, 17). The more excellent name (1:4) that Jesus has inherited is now revealed. He is crowned with glory and honor (2:9), signifying his new entitlement to the office of High Priest (Vanhoye 1986, 85–87). This is a new office he won by his close identification with humankind in his participation in the deepest agony of human experience. His relationship with the Father (1:14–15), his incarnation, and his passion are the ingredients that fit him for this essential office of mediation between humankind and God. The continuing purpose of the epistle will be to indicate how all the implicit promises of the Old Testament institutions are fulfilled in this new High Priest.

Hebrews 2:17, with its twin notes of Christ as merciful and faithful (RV), provides two issues that will be developed in 3:1–5:10. Christ our High Priest as "faithful," as worthy of trust, and as over the house of God dominates 3:1–4:13. (Here "house" is temple or sanctuary, no longer a material building but an edifice under construction [cf. 1 Pet. 2:5]. At the same time, messianic overtones are present, as Vanhoye [1986, 96–107] points out. Second Samuel 7:14 has been cited at 1:5, with its play on a house for the Davidic succession—in the context, building a temple.) The primary contrast is between Jesus and Moses (3:1–6), while Christ also embodies the final divine authoritative word that is to be believed (2:7–4:13). Hebrews 4:14–5:10 exposits Christ as merciful, as able to be approached; unlike the Old Testament priests, he not only possesses the requisite authority to act but also has an infinite capacity for compassion in the face of humankind's weakness and sin (4:15).

As High Priest, Jesus has passed through the heavens, the different layers of the supernatural spheres that separate humankind from God (Peterson 1982, 76). Now, in a heavenly world which is not of this order

(Heb. 9:11–12), Jesus makes continuous intercession for us (4:14; 7:25). In the Epistle to the Hebrews this heaven is the place of God's dwelling (9:23–24; 12:22–24), the location of the divine throne (1:3, 13), the source of the unshakable kingdom (12:28), the goal of believers in their pilgrimage (12:28–29), the city of the living God (12:22–23), and the dwelling place of the spirits of just human beings made perfect (12:23). Moreover, it is the location of the holy place into which Christ has entered on our behalf (8:2; 9:2, 11–12, 23–26). In contrast to this heavenly sphere is the earthly world, which was created, was upheld by the power of Jesus (1:3; Sharp 1984, 290), but will pass away (1:10–12). In spite of Jesus' exalted character, he is able to sympathize with our weaknesses as he ministers on our behalf (4:15). Through the mediation of Christ, a new relationship in the heavenlies is now available to us (4:16).

In a comparison with the Aaronic high priesthood, the qualifications of Jesus for the priesthood are presented in 5:1–10. Like Aaron's, Christ's priesthood was founded on a divine ordination (5:1–6). Hebrews 5:7–10 treats the measure of Christ's identification with humankind. In accepting the likeness to humanity in suffering, Christ became totally assimilated to humankind (except for identification in sin [4:15]) by his sacrifice of consecration (Vanhoye 1986, 130–33), and thus, always possessing full deity, he achieved perfection. That is, he is fit to mediate in the divine presence.

In 5:11–10:39 the distinctives in the relationship between Christ and the Aaronic priesthood are developed. The readers have a new, qualitatively different High Priest and need to understand these new characteristics. After an exhortation (5:11) on the difficult nature of what is to follow (5:11–6:20), the author again (6:20; cf. 5:6, 10) introduces the topical figure of Melchizedek (cf. the detail of 4Q Melchizedek from cave 11, Qumran; Attridge 1989, 192–94). Melchizedek provides a fitting analogy for the new glorified High Priest. In 7:1–3, Melchizedek, like the glorified (as opposed to incarnate) Christ, possessed no genealogy and had seemingly a priesthood with no end to it (although in the case of Melchizedek, with "no interruption," 5:3).

In 7:1–3 also, the figure of Abraham, with whom Aaron is to be connected, is introduced to indicate (by the payment of tithes to Melchizedek, 7:4–10) the superiority of this priesthood to the Aaronic. Hebrews 7:11–19 develops the distinctiveness of this new priesthood. By law only Aaron's descendants could minister (7:11); this new priesthood proclaimed by God (7:17; cf. Ps. 110:4) must, in this polemic against the Mosaic covenant, mean a sweeping away of previous legal requirements (Vanhoye 1986, 160–69). Thus, since there is a change in the law (7:12) which flows from a covenant base, a new covenant (cf.

8:8–13) is presupposed. With Hebrews 7:27–28 the writer's demonstration of this new approach vested in Jesus has ended. We turn in the next and major discourse of the book (8:1–10:18) to the manner in which this High Priest has opened the way into the heavenly holy of holies.

The Work of the New High Priest (8:1–10:18)

The author explains that with his discussion of the offering accomplished by Christ, explicated on the model of the action of the high priest on the Day of Atonement, he has reached the high point (8:1) of his discussion. Christ's ministry, which has replaced that of the Levitical priesthood, is housed not in the earthly tabernacle but in the heavenly sanctuary where Jesus sits at God's right hand (8:2). Hebrews 8:3–9:10 concerns the abrogation of the Old Testament cult, which was characterized by a multiplicity of sacrifices and an inability to achieve peace for the worshiper. Since gifts and sacrifices identify the system (8:3), it is critical to understand the significance of the offering presented by Jesus. Ministry under the old covenant was provisional only (8:5). But a new and better priesthood has stemmed from a new and better covenant, and covenant inaugurated in this case by the death of Christ. Since such a need was anticipated in the Old Testament, the provisionality of the Sinai covenant was clear. The text of Jeremiah 31:31–34 is brought into play in 8:8–13. Hebrews 9:1–10 appraises the old system, whose climax was the entry of the high priest into the holy of holies on the Day of Atonement (9:6–7). But such a climax, in having to be repeated year by year, was an anticlimax! The verdict is that the old system did not meet human needs (9:9–10).

In 9:11–18 the author turns to Christ and his offering. In Christ and his sacrifice (9:11–14) we have all the essentials for an approach to God: a new High Priest who is a perfected mediator; a greater and more perfect tabernacle—perhaps the glorified Christ, the new temple, reflecting all the holiness previously symbolized by the earthly holy of holies (Vanhoye 1986, 189–96)—as a better sacrifice. To sustain the imagery of the Day of Atonement, we should perhaps see this High Priest as the heavenly or spiritual archetype of the earthly tabernacle (Attridge 1989, 247). Christ, uniting in himself perfected requirements of both victim and priest—a requirement impossible to meet under the old system, in which the priesthood must sacrifice for itself—accomplished by the Holy Spirit (v. 14) perfect atonement for sin. In this way Christ provided the basis for the new relationship, the new covenant concluded, as the Sinai covenant had been, by sacrifice, but now in his own blood (Matt. 26:28). Our assurance of the efficacy of this one sacrifice is obtained from the access into the true holy of holies that Christ achieved by it (v. 24). We may now stand before God (i.e., enter into the heavenly holy of holies, since we are identified with Christ) and rejoice in the prospect of our High Priest's return (vv. 27–28).

In Hebrews 10:1–18 the old system of law, covenant, institutions, is finally written off as ineffective. True priesthood is based not on ritual but on personal obedience (10:5–7). Transformed by his incarnate act of obedience to God and the identification with humanity that the passion exemplified, Christ is now able to transform us (10:10) by his sacrifices, offered once and all-sufficient, which inaugurated the new covenant.

Believers and Jesus (Heb. 2:1–4; 3:7–4:13; 10:19–13:25)

Throughout the Epistle to the Hebrews the author relates aspects of Christology and of Christ's work to the personal lives of believers, demonstrating the effect of Jesus on their lives and exhorting them to faithfulness. Thus, believers receive instruction not only in regard to the *what* of their behavior but also in regard to the *why*.

Hebrews 2:1–4 warns the readers of the epistle to take seriously the implications of the Christology of chapter 1, for the world to come has been subjected to the man Christ Jesus (2:5). This explicit, familiar reference to another age, which is apocalyptic, rabbinic, and Pauline, underscores the nature of the work of Christ. Having begun with creation, the present age is to end with the return of Christ (9:28) and with the transformation of the present world (1:11–12; 12:25–29). It is in the last days of the present age in which we now live (1:2). In classical Judaism the present age and the age to come were successive, but in the New Testament there is a decided overlap between them. Believers now take part in the age to come (6:4–5), but the fulness of this experience will be realized only after the second coming of Christ. On this point the teaching of the epistle is completely consistent with that of the Pauline Epistles. The Christ event has made it clear that the end of the present age is approaching (10:25, 37). The coming age refers to a definite reality that, while it is not yet unfolded, is nonetheless ready and active (Peterson 1982, 53).

Hebrews 3:7–4:13 represents an exhortatory discourse on the nature of the faithfulness believers must display if they are to have rest (*katapausis*) in the presence of God. As the basis for the exhortation, the key word *rest* is an important eschatological concept in the epistle. The rest to which believers look forward is the enjoyment of the presence of God in the heavenly Canaan—the New Testament parallel to the Promised Land of the Old Testament.

In Hebrews 3:7–11 the writer uses Psalm 95, interpreting it within the history of the Davidic monarchy, as an address to the present generation. Israel had failed to enter into the promised rest, for she had never securely occupied the Promised Land, not even as a result of the conquest by David. Though David had held out the possibility of rest after the conquest, and presumably in his own time, not even he had given his people rest. Beyond the political rest achieved under Solomon, the Old Testament contains no further reference to rest as having been achieved, certainly no spiritual rest; therefore, a rest for the people of God still remains as a possibility.

The writer uses Psalm 95 to compare the present generation to those in the desert who wandered towards the Promised Land with the expectation of it but who perished on the way because of unbelief (Heb. 3:18–19). The argument is taken further in 4:1–11. God has not withdrawn the promise of rest (4:1–2), which in verses 3–5 is redefined in terms of the Sabbath rest (*katepausen*; Gen. 2:2 LXX). Since the Promised Land was simply a further extension of the Eden motif, the rest promised by the psalmist is thus the same, the writer argues, as that which had been available to humankind from creation onwards. Creation rest—Sabbath rest—remains as a possibility (v. 9), but the enjoyment of God's presence is now to be found in Christ, in whom we anticipate the life to come. The writer thus calls pilgrims of the new exodus to march onwards as the new-wilderness people of God to the heavenly rest.

Hebrews 10:19–25 urges believers to use the knowledge of Christ's sacrificial offering, by which humankind has been cleansed and consecrated, to help them take hold of the present benefits of his sacrifice. Through faith, believers already share in the eschatological life of the new age. The flesh of Christ is the new veil through which believers may penetrate into the presence of God (10:20), for Christ's death has opened the way into the heavenly sanctuary. Perfection, that is, drawing near to God, is the reception of eschatological blessing (11:40); such activity, which will characterize the eschaton, finds its expression now in congregational worship (10:25). Humankind will be perfected in relation to God when the promises of the new covenant are realized in personal experience (Peterson 1982, 155).

Hebrews 12:18–24 presents an eschatological panorama that contrasts the two covenants, two mediators, and two cults mentioned earlier in the epistle and relates the old and the new people of God (Käsemann 1984, 57). Verses 18–21 focus on the conclusion of the Sinai covenant by directing us to the holy mountain of Sinai, the dwelling place of the Deity. To reinforce the terror induced by this theophany, the writer reminds us of the time when Moses quailed before God (v. 21; cf. Deut. 9:19). How unlike this scene is the one presented in verses 22–24, which describes the great company as standing before the throne of God, the judge, and before the Son in the assembly of the end-time *ekklēsia*. In verse 23 the writer identifies those in the assembly as "firstborn," the term for elective privilege found in Exodus 4:22. Thus, the company of the redeemed, which has been founded upon the promises carried by Israel, is the triumphant church of the end.

What is described in verses 22–24 is the new covenant's conclusion, as based on the model of Sinai. The new covenant is thus a perfected Sinaitic covenant by which Israel's vocation will finally be realized and the complete people of God, Jew and Gentile, will be assembled. Those involved—angels, assembled participants, presiding Deity, and mediator—are reminiscent of the *qāhāl* Yahweh assembled at Sinai. By this picture, the recipients of the epistle are reminded of what lies ahead for them as God's people on the move. Jesus perfected, the one completely fitted for his heavenly role, now stands in the congregation of his many brethren. What had been anticipated liturgically in 2:12 will now occur: believers perfected by the sacrifice of Christ, that is, completely fitted for access to and presence in the heavenly city, will stand before the Deity awaiting scrutiny. The reference in verse 23 to "the spirits of righteous men made perfect" is to this heavenly company as justified by the work of Christ. The precise language grows out of the writer's conviction that the verdict to be pronounced upon those assembled can be nothing other than divine favor and acceptance, a verdict anticipated in the gift of Christian forgiveness.

In the striking imagery of Hebrews 12:18–24 is sketched the goal of the heavenly Jerusalem to which the pilgrim people are moving. In verses 22–24 the writer is at pains to stress that the pattern of Sinai has repeated itself whereby Israel, the firstborn chastened by discipline, has been assembled, approved by God, sprinkled with covenant blood by the imposition of a mediator, and drawn into fellowship. Whereas the blood of Abel caused division (v. 24), that of Jesus brings reconciliation.

At the end of the Epistle to the Hebrews the eschatological paradox remains, for we pilgrims have arrived at the city (12:22) that we still seek (13:14). The new covenant has been concluded in verses 18–24, but the focus is upon Zion as a counterpoint to Sinai. Beyond the conclusion of the covenant, there is no advancement to the Promised Land. In this pilgrim epistle Canaan and rest for the people of God still beckon us on; the epistle concludes with a forward look. We still search for the city whose maker and builder is God. The primary eschatological event, the death of Christ, has placed us in the last days, which will be brought to a close by the return of Christ. At that time the cosmos will be changed, Christ will reign over his enemies, and believers will enter into their promised inheritance. Thus, the present is not a time for wavering but for decisive commitment to the apostle and High Priest of our confession.

Epistle of James

The letter of James addresses Jewish Christians as the restored Israel, as the twelve tribes of the Dispersion soon to be gathered (1:1). In the epistle exists a strong link between ethics and eschatology, and indeed this link is the distinguishing feature of James.

The brother of Jesus begins by exhorting success in the fiery trial to come, for such triumph will mean the reception of the crown of life (1:12), that is, membership in the kingdom of God (2:5). Largely concerned with the return of Jesus in judgment, James depicts Jesus the Judge as standing at the door (5:9). Thus, the inbreaking of the new age is imminent. Indeed, the eschatological judgment of the persecutors of the poor is so near that their wealth is already moth-eaten and rusted (5:1–3; Davids 1982, 38). James equates the coming of the Lord with the coming of God (5:1–8) and does not consider any question of the delay of the second coming or concerns about it. Moreover, he presents the coming day as the reason for endurance (5:7). The way to prepare for this coming is to exhibit in the present a life of firm Christian character, a message that repeats the one in Mark 13 where it is taught that robustness of faith is shown by works of character produced during the period of waiting.

Epistles of Peter

Peter Davids writes, "The whole of 1 Peter is characterized by an eschatological, even an apocalyptic focus" (1990, 15). The controlling metaphor of the letter, found in the very first verse, is the Diaspora. Recipients of the letter have embarked, according to Peter, upon an eschatological journey. Graphically described in 1:3–12, this journey commences with the recipients' rebirth and ends with their reception of salvation in the eschaton. Though the rebirth has already taken place, the reception of salvation is future. Between these two lies the present journey in which manifold temptations engender grief (v. 6). In verses 7–9 Peter contrasts the present time of testing with the joyful moment when the destination is reached. This destination had been studied previously by the Hebrew prophets of old (v. 10), who revealed that the sufferings of Christ would be followed by glory (v. 11). And this message has been announced again (v. 12). In general, Peter's concern is with the present journey of those whom he addresses.

The issue in 2 Peter is the incursion of false teachers who are apparently backslidden Christians (2:1, 5, 20–22). They have gained support (2:1–3a, 14, 18) especially from those who were weak or new in the faith (2:14, 18), though their teaching also troubles the mature (3:17). Eschatological scepticism underlies the false teachers' doctrine: they had expected the judgment of the day of the Lord (3:10) during the lifetime of the first generation who had passed away (3:4). The major outgrowth of their denial of judgment may have been a misinterpretation of Pauline doctrine (3:16). These false teachers will experience judgment (2:1, 3, 12, 17) and their destruction will come swiftly (2:1). Indeed, their very presence and their scoffing are signs of the last days (3:3). The present audience will also witness Christ's return in judgment (3:11–14), a detail that appears to refer to the fall of Jerusalem, the end of Israel's age.

The Work of Christ (1 Pet. 3:18–22)

Eschatology and Christ's work converge in the difficult passage found in 1 Peter 3:18–22. Though the passage gives rise to many interpretations, it is best taken in the context of examples of godly conduct in the face of persecution. Having appealed to the death and resurrection of Christ in verse 18, Peter continues with these words: "He went and preached to the spirits in prison who disobeyed long ago when God waited patiently in the days of Noah while the ark was being built. In it only a few people, eight in all, were saved through water" (vv. 19–20). These verses are generally taken to refer to Christ's activity during the period between his death and resurrection in a preaching ministry to (1) the angels (sons of God) imprisoned for the offenses reported in Genesis 6:2–4 (1 Enoch 6–7), (2) the dead of Noah's day, or (3) the dead of the Old Testament in general. Some expositors view verses 19–20 as a reference to the postascension preaching of Christ's triumph to the powers of evil, who ultimately stood behind the persecutors of Peter's day (Dalton 1965, 141–42). Still others interpret the verses to mean that in the days of Noah the preexistent Christ preached to the "spirits," that is, to disembodied human spirits (Dalton 1965, 145–46). Though Christ had preached to them when they were embodied, they had failed to respond and are now in prison (cf. 4:6). As a result of the preaching, only a few were saved. The point of the passage, indeed from verse 13 on, is steadfastness under persecution and the encouragement that promotes it (Feinberg 1986, 303–36).

Exhortation for Living in the End Time
(1 Pet. 2:4–10; chap. 4)

In 1 Peter 2:4–10, which is found in a context of an appeal for holiness (1:13–2:10), Peter refers to the construction of a new worshiping community. Note the emphasis on God's elective purposes in verses 6–9—through allusions to the stone in verses 6–8 (cf. Isa. 28:16; Ps. 118:22; Isa. 8:14; Elliott 1966, 217–18) and to the chosen in verse 9 (cf.

Exod. 19:4–6). What we find in these verses are images of spiritual
growth, not a sustained analogy of the community as a temple (*oikos* in
v. 5, which elsewhere in the New Testament is never used as a technical
term to denote the temple; Elliott 1966, 157–59). The new community
of priests will demonstrate their role by enduring the spiritual sacrifices
that the social code in 1 Peter demands.

Peter is much concerned with the persecution experienced by believers. As he sees it, however, the present crisis of faith precedes an eschatological judgment, which is itself a prelude to the coming salvation of
the people of God (2:12; 3:16; 4:4–5, 17–18). First Peter 4:1–11 exhorts
believers to constancy in this end of time and offers the completed sufferings of Christ and their glorious results as encouragement to cease
with sin. With the end in view believers are to endure their sufferings
since Christ himself "suffered in the flesh" (4:1 NRSV). Indeed, believers
live in the light of an imminent end (v. 7). Whether this end refers to the
imminent return of Christ or, better, to the fall of Jerusalem and the end
of the Jewish age is a matter of debate. Still the fiery ordeal is coming
(vv. 12–19), and believers must share in the messianic sufferings of the
end (i.e., the sufferings that must precede the revelation or return of
Christ; Davids 1990, 15). Thus, suffering in 1 Peter has an eschatological focus. At the last judgment not only will the living be judged, but
also those who have died in the meantime (4:6; the dead seem to be
those Christians who have died subsequent to their having heard the
gospel).

The Day of the Lord (2 Pet. 3)

All-pervasive throughout 2 Peter is the impending day of the Lord. In
the third chapter Peter addresses the problem of the so-called delay of
the "coming" which Jesus promised, treating the delay in the manner of
Mark 13 and 2 Thessalonians 2 (Moore 1966, 152) and appealing to the
prophets and the patriarchs of the old covenant as witnesses to God's
fidelity to his intentions. Consider Peter's words in verse 7: "By the
same word the present heavens and earth are reserved for fire, being
kept for the day of judgment and destruction of ungodly men." To what
is Peter referring? It appears that Peter refers, as do Mark and
2 Thessalonians, to the destruction of Jerusalem. Since God had promised in Genesis 8:21 that the world would never again be destroyed, as
it was in the flood, 2 Peter 3:7 refers, not to the end of the world, but to
something more readily discerned by Peter's readers. Though some
may argue that the reference in verse 7 to the passing away of the heavens and earth demands a universal and wide-ranging interpretation, remember that in Matthew 5:18 the phrase refers to the end of the present

age, which was a regular use of the phrase in contemporaneous Jewish literature (Meier 1976, 63). (Note Isa. 51:15–16, in which the planting of the heavens and the laying of the earth's foundations connote the span of the old covenant.) What would perish in A.D. 70 was the Jewish world, and the Jewish age came to an end with the destruction of Jerusalem (cf. Matt. 13:39–40, 49; 24:3; 28:20; 1 Cor. 10:11; Heb. 9:26). Continuing the thought of verse 7, verses 10–13 use spectacular language in a typically apocalyptic presentation of the appearance of God in judgment (cf. Isa. 13:10–13; 24:19; 34:4; 64:1–4; 66:16; Mic. 1:4). We are also reminded that biblical writers regularly used end-of-the-world language metaphorically to refer to what they well knew was not the end of the world (Caird 1980, 256).

In verse 8 Peter reminds his readers of the impossibility of endeavoring to anticipate God's timing. When the appointed time comes, it will appear with destructive suddenness (v. 10). As Jesus does in Mark 13:32, Peter denies that he has any precise knowledge of the times. The balance between imminence of and ignorance of the end found in Mark 13 and 2 Thessalonians 2 is retained here (Moore 1966, 154). What the present time indicates is God's patience (v. 15), for the delay means salvation for those who hear and accept the gospel (cf. Mark 13:10).

Epistle of Jude

The Epistle of Jude, the brother of James and the Lord, is directed against false teachers who threaten to mislead believers. The major theme of the letter, which exhorts those called to contend for the faith, is stated in verses 3–4 and taken up again in verses 20–23. Verses 5–19 argue for the necessity of such contention in light of the activity of these false teachers, who are the ungodly people of the last days against whom Scripture constantly warns.

The four main sections within verses 5–19 (vv. 5–7, 11, 14–15, 17–18) represent false teaching previously offered to Israel; each is followed by a section of interpretation relating to divine judgment or expected personal reaction (vv. 8–10, 12–13, 16, 19). Throughout the short letter are sustained references to 1 Enoch, in which the prospect of divine judgment to overwhelm the present evil age is the main theme. Jude argues in verses 5–19 that the opponents, the false teachers, will be judged by the coming of the Lord. And to what does this coming refer? The close relationship of Jude and 2 Peter and the probable early date of each indicate that the coming refers as likely to the fall of Jerusalem as to the second coming.

13

Apocalyptic Eschatology

When used in conjunction with the writings of the New Testament, the phrase *apocalyptic eschatology* refers in the main to the Revelation to John. An analysis of what it means to be a citizen of the New Jerusalem in a Babylon-dominated world order (Mulholland 1990, 88), the book seeks to encourage Christians who are threatened by persecution by putting their present difficulties into an eschatological context. In 1:1 the book is identified as a revelation, an unveiling, and as such is not a general truth that can be obtained by reflection upon one's world. The truth contained in the book is one that must have been given, as were the truths given to the prophets. Not surprisingly then in 1:3 John refers to the book as a prophecy, nowhere distinguishing, however, between prophecy and the apocalyptic symbolism by which communication in the book is effected. If the differences between apocalyptic and prophecy are overall mood and the perception of how God speaks, then Revelation has more affinity with the former.

The Book of Revelation aims to lay bare for persecuted Christians the meaning of the present in the context of history's march to its consummation; it begins with the redeemed in tribulation and ends with cosmic reconciliation. John mentions only one earthly act of Jesus— his death—for it is pivotal for the understanding of all history. Jesus' death was God's testimony to divine control over history, for in the death of Jesus, the Lamb, God conquered death. One problem that the people of God have always faced is the juxtaposition of evil and the will of God. In the book John reveals this to the new people of God: God knows that evil seems to triumph in this world, but God is doing something about it. For John, the new people of God have without doubt inherited the promises formerly directed to national Israel. Indeed, in 1:6, 5:10, and 20:6 John applies to believers Adam's and Israel's priestly and royal legacy.

At the core of the Revelation to John is a central narrative (1:9–22:5), which is preceded by general (1:1–3) and christological (1:4–8) introductions and followed by general (22:6–15) and christological (22:16–21) conclusions. Through three cycles of ever-intensifying judgment, John relates a classic biblical story of cosmic combat in which the empires of the world embody the demonic threat of chaos against order. Two final acts of judgment conclude the narrative: one culminates in the one-thousand-year reign, which is tied to Jesus' death, and the other in the judgment of the great white throne, which is linked to the parousia. Of these judgments, one demonstrates the victory of the true Messiah over the false one, and the other shows the victory of the only true God over the aboriginal power of evil, that is, Satan.

Understanding Jesus (Rev. 1)

Christology and the role of Jesus in the continuity of history hold the key to understanding the Book of Revelation. Indeed, the very first verse identifies the book as a revelation *concerning Jesus* of events divinely destined to come to pass. John ascribes three titles to Jesus in verse 5: Jesus is "the faithful witness, the firstborn from the dead, and the ruler of the kings of the earth." As the faithful witness, Jesus is the legatee to Israel's role (cf. Isa. 49:6) and by his resurrection the inaugurator and representative of the new creation. The title *ruler of the kings* may refer to Christ's rule over believers, who in this new messianic age have assumed the role that was Adam's and Israel's by virtue of Exodus 19:6 (Rev. 1:6). John reveals Christ's activity regarding humankind in verses 5b–6a: he loves us, has ransomed us, and consequentially has installed us to kingship (Fiorenza 1974, 222–25). However, what Christ has done will be complemented and thus documented as complete by Christ's second coming, to which end the book looks as the consolation offered in the time of trial. Jesus will come as he had gone—with clouds (1:7), the emblems of Deity as the supreme judgment figure of the end, the Son of man (cf. Dan. 7:13).

The vision of the exalted Son of man in Revelation 1:9–20 sets the christological tone for the judgment of the world and the vindication of the saints revealed in the book. Drawn from Zechariah 4, the vision of the golden candlesticks in 1:12–16 identifies the redeemed in the present, dark world as the new temple, which reflects the light received from Jesus. At once the vision turns to indicate the nature of the Son of man, for it is upon his worth that the people of God are totally dependent. Jesus is clothed in a garment normally associated with the high priest (Mulholland 1990, 81). Both Jesus' priesthood and messiahship, with which he is identified later in this vision, define the expectations fostered originally for Israel that Christians, as joint heirs with Jesus, are to entertain (1:6; 5:10; 20:6; 22:4–5; cf. Exod. 19:5–6). With head and hair as white as pure snow (1:14), Jesus appears as the Ancient of Days—the end-time Judge—the divine figure of Daniel 7:9. With eyes as flames of fire and feet like burnished brass, Christ moves in the midst of the churches with a divine presence and a moral purity that befit the Lord of the churches. Proceeding out of the Son's mouth is a sword (v. 16). This imagery, which is drawn from Isaiah 11:4 and 49:2, identifies the Son of man with the Servant and with the messianic shoot of David (Beale 1984, 162). Verse 16 ends with a description of his face: "His face was like the sun shining in all its brilliance" (cf. Matt. 17:2).

There can be no doubt about the identity of the Son of man, the one with whom we must deal: this is the victorious Christ, risen and exalted and now represented in the world by his people. Revelation 1:17–18 completes the identification. This is God, "the First and the Last" (cf. Isa. 41:4; 44:6; 48:12), "the Living One" elevated from death by the chaining and imprisonment of death and of Hades. The vision is of the Son of man's glorious fulfilment of his office as messianic King, and verse 20 discloses the eschatological mystery of the seven lampstands and stars. In the remainder of the book, John reveals the manner in which the vision becomes a reality.

Understanding the Present (Rev. 2–5)

Chapters 2–3 represent seven letters, which describe the fate of the struggling people of God—saints struggling with temptation and persecution. Addressed to extant churches of western Asia, the letters must be regarded as comprehensively representative of church life in John's time. Seductions and perils of the era that threatened the believing community include materialism (3:17), persecution (2:13), false teaching (2:14–15), sexual immorality (2:20), and apathy (3:16). In chapters 4–5 the focus turns toward heaven in a vision of the council as it proceeds to close out the historical period. The vision is a logical extension of the commission given to Christ in chapter 1, for it presents the universal reign of the Son of man with the saints as accomplished. Thus, the description of Christ's people exposed in the world, the struggling seven churches of Asia, who are powerful in all their weakness (chaps. 2–3), is flanked by what will be (chap. 1 and chaps. 4–5).

Since a door in heaven has been opened by Christ's sacrifice, in chapter 4 John, like one of the Old Testament prophets, is called up into the heavenly council, where he is ushered into the very center of reality—the throne room of the heavens (Minear 1981, 69). But this particular scene, dominated as it is by the presentation of the throne and the surrounding entourage, is without parallel among Jewish apocalytic visions. Twenty-four elders, who represent the citizenry of the New Jerusalem while symbolizing the elect community of both Testaments and God's completed purposes, surround the throne (Rev. 4:4; Hurtado 1985, 114). Encircling the throne is a rainbow, which assures us the vision is the logical result of God's covenant pledge to Noah (4:3b; Gen. 9:13). God's purposes for creation have prevailed! Crowned as kings and vested in white robes as priests, the elders are fitting successors of elect Israel (4:4b; cf. Exod. 19:5–6). Moreover, they participate in the vision of God, as did the ancient elders of Israel at the conclusion of the covenant at Sinai (Exod. 24:10). The four living creatures positioned around the throne represent the totality of life in the created order (4:6b–8), while the sea of glass before the throne is the chaos threat now tamed and calmed (v. 6a). As God had always intended, perfect order finally prevails.

The scene John describes in chapters 4–5 of the one God in heaven presiding over ordered creation, bears witness to clear echoes from the Old Testament. Note the correspondence between the depiction of the heavenly groups' worship of God as Creator in 4:8 and Isaiah's vision in 6:2–3. Moreover, John's vision represents fulfilment of the vision in Daniel 7 in which the kingdom is given to the Son of man, who will now reign with the saints (Beale 1984, 227). On the analogy of Daniel 7, then, we would expect books to be opened, judgment to be passed, and the kingdoms of this world to become the kingdoms of Christ. And indeed the divine plan for the rule of the saints as revealed by John is set against the background of God's sovereign purposes for creation, which will come to pass when the scroll is opened by the only one who is worthy, the Lamb (Rev. 5:1–5).

The idyllic creation picture of chapter 4 is balanced by redemption in chapter 5. It is Jesus, the slain Lamb, who effects the redemption; however, there is another characterization of Jesus in the chapter. John first introduces Jesus as a lion, Israel's powerful Messiah, the fulfilment of God's intentions as expressed through Israel (v. 5). Because of the necessity of redemption, however, the lion of Israel is replaced by and is henceforth to be understood in terms of the lamb, a multivalent image that here suggests the securing of the divine purposes will be through suffering and sacrifice, not power. Moreover, the depiction of Jesus as the Lamb is paradoxical, for he is equipped with the plenitude of power in the form of seven horns and with divine omniscience in the form of seven eyes. Having conquered death, Jesus is victorious, alone worthy to open the sealed book (vv. 6–9). By virtue of his worthiness, Jesus is aligned with the Creator in worship (vv. 9–10; cf. vv. 12–13; van Unnik 1970, 460; cf. Carnegie 1982, 251). Thus, John pictures the redemptive work of Christ as the further unfolding of God's purposes for creation, for redemption is the act of new creation.

As the lion of Judah and the root of David, Jesus is preeminently Israel's Messiah. In Revelation 5:6, however, Jesus stands at the place of power, at the right hand of the throne, as a lamb slain, that is, sacrificed but resurrected (Guthrie 1987, 48). And the image of the slain lamb speaks not only of sacrifice but also of struggle and conflict. Thus, the emphasis is not upon Jesus' elevation or enthronement but upon the judgments that will be unleashed by the opening of the book. The image of the lamb has roots in Isaiah 53:7 as well as in Jewish apocalyptic, which viewed the people of God as God's flock and the deliverer as David, the lamb who became a great horned ram—a powerful conqueror (1 Enoch 90:6–42). As revealed through John, Christ now reigns as heavenly regent and Messiah, and his people will overcome the world in spite of the judgments, struggles, and conflict that will test the Christian community. As the Lamb, Jesus is the prototype of the Christian martyrs of the scroll, which is sealed with seven seals representing what must occur before the eternal heavenly Sabbath in the New Jerusalem.

God's Plan (Rev. 6:1–22:5)

In Revelation 6:1–22:5 John unveils the significance of world history in the light of God's cosmic intention on the basis of Christ's sacrifice to restore creation. What this restoration will mean is the reign of the redeemed in the kingdom of God upon earth and the final conversion of the nations. Wherever the inner dynamics of history are examined is revealed the collision between order and chaos with evil intensifying as the world continues. In the three cycles of calamities that follow in chapters 6–16, the repetition of the problems with which our world has been continually afflicted makes it clear that only by divine imposition of the final chapters of the book can the search for order be concluded.

Cycles of Conflict (Rev. 6–16)

Through a sequence of seals, trumpets, and bowls, chapters 6–16 present three windows into the inner meaning of history. The presentation is cyclical, for human and demonic reaction to divine intention is unvarying; however, each sequence presents a different and a more profound perspective on history. The judgments increase in intensity. The cycle of seals is clearly preliminary; the contents at the scroll (chap. 5) cannot be revealed until the last seal is broken (Ulfgard 1989, 28). The events in Revelation 6:1–7:17 serve as an overture to the following visions. As Hakan Ulfgard (1989, 28) points out, no real action occurs until the sixth seal is broken and the world is confronted by the wrath of God. In the series that follow, judgments upon earth take place with increasing intensity, so that the judgment in chapter 19 is more complete than in 14:14–20. In chapters 8–14 the judgments are only partial, but in chapters 15–19 they are complete and final. But as the judgments increase in intensity there is, strangely, less inclination by the world to repent.

Inaugurated by a divine personage, such as the Lamb or angels, each sequence of seven disasters is stereotypical, having been drawn from familiar apocalyptic materials found in the Old and New Testaments. The first four disasters in each sequence affect the natural world or political structures; the fifth and sixth disasters, the moral or religious realms (O'Donovan 1986, 72). Consider the first sequence in Revelation 6:1–17 and 8:1–5. The first four seals, inspired by visions of the four horsemen of Zechariah (Rev. 6:1–8; cf. Zech. 1:8–10), represent the result of some form of human wickedness. Yet, the war, international strife, famine, and pestilence are all mysteriously part of God's redemptive plan. The fifth seal, which attests to past and future martyrs, bears witness to the context of persecution in which the Book of Revelation was written (6:9–11) and to the accompanying, preoccupying puzzle for the people of God, that is, Christ's triumph seemed to bring suffering to them. The first five seals have a this-worldly quality, but the sixth is cosmic in scope (vv. 12–16). These cosmic disasters presage the expectation of the final day of divine judgment.

Chapter 7 represents an interlude of two visions before the climactic seventh seal is opened. In the first vision (vv. 1–8), the elect are sealed as disaster is held back by the four angels who hold in check the four winds of the earth. In the second (vv. 9–17), the elect have been gathered by the Lamb and are rejoicing in his victory "over the evil powers, and in their worship before the throne their royal and priestly dignity is displayed" (Ulfgard 1986, 78). Whereas the first vision signifies the fulfilment of the covenantal blessings promised to Israel in the Old Testament, the second denotes consummation of the new covenant.

With the breaking of the seventh seal in Revelation 8:1–5, we expect the end, but there is a pause before John reveals another sequence. There is a suspenseful silence in heaven for the duration of about half an hour in which the prayers of the saints are heard and divine judgment is held suspended. Standing with a censer at the altar (v. 3), an angel anticipates the divine judgment brought on by the persecution of the people of God. The sequence of the trumpets follows in 8:6–9:21 and 11:15.

The first four trumpets usher in a list of supernatural disasters designed to plunge the world into suffering: hail and fire, the sea turned into blood, the pollution of the waters by a falling star typifying Babylon (cf. Isa. 14:12–15), and the sky darkened. Similarities between these disasters and the first, seventh, and ninth plagues in Exodus (cf. Exod. 7:14–9:35; 10:21–29) point to a new exodus for the people of God. With the first four trumpets, the earth is purged, and one-third of the world is affected. Then an eagle, which signifies God's providential care (cf. Exod. 19:4) appears in midheaven to announce the doom of the last three trumpets—the day of Yahweh's wrath to come as a cosmic catastrophe (v. 13). With the sounding of the fifth trumpet, an angel falls from heaven (9:1–12), which seems to echo the fall of the Day Star in Isaiah 14:12–15 (NRSV). The angel then uses a key given by God to open the bottomless pit, that is, the accumulation of human evil. Thus, this infernal reservoir of evil will once again influence humanity for a short period of time. Then demonic beings, likened to those emerging in the locust plague of Joel 1–2, appear (9:3–11). The sounding of the sixth trumpet in 9:13–21 releases four angels bound at the Euphrates. This act leads to the onset of hordes from beyond the Euphrates, which draws on the Gog myth of Ezekiel 38–39 while doubtlessly alluding in cosmic terms to the political threats to the Roman Empire in John's day. Though the ultimate threat from the East is activated and is cosmically transformed into an Armageddon, the decimation from the ensuing plagues does not result in humankind's repentance. The warnings accruing from the event go unheeded.

Revelation 10:11–14 provides an interlude between the sixth and seventh trumpets, bringing to an end the warning but indecisive judgments of the seals and trumpets which failed to compel the world to repentance. The mighty angel, who comes down placing his right foot on the sea and his left foot on the land, puts the whole world under the sphere of God's judgment (10:1–3). Moreover, the hidden purposes of God in judgment, the "mystery" of verse 7, are now to be revealed. First, however, John is recommissioned by eating the scroll in the hand of the angel (10:8–11). The final revelation now begins. The scroll's bittersweet nature signifies the mixture of woe and triumph that it contains and anticipates what is to follow. In 11:1–2 John is told to measure the temple, whereby the people of God are put under divine protection in the coming tribulation. However, the trampling of the holy city in verse 2c indicates that martyrdom will reach believers, whose vulnerability is exposed since the area surrounding the temple is given to the Gentiles for a time. Two witnesses, whom John presents in terms recalling the prophetic features of Moses and Elijah, prophesy during the tribulation (vv. 3–6). By their kingly and priestly features (cf. Zech 3:1–4:14), the two represent the elect, that is, the redeemed in their ideal form. However, evil from the abyss eventually overtakes the two, and their bodies are left in the street of the martyr center—the city where Christ died, the symbol of opposition to the people of God, the unnamed Jerusalem (vv. 7–8). At the hands of the world, the witnesses meet the same fate as Jesus. To proclaim the truth of God in this world means death for the believers, of which the witnesses are symbols. Then, as Jesus had been, the two are resurrected and triumphantly carried up to heaven in a cloud (vv. 11–12). In verse 13 the interlude ends with an earthquake, which indicates the divine provenance of what is taking place.

In Revelation 11:15 the seventh trumpet sounds. Won by divine adherence to the purposes of election by which a people of God had been decreed, the victory that overcomes the world reveals the triumph of God's people through tribulation (vv. 15–19). Now is the time for the world to become the kingdom of our God and his Christ. This is the time God has chosen to usher in the kingdom of the Messiah, and for this purpose the seventh trumpet is blown. As the world passes back to its true owner, the Messiah is about to appear. The hymn in verses 17–18, which alludes to Psalm 2, foreshadows the remaining content of John's revelation. God's wrath is to come upon the nations for the persecution of the people of God. The dead will be judged, the righteous will receive their rewards, and the earth will be rescued from the hands of her destroyers. Then heaven will be opened. As the vision of the ark in verse 19 makes clear, the openness is to the very throne room of God. The heavenly vision that had been sustained from chapter 4 through 11 now ends. To this point, John's assessment has been general, that is, representing the traditional difficulties encountered by believers amid political opposition and in the face of the realities of a fallen world. Much of what John writes from this point to the end of chapter 15 describes the demonic scenario characteristic of the people of God in his day.

The great parenthesis of chapters 12–14 illuminates the struggle between the people of God and the forces of darkness. In Revelation 12:1–6 John's survey of salvation history moves to the birth, death, and resurrection of the Messiah, born of Mother Israel. By the Messiah's victory and ascension, the dragon, that is, Satan, and his hordes are overcome by the blood of the Lamb and are cast out of heaven down to earth (vv. 7–9), where the dragon looks for an earthly form in which to operate (vv. 13–17). Satan will wreak havoc on the earth in the short time left to him. The saints, however, can defeat him (12:11) by virtue of their steadfast trust in Christ's salvific victory. The form Satan takes is empire as an eschatological phenomenon (O'Donovan 1986, 79); John calls it "a beast" (13:1). The beast that arises from the sea—the abyss of disorder overcome by creation—compounds the four empires of Daniel 7 into one demonic imperium (13:1–2a), which represents the diabolical and subtle deceptions of the world systems as messianic replacements of every age. Already such deceptions have received their death-blow in the cross of Christ, although demonic political disorder follows Christ's death. This upheaval is the reverse of what happens in Daniel 7, where disorder is brought to an end by the coming of the Son of man. Thus, the dragon confers upon the beast an authority as an antimessianic force (v. 2b). Since the empire imposes order on chaos (vv. 4–9), it appears there is a political resurrection. However, the achieved order is gained by a crude imitation of the good (O'Donovan 1986, 80). The false prophet of imperial idealogy and rationale in 13:11–15—the beast coming up from the land—joins with the false Christ in the service of the primeval power of evil. All adherents of this evil trinity are then sealed in parody of the Christian sacrament (13:16–17). In John's time, the manifestation of such evil was the demand for emperor worship. Although the beast appears powerful and compelling, it is in reality only a demonic parody of incompleteness with a number (666) that symbolizes human imperfection (v. 18).

In the interlude of chapter 14 John reveals the force poised to counter the beast. The Lamb and the first fruits of the gospel, all the redeemed of the Lord, appear as conquerors on Mount Zion (14:1–5; cf. Heb. 12:18–24). Verses 6–13 proclaim the efficacy of the eternal gospel, that is, the one that relates to the age to come, in its condemnation of the world and its power over the death of the saints. After this affirmation that all the demonic strategies to destroy the people of God have failed, John presents his vision of the end, the proclamation of the last judgment over which the Son of man presides as royal harvester (vv. 14–20) and of Christ's second advent (15:1–4).

Acknowledging the progress of redemption from the old to the new covenant, the summary of the multitude's new-exodus triumph in Revelation 14:1–5 and the new Song of the Sea in 15:3–4 (cf. Exod. 15:1–18) anticipate the final sequence of God's wrath (15:5–16:21). It begins with judgment decreed by the law of the divine covenant (15:5). In recognition of the appropriateness of the summation of world judgments to follow in the plagues, one of the four living creatures delivers the bowls to the waiting angels (15:6–8). As ineffective in securing repentance as were the Exodus plagues, those issuing from the first four bowls convey the expected series of natural disasters that affect the earth, sea, rivers, and sky (16:1–9). Doom must reach its climax. This time there is no interruption after the sixth plague. The final three plagues in 16:10–21 concern the collapse of the world system under its own weight: the beast is dethroned.

Approach of the End (Rev. 17:1–19:10)

As the climax of the Book of Revelation approaches, John reveals details of the end as viewed from different vantage points. That is, the end of the present world order (Rev. 17:1–19:10) gives way synchronously to the picture of the final judgment of God in Christ (19:11–20:15) and then to the advent of the New Jerusalem (21:1–22:9; cf. Mulholland 1990, 276).

In chapter 17 John examines the collapse of decadent world imperialism, which he defines as fornication in verses 1–2 (O'Donovan 1986, 87). Though the empire of John's time was Rome, he calls it Babylon (v. 5) to demonstrate continuity with Israel's experience with imperialism and to document the continuity in imperial ideology between Babylon and Rome. Astride the military and commercial pathways of the Mediterranean, "seated upon many waters" (v. 1 rsv), Babylon rules the world. In verse 5 John identifies Babylon as the harlot she is—one founded on an idealogy that gave rise to both her power and her evil (vv. 3–4). But Babylon's rule is not forever, for absolute power that is corrupt must return to the abyss from which it came (vv. 6–8). Through the image of the seven mountains on which the harlot sits, John reveals that there is further dominion by Rome to come (vv. 9–11), for the empire will be backed by the ten constituent powers that will give way to imperialism (vv. 11–13). For the short time that this final evil reign holds sway, it will be supported by a united world power structure, which will make unceasing attacks on the people of God (v. 14). But, says John in verses 15–18, the adherents of the structure will inevitably turn against the empire that nourished them by offering their purest worship to the beast in their assault, for "predatory power collapses in upon itself" (O'Donovan 1986, 88).

In chapter 18 John reveals that the fall of Babylon will be accompanied by a lament. By using details from the lament over mercantile Tyre found in Ezekiel 27 and the prophecy of conquering Babylon's demise in Jeremiah 51, John makes clear that the source of Rome's world authority had been her commercial and military power, one feeding the other. Bewailed by those in authority (vv. 1–10) and in commerce and trade (vv. 11–20), the end of Babylon means the end of the world's social system as we know it, including the demise of crafts and culture (vv. 21–24). But this end of the kingdom of Antichrist ushers in the advent of the kingdom of God, and heaven celebrates the coming reign of God and the marriage of the Lamb (19:1–8). Babylon must give way to the inauguration of the new society.

Advent of the Kingdom of God (Rev. 19:11–20:15)

Once the doors of heaven are flung open wide, Christ rides on to victory mounted on a white charger, and thus exercising the power of purity (Rev. 19:11). Commissioned to undertake the kingship over all creation that had been usurped by evil, Christ defeats his enemies by judging them in righteousness. The character of his life qualifies him to judge, and his eyes penetrate the secrets of all hearts (vv. 11–12). John depicts Jesus, standing in the blood of his own sacrifice, as the Word, the divine communication to this world (v. 13). Since Jesus met victory through the spilling of his own blood, the decisive battle has been fought (cf. 12:7–9). No other battle against evil is expected. The heavenly conquerors who accompany Christ are dressed, not for battle, but for a wedding (v. 14).

The only weapon Christ needs is the sword of his mouth, that is, the proclamation of the gospel—before which nations collapse (v. 15). Ruling with an iron scepter, Jesus strikes down the nations and tramples the winepress of God's wrath (v. 15; cf. Ps. 2:9; Isa. 11:3; 63:1–6). He wrests the kingship usurped over the earth from the anti-God powers as true King of Kings—this name of absolute kingship is written on his garment and on his thigh, where a sword would normally hang (v. 16). The announcement of God's great feast in verse 17 (cf. Ezek. 39:4, 17–20) contrasts grimly to the invitation to the marriage supper of the Lamb in verse 9. By announcing the coming carnage to the birds of heaven, the angel discloses the futility of resistance. Utterly powerless, the Antichrist and the false prophet are seized and thrown into the lake of fire, and their followers are slain by the sword—the announced word of judgment (vv. 19–21).

What more could possibly happen? As we know from chapter 20, four scenes are yet to come: (1) the binding of Satan (vv. 1–3), (2) the heavenly rule of the saints in the period from Christ's resurrection to the parousia (vv. 4–6), (3) the release of Satan and his demise (vv. 7–10), and (4) the final judgment (vv. 11–15). It is a mistake, however, to assume that the scenes in chapter 20 necessarily follow 19:11–21 in chronological sequence, for some appear to recapitulate events previously unveiled by John. (See White 1989 for a discussion of the problem of chronological sequence and the evidence for recapitulation.)

Revelation 20:1–3, which precedes 19:11–21 in time, describes measures taken to prevent the deceptions of Satan against the nations. It takes only an angel to constrain the dragon and lock him in the abyss for the duration of the Christian age. Extending from verse 1 to verse 6, the Christian age is the Sabbath period into which the faithful have entered with Christ: "They came to life and reigned with Christ a thousand years" (v. 4d). What John emphasizes in the sentence is not the duration but the nature of the reign. (Note that all 2 Enoch 33:1 claims is that there is a world pause of one thousand years. It does not say that it is a world pause between death and life before the advent of the new world.)

In Revelation 20:4–6 John describes his vision regarding the heavenly rule of the redeemed. Difficulties abound in verse 4. Who are the "they" who are seated on the thrones, and what relationship do they bear to the "them" to whom judgment was given? And how does this first clause relate to the remainder of the verse? I take the vague subject of the first verb in 20:4 to be the redeemed host with Christ and to be identical with "them," the indirect object of the first clause. I suggest that their precise identification is then made by the two groups to which the remainder of the verse refers. "Judgment" (Gk. *krima*) is to be taken in the Old Testament sense of dominion (Balz and Schneider 1991, 2:317); "judgment," "reigning," and "sitting on thrones" are virtually synonymous in the Old Testament (Ulfgard 1989, 59 n. 252). The two groups to which the remainder of the verse refers are *both* the souls of those executed and those who had not worshiped or borne the image of the beast. They came to life and reigned with the Messiah as kings and priests in what is described as the first resurrection.

Those who take part in the first resurrection (v. 5) have no share in the second (spiritual) death (20:6, which presumes a first, physical death). The second (spiritual) death is referred to in 20:11–15, where the physical resurrection (and thus a second resurrection for those involved in the activities of 20:4) of all for judgment is described. The assumption in 20:11–15 seems to be that those destined for the second spiritual death—which follows on a first physical death—had no part in the first (spiritual) resurrection.

The content of the "first resurrection" (20:5) appears to be living and reigning with Christ as kings and priests. But this is the content of present Christian experience (1:6; 5:10) and thus the first resurrection refers to entry into Christian belief through conversion/initiation and not specifically to martyrdom. Thus the term *first resurrection* is to be interpreted spiritually and it is no argument against this view that it requires "to live" (Gk. *zao*) to be taken in two different senses in verses 4 and 5, since two entirely different experiences are being referred to (Ulfgard 1989, 58–65). The thousand-year reign is a symbolic period of ultimate, heavenly security. Thus, the binding of Satan, the resurrection of the saints, and the thousand-year reign are metaphors for the present situation of Christians. As expected, the day of the Lord has quelled all opposition and brought peace for believers.

The final end of Satan, projected in the millennial restraint of 20:1–3, is described in 20:7–10, which generally recapitulates the action of 19:11–21. Specifically, 19:17–21 narrates the demise of the beast and the false prophet at the second coming, and 20:7–10, the demise of Satan at the same time. Before his end, Satan makes a last attempt to destroy the beloved city, the camp of the saints (v. 9). But this last attack upon the millennial congregation, the Armageddon assault (cf. 19:17–18), comes to nothing. Since the language of 19:17–18 and 20:7–10 draws upon the Gog and Magog oracles of Ezekiel 38–39, these two battle scenes in chapters 19–20 are parallel expansions of chapters 15–16, in which the same imagery is used and which had also taken us to the end (White 1989, 327). In 20:7–10 the release of Satan, the mobilization of Gog and Magog, the attack upon the redeemed, and the casting of Satan into the lake of fire all serve to magnify the power of Christ in the final era and to reassure the reigning saints of their security.

Revelation 20:11–15 describes that world judgment along with the resurrection of the dead, thereby satisfying Jewish and Christian expectations. The judgment scene is drawn from the one in Daniel 7:9–10. Though John does not identify the judge, the correspondence to Daniel leads to the conclusion that the judge is God. Jesus is the chief witness. Beginning in verse 12 John describes the resurrection of all the dead. With this, the old creation disappears. When the record books are opened, all the godly and the ungodly are judged by their deeds. What is in these books? The content is determined by what God decides to remember and what God decides to forget (18:5). At the same time, the gracious, predestining purposes of God are operating, for the book of life, the Lamb's book, is also opened. Note that John does not reveal the nature of the judgment of the unsaved. Then the true and final enemies of humankind and God—death and Hades—are cast into the lake of fire. Since death loses its power, the character of this world is undone and must be replaced.

The New Jerusalem (Rev. 21:1–22:5)

The New Jerusalem that descends from heaven in Revelation 21:2 is an offset to Babylon and to the politically disordered society resulting from the fall as well as to the seven churches of Revelation (Colin Hemer in Court 1979, 156). Though it was expected in Jewish thought that a heavenly paradise would appear on earth for Adam, whose role the Messiah had taken as the Second Adam (Charles 1920, 2:158; 1 Enoch 90:29; 2 Apoc. Bar. 4:3; 2 Esd. 7:26; 10:54; 13:36), there is no biblical anticipation of such a descent prior to Revelation 21. The holy city is the concrete form of all that is new (*kainos*) since God is now in the midst of it. Note, however, that the word *kainos* suggests qualitative continuity with the expectations held for the old Jerusalem.

What is this New Jerusalem? It is not "the Jerusalem that is above" of Galatians 4:26, for there is no evidence that the New Jerusalem is the heavenly congregation coming to earth. John's description of the city in Revelation 21:9–27 has some affinity with the description of the temple in Ezekiel 40–48, but John's emphasis is on the city as a place where God dwells (21:13). Indeed, the New Jerusalem appears to encompass people (the redeemed), place (the New Creation), and presence (the immediate being of God) and thus to be identical with the kingdom of God. It is the renewed world, a paradise, a holy city, a temple, the cosmic mountain joining heaven and earth, the eschatological expectations of the whole Bible now realized (Bauckham 1993, 132–43). God in his gracious glory, the Shechinah, will dwell there. Every part of the entire city reflects the divine nature, for its existence is traced directly to supernatural action. Since the New Jerusalem comes down from God and is filled with his glory, it is at once a temple and a city. Described in terms once reserved for Israel's kings, the conquerors exercise rule in the New Jerusalem (21:7; cf. 2 Sam. 7:14; Ps. 2:7). However, their rule is manifest, not by subjugation of others, but by salvation and full life. The exclusions of Revelation 21:8, 21:27, and 22:15 are not details relating to the city; rather, they are warnings to John's congregation.

The advent of the New Jerusalem fulfils the eschatological expectations associated with Zion in the Old Testament—that of the world united in redemption and of the saved community as the one new people of God undivided by the consequences of Genesis 3–11. That God will henceforth permanently dwell in the midst of his people (Rev. 21:3) also fulfils the temple theology of both Testaments. In 21:3 John uses a familiar old-covenant formula: "They will be his people, and God himself will . . . be their God." Through the use of this formula, John indicates that the New Jerusalem is the consummation of the new covenant initiated by the death of Christ, when Jew and Gentile live in perfect harmony, when the redeemed live in community, as suggested by the image of the city (Guthrie 1987, 90). Moreover, with the passing away of the first heaven, the first earth, and the principle of opposition—the sea—the onset of the new creation is heralded. Thus, the separation between heaven and earth and the binary disjunctions of the first creation are forever gone.

In 21:9–22:5 John reveals details of the New Jerusalem. Fulfilling the expectations of Ezekiel 40:1–2, the city is God's gift as bride for the Lamb. Therefore, the city's origins are to be traced to the self-sacrifice of the Lamb. John is introduced to the city by the same angel who had poured out the bowls of wrath on the antithesis of the bride, the great harlot Babylon (21:9–10; cf. 17:1–2; Minear 1981, 136). John reveals in 21:12 that the city has twelve gates that correspond to the twelve tribes of Israel; thus, the city is the result of specific promises made by God to the believing communities (Minear 1981, 137). Moreover, the stories of all the saints coalesce in a hope for this new city. The symbolism in John's description seems clear: That the foundations are the twelve apostles indicates the nature of the message that provides entrance. That the names of the twelve tribes are written on the gates indicates that the salvation the city provides is of the Jews. Taken together, the detail on the gates and on the foundations signifies total covenant fulfilment.

In Revelation 21:15–17 John bursts the bonds of language in trying to give expression to what is inexpressible. The city is a perfect cube reaching from heaven to earth, like the tower of Genesis 11, and is thus the new Holy of Holies. But there is a difference. The Holy of Holies was used episodically by Israel's high priest; however, in the city the new community will be unceasingly involved. Despite the measurements John provides in verses 15–17, there is no way to adequately represent his vision. The fabric of the city is gold (v. 18), but this is no earthly gold, for it is as bright as clear glass, shining with the reflected glory of God. The twelve gems that comprise the foundations of the city appear to relate to the twelve that decorated the breastplate of the high priest and to the identical jewels worn by the king of Tyre (vv. 19–20; cf. Ezek. 28:13 LXX). The pearly gates remind us of a prophecy by Isaiah (v. 21; cf. Isa. 54:11–12). These various correspondences and echoes serve to demonstrate that the present vision is the consummation of all those hopes, lest any detail of Old Testament expectation should have been omitted.

Amid the measurements and descriptions of what John saw, he tells us in verse 22 of something he did not see—a temple. This implies the sanctification of the whole world order (cf. Zech. 14:20–21) and the relevance of the city to all social and political institutions. Verse 24 implies that the nations have been converted and that the full blessings of the Abrahamic covenant have now been received by the world. From this verse we know further that nothing of the old order which has value is prevented from entering the city. Indeed, the gates are always open. They do not point to a world outside.

In Revelation 22:1–5 John presents the heavenly state of the New Jerusalem from a different point of view, that is, in terms of Ezekiel 47:1–12 and of Eden. Ezekiel's river of life is now the fertilizing force in the New Eden. With the curse of the fall having been removed (v. 3), the divine intention of Genesis 1–2 is recaptured. Moreover, the kingly and priestly motifs of Exodus 19:5–6 reappear in verses 4–5. Jesus' name will be on the believers' foreheads as a priestly symbol (cf. Exod. 28:38), and this redeemed people of God will reign for ever.

Exhortations for the Present (Rev. 22:6–21)

In the epilog of Revelation 22:6–21 John and his guide are outside the city, that is, in the present reality to which they have come. Sanctioned by Jesus as faithful and true (v. 6), the prophecy is to remain open for all to read, for the time is short until Jesus comes again (vv. 7, 10).

At the end of the canon, we have returned to the beginning with an overplus. The divisions inherent within human society since Babel have been removed. The new people of God, Jews and Gentiles together, have been located in a new sacred space. This is the very end to which the tentative beginning of Genesis 1–2 had pointed. The carriers of the hope had progressed from Adam to Israel and then to Christ. Through the sacrifice of the Lamb, believers will rule as kings and priests, taking on the role that Adam had forfeited and fulfilling the mandate given to Israel at Sinai (Exod. 19:5–6). The immortality of these new people will not be provisional, as Adam's was, for they have seen the face of the Lamb, the image into which they have been transformed, and they will be eternally in his presence. The history of salvation has ended, and the journey has been long. We have moved from creation and Adam to Israel and redemption, to Jesus as suffering Israel, to the creation of a new people of God through the cross and resurrection of Jesus. We have moved through the call of the Gentiles to come into the new people of God, through the difficulties of the overlap of the ages, into the reality of the new age itself.

The biblical search for order is now at an end. Though the divine intention for humankind and the world had been signaled by Genesis 1–2, God patiently bore with sinful humankind until finally imposing order at the end of the canon. The movement in the Bible from creation to the new creation was made possible only by the fact that God was in Christ, in the historical factor of the cross outside the city of Jerusalem in the midpoint of salvation history, reconciling the world unto himself.

Bibliography

Aharoni, R. 1977. "The Gog Prophecy and the Book of Ezekiel." HAR 1:1–27.

Allison, D. C. 1985. *The End of the Ages Has Come: An Early Interpretation of the Passion and Resurrection of Jesus*. Philadelphia: Fortress.

Ambrozic, A. M. 1972. *The Hidden Kingdom: A Redaction-Critical Study of the References to the Kingdom of God in Mark's Gospel. CBQMS* 2. Washington, D.C.: Catholic Biblical Association.

Attridge, H. W. 1989. *The Epistle to the Hebrews*. Philadelphia: Fortress.

Baldwin, J. 1978. *Daniel: An Introduction and Commentary*. Leicester: Inter-Varsity.

Balz, H., and Schneider, G., eds. 1991. *The Exegetical Dictionary of the New Testament*. Grand Rapids: Eerdmans. English translation of *Exegetisches Wörterbuch zum Neuen Testament*, Stuttgart, 1981.

Banks, R. J. 1979. *Paul's Idea of Community: The Early House Churches in Their Historical Setting*. Sydney: Anzea.

Barrett, C. K. 1956. "The Eschatology of the Epistle to the Hebrews." In *The Background of the New Testament and Its Eschatology*, ed. W. D. Davies and D. Daube, 363–93. Cambridge: Cambridge University Press.

Bassler, J. M. 1982. *Divine Impartiality: Paul and a Theological Axiom*. SBLDS 59. Chico, Calif.: Scholars.

Bauckham, R. 1993. *The Theology of the Book of Revelation*. Cambridge: Cambridge University Press.

Bauer, D. R. 1988. *The Structure of Matthew's Gospel: A Study in Literary Design*. ISNTSup 31. Sheffield: Almond.

Baur, F. C. 1873. *Paul, the Apostle of Jesus Christ*. Vol. 1. London and Edinburgh: Williams and Norgate.

Beale, G. K. 1984. *The Use of Daniel in Jewish Apocalyptic Literature and in the Revelation of St. John*. Lanham, Md.: University Press of America.

———. 1989. "The Old Testament Background of Reconciliation in 2 Corinthians 5–7 and Its Bearing on the Literary Problem of 2 Corinthians 6:14–7:1." *NTS* 35:550–81.

Beasley-Murray, G. R. 1986. *Jesus and the Kingdom of God*. Exeter: Paternoster.

Beker, J. C. 1980. *Paul the Apostle: The Triumph of God in Life and Thought.* Philadelphia: Fortress.

Best, E. 1972. *A Commentary on the First and Second Epistles to the Thessalonians.* London: A. & C. Black.

Beuken, W. A. M. 1972. "Mišpāt; The First Servant Song and Its Context." *VT* 22:1–30.

———. 1974. "Isaiah liv: The Multiple Identity of the Person Addressed." *OTS* 19:29–70.

Bird, P. A. 1981. "'Male and Female He Created Them': Gen. 1:27b in the Context of the Priestly Account of Creation." *HTR* 74:129–59.

Blank, J. 1964. *Krisis: Untersuchungen zur johanneischen Christologie und Eschatologie.* Freiburg, Ger.: Lambertus.

Bowers, W. P. 1976. "Studies in Paul's Understanding of His Mission." Dissertation, University of Cambridge.

Bowker, J. W. 1974. "Mystery and Parable: Mark 4:1–20." *JTS* 25:300–317.

Braun, M. A. 1977. "James' Use of Amos at the Jerusalem Council: Steps toward a Possible Solution of the Textual and Theological Problems (Acts 15)." *JETS* 20:113–21.

Brawley, R. L. 1987. *Luke-Acts and the Jews: Conflict, Apology, and Conciliation.* SBLDS 33. Atlanta: Scholars.

Brown, R. E. 1967. "The Paraclete in the Fourth Gospel." *NTS* 13:113–32.

———. 1977. *The Birth of the Messiah: A Commentary on the Infancy Narratives in Matthew and Luke.* Garden City, N.Y.: Doubleday.

Bruce, F. F. 1974. "The Speeches in Acts—Thirty Years After." In *Reconciliation and Hope; New Testament Essays on Atonement and Eschatology Presented to L. L. Morris on His 60th Birthday,* ed. R. Banks, 53–68. Grand Rapids: Eerdmans.

———. 1977. *Paul: Apostle of the Free Spirit.* Exeter: Paternoster.

———. 1982. *1 & 2 Thessalonians.* Waco: Word.

Bultmann, R. 1952, 1955. *Theology of the New Testament.* 2 vols. Translated by Kendrick Grobel. London: SCM.

Burnett, F. W. 1981. *The Testament of Jesus-Sophia: A Redaction-Critical Study of the Eschatological Discourse in Matthew.* Lanham, Md.: University Press of America.

Burney, C. F. 1925–26. "Christ as the *Arche* of Creation." *JTS* 27:160–77.

Byrne, B. 1981. "Living Out the Righteousness of God: The Contribution of Rom. 6.1–8.13 to an Understanding of Paul's Ethical Presuppositions." *CBQ,* 43:557–81, 61.

Caird, G. B. 1969. *Paul's Letters from Prison: Ephesians, Philippians, Colossians, Philemon.* Oxford: Oxford University Press.

———. 1980. *The Language and Imagery of the Bible.* London: Duckworth.

Calvin, J. 1949. *The Gospel According to St. John.* Vol. 2, 12–21. Translated by William Pringle. Grand Rapids: Eerdmans.

Caragounis, C. C. 1977. *The Ephesian Mysterion: Meaning and Content.* ConBNT 8. Lund, Swed.: Gleerup.

———. 1986. *The Son of Man: Vision and Interpretation.* WUNT 38. Tübingen, Ger.: J. C. B. Mohr.

Carlson, R. A. 1964. *David the Chosen King: A Traditio-Historical Approach to the Second Book of Samuel.* Uppsala, Swed.: Almquist and Wiksell.

Carnegie, D. R. 1982. "Worthy Is the Lamb: The Hymns in the Revelation." In *Christ the Lord: Studies in Christology Presented to Donald Guthrie,* ed. H. H. Rowdon, 243–56. Leicester: Inter-Varsity.

Carroll, J. T. 1988. *Response to the End of History: Eschatology and Situation in Luke-Acts.* SBLDS 92. Atlanta: Scholars.

Carroll, R. P. 1979. "Twilight of Prophecy or Dawn of Apocalyptic." *JSOT* 14:3–35.

Casey, M. 1979. *Son of Man: The Interpretation and Influence of Daniel 7.* London: SPCK.

Catchpole, D. R. 1979. "The Poor on Earth and the Son of Man in Heaven." *BJRL* 61:355–97.

Charles, R. H. 1920. *Revelation.* 2 vols. ICC. Edinburgh: T. and T. Clark.

Childs, B. S. 1974. *The Book of Exodus: A Critical, Theological Commentary.* Philadelphia: Westminster.

Chilton, B. D. 1978. "Regnum Dei Deus Est." *SJT* 31:261–70.

Clark, W. M. 1969. "A Legal Background to the Yahwist's Use of 'Good and Evil' in Genesis 2–3." *JBL* 88:266–78.

Clifford, R. J. 1972. *The Cosmic Mountain in Canaan and the Old Testament.* HSM 4. Cambridge: Harvard University Press.

———. 1983. "Isaiah 55: Invitation to a Feast." In *The Word of the Lord Shall Go Forth: Essays in Honor of David Noel Freedman in Celebration of His Sixtieth Birthday,* ed. C. L. Meyers and M. O'Connor, 27–35. Winona Lake, Ind.: Eisenbrauns.

———. 1984. *Fair-Spoken and Persuading: An Interpretation of Second Isaiah.* New York: Paulist.

Clines, D. J. A. 1967. "The Image of God in Man." *TynB* 18:53–103.

———. 1976. *I, He, We, and They: A Literary Approach to Isaiah 53.* Sheffield: JSOT.

Collins, J. J. 1974. "Apocalyptic Eschatology as the Transcendence of Death." *CBQ* 36:21–43.

———. 1977. *The Apocalyptic Vision of the Book of Daniel.* HSM 16. Missoula, Mont.: Scholars.

———. 1981. "Apocalyptic Genre and Mythic Allusions in Daniel." *JSOT* 21:83–100.

Combrink, H. J. B. 1983. "The Structure of the Gospel of Matthew as Narrative." *TynB* 34:61–90.

Court, J. M. 1979. *Myth and History in the Book of the Revelation.* London: SPCK.

Cranfield, C. E. B. 1959. *The Gospel According to Saint Mark: An Introduction and Commentary.* Cambridge: Cambridge University Press.

———. 1975. *A Critical and Exegetical Commentary on the Epistle to the Romans.* Vol. 1, *Introduction and Commentary on Romans 1–8.* Edinburgh: T. and T. Clark.

Culpepper, R. A. 1980. "The Pivot of John's Prologue." *NTS* 27:1–31.

Dahl, N. A. 1958. "'A People for His Name' (Acts XV. 14)." *NTS* 4:319–27.

Dalton, W. J. 1965. *Christ's Proclamation to the Spirits: A Study of 1 Peter 3:18–4:6.* AnBib 93. Rome: Biblical Institute Press.

Davids, P. H. 1982. *Commentary on James.* NIGTC 39. Exeter: Paternoster.

———. 1990. *The First Epistle of Peter.* NICNT. Grand Rapids: Eerdmans.

Davies, P. R. 1985. *Daniel.* Sheffield: JSOT.

Davies, W. D., and D. C. Allison. 1988. *The Gospel According to St. Matthew.* ICC 1. Edinburgh: T. and T. Clark.

Day, J. 1985. *God's Conflict with the Dragon and the Sea: Echoes of a Canaanite Myth in the Old Testament.* Cambridge: Cambridge University Press.

De Boer, M. C. 1988. *The Defeat of Death.* JSNTSup 22. Sheffield: JSOT.

Deidun, T. J. 1981. *New Covenant Morality in Paul.* AnBib 89. Rome: Biblical Institute Press.

de Jonge, M. 1973. "Jesus as Prophet and King in the Fourth Gospel." *ETL* 49:160–77.

Delcor, M. 1971. *Le Livre de Daniel.* Paris: Gabalda.

Dodd, C. H. 1954. *The Interpretation of the Fourth Gospel.* Cambridge: Cambridge University Press.

Donaldson, T. L. 1985. *Jesus on the Mountain: A Study in Matthean Theology.* JSNTSup 8. Sheffield: JSOT.

Donfried, K. P. 1970. "A Short Note on Romans 16." *JBL* 89:441–49.

Duff, N. J. 1989. "The Significance of Pauline Apocalyptic for Theological Ethics." In *Apocalyptic and the New Testament: Essays in Honour of J. L. Martyn,* ed. J. Marcus and M. L. Soards, 279–96. JSNTSup 24. Sheffield: JSOT.

Dumbrell, W. J. "The Logic of the Role of the Law in Matt. 5:1–20." *NovT* 23:1–21.

———. 1984. *Covenant and Creation.* Exeter: Paternoster.

Dunn, J. D. G. 1980. *Christology in the Making: A New Testament Inquiry into the Origins of the Doctrine of Incarnation.* Philadelphia: Westminster.

———. 1987. "A Light to the Gentiles: The Significance of the Damascus Road Christophany for Paul." In *The Glory of Christ in the New Testament: Studies in Christology in Memory of George Bradford Caird,* ed. L. D. Hurst and N. T. Wright, 251–66. Oxford: Clarendon.

Durham, J. I. 1987. *Exodus.* Word Biblical Commentary 3. Waco: Word.

Elliot, J. H. 1966. *The Elect and the Holy: An Exegetical Examination of 1 Peter 2:4–10 and the Phrase βασίλειον ἱράτευμα.* NovTSup 12. Leiden: Brill.

Elliott, N. 1990. *The Rhetoric of Romans.* JSNTSup 45. Sheffield: JSOT.

Eslinger, L. 1983. "Viewpoints and Point of View in 1 Samuel 8–12." *JSOT* 26:61–76.

Fee, G. D. 1987. *The First Epistle to the Corinthians.* NICNT. Grand Rapids: Eerdmans.

Feinberg, J. S. 1986. "1 Peter 3:18–20, Ancient Mythology, and the Intermediate State." *WTJ* 48:303–36.

Feinberg, P. D. 1981. "An Exegetical and Theological Study of Daniel 9:24–27." In *Tradition and Testament: Essays in Honor of Charles Lee Feinberg,* ed. J. S. Feinberg and P. D. Feinberg, 189–220. Chicago: Moody.

Ferch, A. J. 1979. *The Son of Man in Daniel 7.* Berrien Springs, Mich.: Andrews University Press.

Fiorenza, E. 1972. *Priester fuer Gott.* NTAbh NF 10. Münster, Ger.: Aschendorff.

———. 1974. "Redemption as Liberation: Apoc 1:5f. and 5:9f." *CBQ* 36:220–32.

Fitzmyer, J. A. 1979. "The New Testament Title 'Son of Man' Philologically Considered." In *A Wandering Aramean: Collected Aramaic Essays*, 143–60. Missoula, Mont.: Scholars.

Foerster, W. 1964. "ἁρπάζω." In *TDNT* 1:472–74.

Fokkelman, J. P. 1975. *Narrative Art in Genesis*. Assen, Neth.: Van Gorcum.

Forestell, J. T. 1974. *The Word of the Cross: Salvation as Revelation in the Fourth Gospel*. AnBib 51. Rome: Biblical Institute Press.

France, R. T. 1971. *Jesus and the Old Testament: His Application of Old Testament Passages to Himself and His Mission*. London: Tyndale.

———. 1984. "The Church and the Kingdom of God." In *Biblical Interpretation and the Church: The Problem of Contextualization*, ed. D. A. Carson, 30–44. Exeter: Paternoster.

Frankfort, H. 1948. *Kingship and the Gods: A Study of Ancient Near Eastern Religion as the Integration of Society and Nature*. Chicago: University of Chicago Press.

Franklin, E. 1975. *Christ the Lord: A Study in the Purpose and Theology of Luke-Acts*. Philadelphia: Westminster.

Gaston, L. 1970. *No Stone on Another: Studies in the Significance of the Fall of Jerusalem in the Synoptic Gospels*. NovTSup 23. Leiden: Brill.

Giblin, C. H. 1985. *The Destruction of Jerusalem According to St. Luke's Gospel: A Historical-Typological Moral*. AnBib 107. Rome: Biblical Institute Press.

Gibson, J. C. L. 1981. *Genesis*. Daily Study Bible 1. Philadelphia: Westminster.

Gillman, J. A. 1988. "A Thematic Comparison: 1 Cor 15:50–57 and 2 Cor 5:1–5." *JBL* 107:439–54.

Gitay, Y. 1981. *Prophecy and Persuasion: A Study of Isaiah 40–48*. Bonn: Linguistica Biblica.

Goldingay, J. 1989. *Daniel*. Word Biblical Commentary 30. Waco: Word.

Gowan, D. E. 1987. *Eschatology in the Old Testament*. Edinburgh: T. and T. Clark.

Greenberg, M. 1984. "The Design and Themes of Ezekiel's Program of Restoration." *Int* 38:181–208.

Groenbaek, J. H. 1985. "Baal's Battle with Yam: A Canaanite Creation Fight." *JSOT* 33:27–44.

Grudem, W. A. 1982. *The Gift of Prophecy in 1 Corinthians*. Lanham, Md.: University Press of America.

Guelich, R. A. 1976. "The Matthean Beatitudes: 'Entrance Requirements' or Eschatological Blessings?" *JBL* 95:415–34.

———. 1982. "The Beginning of the Gospel." *BR* 27:5–15.

Gundry, R. H. 1967. "In My Father's House Are Many Μοναί (John 14:2)." *ZNW* 58:68–72.

———. 1987. "The Hellenization of Dominical Tradition and Christianization of Jewish Tradition in the Eschatology of 1–2 Thessalonians." *NTS* 33:161–78.

Guthrie, D. 1983. *The Letter to the Hebrews: An Introduction and Commentary*. Leicester: Inter-Varsity.

———. 1987. *The Relevance of John's Apocalypse*. Exeter: Paternoster.

Hahn, F. 1969. *The Titles of Jesus in Christology: Their History in Early Christianity*. Translated by Harold Knight and George Ogg. London: Lutterworth.

Hansen, G. W. 1989. *Abraham in Galatians: Epistolary and Rhetorical Contexts*. JSNTSup 29. Sheffield: JSOT.

Hanson, P. D. 1975. *The Dawn of Apocalyptic*. Philadelphia: Fortress.

Hare, D. R. A. 1967. *The Theme of Jewish Persecution of Christians in the Gospel According to Saint Matthew*. SNTSMS 6. Cambridge: Cambridge University Press.

Harris, M. J. 1983. *Raised Immortal: Resurrection and Immortality in the New Testament*. London: Marshall, Morgan and Scott.

———. 1990. *From Grave to Glory: Resurrection in the New Testament*. Grand Rapids: Zondervan.

Harvey, A. E. 1982. *Jesus and the Constraints of History*. London: Duckworth.

Hasel, G. F. 1974. *The Remnant: The History and Theology of the Remnant Idea from Genesis to Isaiah*. 2d ed. Berrien Springs, Mich.: Andrews University Press.

Hatton, H. J., and D. J. Clark. 1975. "From the Harp to the Sitar." *BT* 26:132–38.

Hays, R. H. 1985. "'Have We Found Abraham to Be Our Forefather According to the Flesh': A Reconsideration of Rom. 4:1." *NovT* 27:76–98.

Heidel, A. 1961. *The Babylonian Genesis: The Story of Creation*. 6th ed. Chicago: University of Chicago Press.

Hill, C. E. 1988. "Paul's Understanding of Christ's Kingdom in 1 Corinthians 15:20–28." *NovT* 30:297–320.

Hoehner, H. W. 1975. "Chronological Aspects of the Life of Christ, Pt 6: Daniel's Seventy Weeks and New Testament Chronology." *BSac* 132:47–65.

Holladay, W. L. 1978. *Isaiah, Scroll of Prophetic Heritage*. Grand Rapids: Eerdmans.

Hollenberg, D. E. 1969. "Nationalism and 'the Nations' in Isaiah x1–1v." *VT* 19:26–36.

Hooker, M. D. 1967. *The Son of Man in Mark: A Study of the Background of the Term "Son of Man" and Its Use in St. Mark's Gospel*. London: SPCK.

———. 1982. "Trial and Tribulation in Mark 13." *BJRL* 65:78–99.

Hort, F. J. 1900. *The Christian Ecclesia*. London: Macmillan.

Hughes, G. 1979. *Hebrews and Hermeneutics: The Epistle to the Hebrews as a New Testament Example of Biblical Interpretation*. Cambridge: SNTSMS 36. Cambridge University Press.

Hultgren, A. J. 1982. "The Johannine Footwashing (John 13:1–11) as Symbol of Eschatological Hospitality." *NTS* 28:539–46.

Hunter, A. V. 1982. *Seek the Lord!* Baltimore: St. Mary's Seminary and University.

Hurtado, L. W. 1985. "Revelation 4–5 in the Light of Jewish Apocalyptic Analogies." *JSNT* 25:105–24.

Hutter, M. 1986. "Adam als Gärtner und König (Gen. 2:8, 15)." *BZ* 30:258–62.

Janzen, W. 1965. "ʾAšrê in the Old Testament." *HTR* 58:215–26.

Jeremias, Joachim. 1926. *Golgotha*. Leipzig: Pfeiffer.

———. 1967. "λιθος." In *TDNT* 4:268–80.

———. 1971. *New Testament Theology*. Vol. 1, *The Proclamation of Jesus*. Trans. J. Bowden. London: SCM.

Jeremias, Jörg. 1972. מִשְׁפַּט im ersten Gottesknechtslied (Jes. 42:1–4)." *VT* 22:31–42.

Jervell, J. 1972. *Luke and the People of God: A New Look at Luke-Acts.* Minneapolis: Augsburg.

———. 1984. *The Unknown Paul: Essays on Luke-Acts and Early Christian History.* Minneapolis: Augsburg.

Johnson, L. T. 1977. *The Literary Function of Possessions in Luke-Acts.* SBLDS 39. Missoula, Mont.: Scholars.

———. 1982. "The Lukan Kingship Parable (Lk 19:11–27)." *NovT* 24:139–59.

Juel, D. 1977. *Messiah and Temple: The Trial of Jesus in the Gospel of Mark.* SBLDS 31. Missoula, Mont.: Scholars.

Kaiser, O. 1972. *Isaiah 1–12: A Commentary.* London: SCM.

Kaiser, W. C., Jr. 1974. "The Blessing of David: The Charter for Humanity." In *The Law and the Prophets: Old Testament Studies in Honor of O. T. Allis,* ed. J. H. Skilton, 298–318. Nutley, N.J.: Presbyterian and Reformed.

———. 1983. *Toward Old Testament Ethics.* Grand Rapids: Zondervan.

Käsemann, E. 1969. *New Testament Questions of Today.* Philadelphia: Fortress.

———. 1984. *The Wandering People of God: An Investigation of the Letter to the Hebrews.* Trans. R. A. Harrisville and I. L. Sandberg. Minneapolis: Augsburg.

Keck, L. E. 1966. "The Introduction to Mark's Gospel." *NTS* 12:352–70.

Kee, H. C. 1968. "The Terminology of Mark's Exorcism Stories." *NTS* 14:232–46.

Keil, C. F., and F. Delitzsch. 1975. *Commentary on the Old Testament.* Vol. 1, *The Pentateuch.* Grand Rapids: Eerdmans.

Kelly, J. N. D. 1963. *A Commentary on the Pastoral Epistles (1 Timothy, 2 Timothy, Titus).* London: Adam and Charles Black.

Kik, J. M. 1948. *Matthew XXIV: An Exposition.* Philadelphia: Presbyterian and Reformed.

Kim, S. 1982. *The Origin of Paul's Gospel.* Grand Rapids: Eerdmans.

———. 1983. *The "Son of Man" as Son of God.* WUNT 30. Tübingen, Ger.: J. C. B. Mohr.

Knierim, R. P. 1968. "The Messianic Concept in the First Book of Samuel." In *Jesus and the Historian, Written in Honor of Ernest Cadman Colwell,* ed. F. T. Trotter, 20–51. Philadelphia: Westminster.

Köhler, L., and W. Baumgartner. 1958. *Lexicon in Veteris Testamenti Libros.* Leiden: Brill.

Kourie, C. E. T. 1987. "'In Christ' and Related Expressions in Paul." *Th Ev* 20:33–43.

Krodel, G. 1986. *Acts.* Minneapolis: Augsburg.

Levenson, J. D. 1976. *Theology of the Program of Restoration of Ezekiel 40–48.* HSM 10. Missoula, Mont.: Scholars.

———. 1985. *Sinai and Zion: An Entry into the Jewish Bible.* Minneapolis: Winston.

Lewis, C. S. 1962. *The Problem of Pain.* New York: Macmillan.

Lincoln, A. T. 1981. *Paradise Now and Not Yet: Studies in the Role of the Heavenly Dimension in Paul's Thought with Special Reference to His Eschatology.* SNTSMS 43. Cambridge: Cambridge University Press.

————. 1985. "Theology and History in the Interpretation of Luke's Pentecost." *ExpT* 96:204–9.

Lindars, B., ed. 1972. *The Gospel of John*. New Century Bible. London: Oliphants.

————. 1983. *Jesus, Son of Man: A Fresh Examination of the Son of Man Sayings in the Gospels in the Light of Recent Research*. London: SPCK.

Lohfink, N. H. 1969. *The Christian Meaning of the Old Testament*. London: Burns and Oates.

McCarter, P. K. 1984. *II Samuel: A New Translation with Introduction, Notes, and Commentary*. Anchor Bible. Garden City, N.Y.: Doubleday.

McCarthy, D. J. 1972. "*Bĕrît* and Covenant in the Deuteronomic History." VTSup 23:65–85.

McConville, J. G. 1979. "God's 'Name' and God's 'Glory.'" *TynB* 30:149–63.

McCurley, F. R. 1983. *Ancient Myths and the Biblical Faith: Scriptural Transformations*. Philadelphia: Fortress.

McKane, W. S. 1982. "The Eschatology of Jewish Apocalyptic." *OTWSA* 25:79–91.

Maddox, R. 1968. "The Function of the Son of Man According to the Synoptic Gospels." *NTS* 15:45–74.

————. 1982. *The Purpose of Luke-Acts*. Edinburgh: T. and T. Clark.

Malamat, A. 1976. "Charismatic Leadership in the Book of Judges." In *Magnalia Dei, The Mighty Acts of God: Essays on the Bible and Archaeology in Memory of G. Ernest Wright*, ed. F. M. Cross, W. E. Lemke, and P. D. Miller, 152–68. Garden City, N.Y.: Doubleday.

Marshall, I. H. 1978. *The Gospel of Luke: A Commentary on the Greek Text*. Exeter: Paternoster.

————. 1985. "The Hope of a New Age: The Kingdom of God in the New Testament." *Themelios*, n.s. 11, no. 3:5–15.

Martin, R. P. 1972. *Mark, Evangelist and Theologian*. Grand Rapids: Zondervan.

Mearns, C. L. 1981. "Early Eschatological Development in Paul: The Evidence of I and II Thessalonians." *NTS* 27:137–57.

Meeks, W. A. 1967. *The Prophet-King: Moses Traditions and the Johannine Christology*. NovTSup 14. Leiden: Brill.

Meier, J. P. 1976. *Law and History in Matthew's Gospel: A Redactional Study of Mt. 5:17–48*. AnBib 71. Rome: Biblical Institute Press.

Mettinger, T. N. D. 1974. "Abbild oder Urbild? Imago Dei in traditionsgeschichtlicher Sicht." *ZAW* 86:403–24.

————. 1976. *King and Messiah: The Civil and Sacral Legitimation of the Israelite Kings*. ConBOT 8. Lund, Swed.: Gleerup.

Meyer, B. F. 1979. *The Aims of Jesus*. London: SCM.

Meyer, M., ed. 1992. *The Gospel of Thomas: The Hidden Sayings of Jesus*. San Francisco: Harper.

Michaels, J. R. 1983. *John*. A Good News Commentary. San Francisco: Harper and Row.

Miller, P. D., Jr. 1969. "The Gift of God: The Deuteronomic Theology of the Land." *Int* 23:451–65.

Minear, P. S. 1981. *New Testament Apocalyptic*. Nashville: Abingdon.

Moberly, R. W. L. 1983. *At the Mountain of God*. JSOTSup 22. Sheffield: JSOT.

Moessner, D. P. 1988. "Paul in Acts: Preacher of Eschatological Repentance to Israel." *NTS* 34:96–104.

Moloney, F. J. 1978. *The Johannine Son of Man*. 2d ed. Biblioteca de Scienze Religiose 14. Rome: LAS.

Monsengwo-Pasinya, L. 1980. "Deux textes messianiques de la Septante: Gn 49,10 et Ez 21,32." *Bib* 61:357–76.

Moore, A. L. 1966. *The Parousia in the New Testament*. NovTSup 13. Leiden: Brill.

Moore, G. F. 1932. *Judaism in the First Centuries of the Christian Era*. Cambridge: Harvard University Press.

Moule, C. F. D. 1970. "Further Reflections on Philippians 2:5–11." In *Apostolic History and the Gospel, Biblical and Historical Essays Presented to F. F. Bruce on His 60th Birthday*, ed. W. W. Gasque and R. P. Martin, 264–76. Exeter: Paternoster.

———. 1974. "Neglected Features in the Problem of the 'Son of Man.'" In *Neues Testament und Kirche, fuer Rudolf Schnackenburg*, ed. J. Gnilka, 413–28. Freiburg, Ger.: Herder.

Mulholland, M. R., Jr. 1990. *Revelation: Holy Living in an Unholy Land*. Grand Rapids: Zondervan.

Neyrey, J. H. 1981. "John 3: A Debate over Johannine Epistemology and Christology." *NovT* 23:115–27.

———. 1985. *The Passion According to Luke: A Redaction Study of Luke's Soteriology*. New York: Paulist.

Nicholson, G. C. 1983. *Death as Departure: The Johannine Descent-Ascent Schema*. SBLDS 63. Chico, Calif.: Scholars.

Nickelsburg, G. W. E. 1972. *Resurrection, Immortality, and Eternal Life in Intertestamental Judaism*. Cambridge: Harvard University Press.

Niditch, S. 1986. "Ezekiel 40–48 in a Visionary Context." *CBQ* 48:208–24.

Nolan, B. M. 1979. *The Royal Son of God*. OBO 23. Göttingen, Ger.: Vandenhoeck and Ruprecht.

Nolland, J. 1979. "Impressed Unbelievers as a Witness to Christ (Luke 4:22a)." *JBL* 98:219–29.

———. 1980. "A Fresh Look at Acts 15:10." *NTS* 27:105–15.

———. 1989. *Luke 1–9:20*. Dallas: Word.

O'Donovan, O. 1986. "The Political Thought of the Book of Revelation." *TynB* 37:61–94.

Osborne, G. R. 1991. *The Hermeneutical Spiral*. Downers Grove, Ill.: Inter-Varsity.

O'Toole, R. F. 1978. "Luke's Notion of 'Be Imitators of Me as I Am of Christ' in Acts 25–26." *BTB* 8:155–61.

Pancaro, S. 1975a. *The Law in the Fourth Gospel: The Torah and the Gospel, Moses and Jesus, Judaism and Christianity According to John*. NovTSup 42. Leiden: Brill.

———. 1975b. "The Relationship of the Church to Israel in the Gospel of St. John." *NTS* 21:396–405.

Parker, J. 1978. *The Concept of Apokatastasis in Acts: A Study in Primitive Christian Theology*. Austin: Schola Press.

Parsons, M. C. 1987. *The Departure of Jesus in Luke-Acts: The Ascension Narratives in Context*. JSNTSup 21. Sheffield: JSOT.

Parsons, Michael. 1988. "'In Christ' in Paul." *Vox Ev* 18:25–44.

Parunak, H. v. D. 1980. "The Literary Architecture of Ezekiel's *mar> ôt >elōhîm*." *JBL* 99:61–74.

Patai, R. 1947. *Man and Temple in Ancient Jewish Myth and Ritual*. London: Nelson.

Patte, D. 1987. *The Gospel According to Matthew: A Structural Commentary on Matthew's Faith*. Philadelphia: Fortress.

Patterson, J. W. 1983. "Thermodynamics and Evolution." In *Scientists Confront Creationism*, ed. L. R. Godfrey, 99–116. New York: Norton.

Peterson, D. G. 1982. *Hebrews and Perfection: An Examination of the Concept of Perfection in the Epistle to the Hebrews*. SNTSMS 47. Cambridge: Cambridge University Press.

Pfitzner, V. C. 1983. *Hebrews*. Adelaide: Lutheran.

Phillips, A. 1979. "Torah and Mishpat: A Light to the Peoples." In *Witness to the Spirit: Essays in Revelation, Spirit, Redemption*, ed. W. Harrington, 112–32. Manchester: Koinonia Press.

Plevnik, J. 1975. "The Parousia as Implications of Christ's Resurrection (An Exegesis of 1 Thess 4:13–18)." In *Word and Spirit, Essays in Honor of David Michael Stanley, SJ, on His 60th Birthday*, ed J. Plevnik, 199–277. Willowdale, Ont.: Regis College Press.

Porter, P. A. 1983. *Metaphors and Monsters: A Literary Critical Study of Daniel 7 and 8*. Lund, Swed.: Gleerup.

Pritchard, J. B., ed. 1969. *Ancient Near Eastern Texts Relating to the Old Testament*. 3d ed. Princeton, N. J.: Princeton University Press.

Pryor, J. W. 1990. "Jesus and Israel in the Fourth Gospel—John 1:11." *NovT* 32:201–18.

Przybylski, B. 1980. *Righteousness in Matthew and His World of Thought*. SNTSMS 41. Cambridge: Cambridge University Press.

Rabbinowitz, L. 1971. "Salt." In *EncJud* 14:710–11.

Richard, E. 1984. "The Divine Purpose: The Jews and the Gentile Mission (Acts 15)." In *Luke-Acts: New Perspectives from the Society of Biblical Literature Seminar*, ed. C. H. Talbert, 188–209. New York: Crossroad NY.

Riches, J. K. 1980. *Jesus and the Transformation of Judaism*. London: Darton, Longman and Todd.

Ridderbos, H. N. 1975. *Paul: An Outline of His Theology*. Trans. J. R. de Witt. Grand Rapids: Eerdmans.

Robinson, D. W. B. 1964. "II Thess 2:6:1 'That Which Restrains' or 'That Which Holds Sway'?" In *SE*, ed. F. L. Cross, 2:635–38. Berlin: Akademie-Verlag.

———. 1965. "The Distinction Between Jewish and Gentile Believers in Galatians." *ABR* 13:29–48.

———. 1967. "The Salvation of Israel in Romans 9–11." *RTR* 26:81–96.

Robinson, G. 1980. "The Idea of Rest in the Old Testament and the Search for the Basic Character of Sabbath." *ZAW* 92:32–42.

Robinson, J. A. T. 1956. "Expository Problems: The Second Coming—Mark 14:62." *ExpT* 67:336–40.

———. 1961. *Twelve New Testament Studies*. London: SCM.

Robinson, J. M. 1982. *The Problem of History in Mark and Other Marcan Studies*. Philadelphia: Fortress.

Sakenfeld, K. D. 1975. "The Problem of Divine Forgiveness in Numbers 14." *CBQ* 37:317–30.

Sanders, E. P. 1977. *Paul and Palestinian Judaism: A Comparison of Patterns of Religion*. Philadelphia: Fortress.

Sanders, J. T. 1984. "The Salvation of the Jews in Luke–Acts." In *Luke-Acts: New Perspectives from the Society of Biblical Literature Seminar*, ed. C. H. Talbert, 104–28. New York: Crossroad.

———. 1987. *The Jews in Luke-Acts*. London: SCM.

Sarna, N. H. 1971. "Abraham." In *EncJud* 2:111–15.

Sawyer, J. F. A. 1984. *Isaiah*. Vol. 1, *Chps. 1–32*. Daily Study Bible. Philadelphia: Westminster.

Schaberg, J. 1982. *The Father, the Son, and the Holy Spirit: The Triadic Phrase in Matthew 28:19b*. SBLDS 61. Chico, Calif.: Scholars.

Schnackenburg, R. 1968–82. *The Gospel According to St. John*. 3 vols. London: Burns and Oates.

Schreiner, T. 1989. "The Abolition and Fulfillment of the Law in Paul." *JSNT* 35:47–74.

Schweitzer, A. 1931. *The Mysticism of Paul the Apostle*. Trans. W. Montgomery. London: Adam and Charles Black.

Seccombe, D. P. 1982. *Possessions and the Poor in Luke-Acts*. SNTSU 6. Linz, Aus.: Albert Fuchs.

Sharp, J. R. 1984. "Philonism and the Eschatology of Hebrews: Another Look." *E Asia J Th* 2:289–98.

Snodgrass, K. R. 1986. "Justification by Grace to the Doers: An Analysis of the Place of Romans 2 in the Theology of Paul." *NTS* 32:72–93.

Soares Prabhu, G. M. 1976. *The Formulary Quotations in the Infancy Narrative of Matthew*. AnBib 63. Rome: Biblical Institute Press.

Stendahl, K. 1963. "The Apostle Paul and the Introspective Conscience of the West." *HTR* 56:199–216.

———. 1960. "'Quis et Unde': An Analysis of Matt. 1–2." In *Judentum, Urchristentum, Kirche*, ed. W. Eltester, 94–105. BZNW26. Berlin: Töpelmann.

Stenning, J. F., ed. 1947. *The Targum of Isaiah*. Oxford: Clarendon.

Strack, H. L., and P. Billerbeck. 1922. *Kommentar zum Neuen Testament aus Talmud und Midrasch*. Vol. 1. Munich: C. H. Beck.

Stuhlmueller, C. 1970. *Creative Redemption in Deutero-Isaiah*. Rome: Biblical Institute Press.

Sweeney, M. A. 1988. *Isaiah 1–4 and Post-Exilic Understanding of the Isaianic Tradition*. BZAW 171. Berlin: Walter de Gruyter.

Swetnam, J. 1972. "Form and Content in Hebrews 1–6." *Bib* 53:368–85.

Tannehill, R. C. 1985. "Israel in Luke-Acts: A Tragic Story." *JBL* 104:69–85.

Tasker, R. V. G. 1961. *The Gospel According to St. Matthew: An Introduction and Commentary*. London: Tyndale.

Thompson, J. W. 1976. "The Structure and Purpose of the Catena in Heb 1:5–13." *CBQ* 38:352–63.

Tiede, D. L. 1980. *Prophecy and History in Luke-Acts*. Philadelphia: Fortress.

————. 1986. "The Exaltation of Jesus and the Restoration of Israel in Acts 1." *HTR* 79:278–86.

Tödt, H. E. 1965. *The Son of Man in the Synoptic Tradition*. London: SCM.

Travis, S. H. 1986. *Christ and the Judgment of God*. Basingstoke, U.K.: Marshall Morgan and Scott.

Trilling, W. 1964. *Das Wahre Israel: Studien zur Theologie des Matthaus-Evangeliums*. SANT 10. Munich: Kosel-Verlag.

Trites, A. A. 1977. *The New Testament Concept of Witness*. SNTSMS 31. Cambridge: Cambridge University Press.

Tuckett, C. M. 1982. "The Present Son of Man (Mk 2:10, 28)." *JSNT* 14:58–81.

Turner, M. M. B. 1981. "Jesus and the Spirit in Lucan Perspective." *TynB* 32:3–42.

————. 1982. "The Spirit of Christ and Christology." In *Christ the Lord: Studies in Christology Presented to Donald Guthrie*, ed. H. H. Rowdon, 168–90. Leicester: Inter-Varsity.

Tyson, J. B. 1992. *Images of Judaism in Luke-Acts*. Columbia, S. C.: University of South Carolina Press.

Ulfgard, H. 1989. *Feast and Future: Revelation 7:9–17 and the Feast of Tabernacles*. Lund: Almqvist and Wiksell.

van Unnik, W. C. 1970. "Worthy Is the Lamb: The Background of Apoc 5." In *Melanges bibliques en hommage au R. P. Bidaux*, ed. A. Deschamps et al., 445–61. Gembloux, Belg.: Duculot.

Vannoy, J. R. 1978. *Covenant Renewal at Gilgal: A Study of 1 Sam 11:14–12:15*. Cherry Hill, N.J.: Mack.

Vanhoye, A. 1986. *Old Testament and the New Priest: According to the New Testament*. Translated by J. BErnard Orchard, OSV. Petersham, Mass.: St. Bede's Publications.

Vellanickal, M. 1977. *The Divine Sonship of Christians in the Johannine Writings*. AnBib 72. Rome: Biblical Institute Press.

Vermes, G. 1973. *Jesus the Jew: A Historian's Reading of the Gospel*. London: Collins.

Via, D. O. 1987. "Ethical Responsibility and Human Wholeness in Matt 25:31–46." *HTR* 80:79–100.

von Rad, G. 1965. *Theology of the Old Testament*. Vol. 2, *The Prophets*. Trans. D. M. G. Stalker. London: Oliver and Boyd.

————. 1972. *Wisdom in Israel*. London: SCM.

Vorster, W. S. 1973. "A Messianic Interpretation of Gen 3:15: A Methodological Problem." *OTWSA* 116:108–18.

Wainwright, A. W. 1977. "Luke and the Restoration of the Kingdom to Israel." *ExpT* 89:76–79.

Wallace, H. N. 1985. *The Eden Narrative*. HSM 32. Atlanta: Scholars.

Walsh, J. T. 1977. "Genesis 2:4b–3:24: A Synchronic Approach." *JBL* 96:161–77.

Ward, J. M. 1978. "The Servant's Knowledge in Isaiah 40–55." In *Israelite Wisdom: Theological and Literary Essays in Honor of Samuel Terrien*, ed. J. G. Gammie et al., 121–36. Missoula, Mont.: Scholars.

Ware, P. 1979. "The Coming of the Lord: Eschatology and 1 Thessalonians." *Res Q* 22:109–20.

Watson, F. S. 1986. *Paul, Judaism, and the Gentiles: A Sociological Approach.* SNTSMS 56. Cambridge: Cambridge University Press.

Watts, R. E. 1990. "Consolation or Confrontation? Isaiah 40–55 and the Delay of the New Exodus." *TynB* 41:31–59.

Weinfeld, M. 1972. *Deuteronomy and the Deuteronomic School.* Oxford: Clarendon.

———. 1981. "Sabbath, Temple and Enthronement of the Lord—The Problem of the Sitz im Leben of Gen. 1:1–2:3." In *Melanges bibliques et orientaux en l'honneur de M. Henri Cazelles*, ed. A. Caquot and M. Delcor, 501–12. AOAT 212. Kevelaer, Ger.: Butzon and Becker.

Weiss, M. 1966. "The Origin of the 'Day of the Lord' Reconsidered." *HUCA* 37:29–60.

Wenham, D. 1984. *The Rediscovery of Jesus' Eschatological Discourse.* Sheffield: JSOT.

Wenham, G. 1971. "Deuteronomy and the Central Sanctuary." *TynB* 22:103–18.

———. 1987. *Genesis 1–15.* Word Biblical Commentary 1. Waco: Word.

Westcott, B. F. 1958. *The Gospel According to St. John.* London: Clarke.

Westermann, C. 1984. *Genesis 1–11: A Commentary.* Trans. J. J. Scullion. Minneapolis: Augsburg.

White, R. F. 1989. "Reexamining the Evidence for Recapitulation in Rev. 20:1–10." *WTJ* 51:319–44.

Williams, D. J. 1991. *First and Second Thessalonians.* NIBCS. Peabody, Mass.: Hendrickson.

Williams, S. K. 1980. "The 'Righteousness of God' in Romans." *JBL* 99:241–90.

Williamson, H. G. M. 1977. "Eschatology in Chronicles." *TynB* 28:115–54.

Wilson, A. 1986. *The Nations in Deutero-Isaiah: A Study on Composition and Structure.* Lewiston, N.Y.: Edwin Mellen.

Wilson, S. G. 1973. *The Gentiles and the Gentile Mission in Luke-Acts.* SNTSMS 23. Cambridge: Cambridge University Press.

———. 1979. *Luke and the Pastoral Epistles.* London: SPCK.

———. 1983. *Luke and the Law.* SNTSMS 50. Cambridge: Cambridge University Press.

Wolff, H. W. 1966. "The Kerygma of the Yahwist." *Int* 20:131–58.

Woll, D. 1980. "The Departure of 'The Way': The First Farewell Discourse in the Gospel of John." *JBL* 99:225–39.

Wright, N. T. 1980. "Justification: The Biblical Basis and Its Relevance." In *The Great Acquittal: Justification by Faith and Current Christian Thought*, ed. G. Reid, 13–37. Glasgow: William Collins.

———. 1983. "Adam in Pauline Christology." *SBLSP* 22:359–89.

———. 1985. "Jesus, Israel and the Cross." *SBLSP* 24:75–95.

———. 1986. *The Epistles of Paul to the Colossians and to Philemon.* Leicester: Inter-Varsity.

———. 1988a. "Jesus." In *New Dictionary of Theology*, ed. S. B. Ferguson and D. F. Wright, 348–51. Leicester: Inter-Varsity.

———. 1988b. *Jesus in History and Theology.* Audiotapes of public lectures presented at Vancouver Summer School, Regent College, Vancouver, B.C., Canada, July.

———. 1988c. "Paul." *In New Dictionary of Theology*, ed. S. B. Ferguson and D. F. Wright, 496–99. Leicester: Inter-Varsity.

———. 1992. *The New Testament and the People of God*. London: SPCK.

Yates, R. 1980. "The Powers of Evil in the New Testament." *EvQ* 52:97–111.

Ziesler, J. A. 1981–82. "Salvation Proclaimed: Romans 3:21–26." *ExpT* 93:356–59.

———. 1983. *Pauline Christianity*. Oxford: Oxford University Press.

Index of Subjects

Abrahamic covenant, 35, 39, 43, 44, 72, 80, 95, 225, 268, 293, 295
universality, 84
Abrahamic promises, 52, 83–84, 104, 124, 162, 225, 273
Abram, 32
call, 33–34
change of name, 35
Adam, 260, 275, 286, 287–88, 343
and Israel, 10, 29, 275–76
as priest-king, 25, 29
provisional immortality, 346
Adoption, 297
Age, 260
Christian, 342
to come, 272–73, 322
eschatological, 128–29
present, 11, 132, 272–73
Aharoni, R., 105
Ahaz, 86, 89
Alexander the Great, 144, 148
Alienation, 36
Allison, D. C., 164, 187
Ambrozic, A. M., 182, 184, 199
Ammonites, 63
Ancient of Days, 142, 143, 333
Ancient Near East, 16, 24, 46, 82, 137
Angels, 164, 202, 284–85, 306, 312, 319, 336, 337
Anointing, 62–65
Antichrist, 140, 142, 147, 314, 340
Antiochus III, 148
Antiochus IV Epiphanes, 144, 146, 148, 150, 314
Apathy, 333
Apocalyptic, 127, 131–36, 140–41, 185–86, 195, 328
eschatology, 10, 331

and history, 140–41
Jewish, 299
and prophecy, 132, 133–34, 136, 331
Apostasy, 49, 54, 59, 77, 78, 80, 233, 313, 315
Ark of the covenant, 60, 67–70, 97
Armageddon, 273, 337, 343
Artaxerxes, 145–46
Asceticism, 306
Asherah, 77
Assyria, 68, 79, 91
Atonement, 101, 120, 121, 272, 276
Attridge, H. W., 320, 321
Augustine, 263
Authority, 237
Autonomy, 27

Baal, 16, 40, 42, 76–78, 105
Babylon, 48, 91, 97–98, 105, 112, 114, 135, 137–40, 337, 340–41
wickedness, 137–38
Baldwin, J., 136
Balz, H., 342
Banks, R. J., 267
Baptism, 162–63, 178, 281, 284, 286–87, 299, 303
Barnabas, 229
Barrett, C. K., 318
Bassler, J. M., 271
Bathsheba, 156, 157
Bauckham, R., 344
Bauer, D. R., 159, 164
Baumgartner, W., 21
Baur, F. C., 269
Beale, G. K., 333, 334
Beasley-Murray, G. R., 172, 195, 196
Beast, 339–40
Beatitudes, 164–69

Beginning, 306–7
Beker, J. C., 271
Best, E., 310, 312
Bethlehem, 159
Beuken, W. A. M., 116, 122
Billerbeck, P., 163
Bird, P. A., 18, 19
Blessings, 28, 34–35, 54, 164
Body
   earthly, 290
   natural, 287
   resurrection, 290–91
   spiritual, 287
Body of Christ, 282–84, 301–2, 303
Bowers, W. P., 259, 262
Bowker, John, 199
Branch, 86
Braun, M. A., 230
Brawley, R. L., 211
Bride of Christ, 303
Brown, R. E., 255
Bruce, F. F., 226, 291
Bultmann, R., 191
Burnett, F. W., 175
Burney, C. F., 306
Byrne, B., 276

Caird, G. B., 304, 305
Calvin, J., 257
Canaan
   conquest, 19
   and the garden, 29
   gods of, 76–77
   heavenly, 55, 323
   new, 224
   as sanctuary, 25
Caragounis, C. C., 143, 297
Carlson, R. A., 67, 70
Carroll, J. T., 208
Carroll, R. P., 132, 134
Casey, M., 143
Chaos, 16–17, 42, 82, 94, 277, 334, 339
   city, 93
   dragon, 40–41
   sea, 40
Charismatic, 59
Charles, R. H., 343
Children of God, 237
Childs, Brevard, 48
Chilton, B. D., 187
Christ (title), 156–57, 195, 250
Christianity:
   continuation of Israel, 278
   and Judaism, 229–30, 232–33, 265, 269

Church, 12, 172–73, 214, 266–68, 281, 282, 296, 298, 301–3, 307–8
   and Israel, 225–26
   unity, 302–3
Circumcision, 100, 178, 228, 263, 294
City of God, 93, 105. *See also* Jerusalem; Zion
City on a hill, 166–67
Clark, D. J., 165
Clark, W. M., 27
Cleansing, 162, 244
Clifford, R. J., 82, 113, 122
Cloud, 86, 311–12
Collins, J. J., 131, 143
Combrink, H. J. B., 157
Comfort, 111–12
Community, 204
Conditional immortality, 26
Conquest, 53, 105–8
Consummation, 188
Cosmologies, in ancient Near East, 16, 40, 41, 42
Covenant, 10, 30–32, 39, 43, 46–47, 84, 92, 240
   code, 46–47
   conditionality, 43, 71
   and kingship, 63, 64–65, 69
   of peace, 121, 123
   promissory, 43
   renewal, 130–31, 160, 161, 182–83
   See also New covenant; Sinai covenant
Cranfield, C. E. B., 276
Creation, 15–18, 42
   completion, 23
   continuance, 31
   goodness, 20
   hope, 276–77
   "perfected," 20–22
   purpose, 12, 307, 334–35
   and redemption, 42, 308, 334, 335
   restoration, 297
Cross, 173, 191, 247
Culpepper, R. A., 237
Curses, 27–29, 34–35, 54, 131
Cyrus of Persia, 114–15, 118, 119, 145–46

Dahl, N. A., 230
Dalton, W. J., 327
Darius I, 145
Darkness, 298
David, 62, 63–64, 66–73, 69–70, 150, 159–60
Davidic covenant, 43, 70–72, 98–99, 122

Davidic kingship, 37, 41, 70–71, 87–88, 90–91, 107, 155, 156–57, 158, 185–86, 196, 227
Davids, P. H., 317, 326
Davies, P. R., 136
Davies, W. D., 164
Day, J., 40
Day of Atonement, 272, 322
Day of the Lord, 94, 108–9, 119, 130, 131, 143, 176, 179, 217, 312–13, 327, 343
De Boer, M. C., 284, 285
de Jonge, M., 243
Death, 149, 286–88, 290, 291–92, 331, 343
    spiritual, 342
Decalogue. *See* Ten Commandments
Decay, 20–22
Defilement, 138
Deidun, T. J., 295
Delcor, M., 149
Delitzsch, F., 24
Demonic, 339
Determinism, 132, 135
Diaspora, 326
Disciples, commissioning, 177–78
Discipleship, 200
Disembodiment, 291
Disorder, 313, 339
    of Babel, 34
    during time of judges, 59
    See also Chaos
Divine warrior, 40, 42, 110, 129
Dodd, C. H., 195, 241
Dominion, 19–20, 22, 25–26, 29
    and kingship, 73
Donaldson, T. L., 163
Donfried, K. P., 269
Dreams, 138–40
Dualism
    in apocalyptic, 132, 135
    in Paul, 260–61
Duff, N. J., 261
Dumbrell, W. J., 30–31, 43, 166
Dunn, J. D. G., 262, 271
Durham, J. I., 46

Earthquakes, 174
Ecclesiology. *See* Church
Eden, 23–26, 29, 49, 54, 55, 73, 82, 104, 106, 277, 323
    new, 110
    recaptured, 102
Egypt, 19, 24, 62, 90, 160
El, 41, 82, 142
Election, 44–45, 60, 64, 86, 172, 278, 297, 338

Eli, 60–61
Elijah, 76–78, 130–31, 161, 182–83, 201, 208, 213, 227, 338
Elisha, 213
Elliott, J. H., 327
Elliott, N., 268, 271
Empires, 140–41
Endurance, 326
Entropy, 21
Enuma Elish, 16, 40, 41
Eschatological Jerusalem. *See* New Jerusalem
Eschatology
    broader meaning, 9
    and ethics, 326
    future, 274, 280, 284, 305
    Jewish, 227, 260
    and kingship, 72
    narrower meaning, 9
    New Testament, 49
    Old Testament, 48–49
    overrealized, 280, 284
    realized, 274, 292, 296, 305, 310
    universal, 83–84
Essenes, 186
Eternal life, 247
Ethics, 326
Ethnos, 175
Evil, 17, 21–22
Exile, 84, 87, 97–98, 99, 110, 146–47, 156, 159, 186, 212, 276
    return from, 127–28
Exodus, 105–8, 224
    goal, 43–44
    as new creation, 42
    and redemption, 41
Exorcism, 189–90

Faith, 136, 265, 293–94
Faithfulness, 92, 116, 166, 323
Fall, 21–22, 23, 26–29, 30, 183, 276–77
False teachers, 315–16, 326, 328–29, 333
Feast of First Fruits, 53
Feast of Tabernacles, 248
Fee, G. D., 287
Feinberg, J. S., 327
Feinberg, P. D., 147
Fertility, 25, 110, 123
Fiorenza, E., 44, 45, 332
Fire, 86, 162, 223
Firstborn, 325
Fitzmyer, J. A., 191
Flesh, 109, 294
Flood, 31, 32, 327
Fokkelman, J. P., 32, 36

Foreigners, 123–24
Forestell, J. T., 254, 256
Forgiveness, 80, 84, 101–2, 162, 195, 258, 271
Four (number), 141
Four winds, 141–42
Fourteen (number), 157
France, R. T., 189, 201
Frankfort, H., 67
Franklin, E., 209, 215, 222

Gabriel (angel), 143, 144–45, 208
Gap theory, 16
Garden of Eden. *See* Eden
Gaston, L., 215, 217
Genre, 131, 135
Gentiles, 52, 95, 102, 110, 116, 117, 124, 159, 175, 186, 209, 217, 220–21, 226, 230, 232, 233–34, 277–80, 346
    age of, 137
    and Israel, 315
    mission to, 229–32
    Paul's mission to, 262, 263
    reconciliation with Jews, 296–98, 302
Giblin, H. C., 216
Gideon, 57–58
Gilgamesh epic, 24
Gillman, J. A., 290
Glorification, 252
Glory, 239, 252
God
    blessed, 297
    changelessness, 114
    control of history, 107, 132, 138, 141, 150
    dealings with nations, 113–14
    faithfulness, 131
    grace, 50
    kingship, 40, 42, 113
    lordship, 46, 117
    patience, 328
    purposes in creation, 334–35
    rest, 22–23
    righteousness, 122, 270–71
    shepherd, 40
    sovereignty, 16, 17, 44, 47–48, 53, 113, 118, 139, 141, 160, 164, 185, 187, 188
    vengeance, 217
    wisdom, 113
    wrath, 270–71, 292, 309
Gog, 105, 337, 343
Golden calf, 48, 49, 52, 238, 240
Goldingay, J., 144
Gospel, 181–82, 183–84, 269–71, 285, 341

Gowan, D. E., 92, 152
Grace, 258, 261, 297
Greece, 140, 144
Grudem, W. A., 302
Guelich, R. A., 165, 181
Gundry, R. H., 313
Guthrie, D., 335, 344

Hahn, F., 191
Hanson, P. D., 129, 130, 133–34
Hare, D. R. A., 165
Harlot, 340
Harris, M. J., 291, 292
Harvey, A. E., 214
Hasel, G. F., 87
Hatton, H. J., 165
Hays, R. H., 273
Healing, 171, 190, 197
Heart, 100–101, 104
Hemer, C. J., 343
Herod, 159–60
Hezekiah, 81, 89
High priest, 320–21
Hill, C. E., 286
History, 150, 335–36
    apocalyptic perspective, 132–34, 140–41
    divine control, 188
    and eschatology, 149
    goal, 9
    human control, 140
    progress, 134
Hittites, 62
Hoehner, H. W., 146
Holiness, 48, 122, 303, 327
Holladay, W. L., 91
Hollenberg, D. E., 116
Holy of Holies, 48, 321
Holy Spirit, 17, 18, 63–64, 91–92, 102, 109, 115, 162, 163, 189–90, 197, 219–25, 257–58, 290, 302–3
    earnest, 315
    fruits, 295
    and kingdom, 188, 219, 302
    in ministry of Jesus, 183, 211–12, 241
    and new birth, 244
    Paraclete, 254–56
    and servant, 124
Holy war, 66, 109, 311
Hooker, M. D., 194, 201
Hope, 80, 111, 152, 303, 314
    apocalyptic, 132–33, 136, 147
    of creation, 276–77
    and loss, 174–75
Hopelessness, 298

Hort, F. J., 172
Hughes, P. E., 318
Hultgren, A. J., 254
Humankind, 194–95
    creation, 18–20
    dominion, 277
    rest, 23
Hunter, A. V., 79
Hutter, M., 24

Idolatry, 51, 61, 228
Ignorance, 298
Image
    of Christ, 346
    of God, 18–20, 140
Immanuel, 89, 178
Immortality, 26, 291, 346
"In Christ," 280–82
Indicative and imperative, 315
Individualism, 59, 97, 102, 119, 152
Inheritance, 53, 122
Institutionalism, 136
Integrity, 165
Intermediate state, 291
Intuitiveness, 18
Irenaeus, 28
Isaac, 35
Ishmael, 35
Israel, 33, 49, 86, 225, 233, 278
    and Adam, 10, 29, 45, 54
    and the church, 225–26, 279
    disobedience, 11
    election, 76, 102, 265
    failure, 275
    and Gentiles, 315
    holy nation, 240
    hope, 52, 103, 230, 234
    judgment, 172, 233
    obedience, 103
    people, 33–34
    priestly kingdom, 47, 240
    rejection, 167, 258
    response to Jesus, 169–71, 227–28
    restoration, 232, 258
    salvation, 207, 277–80
    treasured possession, 44–45
    vocation, 39, 43–46, 155, 178

Jacob, 36, 157
James, 230–31
Jeremias, Joachim, 162, 172, 302
Jeremias, Jörg, 116
Jerusalem, 10, 43, 66–69, 71, 86, 92–94, 95,
    159, 295

destruction in A.D. 70, 170, 175–76, 185,
    201–2, 215–17, 226, 234, 314, 328,
    329
fall during exile, 10, 97, 103, 276
heavenly, 55, 296
punishment, 78
rejection, 80–81
restoration, 118, 123, 125, 127, 226–27,
    296
under Solomon, 75–76
world center, 128–30, 187
Jerusalem Council, 231
Jervell, J., 226, 232, 233
Jesus Christ
    ascension, 214, 219, 222, 225, 252, 254
    baptism, 160, 162–63, 183, 189, 211
    birth, 89, 155–58
    crucifixion, 251, 252–53
    death, 11, 102, 177–78, 214, 254,
        272–73, 331
    descent into hell, 300
    entry into Jerusalem, 174–75, 251–52
    exaltation, 252, 299–300, 304
    fulfilment of Old Testament, 178, 210
    genealogy, 156–58
    goal of creation, 307
    High Priest, 320–23
    humanity, 288, 319
    humiliation, 304, 319–20
    image of God, 307
    incarnation, 237–38, 239, 245, 304,
        306–7
    king, 73, 181, 256
    lamb, 241, 334–35
    light of the world, 248–49, 250
    Lion of Judah, 335
    lordship, 225, 304, 311, 319
    messiah, 10, 64, 121, 170–72, 177–78,
        179, 207, 248–50, 262
    messianic secret, 197–98
    ministry, 164, 172, 210, 238
    miracles, 200, 213
    and Moses, 247
    as new Israel, 178–79, 205
    post-resurrection appearances, 218–19,
        222
    preaching, 214–15
    as prophet, 212–14, 250
    resurrection, 177, 203, 225, 251, 256,
        285–86
    role in creation, 306–7
    root of David, 335
    second Adam, 10, 11, 275–76, 277, 305,
        307, 343

second coming, 275, 299, 304, 308,
    309–10, 313, 323, 325, 326, 329, 339
sonship, 240–41, 245
suffering, 165, 177, 198, 201, 204, 226,
    319, 328
supremacy, 306–8, 318
teaching, 171, 200, 212
temptations, 163–64, 178, 183, 189,
    190, 210–11
titles, 181
transfiguration, 174, 201, 213, 227
trial, 203–4
unity with Father, 249–50, 319
wilderness experience, 160, 163–64,
    183
Jewish law, 223, 263–65, 306
Jews
    reconciliation with Gentiles, 296–98,
        302
    relationship with Gentiles, 292–94
John the Baptist, 160, 161–63, 170, 175,
    181–83, 186, 188, 209, 213, 241
Johnson, L. T., 213, 215
Jonah, 171
Joseph, 36–37, 157–58
Joseph (father of Jesus), 157
Josianic reforms, 94, 98, 100
Jotham, 58, 86
Jubilee, 211–12
Judah, blessing, 36–37
Judaism, 263–65, 265
    and Christianity, 229–30, 232–33,
        262–63, 265, 269
    intertestamental, 288, 296, 298
    response to Jesus, 243, 245
    use of law, 265
Judas Maccabeus, 174
Judges, 57–59, 61, 65
Judgment, 79–81, 84, 90, 92–95, 103,
    108–10, 115, 139, 142–44, 161–62,
    176–77, 179, 195, 204, 218, 247, 309,
    312–13, 326, 328, 335–36, 342, 343
Juel, D., 203, 204
Justice, 115–16, 124
Justification, 263–64, 265, 269, 274–75,
    294, 315

Kaiser, W. C., 91
Käsemann, E., 261, 323
Keck, L. E., 184
Keil, C. F., 24
Kelly, J. N. D., 316
Kim, S., 192, 193
King, 61, 90, 103
Kingdom, 45, 215, 217

of priests, 45, 46
Kingdom of God, 9, 12, 45–46, 94, 102,
    105, 110, 128, 139–40, 141, 144, 148,
    151, 152, 163, 179, 181, 183, 187,
    196–97, 198, 200–201, 302, 340–41
    keys, 173
    modeled in temple, 238
    and Spirit, 219
    teaching of Jesus, 164–65, 184–89
Kingship, 57–59, 61–62, 99, 113
    and covenant, 63, 64–65, 69
    divine, 87–88
    and eschatology, 72
    messianic, 64, 73, 87, 90–92
    and prophecy, 66
Knierim, R. P., 66
Knowledge, of good and evil, 26–27
Köhler, L., 21
Kourie, C. E. T., 281
Krodel, G., 229, 232, 233

Lamb, 336, 341, 344–45, 346
    of God, 334–35
    marriage supper, 341
Land, 37, 97
Last Adam, 109, 260, 287–88. *See also*
    Jesus Christ, second Adam
Last days, 81, 83–84, 141, 220–21, 224, 271,
    315–16, 318, 326, 327–28
Last Supper, 218
Law, 167, 231, 240, 265–66, 293–94
    and Spirit, 223
    See also Jewish law; Mosaic law
Lazarus, 251
Leadership, 87
Levenson, J. D., 82, 105
Leviathan, 94
Lewis, C. S., 22
Liberation, 297
Libertarianism, 284
Light, 165–69
Lincoln, 223, 284, 285, 287, 288, 296, 300,
    302, 305
Lindars, 258
Locusts, plague, 109–10
Logos, 235, 236, 237–41, 242, 245
Lohfink, N. H., 29
Lord's Supper, 282–83, 284
Love, 295
Luther, M., 263–64

Maccabean revolt, 148, 150
McCarter, P. K., 68
McConville, J. G., 50
McCurley, F. R., 41

McKane, W. S., 132
Maddox, R., 172, 214
Magog, 343
Malamat, A., 58
Man of lawlessness, 313–14
Manna, 246
Mantic wisdom, 135, 141
Marduk, 16, 40, 41, 48, 112
Marriage, and covenant, 121
Marshall, I. H., 187, 217, 218, 219
Martin, R. P., 198
Martyrdom, 337–38
Mary, 156–57
Materialism, 130, 333
Mearns, C. L., 314
Mediator, 50, 101, 240
Meeks, W. A., 204, 256
Meier, J. P., 168, 328
Melchizedek, 211, 321
Mercy seat, 272
Mesopotamia, 19, 24, 40, 41, 42, 48, 62,
  116
Messiah, 28, 37, 60, 62–63, 92, 120–21,
  147, 191, 193–94, 195–98, 197,
  208–10, 214
  and Mosaic law, 293–95
  titles, 90–91
Mettinger, T. N. D., 19
Meyer, B. F., 161, 169, 172, 187, 189, 196
Meyer, M., 166
Michael (angel), 143, 148–49
Michaels, J. R., 250
Miller, P. D., 53
Minear, P. S., 334, 345
Miracles, 190, 197
Moberly, R. W. L., 50
Moessner, D. P., 233
Moloney, F. J., 254
Monarchy, 58–59, 60, 106
Monsengwo-Pasinya, L., 36
Moore, A. L., 328
Moore, G. F., 265
Mosaic covenant. *See* Sinai covenant
Mosaic law, 46, 266, 292–93
Moses, 201, 227, 338
  call, 39
  glory, 289–90
  mediator, 49–51, 238–40
  typology, 77
  veiling, 51, 289
Mot, 76
Moule, C. F. D., 192, 304
Mount Carmel, 77
Mount of Olives, 176–77
Mountain, 41, 82, 140, 163–64

Mulholland, M. R., 331, 333, 340
Mystery, 297–98
Myth, 133

Nathan, 69
Nathanael, 242
Nation, 45, 52
  Israel as, 33–34
Nationalism, 97, 117, 136, 187, 191, 200
Natural-spiritual distinction, 287–89
Nazareth, 160
Nebuchadnezzar, 37, 71, 97–98, 137–40,
  192
New age, 10, 11, 101, 108, 123–24, 125,
  127, 224–25, 260–61, 271, 273, 275,
  281, 289, 317, 325
New birth, 237, 243–44
New community, 237, 238, 240, 258
New covenant, 31, 43, 97, 98–102, 104,
  110, 116, 117, 121, 151, 169, 201,
  240, 289, 296, 321–24
  consummation, 336, 344
  inwardness, 100
New creation, 29, 31, 33, 81, 83, 102, 109,
  123, 124, 184, 236, 269, 274, 278, 306,
  308, 344, 346
New Eden, 10, 122, 345
New exodus, 99, 102, 103, 112, 112–13,
  113, 119, 123, 151, 156, 160, 240, 337,
  339
New Israel, 104, 121, 159
New Jerusalem, 10, 32, 79–81, 92, 102, 108,
  124, 129, 149, 274, 340, 343–45
New life, 244
New man, 301
New temple, 103, 108, 130, 173
Neyrey, J. H., 218, 243-
Nicholson, G. C., 244, 246
Nickelsburg, G. W. E., 148
Nicodemus, 243–45
Noah, 121, 327
Noahic covenant, 30–31
Nolan, B. M, 159
Nolland, J., 212, 230
Now and not-yet, 188, 267, 299, 300, 301,
  303–4, 310, 315

Obedience, 103, 104, 265
O'Donovan, O., 336, 339, 340
Oikos, 328
Old covenant. *See* Sinai covenant
Onias III, 146
Order, 334, 346
  and chaos, 335
  of creation, 26, 31

and redemption, 42
Osborne, G. R., 136
O'Toole, R. F., 231

Pain, 20–22, 28
Pancaro, S., 240, 242
Parables, 171, 177, 187, 198–200
Parousia, 158, 226, 284, 286, 290–91, 292, 309–12, 313, 316
  See also Jesus Christ, second coming
Parsons, M. C., 233
Parsons, Michael, 281
Passover, 40
Passover Lamb, 241
Patai, R., 172
Patriarchs, 35
Patte, D., 171
Patterson, J. W., 21
Paul
  call, 261–62, 263, 264
  conversion, 229
  Damascus road experience, 260, 261, 263, 266
  mission, 229–32, 233–34
Peace, 68, 92, 104–5, 315
Pentecost, 11, 109, 162, 223–25, 257–58
  of Gentiles, 229
Perfection, 315, 318, 323–25
Persecution, 165, 170, 317, 327, 328, 331, 333, 336
Perseverance, 304, 318
Persia, 140, 144, 148
Peter, 172–74, 224–27, 229, 230–31
Peterson, D. G., 320, 323
Pfitzner, V. C., 318
Pharaoh, 160
Pharisees, 169, 185, 215, 216, 243–44
Philistines, 60–61, 65–66, 69
Phillips, A., 124
Philo, 185, 298
Pilgrimage, 124, 317, 318, 325
  to Zion, 76, 83, 95
Plagues, 337, 339
Plevnik, J., 311, 312
Poor, 124, 165, 212
Powers. *See* Principalities and powers
Predestination, 297
Pride, 85
Priesthood, 101, 106–7
Prince, 103
Principalities and powers, 260–61, 298–301, 305, 306
Pritchard, J. B., 24
Promise, 37, 53
  and law, 293

Promised land, 39, 40, 41, 47, 49, 53–54, 54, 69, 72, 92, 98, 99, 104, 167, 239, 317, 318, 324, 325
Prophet, prophecy, 65–66, 78, 101, 224, 227
  and apocalyptic, 132, 133–34, 136, 331
  eschatology, 10, 83–84
  messianic, 89
  Mosaic office, 62
  theology, 43
Propitiation, 272
Providence, 139, 337
Przbylski, B., 169

Qumran, 162, 163, 172, 185, 186, 193, 196, 211, 300, 311

Rabbi Akiba, 142
Rachel, 160
Rahab, 156, 157
Rainbow, 31, 334
Reason, 18, 236
Recapitulation, 341, 343
Reconciliation, 273–74, 292, 302, 303, 308, 325, 346
Redemption, 9, 43, 271–72, 297, 307
Remembering, 101
Remnant, 52, 76–78, 79, 80, 85, 86–87, 90, 94, 95, 109, 119, 124, 130, 186, 230, 233–34, 278, 279
Repentance, 87, 131, 161, 182–83, 189
Rest, 48–49, 54, 122, 239, 323–24
  for David, 68–69, 72, 324
  for Solomon, 75
Restoration, 43, 73, 79, 91–92, 94, 103–5, 106, 110, 225, 232, 335
Resurrection, 93, 104, 149, 171, 185, 186, 247, 250–51, 285–89, 291–92, 312, 342–43
  in apocalyptic, 135
  bodily, 286–89, 291
  first, 342
  future, 280, 284, 286, 310
  second, 342
  spiritual, 292
Revelation, 41, 131–32, 240–41
Richard, E., 233
Righteousness, 92, 122, 139, 169, 255, 293–94
River of life, 345
River of paradise, 82
Robinson, D. W. B., 278, 279, 296, 314
Robinson, G., 23, 48
Robinson, J. A. T., 226
Robinson, James, 190

Roman Empire, 140, 337, 340
Rome, 295
Ruth, 156, 157

Sabbath, 15, 22–23, 48–49, 170, 195, 324,
    335, 342
Sacrifice, 321, 334–35
Saints, 143–44
Sakenfeld, K. D., 50
Salt, 165–69
Salvation, 79, 95, 108, 218, 225, 229, 230,
    235, 248, 278, 315
    future, 275
    unity, 246
    universal, 169
Salvation history, 33, 346
Samaria, Samaritans, 229, 243, 245–46
Samuel, 60–61, 63, 65–66
Sanctification, 265, 274, 294
Sanctuary, 25, 41–42, 54, 322
Sanders, E. P., 264–65
Sanders, J. T., 233
Sarah, 35
Sarna, N. H.,35
Satan, 148, 189–90, 210, 212, 217, 253,
    260, 338–39, 341, 343
Saul (king), 62–66
Sawyer, J. F. A., 93
Schaberg, J., 192
Schnackenburg, R., 237, 246, 248, 254
Schneider, G., 342
Schreiner, T., 293, 294
Schweitzer, A., 281
Sea, 40, 141–42, 339
Seccombe, D. P., 212
Second exodus. *See* New exodus
Second temple. *See* New temple
Seed, 27–28
Seleucids, 144, 148
Self-forgetfulness, 169
Sermon on the Mount, 164, 170
Serpent, 26, 27–28
Servant, 84, 111–23, 149, 178, 241, 275
    active obedience, 118–19
    death, 121–23, 125
    exaltation, 120
    and Messiah, 115
    suffering, 118–19, 123, 227
Seven (number), 147
Seventy weeks of years, 144–47
Sexual immorality, 333
Shades, 93
Sharp, J. R., 321
Shepherd, 40, 103, 113, 249–50
Shiloh, 60–61, 69

Shinar, 137–38
Simeon, 209, 234
Sin, 101–2, 263–64, 294, 298
    as power, 261
    spread, 32–33
Sinai, 240–41
Sinai covenant, 39, 42–47, 50, 51–52, 61,
    72, 99–101, 104, 289, 292–94, 295,
    311, 322, 323
    and New Covenant, 296
Sleep, 149
Snaith, N. H., 116
Snodgrass, K. R., 274
Soares Prabhu, G. M., 158
Sodom and Gomorrah, 35
Solomon, 62, 70–71, 75, 150
Son of Abraham, 156, 158
Son of David, 156, 157, 158, 179, 191
Son of God, 42, 155, 159, 163, 179, 191,
    193, 204, 205
Son of man, 25, 142–43, 171–72, 173–74,
    176–77, 178, 179, 191–95, 204, 214,
    218, 242, 245, 247–48, 253, 333, 339
Song of Hannah, 60
Song of the Sea, 40, 42, 339
Song of Simeon, 209
Song of the Vineyard, 94
Song of Zechariah, 208
Sonship, 72, 237, 240–41
Soteriology, 12
Spirit and flesh, 101, 109
Spiritual gifts, 283, 303
Spiritual warfare, 298–301
Spiritual weapons, 300
Stendahl, K., 157, 159, 263–64
Stenning, J. F., 203
Stephen, 227–28
Sterility, 123
Stewardship, 29, 277
Stoics, 236
Strack, H. L., 163
Stuhlmueller, C., 112
Suffering, 20–22, 28, 103, 165, 173,
    191–92, 193, 195, 217–18, 290, 317,
    328, 334–35, 336
    of Jerusalem, 112
Sumerian myths, 24
Suzerain, 43
Sweeney, M.A., 85, 91
Symbolism, 136, 141, 147, 331
Syncretism, 76
Syria, 62

Tabernacle, 47–48, 50, 53, 238–39
Tamar, 156, 157

Tannehill, R. C., 228
Targum, 120–21, 173, 185, 203
Temple, 10, 41–42, 44, 47, 49, 67–71, 83,
        97, 98, 105–8, 137, 163–64, 174–75,
        203–5, 238, 301, 302, 344
    destruction, 110
    rebuilding, 118, 127–29, 151
    See also New temple
Temple Vision, 103, 105–8
Ten Commandments, 46–47, 295
Tent, 290
Tent of meeting, 50
Theocracy, 42, 46
Theophany, 50, 54, 77–78, 239, 312
Thousand-year reign, 342
Thrones, 142
Tiamat, 40, 41
Tiede, D. L., 220, 223
Tödt, H. E., 192
Tongues, 285
Torah, 116, 124, 167, 276, 278, 308
Tower of Babel, 32–33, 137–38, 223, 345
    reversal, 85, 95, 346
Transformation, 289, 290–91, 305, 309
Tree of knowledge, 24
Tree of life, 24, 106, 172
Tribulation, 256, 337–38
Trilling, W., 167
Trites, A. A., 247
Trumpet, 311
Truth, 240, 255
Turner, M. M. B., 211–12, 223, 224
Two ages, 133, 260–61, 272–73, 280, 291
Tyson, J. B., 233

Ulfgard, H., 336

Valley of dry bones, 104
van Unnik, W. C., 335
Vanhoye, A., 320, 321, 322
Vannoy, J.R., 63, 64
Vellanickal, M., 235, 236
Vermes, G., 191, 196
Vindication, 143–44, 193, 204, 217, 229,
        242
Virgin, 158
Vocation, 167
von Rad, G., 91, 134
Vorster, W. S., 27

Wainwright, A. W., 226
Wallace, H. N., 24

Walsh, J. T., 26
Ward, J. M., 120
Ware, P., 311
Watson, F. S., 263
Watts, R. E., 119
Weber, Max, 59
Weinfeld, M., 24, 43, 48
Weiss, M., 108
Wenham, D., 202
Wenham, G., 19, 54
Westcott, B. F., 257–58
Westermann, C., 19, 20
White, R. F., 341, 343
Wickedness, 336
Wild beasts, 141–42, 183
Wilderness, 160, 163–64, 178
Williams, D. J., 314
Williams, S. K., 270
Williamson, H. G. M., 150
Wilson, A., 111, 117–18, 121, 122
Wilson, S. G., 221, 230, 231, 315
Wind, 223, 244
Wisdom, 18, 137, 166, 236, 297, 307, 308
    of Solomon, 76
Wisdom movement, 134–35
Woll, D., 254
Word of God, 112–13, 198–99
Works righteousness, 274, 278
World, 236, 260
Worldviews, 139
Worship, 25, 45, 47–48, 49, 60, 85, 108,
        125, 239, 318
Wrede, William, 197
Wright, N. T., 106, 175, 178, 179, 185, 186,
        189, 193, 200, 204, 205, 274, 275, 276,
        288, 309

Yahweh, 39
Yamm, 40, 42
Yates, R., 298

Zadok, 106–7
Zeus, 148
Ziggurat, 41
Zion, 79, 81–86, 93–94, 105, 122–23,
        172–73, 339, 344
    eschatology, 140
    inviolability, 167
    restoration, 124, 125
    reversal of Babel, 85
    world center, 166
Zion theology, 75–76, 95

Index of Scripture

Genesis

1–2   10, 11, 12, 22, 32, 37, 45, 277, 346
1–3   9, 15, 29
1–12   275
1–2:4a   15
1:1   16, 236, 306, 307
1:2   16, 17, 141
1:3   33
1:3–31   17
1:26–28   18, 19, 31, 140, 195, 205, 225, 286
1:26–27   306, 319
1:26   25
1:28   31
1:31   20, 21, 22
2   22, 23, 26, 29, 41, 49
2–3   25, 320
2:1–3   17
2:1–4a   22, 49
2:2–3   23
2:2   324
2:4b–3:24   23
2:7   104, 257, 287
2:8a   25
2:9–17   25
2:15   26
2:16–17   26
2:18–25   26
3   26
3–11   33, 34, 73, 344
3:5   26
3:6–7   27

3:14   34
3:14–19   24, 27
3:16   28
3:16–19   25
3:17   29, 34
3:17–19   277
3:18–19   28
3:22   25, 27
3:23   26
3:24   24
4:11   34
5:3   18
5:29   28, 34
6:2   237
6:2–4   326
6:17–18   30–32
8:1   101
8:9–12   163
8:21   31, 328
9:1   31
9:6   18
9:7   31
9:8–17   30, 31
9:9   31
9:10   31
9:11   31
9:13   31, 334
9:17   31
9:25   34
10   214
11   33, 345
11:1–9   32–33, 223
11:2   137
11:3   34
11:4   32, 33
11:7   85
11:10–32   32
12:1–3   33, 35, 52, 72, 293

12:2   34, 45, 70, 275
14:18   320
15:1–17   35
15:18   35, 70
17:2   275
17:4–6   35
17:7   31, 275
17:9–10   44
17:19   31
17:19–21   35
17:21   31
18:1–19   121
18:18   35
21:22–23   30
22:2   240
22:15–18   36
22:16   240
22:17   121
22:17–18   275
22:18   35
25:19–35:29   36
26:2–5   36
26:4   35
26:24   36
26:26–33   30
27:27–28   28
27:35   242
28:3   275
28:10–17   36
28:12   242
28:13–15   36
28:14   35
30:23–24   36
31:43–54   30
32   36
34:3   111
35:9–12   36
35:11–12   275

37–50   36, 157
41:57   36
45:1–11   36
47:27   275
48:4   275
49:1   83
49:10   36, 37, 196
49:11   216

Exodus

1–4   39
1:12   39
2:24   44
3:12   43
3:13–15   50, 52
3:14   239
4:22   72, 163, 237, 307, 325
6:1–8   52
6:4   31
6:4–5   44
6:7   100, 104, 111
7:8–13:16   40
7:14–9:35   337
10:21–29   337
14   40
15   42
15:1–18   40, 339
15:13   121
15:17   25, 41, 47, 84, 118, 203, 238
15:17–18   185
15:18   42
19   26
19–20   50
19–23   47
19–24   43

19–34   51, 52, 289
19:1–3a   43
19:3–6   130
19:3b–6   43, 52,
   109, 120
19:4   337
19:4–6   45, 328
19:5   46
19:5–6   29, 44,
   101, 333, 334,
   346
19:6   47, 72, 104,
   122, 240, 332
19:10–18   311
20   240
20–23   46, 293
20:8–11   48
21:1   46
23:20   41, 182
24   238
24:1   201
24:2   201
24:10   334
24:15–16   48
24:16   201
24:18   77
25–31   47
25:8   40
25:9   47, 105
28:17–20   25
28:38   346
30:35   166
31:12–17   48
32   48, 49, 275
32:25–29   77
32:32   142
33–34   49, 50, 240
33:1–2   50
33:3b   50
33:7–11   50, 201
33:12–17   50
33:14   238
33:17–20   239
33:18–23   50
33:22   77
34   48, 105, 238
34:1   51
34:1–7   50
34:6   121
34:8–9   50
34:10   50, 51
34:11–26   51
34:27   51
34:28b   51
34:29–35   51, 289

35–40   48, 53
35:1–3   48
35:3   22
40:34   238

Leviticus
2:13   166
10:17   121
17   230
25:8–10   211
25:43   19
25:46   19
25:53   19
26:9   31
26:12   100, 111

Numbers
6   160
10:35–36   69
11:29   101, 109,
   224
18:1   121
18:19   166
18:23   121
23:21   185
24:7   185
24:17   159
32:22   19
32:29   19
34:1–12   107

Deuteronomy
3:20   54
6:4–6   100
7:6   44
7:14   53
7:15   53
8:2   163
8:7   53
8:12–14   68
8:16   163
8:18   31
8:24–27   58
9:19   324
11:11–12   53
11:17   28
11:18   100
11:24   70
12:2–4   54
12:5–11   75
12:5–12   54
12:11   69, 71
14:2   44
17:14–20   61
18:15   227

23:1–8   123
25:19   54
26   53, 54
26:18   44
27:15–26   28
28   54
28:11   28
30:6   100
32:28   34
32:35–36   217
32:39   217
32:43   319
33:2   106
33:3   143
33:29   164

Joshua
5:14   149
18:1   107

Judges
2:20   34
3:27   311
5:4–5   106
5:20   149
6:34   17, 311
7:15–25   90
8:18   57
8:22–28   57–58
9   58
11:34   240
14:6   17
19:3   111
21:25   58, 59

1 Samuel
1–3   69
1–7   60
1:19–20   101
4   68
4–6   61
4:8   60
5:6   60
6:6   60
7   61
7:13   69
8   62
8–12   61, 63
8:16   216
9   62
9–12   63
10–11   62
10:1   63
10:8   65, 66
10:10   63

10:12   64
11   63
11:11–12   63
11:14   65
11:14–15   64
11:15   65
12   65
12:8   41
13   65, 66
13–15   65
13:3   311
13:14   62
14   66
15   66
16 - 2 Sam.5   66
16:1   63
16:1–13   115
16:13   63
16:14   63
17   63, 64
17:45   186
17:45–47   66
17:55   148
25:30   62
31   66

2 Samuel
2:1–4   66
5:1–5   66
5:2   62, 69, 159
5:7–9   66
5:17–25   66
6   66, 67
6:1–15   70
6:13   68
6:15   68
6:17   68
6:20–23   68
6:21   62
7   67, 68, 69, 70,
   71, 72
7:8   62
7:12–13   208
7:13   203
7:14   90, 237, 319,
   320, 344
7:16   89, 166
11:3   157
12:24   112
14:7   116
19:7   111
23:1   91
23:5   71
23:34   157
24   60

1 Kings

1–11 75
1:19 148
1:33 216
1:35 62
2:4 71
4:20 75
4:34 76
5:3 70
5:4–5 75
8:10 75
8:25 71
9:4–5 71
10 76
11:11 44
14:7 62
16:2 62
17–19 76
17:17–24 213
18:19 77
18:21 77, 161
18:29 77
18:30–32 77
18:38 77
18:40 77
18:45 77
19:2–3 77
19:4–8 77
19:9 77
19:10 77, 78
19:12 78
19:13 78
19:14 78
19:15–17 78
19:18 78
22:19 298

2 Kings

4:13 148
5 213
9:13 216
15:29 90
20:5 62
22 174
23:3 31
23:30 63
25:4 24
25:19 148
25:27–30 138

1 Chronicles

17:12 203
22:8 70
22:18 19

28:3 70
29:3 44

2 Chronicles

9 151
11:22 62
13:5 166
15:8 64
24:4 64
28:10 19
29–30 174
36:22–23 150, 151

Ezra

1–2 145
1:1–3 150
4:14 166
5:8–6:13 145
7:12–26 146

Nehemiah

2:1–8 146
3:15 24
5:5 19

Esther

8:11 148
9:16 148

Job

1:6 237
2:1 237, 298
5:17 164
7:12 16, 141
7:21 149
14:12 149
20:11 149
26:12 16, 141
33:4 17
38:7 237, 298

Psalms

2 338
2:4–7 82
2:7 90, 163, 183, 237, 319, 344
2:9 341
8 19
8:4–6 319
8:5 192
8:6–8 286
16:3 143
16:8–11 225
22:1 179
24:7–10 83

29:1 237
34:9 143
36:8–9 82
37:31 100
40:9 184
41:13 208
45:6 91
45:6–7 319
46:3 82
46:5 83
46:6 82
46:7 83
46:11 83
47 83, 118, 185
48:1–2 82
48:4–7 82
50 82
51:10, 17 100
56:8 142
68:8 106
68:11 184
68:18 300
68:29–33 118
68:30 141
69:28 142, 149
72:8–11 83
72:18 208
73:1 100
74:12–17 42
74:13 16, 141
74:19 141
76:2 83
76:3 82
76:5–8 82
78:10 44
78:54 25, 41
78:68 82
82 82
82:6 237, 250
89:3 115
89:5–7 82
89:5–12 42
89:6 237
89:6–8 40
89:9–10 41
89:19–37 41
89:26–27 90
89:27 307
89:29–32 71
89:33–37 71
93 42, 83, 185
93:3–4 16
93:5 82
95 323, 324
96–97 83

96–98 118
96–99 185
96:2 184
97:7 319
99 83
102:12–22 83
102:25–27 319
103:3–4 158
103:18 44
104:1–9 42
104:4 319
106:48 208
110:1 204, 225, 286, 319
110:4 72
114 161
118:22 178, 327
118:22–23 201
132 83
132:12 44, 71
132:13 82
135:4 44
135:21 208
137:9 216
139:7 17

Proverbs

3:18 24
8:22 306, 307
8:27–31 307
8:30 18
9:10 143
11:30 24
13:12 24
15:4 24
22:11 100
24:30–31 24
30:3 143
40:8 100

Ecclesiastes

2:8 44

Isaiah

1 84
1–39 80, 81, 87, 94, 110
1:2 163, 237
1:4 34
1:8 79
1:10–20 88
1:11–13a 80
1:15 80
1:18–20 80
1:21 94

1:24–26 87
1:25 162
1:29–30 85
2:1–4 84
2:2 82, 130
2:2–4 46, 76, 81,
    83, 85, 102, 116,
    118, 123, 151,
    159, 166
2:2–5 80
2:3–4 82
2:4 109
2:5–22 85
2:12–16 85
2:19–21 277
3 85
3–35 94
3:26 216
4:2–3 87
4:2–6 85, 86
4:3 149
4:4 100
5–12 92
5:1–7 94
5:5 24
6 200
6–9 88
6–11 87
6:1 87, 88
6:1–4 106
6:2–3 334
6:3 87, 88
6:4 87
6:5 88
6:8–13 88
6:8 82
6:9–10 198, 233,
    234, 253, 258
6:9–13 199
6:10 252
6:11 86
6:13 86, 87, 91
7–11 85, 89
7:1–3 89
7:1–9 87, 94
7:3 86
7:4 89
7:7–9 89
7:11–13 89
7:14 90
7:14–16 64, 158
7:14–17 89
7:15–25 90
8 90
8:14 327

9:1–7 64, 85, 90,
    91
9:8–10:4 91
9:25–26 100
10:5–34 91
10:6 33
10:20–23 87
10:22 278
10:27d–32 94
10:33–34 94
11 64, 90, 124
11:1–9 196
11:1 91, 160
11:2 91, 92
11:3 341
11:3b 92
11:4 333
11:4d 92
11:6–8 183
11:6–9 82, 92
11:9 83
11:10 92, 173
11:11–12 92
11:13–16 92
13 108
13–23 92
13:9–11 277
13:10 202
13:10–13 329
14:6 19
14:12–15 337
14:26–27 82
14:28–32 94
14:32 83
19:1 202
22:20–22 173
24–27 92, 93
24:1–6 93
24:10 94
24:14–16 93
24:17–20 93
24:19 329
24:21–23 93
25:1–5 93
25:6–10a 93
26:1–6 93
26:7–19 93
26:14 149
26:19 149
27:1 82, 94
27:2–6 94
27:7–8 94
27:9 94
27:12–13 94
27:13 311

28–35 94
28:5–6 87
28:16 83, 172,
    173, 327
29:1–4 94
29:5–8 94
29:18 249
30:15–17 87
30:27–33 94
31:1–9 94
31:33 100
32:13–14 94
32:15 212
33:17–24 94
33:21 82
34:4 202, 329
35 118
35:1–10 83
35:5 249
36–38 88
39 81
39:5–7 110
40–55 43, 64, 111,
    112, 113, 117,
    119, 120, 123,
    127, 151, 161,
    186, 227, 275
40–66 81, 87, 97,
    110, 125, 262
40:1–2 112, 113
40:1–11 81, 110,
    111, 116
40:3 161, 182, 184
40:3–5 112, 130
40:6–8 112
40:9–11 112, 113
40:12–41:29 115
40:12–48:22 113
40:18–31 114
40:27 115
41:1 115
41:1–4 114
41:4 333
41:5–7 114
41:8–13 114
41:8–9 119
41:9–10 117
41:11 117
41:14–20 114
41:17–20 118, 212
41:20 119
41:21–29 114
41:27 184
41:27–29 116
42:1 116, 163, 183

42:1–4 111, 113,
    115, 117, 123,
    171, 178, 261
42:1–9 119
42:2–3 116
42:4 116
42:5–9 117
42:6 84
42:7 249
42:12 118
42:16 112
43:10 220, 249
43:16–19 112
43:17 116
44:1 119
44:3–5 212
44:6 333
44:26 146
44:28 118, 146
45:1 146
45:4 119
45:4–5 118
45:13 118
45:14 117, 120
45:20–25 120
45:22 117
48:12 333
49 117
49–55 119
49:1 261
49:1–6 111
49:1–52:12 113
49:2 333
49:6 84, 220, 221,
    223, 261, 262,
    332
49:7 118
49:9–11 118
49:9c–11 112
49:13 212
49:23 117
49:26 117
50:4–9 111, 118
51:3 25
51:5 116
51:7 100
51:9 111
51:9–10 16
51:9–11 42, 133
51:10 112
51:15–16 329
51:17 111
52–53 118
52:7 113, 184,
    187, 211

52:10 113
52:13 118, 149
52:13–53:12 111
52:13–55:13 113
52:15 119
53 123
53:1 253, 258
53:1–9 119, 120
53:5 203
53:7 335
53:12 121, 227
54–55 118, 121, 123
54:1–18 296
54:2 122
54:5 303
54:10 104, 122
54:11a 122
54:11–12 345
54:11b–13 122
54:14–17 122
55 122
55:3–5 117
55:12–13 118, 123
56–66 111, 123, 133, 134
56:7 174
57:15 100
59:20 279
60–62 76, 83
60:1–6 178
60:10–22 124
61 124, 167, 212
61:1 17
61:1–2 211
61:1–3 170, 184
61:1–4 165
61:2b 213
61:4 64
62 124
63:1–6 341
64:1 131
64:1–4 329
65–66 81, 124
65:17–18 83
65:17–19 227
65:25 183
66:16 329
66:20 125
66:21 125
66:23 125

Jeremiah

1:5 97
1:10 97

1:15 105
3:8 303
5:9 34
6:26 240
7 98
7:7 41
7:11 174
16:2–3 41
16:15 220
21:10 214
22:24 128
23:5 86, 209
23:10 28
24:4–7 98
24:6 220
25:11–14 144
25:12 146, 151
26 98
29:10 144, 146
30–31 99
30–33 98
31:9 307
31:15 160
31:31–34 43, 102, 322
31:32 99–100
31:33 122
31:34 101
31:35–37 102
31:38–40 102, 130
33:15 86
34:11 19
34:16 19
34:18 31
39:4 24
50:19 220
51 340
51:39 149
51:57 149
52:7 24

Ezekiel

1 142
1–2 106
1–3 103
1–24 103
3:22 104, 258
4:1–2 216
6:2 214
7 108
8–10 106
8–11 103
10:19 106
13:17 214
15:7 214

16 303
17:14 44
18:31 212
20:33 106
20:34 103
20:40 105
21:27 37
24 103
25–32 103
27 340
28:11–15 82
28:13 345
28:13–14 25
29:3–5 141
29:17 103
32:2 40
32:7–8 202
33–48 103
34 249
34:4 19
34:24 104
34:25–31 104
35:1–36:15 104
36:16–37:4 104
36:24–26 244
36:26–27 212
36:33–36 25
37 244
37:9 258
37:10 258
37:12–14 177
37:14 212
37:15–28 99, 104
37:24–28 105
37:26–27 105
37:27 100
38–39 105, 337, 343
39:4 341
39:9 105
39:12–15 105
39:17–20 341
39:29 212
40–48 103, 105, 107, 174, 344
40:1–43:12 106
43:6–44:3 106
44:4–46:24 106
47:1–2 130
47:1–12 25, 82, 106, 248, 345
47:13–23 106
48:1–7 107
48:8–12 107
48:13–22 107

48:23–29 107
48:32 107
48:35 130

Daniel

1 137
1–6 139
1:4 138
1:7 138
1:21 138
2 138, 141
2:34–35 140
2:37 192
2:44 186
2:46–49 140
3–6 141
3:28 143
4:10–12 199
4:20–22 199
4:34 185
5:5–13 150
5:18 192
6:22 143
7 141, 143, 144, 147, 193, 194, 334
7–12 131
7:8 147
7:9 333
7:9–13 343
7:9–14 142
7:13 174, 178, 191, 202, 204, 332
7:13–14 192, 222, 229
7:14 298
7:23–24 147
7:27 298
8 144
8:9–12 148
8:9–14 227
8:15–16 143
8:23–25 148
9 135, 151
9–12 144
9:21 143
9:24–27 145, 146, 147
10 148
10–12 147
10:2–3 132
10:5–6 143
10:13 149, 298
10:19–21 298

10:21 149
11:1 148
11:2–4 148
11:5–20 148
11:21–45 148
11:31–32 314
12:1 142, 148, 149
12:1–2 312
12:1–3 186
12:2 149
12:3 149
12:4 149

Hosea

1–3 303
2 161
2:14 111
9:10 242
11:1 160

Joel

1–2 337
1:2–2:27 108
1:13–20 110
2 108
2:1–11 109
2:6 217
2:10 110, 202, 217
2:11 110
2:12–17 109
2:18–27 109
2:28 188
2:28–29 212
2:28–32 109, 220, 223, 224
3:1–12 109
3:1–21 108
3:13–16 109
3:15 110, 202
3:16 110
3:17–18 110
3:19–21 109, 110

Amos

1:2 79
5:15 79
5:18 108, 179
8:9 202
8:10 240
9:8–10 79
9:11–12 230
9:11–15 79

Obadiah

1:1–14 110

1:15 110
1:17–21 110

Micah

1:4 329
4–5 79
4:1–4 84
4:1–5 80, 151
4:4 175
4:6–7 87
4:7 80
4:8 80
5:2 159
5:7–9 80, 87
7:7–20 80
7:19 19

Habakkuk

2:4 270, 271
2:11 216
3:3–4 106

Zephaniah

1:1–2:3 94
1:14–16 311
2:4–15 95
2:9 87
3:1–4 95
3:6–8 95
3:9 95
3:10 95
3:11–13 95
3:12–13 87
3:14–17 95

Haggai

1:4–11 128
1:12–14 128
2:1–9 128
2:10–14 128
2:15–19 128
2:20–23 128

Zechariah

1–8 127, 128, 129, 133, 134
1:8–10 336
3:1–4:14 338
3:7 174
3:8 86, 209
3:10 175
4 332
5:5–11 137
6:12 86, 203, 209
8:12 128

9–14 127, 129, 134
9:9 174, 252
12:3 217
12:10 240
13:1–6 130
14:1–5 130
14:4–5 175
14:6–8 130
14:9–10 130
14:11–21 130
14:20–21 345

Malachi

3:1 130, 175, 182
3:16 142
3:16–17 130
3:16–18 149
3:17 44
4:4–6 130, 131
4:5–6 161, 182

Matthew

1–2 155
1:1 197
1:1–17 156, 157, 158
1:6 156
1:18–25 157, 158
1:21 208
2 159–60
2:6 79
2:11 178
3:1–2 184
3:1–12 160
3:1–4:11 160
3:9–12 161–62
3:13–17 162–63
3:17 174
4:1–11 163–64
4:12 164
4:12–25 177
4:17 161, 184
4:17–25:46 164
5:1–7:27 164
5:3–16 165
5:7–10 167
5:10–12 170
5:13–14 166, 178
5:14 167
5:16–20 167
5:17–20 168
5:18 328
5:20 169
5:21–48 169

5:22 177
5:23–24 159
5:47 177
6–7 169
6:33 128
7:21 188
7:28–29 164, 169
7:36 197
8–9 169
8:1–16:12 169
8:4 159
8:10–12 178
8:11–12 179
8:26 197
8:30 197
9:6 194
9:8 194
9:27 197
10 170
10:5–6 155, 178
10:7 188
10:18 178
10:23 188, 192
10:42 177
11:2–3 188, 241
11:2–16:12 170–71
11:5–6 189
11:10 202
11:12 188
11:19 193
11:20–24 178
12:15–21 178
12:23 197
12:28 188, 190
12:32 193
12:38–41 171
12:40 193
12:41–42 178
13–16 171
13:37 192, 193
13:37–43 176
13:39–40 329
13:41 192
13:49 329
15:21–28 178
15:22 197
15:24 155
16 171–74
16:8 171, 172
16:13 173, 193
16:18–28 173
16:28 174, 192
17:1–8 174
17:2 333

17:9   174
18:6   177
18:10   177
18:14   177
18:18   257
19:28   192, 196
20:28   171
20:30–31   197
21:1–22:14   174
21:9   197
21:15   197
21:18–27   175
21:23–22:14   179
21:33–46   175
21:42   178
21:43   155
22:1–14   175
22:42   197
23:13   173, 188
23:29–32   179
23:37–25:46   175
24:3   176, 328
24:26–33   176
24:27   192
24:30   170
24:31   179, 311
24:37   192
24:37–41   176
24:39   192
24:44   192
25:1–13   176
25:13   188
25:14–30   176
25:31   192, 312
25:31–46   176
25:40   177
26–28   177
26:2   193
26:28   322
26:57   203
26:59–68   203
26:61   179
26:64   178
27:46   179
27:51–54   155
28:16–20   155, 158
28:18–20   177–78
28:20   329

Mark

1:1   195
1:1–3   184
1:1–13   181–83
1:2   202
1:2–3   183

1:10   188
1:12   188
1:12–13   189
1:13   190
1:14   181
1:14–28   189
1:14–13:37   183
1:15   184, 188
1:24   190
1:25   190, 197, 200
1:27   190
1:29–34   190
1:34   197
1:35–38   197
1:40–42   190
1:44   197
2:1–3:30   190
2:7   193
2:10   191, 193,
   194, 195
2:19–20   189
2:27–28   195
3:1–5   190
3:10–11   190
3:12   190, 197, 200
3:23   190
3:26   190
3:31–35   198
3:34–35   200
4   198–99
4:10–12   197
4:15   190
5:2   190
5:6   190
5:12   190
5:15   190
5:43   197
6:34   197
7:24   197
8:11   190
8:27   171
8:27–33   198
8:27–13:37   200–
   202
8:28–31   191
8:29   195
8:31   190, 191,
   193, 195, 203
8:31–9:1   190
8:35   184
8:38   191, 192
9:1   188
9:12   193
9:25   190, 197
9:30–50   190

9:31   192, 193, 195
9:41   195
9:50   166
10:2   190
10:29   184
10:32–45   190
10:33   193
10:33–34   195
10:45   26, 193
10:46–52   198
10:47–48   191
11:1–11   198
11:12–14   175
11:15–19   203
11:20–25   175
12:15   190
12:35–37   197
13   175, 198, 314,
   326, 328
13:6   203
13:10   329
13:26   191, 192
13:32   188, 329
14–15   183, 202–5
14:21   193
14:25   188
14:37–42   190
14:61   195
14:62   192, 195,
   198
15:32   195
15:39   181

Luke

1–2   207, 208–10
1:7–8   232
1:32–33   225
1:68   218
1:68–79   225
1:78   209
1:78–79   216
2:29–32   232
2:32   52, 234
2:38   218
2:40   225
3:17   218
3:22   211
4:1   211
4:1–13   210, 212,
   217
4:14   211
4:14–21:38   210
4:16–19   224
4:16–21   211

4:16–30   184, 212,
   232
4:18–19   213
4:24–27   213
4:31–37   212
4:41   213
5:24   194
7:1–8:3   213
7:24   202
9:18   171
9:22   214, 218
9:26   191
9:28–36   213
9:31   174, 201
9:36   214
9:51   218
9:51–19:27   214,
   232
9:52   202
10:9   188
10:13–15   218
10:18   217
10:21   211
11:13   211
11:20   188, 190
11:22   217
12:8   191
12:10   211
12:12   211
12:40   192
12:46   188
13:27   218
14:15–24   215
14:34   166
16:16   188, 215
17:5   215
17:20–22   207
17:20–37   215
17:21   188
17:24   192
17:25   218
17:26   192
17:30   192
18:8   188, 192, 215
19:11   188, 207,
   215
19:19   225
19:27   218
19:28–44   215
19:33   216
19:35   216
19:36   216
19:37–42   216
19:44   214, 216,
   234

19:45–21:38 216–
  17
20:9 207
21:20 202
21:20–28 314
21:31 188
21:36 188, 192
22–24 217
22:3 210
22:7–38 218
22:16 188
22:18 188
22:28 210
22:29–30 196
22:31–32 210
22:54–71 218
23:2 204
23:27–31 218
23:35 218
23:39–43 218
23:46 218
24:4 222
24:7 218
24:21 218, 219
24:26 200, 213,
  214, 219, 226
24:36–49 222
24:44–49 219, 232
24:47 221
24:47–48 222
24:49 222
24:50 222
24:50–53 219
24:51 222
24:52 222
24:53 222

John

1–12 253
1:1–3 236
1:1–6 237
1:1–18 235, 245,
  254
1:10–12 258
1:10–13 236
1:11 243
1:11–12 246
1:12 237, 238,
  239, 258
1:12–13 241
1:13 237
1:14 236, 239
1:14–18 237, 238
1:16–18 240
1:17–18 236

1:19 235
1:19–51 241–42
1:31 258
1:33 257
1:49 256
1:51 243
2–4 258
2:1–11 246
2:13–22 246
3:1–4:42 243–46
3:5 188
3:13 242
3:13–14 253
3:14 247, 252
3:15–16 247
4:21 239
4:22 235
4:46–54 246
5–6 247
5–12 246
5:46 242
6:27 253
7–12 247
7:1 236
7:1–11:44 248–50
7:7 236
7:39 252, 257
8:22–23 236
8:28 245, 253
8:39 237
11:25 251
11:45–12:11 251
11:50 237
11:52 237
12:12–50 251–53
12:13 256
12:32 245
12:37–50 246
12:38 258
12:40 258
13 246
13–17 253–56
13:19 249
14–16 256
14:17 236
15:10 294
15:18–19 236
16:11 253
16:20 236
16:32 236
17:3 247
17:4–5 252
17:18 258
17:21 257
18–20 256–58

18:39–40 250
19:27 236
20:28 242
20:31 235, 250

Acts

1–2 226
1–9 233
1–12 229
1:1–5 219
1:4–5 257
1:2 220
1:3–11 222
1:4 222
1:5 162
1:6 219
1:6–11 220
1:8 221, 222
1:9 222
1:11 312
1:12 222
1:13 222
1:15 223
1:15–26 222
2 109, 162, 173,
  222
2–7 221
2:1–3 223
2:5 223, 232
2:5–11 202
2:11 232
2:12–13 224
2:14 223, 232
2:14–39 224
2:17 228
2:17–18 223
2:22 223
2:24–28 225
2:34–36 225
2:36 262, 269
2:38–39 223
2:39 225
2:41 232
2:47 232
3:1–10 226
3:1–8:1a 225
3:11–26 226
3:13 227
3:17 233
3:19–21 232
3:21–22 227
3:26 227
4:4 232
4:12 299
4:23–31 223

4:24 227
4:25 227
4:27 227
5:14 232
5:31 234
6–12 233
6:1 232
6:7 232
7:1–8:1a 227
7:2–8 228
7:9–14 228
7:16 227
7:20–41 228
7:39 227
7:44 228
7:47 228
7:48 290
7:48–49 228
7:51 228, 233
7:55–56 229
7:56 191, 242
7:60–8:1 226
8–11 221
8:1b–28:31 229
8:4–8 221
8:12 219
8:14–17 173, 223
8:29 223
8:32–35 227
8:39 223
9 266
9:8 227
9:15 221, 231, 262
9:19 227
9:26–29 231
9:35 227
9:42 232
10 173
10:9–16 221
10:19–20 223
10:34–35 231
10:34–38 212
10:38 163
10:43 231
10:44–48 223
10:45 223
11:12 223
11:15–18 223
11:17–18 226
11:19–21 221
11:27–30 231
12–28 233
12:24 233
13–20 221
13:1–19:10 233

13:2   223
13:4   223
13:32–33   225
13:33   227, 231
13:43   233
13:46   233, 234
13:46–51   233
13:47   220, 221,
   261, 262
14:1   233
14:22   219
15   230, 231
15:12–21   221
15:16–18   79
15:21   231
15:36–19:41   231
16:6–7   223
17:4   233
17:11–12   233
17:24   290
18:4   233
18:6   233, 234
18:8   233
19:1–7   223
19:8   219
19:9   233
19:20   233
19:26   233
19:39   266
19:41   266
20:21   226
20:22–23   223
20:25   219
21–26   221
21:6   236
21:15–28:31   231
21:20   233
21:21   313
22:21   231, 262
24:5   232
24:14–15   232
24:19   227
26:4–7   232
26:6   232
26:16–18   261
26:17–18   231, 262
26:20   226
26:22   232
26:23   231
28   221
28:17   232, 234
28:20   234
28:23   219
28:23–24   233
28:25   220

28:25–29   233
28:26–27   234
28:31   219

Romans

1   271
1–8   269
1:1–17   269–71
1:13   268
1:16   34, 277
1:16–18   274
1:17   271
1:18   270
1:18–3:20   268,
   271
2:12–16   176
2:14–16   274
3:20   274
3:21–31   271–72
3:21–4:25   268
3:21–5:11   271
3:27   266
4   273
4:1–25   268
4:16–17   35
5:1–11   273–75
5:12   261
5:12–21   275–76
6:11   281
6:14   294
6:16   261
6:23   261
7:1–6   294
7:8   294
7:11   294
7:14   294
7:21   266
8:3   266
8:18–23   30, 42,
   275, 276–77,
   308
8:18–25   274
8:24–25   275
8:34   286
8:37–39   260
8:38   273, 313
8:38–39   286
9–11   269, 277,
   278
9:4–5   279
9:30–10:4   276
11:25–32   279
13–16   269
13:8–10   294
13:11   275

13:12   300
14–15   294
14:10–12   274
14:17   188
15:15–29   280
15:16   234
15:19   202, 295
15:22–24   268
15:25   234
15:25–26   268
15:25–27   231
15:27–28   295
16:3   281
16:4   267
16:16   267

1 Corinthians

1:2   280–81
1:7   284
1:12   284
1:16–17   284
1:18   275
1:19–27   284
1:23   272
1:29   284
1:31   284
2:2   272
2:8   298
3:1   287
3:13–15   274
3:18   291
3:18–23   284
3:22   313
4:5   284
4:6   284
4:7   284
4:8   284
4:18–19   284
5–6   295
5:2   284
5:6   284
6:12   284
6:13–15   284
6:15–17   282
6:19   302
7:11   273
7:26   313
7:31   261
8:1–3   284
8:7   284
9:20   294
10:1–12   162
10:3–4   284
10:7–8   295
10:11   261, 329

10:14–22   282
11:17–34   282
11:18   267
12   283
12–14   284
12:1   287
12:27   282
13:4   284
14:37   287
15   284–89, 291,
   292
15:1–5   273
15:2   275
15:10   264
15:20–28   275
15:24–28   299
15:29   284
15:34   284
15:45   109
15:47–49   290
15:52   311
16:1–4   234

2 Corinthians

2:15   275
3:1   289
3:1–6   304
3:7–11   294
3:7–18   51, 289
3:13–16   240
3:18   288, 290
4:4   260
4:7–5:21   290–92
5   273
5:17   274, 281
5:18–21   274
5:19   260
6:2   275
6:7   300
6:16–7:1   302
10:3–5   300
11:2   303
11:13   304

Galatians

1–2   292
1:4   272, 313
1:13   267
1:13–14   262
1:15–16   261
1:17–18   295
2:10   295
2:11–13   304
2:11–14   294

3   266, 292–95, 296
3:6–18   171
3:10   263
3:16   28
3:19   276
3:28   281
4:4–5   294
4:10   294
4:25   296
4:26   295–96, 344
4:27   296
5:16–21   188
5:22   295
6:16   234

Ephesians

1:3–14   297
1:10   301
1:14   267
1:20   299
1:20–21   260
1:20–2:10   286
1:21   272, 299
1:22–23   282, 301
2:1–10   301
2:5   297
2:5–6   267, 296
2:6   281
2:7   260, 267
2:11–19   274
2:11–22   268, 302
2:14–15   298
2:15   278
3:1–13   297–98
3:6   262
3:10   267, 307
3:19   301
3:21   267
4:1–16   302–3
4:8–10   300
4:10   301
4:13   301, 302
4:24   278
4:30   301
5:22–33   303
5:23   267
5:25   267, 268
5:29   267
5:32   267
6:10–20   300
6:12   273, 299

Philippians

1:21   304

1:27–2:4   305
2:6–11   304
3:3–6   304
3:6   264
3:7–14   304
3:9   270
3:12   305
3:12–16   304
3:13   264
3:17–20   305
3:20   302
3:20–21   286, 304

Colossians

1:9–2:7   267
1:15–20   19, 42, 275, 306–8
1:16   299
1:20   32, 184, 274
1:20–22   273, 274
1:24–2:5   308
2:3   306
2:6–23   308
2:10   299
2:11   290
2:12   296
2:13   297
2:14–15   299
2:15   273, 299, 308
2:16   294
2:20   299
3:1   297, 299
3:1–3   296
3:1–4   308, 309
3:3   267, 281
3:5–11   309
3:10   278, 308
3:12–17   309
4:15   267

1 Thessalonians

1:1   266
1:9b–10   309
1:10   310, 311
3:13   311
4:11   309
4:13–5:11   310–13
4:16   281
5:6–11   314
5:8   275, 300
5:9–10   272
5:10   292
5:12–22   314, 315
5:14   309

2 Thessalonians

2   328, 329
2:1–12   313–14
2:3   311
3:1–5   314
3:6–15   309, 313, 314, 315

1 Timothy

4:1–6   315
6:14–15   315

2 Timothy

3:1   313
3:1–9   315
3:5   316

Titus

2:12–13   315
2:13   316

Hebrews

1–2   286, 320
1–7   318, 319
1:2   323
1:3   321
1:4   320
1:5   320
1:10–12   321
1:11–12   323
1:13   321
1:14–15   320
2:7–4:13   320
2:1–4   323
2:5   323
2:6   191
2:9   320
2:11–12   320
2:12   324
2:17   320
3:1–4:13   320
3:1–5:10   320
3:1–6   320
3:7–4:13   323–25
4:1   318
4:9   49
4:11   318
4:14–5:10   320
4:14   321
4:15   320, 321
4:16   321
5:1–10   321
5:11–10:39   321
6:4–5   323

6:20   321
7   320
7:1–10   321
7:11–28   321
7:22   318
7:25   321
8–10   318
8:1–10:18   321–23
8:2   321
8:6–13   318
9:2   321
9:9   313
9:11   290
9:11–12   321
9:23–26   321
9:24   290
9:26   176, 329
9:28   323
10:16–18   318
10:19–25   324
10:25   323
10:37   323
11:40   323
12:1–2   305
12:2   318
12:18–24   296, 318, 320, 323, 325, 339
12:22–24   321
12:25–29   321, 323
12:28   321
13:14   320, 325

James

1:1   326
1:12   326
2:5   326
5:1–8   326
5:7   317
5:9   326

1 Peter

1:3–12   326
1:4   26, 29
2:5   320
2:12   328
3:16   328
3:18–22   327
4   328
4:6   327

2 Peter

2   326
2:1   326, 327
2:3   237

2:5   326
2:12   237
2:14   326
2:17   237
2:18   326
2:20–22   326
3   327
3:3   327
3:4   327
3:7   328
3:8   329
3:10   327
3:11–14   327
3:16   327
3:17   327

1 John

2:1   255

Jude

3–4   329
5–19   329
20–23   329

Revelation

1   322–33
1:1   331

1:3   331
1:6   52, 342
1:9–22:5   332
1:13   191
2–5   333–35
3:12   102
5   336
5:10   52, 332, 333, 342
6   217
6–16   336–40
6:1–22:5   335
6:1   312
6:3   312
6:5   312
6:7   312
10:11–14   337
11:11–12   312
12:7   253
14:6–7   184
14:14   191
15–16   343
15–19   336
17:1–2   345
17:1–19:10   340–41
19   336

19:11–20:15   340, 341–43
19:13   236
20:6   52, 332, 333
21   122
21–22   11, 21, 49
21:1   17
21:1–22:5   227, 343–46
21:1–22:9   340
21:2   32, 274
21:2–4   102
22:4–5   333
22:6–15   332
22:6–21   346
22:15   344
22:16–21   332

Apocryphal/
Deuterocanonical
References (listed
alphabetically)

2 Baruch

14:17–19   45
67   217

2 Esdras

7:26   267, 321, 343
10:54   343
13:36   321, 343

1 Maccabees

1:20–28   146
1:54   146
3   217
4:36–59   174
13:51   252

2 Maccabees

10:1–8   174

Sirach

24:8   307

Tobit

13:16   267

Wisdom of
Solomon

6:4   185
6:22   307
9:1–2   236
9:8   321
10:10   185

Printed in Great Britain
by Amazon